MODERN EAST ASIA:
ESSAYS IN INTERPRETATION

Modern East Asia:

VOLUME EDITOR
JAMES B. CROWLEY
YALE UNIVERSITY

HARCOURT, BRACE & WORLD, INC.

NEW YORK   CHICAGO   SAN FRANCISCO   ATLANTA

Essays in Interpretation

CONTRIBUTORS

FREDERIC WAKEMAN, JR.
UNIVERSITY OF CALIFORNIA, BERKELEY

PAUL A. COHEN
WELLESLEY COLLEGE

JOHN WHITNEY HALL
YALE UNIVERSITY

MARIUS B. JANSEN
PRINCETON UNIVERSITY

AKIRA IRIYE
UNIVERSITY OF CHICAGO

ERNEST P. YOUNG
UNIVERSITY OF MICHIGAN

PETER DUUS
HARVARD UNIVERSITY

JEROME B. GRIEDER
BROWN UNIVERSITY

JAMES B. CROWLEY
YALE UNIVERSITY

MAURICE MEISNER
UNIVERSITY OF WISCONSIN

HUGH T. PATRICK
YALE UNIVERSITY

SHINKICHI ETŌ
UNIVERSITY OF TOKYO

UNDER THE GENERAL EDITORSHIP OF
JOHN MORTON BLUM
YALE UNIVERSITY

Modern East Asia: Essays in Interpretation

ISBN: 0-15-561000-7

Library of Congress Catalog Card Number: 75-111320

Printed in the United States of America

NOT too long ago, any volume of essays dealing with China and Japan would have been prefaced by an extended statement extolling the relevance and significance of these societies to the American community. Today, this sort of exhortation seems rather superfluous. It has become increasingly apparent that the past is prologue to the present, and that a focus on present reality affords a means for assessing the past and anticipating the future. One of the most striking realities of this generation is the fact that more Americans have died in combat since 1941 than in all the preceding generations in our history. Further, the greater portion of these have died in a Pacific war, a Korean conflict, and a Vietnam conflagration. Three wars in Asia within thirty years are grim testimony to the relevance of Asia to the United States. We cannot, in this age, afford the luxury of viewing China and Japan as mysterious, esoteric, or alien societies; nor can we assume that the modern experience of these nations concerns only academic specialists and select governmental decision-makers. No less than the history of Europe, the patterns and dynamics of modern Japan and China must become an integral part of our historical consciousness.

Few readers of this volume are apt to question the need for greater knowledge and wider dissemination of information about Asia. Most readers are surely aware that popular ignorance and indifference with respect to China and Japan must be taken into account in any reassessment of America's role in Asia, past and present. Platitudinous though it may be, one must affirm the need for Americans to learn a great deal more about East Asian history. Of course, knowledge of China and Japan is no panacea. It does not guarantee the avoidance of future American wars in Asia, nor does it necessarily provide any insurance against mistaken opinions or inept policies where Asia is concerned. Nonetheless, the most reasonable basis for a national dialogue about America's role in

Asia would be a community that is both knowledgeable about China and Japan and concerned with the evolution of a Western presence in Asia that is not circumscribed by conflict and conditioned by fear. In many respects, this volume of essays is a contribution toward this goal. More particularly, it attempts to present a brief synthesis of modern Chinese and Japanese history.

This is an ambitious undertaking. For this reason, a few comments on the organization and the underlying scheme of the volume are essential. The primary objective, as suggested above, is to furnish readers with the basic facts and central themes in the history of modern China and Japan. To this end, each contributor has synthesized his general approach to a particular period of Chinese or Japanese history. Each contributor is a recognized authority in his area of specialization, and each was given the same assignment: to write a short interpretative essay that would reflect the most recent scholarship in the area, retain the interest of the general reader, and command the respect of the professional scholar. It is for the reader to judge how well the authors have succeeded in this task. We may add, however, that these essays were not structured by any editorial hypothesis or by any fixed set of questions. Notwithstanding this fact, they consistently deal with broad and interlocking themes, thereby affording a wide range of insights and observations on the most popular historical themes—for example, "the traditions of China and Japan," "China's response to the West," "imperialism," "the modernization of Japan," "the Chinese revolution," and "Chinese Communism." The result, in my opinion, is a volume of individual essays that is far more than the sum total of its parts.

In view of the absence of any artificially contrived structure for this volume, it would be improper to seek to impose one in a preface. Similarly, it would be a folly to extrapolate broad generalizations from these essays or to venture any sort of synopsis of the ideas and points of view they contain. It is proper, however, to note that these essays demonstrate the continued relevance of inherited social systems and cultural norms to the momentous changes in China and Japan that have accompanied industrialization, the rise of nationalism, and wars, both civil and foreign. Individually and collectively, these essays confirm the importance of understanding the particular hues and styles of Chinese and Japanese society and how these have influenced "responses" to external factors and the "patterns" of nationalism and industrialization. In brief, these essays represent an introduction and an invitation—an introduction to contemporary academic thinking about modern China and Japan, and an invitation to become engaged with the many unresolved and challenging problems confronting the historian of modern China and Japan.

JAMES B. CROWLEY

Contents

MODERN EAST ASIA:
ESSAYS IN INTERPRETATION

Chronology

CHINA		JAPAN
Ming toleration for Jesuits	1600	Tokugawa hegemony established
Nurhaci consolidates Manchuria	1615	Buke-shohatto (warrior code)
Ch'ing dynasty established	1644	Closed Door policy in force
K'ang-hsi era begins	1662	
Suzerainty over Outer Mongolia	1688	Genroku era begins
	1716	Yoshimune becomes shogun
Control over Tibet	1720	
Ch'ien-lung era begins	1736	End of Kyōhō era
Suzerainty over Burma	1769	Tanuma heads bakufu
Ho Shen runs bureaucracy	1789	Kansei reforms
Suppression of White Lotus Society	1804	First Russian warship in Japanese waters
Rapid growth in opium traffic	1837	Riots led by Ōshio
Opium War begins	1841	Mizuno heads bakufu
Opium War ends; Treaty of Nanking	1842	Tempō reforms
Taiping Rebellion	1850	
Nien rebellion begins	1853	Perry ships end Closed Door policy
Tientsin treaties	1858	Harris commercial treaty with United States
T'ung-chih Restoration	1862	First embassy to Europe
Taiping Rebellion suppressed	1864	Choshu rebellion
Nien rebellion crushed	1868	Meiji Restoration
Northwest Moslem rebellion crushed	1873	Iwakura mission returns
Legations in London and Berlin	1877	Satsuma rebellion, led by Saigō
Treaty of St. Petersburg	1881	Promise of constitution
Li-Itō convention on Korea	1885	Cabinet instituted
	1889	Meiji Constitution
Sino-Japanese War	1894	Sino-Japanese War
Treaty of Shimonoseki	1895	Tripartite intervention
The Hundred Days of reform	1898	Itagaki-Ōkuma cabinet
Boxer Rebellion	1899	British extraterritoriality ends
Yuan Shih-k'ai dominant official	1902	First Anglo-Japanese alliance
	1904	Russo-Japanese War
Ch'ing reforms; Sun Yat-sen organizes revolutionary party (T'ung-meng hui)	1905	Treaty of Portsmouth; second Anglo-Japanese alliance
1911 revolution	1911	Saionji cabinet; tariff autonomy
Ch'ing dynasty abdicates; Yuan Shih-k'ai heads republic	1912	Taishō era begins
Sino-Japanese treaties	1915	Twenty-One Demands on China; Sino-Japanese treaties

CHINA		JAPAN
China enters World War I	1917	Lansing-Ishii agreement
	1918	Hara cabinet; intervention in Siberia
May Fourth movement	1919	Versailles peace settlement
Communist party organized	1921	Washington Conference
Soviets aid Sun Yat-sen	1924	Katō cabinet
Nanking (KMT) government established; Autumn Harvest Uprising	1927	Tanaka cabinet
Mao Tse-tung forms Red Fourth Army	1928	Intervention in Tsinan
Chiang Kai-shek's third anti-Communist campaign	1931	Manchurian crisis
"The Long March"	1934	Okada cabinet
Sian incident	1936	February Twenty-sixth rebellion; Anti-Comintern Pact
	1937	China incident
United front: Chinese Communist party and Nationalist party		
Mao's *On the New Democracy*	1940	Axis alliance
Serious cleavage in united front	1941	Tōjō cabinet; attack on Pearl Harbor
Mao's *On Coalition Government*	1945	Atom bomb attacks and Japanese surrender
	1946	SCAP reforms begin
Renewed civil war	1947	New constitution
	1949	SCAP stresses economic recovery
Maoist victory; Chiang flees to Taiwan		
Korean War; confrontation with United States	1950	Korean War boom
Tibetan occupation legalized	1951	Occupation ends
1954 constitution	1954	Self Defense Force organized
The Great Leap Forward program	1958	Kishi cabinet considers constitutional changes
Withdrawal of Soviet advisers	1960	Anti-Eisenhower riots; mutual security pact with United States
Sino-Indian Border War	1962	Ikeda cabinet accents economic development
Atom bomb explosion	1964	Tokyo Olympics
Red Guard movement	1965	GNP rises to third largest in world
Cultural Revolution moderates	1969	Sato cabinet calls for return of Okinawa

High Ch'ing: 1683–1839

FREDERIC WAKEMAN, JR.

THE Ch'ing dynasty (1644–1911) is not easily seen for itself. Most interpretations—and this essay is no exception—present it through the proscenium arch of the nineteenth century. In the midst of Ch'ing baroque, we hear the distant rumble of Opium War artillery and cannot keep ourselves from asking what in the eighteenth century accounted for China's "failure" in the nineteenth. There is nothing wrong with such a question; those who would try to isolate the eighteenth century from China's later history could easily be accused of antiquarianism. For the moment, though, let us try to pose the High Ch'ing on native ground and seek to understand why Chinese chroniclers then felt their time "unparalleled in history."[1] Such placid self-satisfaction must sound like pride before the fall if we narrowly view eighteenth-century China through the history of its later travail. But, when we realize that Chinese of the 1700's saw themselves as emerging from the disasters of an earlier era, Ch'ing self-esteem no longer seems misplaced. In short, it is impossible to understand the confidence during the *pax sinica* without remembering constantly that it was vividly contrasted with the chaos which accompanied the fall of the preceding Ming dynasty (1368–1644).

Few thoughtful men could forget the tragedies of the late Ming. That dynasty, conceived so splendidly, had begun to lose its hold over the empire as early as 1630. Years of famine had impoverished the Northwest. "Barbarian" Manchus exerted a constant military pressure beyond the Great Wall. Peasants fled revenue collectors. Draftees, cheated out of rations, slew their officers. Bandit groups formed and soon consolidated into large rebel armies that boldly attacked cities. Fitted with fine cap-

[1] Cited in Ho Ping-ti, *Studies on the Population of China, 1368–1953* (Cambridge, Mass.: Harvard University Press, 1959), p. 214.

1

tured mounts and skilled in slashing cavalry tactics, they were more than a match for the clumsy Ming military expeditions sent against them. Within a decade, two rival rebel commanders were powerful enough to be considered potential founders of a new dynasty: a tall, jaundiced man of bestial temperament named Chang Hsien-chung (1605–47) and a slightly more subtle, though nonetheless ferocious, ex-groom named Li Tzu-ch'eng (1605–45), who had lost one eye to an enemy arrow. Leading armies that were swollen with émigrés from the very areas they had overrun, these two rivals moved in and out of the Chihli plain and the Huai River valley almost at will.

The Ming forces were hopelessly slow-moving and badly commanded. While the rebels used peasant foot soldiers only as auxiliaries to their cavalry, the Ming relied heavily on infantrymen. While Chang Hsien-chung and Li Tzu-ch'eng were both professional soldiers-of-fortune, the imperial marshals were usually scholarly gentlemen who knew little of warfare outside the pages of *Sun-tzu*. As campaign after campaign proved indecisive, the government found itself forced to recruit mercenaries— cavalry generals and their private armies who were barely distinguishable from the rebels themselves. These new *condottieri* militarized North China. Local government ceased to exist in many regions when magistrates, appointed to office in isolated districts, found roads blocked by highwaymen or army deserters. Landowners barricaded themselves in armed blockhouses behind mud-ramparted walls or hired their own professional thugs for self-protection. Townsmen and peasants began to fear the approach of any army, whether Ming or rebel, since the soldiers of both sides were equally rapacious. With there being so little to distinguish the supporters of the regime from its attackers, most people north of the Yangtze saw little reason to fight to the death for the existing dynasty.

As these connections between the countryside and the administrative centers were severed, Ming officials in Peking lost touch with rural commands. Thus isolated, the capital could hope for military support only from its own seedy garrison and a force in the Northeast under a general named Wu San-kuei, who was camped at the seaside terminus of the Great Wall, where he confronted the armies of the Manchus. In the spring of 1644, the rebel leader Li Tzu-ch'eng decided the moment had come to capture the capital and dispatched two hundred thousand of his soldiers toward Peking. By the time the emperor had sent an express courier to Wu San-kuei for help, it was too late. On April 23rd Peking was surrounded by rebels, and two days later Li entered the Forbidden City to find the Ming emperor dead by his own hand.

The events of the following forty days, as described in innumerable versions, resemble the plot of a Chinese opera: a beautiful concubine driving men mad with love, riders dashing to and fro with important messages, bribes exchanged, cavalry units meeting on bare fields, officials being tortured. Like all changes of great historical consequence, the fall of the Ming dynasty is thereby reduced to understandable but insignificant events—Richard the Third's horse is slain, and the rule changes hands. However, later Ch'ing dynastic historians gave a more sweeping version of those last months, justifying Manchu intervention at this important juncture. Since, their version ran, the Ming had lost the Mandate of Heaven through misrule, the inhabitants of China were being subjected to the cruelty of a tyrannical bandit leader who had butchered his way to the imperial throne. Dorgon,[2] regent of the Manchu dynasty and commander of its armies, had therefore joined forces with Wu San-kuei to rescue Peking. As the Manchu army approached the capital from the east on January 3, 1644, Li Tzu-ch'eng's rebels burned and looted the city and fled to the west. The Forbidden City now empty, Dorgon placed the young Manchu emperor Shun-chih (reign: 1644–61) on the throne and declared the Ch'ing dynasty the legitimate heir to their lamentably fallen predecessors. In the purple rhetoric of a Manchu prince of the time, "Formerly, the wandering robbers were lawless and wild, recklessly oppressing the people. Our dynasty's numerous, humane, and merciful armies chastised them swiftly and resoundingly, rescuing the people from the water and the fire, bringing peace."[3] The Manchus were saving China from itself and from its own excesses. The world had turned, the cosmic balance had shifted, and another dynastic cycle was about to begin.

Much of this was mere propaganda. In fact, ever since at least 1618—long before peasant rebels arose—the Manchus had set their cap for conquest, and their repeated raids across the Great Wall had done much to create the very problems the Ch'ing now claimed to solve. It was their presence in the North, for example, that had forced the Ming to levy additional taxes and drive the peasantry to arms. But most of the people of North China did not logically connect all of this. They were simply weary of years of civil war. The Ch'ing expulsion of Li Tzu-ch'eng from Peking seemed to promise respite from famine and rapine; hence, Manchu rhetoric did have a ring of truth to it. And if the new Ch'ing dynasty was indeed capable of pacifying China, of wiping out the rebel bands and appointing magistrates who actually took their posts, then many Chinese were likely to accept its right to rule.

All of this may help explain how seventy thousand Ch'ing bannermen

---

[2] Dorgon (1612–50) was one of the many sons of Nurhaci, founder of the Manchu state. By 1644, Dorgon had become virtually the Manchus' sole leader, though Nurhaci's grandson, the Shun-chih Emperor, was nominally their ruler.

[3] Cited in Hsieh Kuo-chen, *Ch'ing-ch'u nung-min ch'i-i tzu-liao chi-lu* (Shanghai: 1956), p. 50.

conquered one hundred fifty million Chinese. It does not mean that the pacification of China was an easy matter. The southerners, unexposed to the direct attacks of rebel forces in the 1630's and proud of a long tradition of opposition to barbarian invaders, resisted fiercely. For decades, Ming remnants hung on along the southeastern coast, and, when most of these loyalists were finally subdued, *their* conquerors (Chinese bannermen who had defected to the Manchus long before the fall of Peking) revolted in turn. But by 1683, sixty-five years after the Manchu invasions had first begun, the Ch'ing Peace was finally realized.

THAT China sinifies its conquerors need not be proved here. Dorgon not only had staffed his ministries with captured Chinese clerks and scholars but had early recognized that the Manchus could hold China only by promising to esteem native officials even more than the Ming had. The Ch'ing Peace, therefore, was a dual one: local order for landlords and tillers of the soil, government appreciation for those who continued to serve conscientiously as civil servants. As the former was an antidote to decades of rural disorder, so the latter was an answer to the years of bureaucratic rivalries, eunuch-led purges, and official obeisance to the capricious Ming emperors.

These promises were paid in double token during the splendid reign of the K'ang-hsi Emperor (1662–1722). As the bandits were (in the euphemism of the *Veritable Records*) "restored to their former professions," as the literati began to take the state examinations once again, as the crumbling waterworks were restored and the corrupt bureaucracy restaffed, China entered one of the most peaceful and productive ages of her history. In the Chinese scale of things, this was not a long period—perhaps at the most only one hundred ten years—but, in men's memories at least, perhaps the best they had ever had.

The majesty of Chinese imperial rule was restored beyond a doubt. The Ming's fourteenth-century chastisement of the Mongols and expulsion of them beyond the Great Wall had never been a complete gesture. The tribesmen did not remain settled there until the latter part of the sixteenth century, when Anda and his Oirat Mongols were finally assuaged with tribute. The Ch'ing, too, had to combine judicious bribes with measured force; but by creating a special office for Central Asian affairs, by marrying into the Mongol aristocracy, and by sharing some of the steppemen's martial values, the dynasty was far better able to ensure continuing peace in Mongolia than the Ming had been. There were eruptions, to be sure, and Central Asia was never entirely at peace; but no Mongol armies rode under the walls of Peking. Instead, Ch'ing expeditions penetrated deep into Central and Southeast Asia. By the end of the Ch'ien-lung Emperor's reign (1736–96), the boundaries of the Chinese empire extended farther than ever before or since: west to the Ili region and the boundaries of Russian Turkestan, southwest to the Himalayas and the border states of India. Tibet was pacified and controlled; Annam was in vassalage, and the rest of Southeast Asia was sending royal tribute; and Korea was once again part of the Chinese sphere of influence.

Within the nation's frontiers, peace and careful rule brought their own benefits. The Grand Canal transport system and the Salt Monopoly were streamlined. Eunuch power was temporarily haltered, and rationalized sanctions and punishments ensured the smooth functioning of the bu-reaucracy.[4] A sophisticated system for auditing government accounts was introduced. Official salaries were raised and the government famine relief system carefully maintained. After 1683, the Ming military levies were abolished, and regular taxes were repeatedly and generously remitted during the following half-century. In fact, by 1712 the head-tax quota had been frozen, and through commutation a Chinese male no longer had to provide corvée for public works. Silver and copper from Europe and Japan flowed into China to be exchanged for raw silk and porcelain. The fertile Yangtze valley continued to develop a lucrative cotton-handicraft industry, while new cash crops like tobacco and sugar cane provided farmers with savings in specie, an insurance against bad crop years of drought or flood. The pace of interregional trade quickly exceeded that under the Ming, with goods passing back and forth across the mountain passes of Kiangsi and Fukien and up and down the canal system of the central valleys. A famous early eighteenth-century author wrote euphorically:

> Houses cluster together like fish-scales and people are as numerous as ants. Since local administration is simple, the district is often quiet. While everywhere on the fields mulberry, hemp and various cereal crops are grown, the streams abound with carp and other fish. Despite the occasional comings and goings of local-government underlings, no household is disturbed. White-haired people, exempt from labor services, listen at leisure to the wind sighing in the pine trees, or birds' speech, or schoolboys' chants. The rest of the adults are all occupied with the plow and the loom.[5]

Above this flourishing society, this land of bucolically contented peasants and elders, the palaces of the capital were crammed and filled with garnered treasures. The master potters and kiln-tenders of the great Ming porcelain factory of Ching-te *chen*, who had been scattered and dispersed by the years of civil war, were slowly regathered. Once more the glaziers

---

[4] I am grateful to Dr. Thomas Metzger of New Hebrew University, Jerusalem, for this observation.

[5] Cited in Ho, *Studies on the Population of China*, p. 211.

turned out the exquisite colored wares of the Ming, now in new shapes and brighter, more enameled tones. Perhaps the purity of Ming pottery was never completely attained, but the Ch'ing had its own special styles and objects of pride. Cloisonné, lacquerware, jade carvings were all commissioned for the emperor. The palaces were refurbished and the walls rebuilt. The land was at peace again.

At its apogee, during the reign of the Ch'ien-lung Emperor, which spanned the eighteenth century, the Ch'ing felt unrivaled. How many other dynasties could claim such a sway of influence, such ubiquitous signs of contentment and wealth? The greatest, the most tangible symbol of all was the Summer Palace, near the Ming tombs west of Peking. Contemporaries were dazzled by the buildings wandering over tens of square miles, by the artificial hills bedecked with gold leaf, and by the gardens filled with twisted trees and pockmarked stones imported at fantastic cost from throughout the world. This was High Ch'ing at the appropriate level of personal grandeur.

The Summer Palace (as distinct from the Imperial Palace in the capital itself) was a human habitat, housing Hung-li, not Ch'ien-lung.[6] In Peking, on the ornate throne of state, the emperor overshadowed the man, for whoever governed civilization did so thanks to broad cultural definitions of rule. Whether Han Chinese or barbarian Manchu, the ruler of China, qua emperor, was defined by his office, conditioned by his public role. His tutors were properly Confucian and his ritual acts the same as those of hundreds of Chinese emperors before him. The spring plowing, the sacrifices on the Altar of Heaven, the vermilion endorsements on state decrees were all generalized symbols of identity. The emperor was the emperor, regardless of race or origin, as long as he fulfilled the proper acts of worship, as long as he seemed to stand—as the philosophers believed he should—between heaven and earth, holding the cosmos in balance, morally radiating his influence over All Under Heaven (T'ien-hsia), by example instructing those beneath him to serve those in his charge as good officials. However, the Chinese emperor was not a god-king in the Egyptian sense; he could do wrong, and his acts were judged personally. But his accomplishments and aberrations were generalized. Emperor after emperor appeared as variations on certain stereotypes: the vicious, perverted, Neronic last emperor or the benevolent sage who walked the streets of his capital in mufti, the better to be near his people. Portraiture became standardized to a certain extent. Ming T'ai-tsu (reign: 1368–98), a crude and ugly ex-monk, appears in paintings as a wise and handsome

[6] The emperor's reign title was Ch'ien-lung. His given name was Hung-li, his princely title Pao, his temple name Kao-tsung, and his posthumous name Ch'ien Huang-ti. To be absolutely correct, one should say, "the Ch'ien-lung Emperor," not "Ch'ien-lung."

A Gazebo of the Summer Palace. *Historical Pictures Service, Chicago.*

sage with great brow and rich mouth. Thus, the office swallowed the man; and the observer's gaze is blurred by a long gallery of look-alikes in ritual robes and pomp, identified by reign, not personal, names.

Because of this, one supposes, individual emperors tried hard to retain their personal identities. They chose peculiar hobbies—carpentry, Turkish dances—to give themselves uniqueness, to be more than part of a line. Thus did the Ch'ing rulers try to keep their individualities alive. For one thing, they were Manchus, which gave them a special identity beyond that generalized symbolism. This was one reason the emperors' ritual hunts beyond the palisades in Manchuria itself were of such importance to the dynasty. The bow had its own poetry, as appealing to some Ch'ing emperors as T'ang tunes played by palace concubines; and earlier days of martial vigor and rough nights on the marches were recalled.

In the same way, the Summer Palace gave the Ch'ien-lung Emperor a more intimate and human setting than the public aspect of the regular Imperial Palace. In the Summer Palace's twisted gardens, where nature was artificially and safely reproduced in civilized guise, the emperor strolled with his retinue of civil officials, his closest counselors and poem-makers. There he practiced his own calligraphy, painted, sipped wine and chatted, penned a line or two (and accepted the authorship of thousands more turned out by a staff of literati). There he was like any cultured gentlemen—but on a forced and monumental scale. His villa grounds intimately enclosed the world. The excitement of a military expedition in distant Tibet could be reproduced in mock maneuvers by his household guards. His bibliophilia and craze for art collecting—both traits of a refined scholar-official—were carried to gigantic extremes. The connoisseurship and cultivated gentility of an eighteenth-century mandarin were amplified enormously. Other men wrote hundreds of poems; he ostensibly authored tens of thousands. Other men collected tens of paintings; he amassed thousands. Other men chose fine silk and ancient ink to immortalize their calligraphy; he had his engraved in gold on slabs of rarest Burmese jade. His tastes did not mock others'; they exceeded and excelled them. It was more than either sinification or glorification—it was personification.

The public role of the emperor was expressed in the formality of the Forbidden City. The Summer Palace's meanders and twisted bridges, its small enclosed spaces and carefully chosen grotesqueries, were reversed in the rigid symmetries of imperial Peking. Here lines were straight and long, a series of squares rather than circles. The perpendiculars ran up from the southern part of the city, through the crowded commercial quarters, into the Manchu districts; then on, square by square, gate by gate, toward the head of the capital, the palace itself, which was elevated in altitude and attitude. It was panoramic, a city of processions and parades, the site of statehood and imperial divinity, and it was fitting that the seat of this power should be forbidden to the outsider, for all formal power in traditional China was held inaccessible and distant behind walls. Even the district yamen, center of magisterial rule, miniaturized this pattern of enclosed squares and high walls. And, as the yamen looked down on the county capital that it governed, so did the Imperial Palace gaze upon the empire at its feet. In this imagery, therefore, power stretched vertically down through layers of officialdom to the market towns of rural China. The term "Central Kingdom" may well express China's notion of its central place in both cosmos and world civilization before the doubts raised by Western contact in the nineteenth century. It does not, however, capture the vertical image of imperial rule symbolized by Peking: the Son of Heaven, High Above, Perpendicular and Raised.

Thus, authority streamed down from the apex. Although mediated by the ruling elite, this power was not distributed in pyramidal fashion, diffused through forty thousand officials, but ideally pressed directly downward, skipping over intermediary layers. The Ch'ing emperors, in fact, were proud of their practice of suddenly addressing themselves to the problems of a given rural district. A county official could, and sometimes did, receive instruction directly from the palace. Such intervention was exceptional, to be sure, but it reflected an important difference of tone between the traditional bureaucracy of China and that of other agrarian empires. The assumption was that all officials were ideally in touch with that imperial source, that the emperor in fact had a hand in every decision instead of delegating authority to intermediaries who could take the power handed them and do with it as they wished.

As paradoxical as it may sound, this model of direct imperial rule theoretically served the Ch'ing as a check on the irregular abuse of power. To Chinese of the eighteenth century, the most prominent example of such a usurpation had taken place during the preceding dynasty. The Ming had ambitiously tried to register every citizen in a rigid system of hereditary occupational categories, the largest of which was a huge militia of almost two million adult males. During the early years of the dynasty, the system seemed to work well enough, but by 1550 it had begun to atrophy. The massive armies were depleted or transformed into coolie corps. Rosters were padded, supplies embezzled. It seemed that the more laws and regulations there were, the greater were the opportunities for abuse. What was to keep a man who faced conscription from bribing his way out of that particular hereditary classification, thereby additionally corrupting the officials who accepted his money?

So complicated a system demanded constant vigilance against corruption and laxness, which meant creating powerful surveillance organs, which in turn increased the dictatorial powers of the throne. Since the Ming emperors feared that regular civil servants would not inform on their colleagues, they preferred to staff police and security offices with trusted eunuchs. Soon, however, these palace servants used their new power either to appropriate offices or to find bureaucratic allies within ordinary administrative agencies. As an emperor came to rely almost entirely on "inner" palace personnel, a barricade was erected between him and "outer" scholar-officials, who could no longer counsel their ruler and hope, in the best Confucian tradition, to act as a moral check on his understandable ambition for absolute power.

No one believed that either eunuch usurpation or imperial tyranny were problems unique to the Ming. Han Confucianists (206 B.C.–220 A.D.)

had warned repeatedly of the evils of corrupt courtiers and had inveighed desperately against the political theories of the legalists, who advocated strict laws and sweeping governmental controls on the populace. This Confucian-legalist debate recurred during subsequent periods, especially in the Northern Sung (960–1126), but the two views were so fundamentally opposed in the abstract that officials were usually content to rule pragmatically according to a "Middle Way" and leave acrimony to the philosophers. Now and again, however, the issues were posed so clearly that even realistic administrators had to consider the question of loose, "moral" rule versus tight, "legal" administration—of letting the people rule themselves under political guidance versus controlling the multiple aspects of social behavior.

The Ch'ing came down on the side of the moralists. Almost as soon as they had established the dynasty, the Manchus abolished the Ming hereditary categories. Furthermore, while continuing to rationalize routine bureaucratic behavior, the great Ch'ing emperors frequently intervened in matters of extraordinary importance. This vertical intervention was also expressed in the opposite direction. That is, while the K'ang-hsi and Ch'ien-lung emperors made decisions that a bureaucracy would normally leave to its staff men, they also expected requests for authority to move back up the hierarchy directly to them. Not all officials were allowed to memorialize the emperor, of course, but those that did on important matters could be relatively sure that their petition would reach the ruler. This constant interchange of directives and intelligence was felt to be the one device that might prevent a recurrence of late Ming conditions, when, as described above, palace officers had simply appropriated the overseeing role of the ruler (one Ming emperor went so far as to see no memorials for over a decade). While this was the immediate reason for the Ch'ing emphasis on direct vertical rule, the continuing cause was the Confucian ideal of face-to-face exchange between ruler and line-official, which was derived from a period of personal feudal relationships in small princely states with populations numbering in the thousands. Needless to say, this method of statecraft was slightly out of date two millennia later, when the population of China was exceeding the two-hundred-million mark. As administration became more complex and the flow of papers a deluge, transmission offices and secretariats were posed athwart this supposedly direct flow and threatened to cut the Ch'ing emperors off from official intelligence. Therefore, extraordinary organs like the Grand Council[7] were created to shunt important policy papers and memorials directly to the ruler. And, when the Grand Council in turn became bu-

---

[7] The Grand Council (Chün-chi ch'u, literally, "Bureau of Military Affairs") was created in 1729 to plan a secret campaign against the Eleuths (Ölöd Mongols). It eventually became the most important office in the government.

reaucratized, later emperors tried to bypass even it. Neither the iron law of routinization nor imperial attempts to break that law were ever entirely carried through, however, and Ch'ing administration was therefore characterized by a compromise between purely bureaucratic decision-making and the ideal of an enlightened monarch, constantly aware of his people's needs.

Vertical rule *and* a strong and sensible emperor thus did serve to keep Ch'ing China from becoming either a conservative's nightmare of absolute and constant governmental interference or a welter of red tape where nothing was ever accomplished. Indeed, one of the striking things about this compromise system was the way in which necessary policies could usually be carried out. The emperor's favorite method was to appoint special commissioners (*ch'in-ch'ai*) who bypassed provincial governors and acted directly for him. These imperial commissioners were guaranteed great discretionary powers which, since immediately derived from the emperor himself, were virtually unquestioned by regular civil servants and which, furthermore, suited the way a commissioner's duties were designated. He was assigned a task and, after generally clearing his proposed tactics with the emperor, given carte blanche to finish the job. If he succeeded, the reward was suitably high, perhaps a noble rank and imperial sinecure. If he failed, exile or worse might be his fate. *How* the job was done was relatively unimportant. This helps account for the later behavior of the one imperial commissioner known to most Western students of Chinese history—Lin Tse-hsu—who involved China in the Opium War (1839–42) largely because his emperor, Tao-kuang (1821–50), failed to foresee that Lin's means of eradicating opium addiction meant armed conflict with England.[8] In short, much depended on the wisdom of the individual emperor himself, whether he was maintaining a compromise system of vertical rule or creating extraordinary ministers for important tasks of state. This was the great strength of the Ch'ing Peace—and its most dangerous weakness. In that sense, the personified monumentalism of the Summer Palace was a more apt symbol of rule than the formal rigor of Peking.

THE imagery of vertical movement was also maintained in another sense. The opportunity for a bureaucratic career open to talent was in itself a device for pulling men of merit up out of their milieu and drawing them into an elite life above village China. Political hopes, ambitions, and desires were all centered on Peking. To become a bureaucrat was to attain

---

[8] This point is, however, open to dispute. See Chang Hsin-pao, *Commissioner Lin and the Opium War* (Cambridge, Mass.: Harvard University Press, 1964), p. 121, and Lin Ch'ung-yung, *Lin Tse-hsu chuan* (Taipei: Chung-hua ta-tien pien-yin hui, 1967), pp. 458–60.

wealth and honor, to "go up to the capital" (*shang-tu*). This focus on upward mobility was hardly unique to the eighteenth century, but it had
become more acute by then.

The High Ch'ing saw the culmination of a crucial social change that
had been in process for approximately a thousand years. Until about 700
A.D., the absolute power of the emperor had been checked by autonomous
local aristocrats, great manor-owning families who sometimes controlled
province-sized portions of the country and, during times of disorder,
allied with warlords to resist a monarch's drive toward unification and
centralization. Such conditions bred perpetual civil war. The T'ang (618–
906), therefore, had tried to break the power of this nobility by recruiting
a loyal bureaucracy through state examinations. The Sung meritocracy
had carried this attack even further. By the year 1000, the aristocratic
lineages of the Northwest had finally lost out to a new elite of literati
centered on the Yangtze valley.

This new, nonascriptive group of civil servants was to be centrally
employed and locally disengaged. Fresh blood would ceaselessly replace
and invigorate old personnel. The high mobility rates of the Ming period,
therefore, were a tribute to the success of this policy and to the efficacy of
the examination system in granting entrée to those who possessed qualifi-
cations of merit, not birth. Looking through official rosters for the entire
Ming reign, one finds only one major Chinese clan with enduring political
influence—a distinct contrast to the noble lineages of the medieval period.
Clearly, the members of this new status group were constantly shifting,
some moving up through the exams to acquire gentry status, others drop-
ping back down to the level of simple landholding or worse.

Only the *attributes* of the elite were fixed. Membership was ostensibly
defined by degree-holding. A man who passed the provincial examinations to become a *chü-jen*, and was thereby allowed to dress in special
clothes or was exempted from common judicial punishments, had acquired *legal* status as a member of the gentry. But a state degree was not
always necessary for gentry *social* status. A way of life—a special "status
manner," which was the product of leisure and wealth—also earned a
man the polite respect and local consideration owing a "gentleman." In
short, if an individual could understand and discuss the classical texts,
write poetry with a fine enough hand, and drop the proper literary allusions in conversation, he became identified as a *hsiang-shen*, a local notable often indistinguishable from a genuine degree-holder. Many have
confused this lower-class deference to the literatus with popular venera-
tion for scholasticism; they forget that learning brought palpable and
tangible rewards. For if state authority in Ch'ing China was aloof and
awesome inside high yamen walls, then access to the magistrate behind
those walls was in itself a derived form of political power.

Let us clarify this by citing a property lawsuit as parable. Mr. Wang, a wealthy but untutored peasant of Kiangsu, claimed title to a piece of fertile land next to the villa of Mr. Ch'en, whose great-grandfather had been a ministry official sixty years earlier. Mr. Ch'en himself held no office, no titles; but he had been tutored in the Classics as a youth and still spent three hours a day in his small study making modest marginal comments on a text of the *Book of Changes* in his own, rather elegant hand. One afternoon a week, he would meet eight close comrades at a temple near the district capital. Wine would be heated and served, philosophical papers presented, and—as dusk came on—poems exchanged or a friend's painted scroll admired.

As the lawsuit developed, Mr. Wang mulled over his options. They were not many. Like any other peasant claimant, he could present himself at the magistrate's gates and plead for justice. Such temerity would probably earn him only a beating from the yamen runners for having dared to disturb the magistrate's nap. On the other hand, he could pay a large sum of money to one of the official law clerks and hope to get a hearing for his case. Naturally, this would appear most irregular from the viewpoint of the authors of the *Ch'ing Statutes*. A competent magistrate was supposed to prevent such petty corruption by staying alert, knowing his district intimately, keeping his finger on the pulse of the people. And how was a magistrate to get this kind of information? A man of his stature could not walk about the streets accosting congee peddlers, asking if they had heard of any bribery cases lately. That would not only demean the necessary dignity of his office but would leave him open to every crackpot with a minor complaint. Since his routine sources of intelligence, the yamen's petty clerks and policemen, were seldom able to resist the blandishments of the highest bidder, he had no recourse but to turn to the one group in the community that he could approach without tarnishing his badges of rank: the gentry. Unfortunately for poor Mr. Wang, these were precisely the sort of men with whom his opponent, Mr. Ch'en, consorted.

Thus, Mr. Ch'en's management of the impending law case was simple, though indirect. First, he paid a call on a fellow member of his poetry club, who also happened to have been a *t'ung-nien*[9] of the local magistrate. This friend was most happy to introduce so cultivated a guest as Mr. Ch'en to the official the following day over tea. Exchanging pleasantries, the two men hit it off well. The magistrate was also enamored of the *Book of Changes* and impressed by Mr. Ch'en's theories about that classic. As Mr. Ch'en was leaving, he asked if he might have the honor

---

[9] Literally, "same year," referring to men who take the state examinations together. This was one of the closest ties among members of the elite, roughly similar to those between American fraternity brothers at the same college.

of presenting the magistrate with a small painting. ("The antique-dealer claimed it's a Sung scroll. It's not, of course. But it is quite a good forgery, and I thought Your Excellency might enjoy looking at such a trinket from so worthless a one as myself.") The official was happy to accept, and the two men parted on the best of terms.

When Mr. Wang discovered that his opponent in the coming lawsuit was an acceptable guest at the judge's own home, he realized how fool-hardy he had been and dropped the matter altogether. Later, he even paid his own visit to Mr. Ch'en, apologizing for having disturbed His Honor. Fortunately, he obsequiously added, *"Ta-jen pu chi hsiao-jen kuo"* ("A great man does not remember the faults of a smaller man").

This is an entirely imaginary incident, drawn from no specific text but symbolic of thousands of such situations and designed to show two things: first, that gentry status could be reduced to a common denominator— power-holding through office or *access* to power-holders—and, second, that people who spoke or thought in ways we now identify with the high culture of China were better able to protect their local interests than those who did not share this language and way of life with Chinese offi-cialdom. Mr. Ch'en's family may not actually have had a power-holder in its ranks for three generations; he himself would not be found on official gentry lists, and he was perhaps registered only as part of a *fu-chia* ("wealthy household"). But he was nonetheless identified with that local elite. This is not to say that Ch'en's ilk was forever protected from the hard end of the stick. A classical education was an expensive proposition and hard to come by. Once established, a family had to hope that con-tinuing generations would produce at least one kinsman with the aptitude and dedication for classical learning. Besides, living up to the gentry way of life (fine wine, copies of the *Book of Changes*, Sung "trinkets") could fritter away a family's fortune. But appearances still told. The Ch'ens of China found it easier to accumulate and hold fortunes than the Wangs, for, although "status manner" and capital were intimately related, the former determined the outcome.

Another aspect of this parable remains to be explained. When Ch'en and Wang began struggling for that piece of property, neither acted cor-poratively. Corporate interest groups did, of course, exist, but they were usually outside the limits of acceptable political behavior. In other parts of China, for example, the two men might have enrolled their kinsmen in the dispute and incited a clan feud. Or Mr. Wang might have turned to a local gang leader and engaged footpads to accost Ch'en some dark night. Ch'en, in turn, might have recruited his own group of vigilantes for self-protection. These activities, however, were criminal examples of cor-porate behavior, existing because other forms of group action, which are usually regarded as legitimate in the West, were forbidden in Ming and

Ch'ing China. For instance, perhaps Mr. Wang could have tried to get together some friends to form a peasants' union. But a petition or two at the yamen and a demonstration protesting bribery in the law courts would probably have been misconstrued as a treasonable riot. Any group of peasants that formed a society for political reasons was automatically suspected by the authorities and likely to be proscribed for inciting revolt. If circumstances were right, considerable pressure might be exerted on a magistrate by threatening a riot; but this was done only in moments of genuine desperation, since the outcome was unpredictable. Besides, even if the magistrate acceded to the threat, Mr. Ch'en would have yet another card to play. Using some other friend, he would try to see that more gifts and pleasantries were exchanged at an even higher level. A prefect or a provincial treasurer, perhaps even a ministry official in Peking, would be approached and the magistrate overridden. Victory would still go to the man with contacts in high places.

Of course, this practice is not unique to eighteenth-century China. How many close friends of the chief of police resist trying to get their parking tickets fixed? The difference lies in emphasis. In China, "fixing," or the use of contacts, was regarded as less of a danger, and therefore as more legitimate, than allowing farmers to form unions. Even Mr. Ch'en —whose poetry club was a perfectly respectable scholastic association above doubt—was not likely to formally summon a gentry committee for help; rather, he would find the one or two liaison men who could put him in touch with a higher bureaucratic figure. Ch'en looked up toward Peking for political help, not around him for potential corporate allies.

In short, the local gentry was not a political estate. But it did, over the hundreds of years of Ming rule, begin to act like a social one. Although the founder of the Ming, Chu Yuan-chang (reign: 1368–98), had tried to destroy the "wealthy households" of the Yangtze basin that he saw as a threat to his control over that important revenue region, his successors felt that such local notables had to be trusted to check the petty despotism of district officials. Therefore, men of local wealth and power were encouraged to supervise rural tax-collection offices in order to prevent clerks and magistrates from growing corrupt. This meant that the power of the gentry itself increased unchecked, and by the late sixteenth century it threatened to become either an interest-seeking political pressure group or a resuscitated feudal elite capable of breaking away from imperial control.

This social estate began to change into a political one when palace interests usurped bureaucratic authority. As eunuchs abused the patronage system and members of the gentry no longer felt that they could look overhead for help, the delicate system of vertical power was thrown out of kilter. Corporately allied for nearly the first time, the gentry began to transform its poetry groups and academies into political clubs, sending in petitions, delivering public speeches, and behaving in a manner entirely familiar to students of eighteenth-century European history.

But this transformation from bureaucratic interest groups into corporate political units was aborted. Supporters of the throne correctly saw it as a threat to independent imperial rule and stepped in before the movement could coalesce. As soon as these supporters applied the usual forms of pressure (accusations of clique interest, disloyalty to the throne, and so forth), the clubs reverted to tried and true methods of defense. The Tung-lin[10] members' habituated mode of response disposed them to play by precisely the same rules as their opponents, searching for support from higher-ups and thus restricting the struggle to the administrative arena. Bureaucratic clienteles, rather than coherent regional and ideological parties, fought for power. Censor Liu (prompted by a governor who is urged by a patron in the Ministry of Rites) impeaches Magistrate T'an for corruption because T'an is the protégé of an official who supports the eunuchs against Liu's friend's patron.

This complicated game of oriental chess was played out with innuendo, but that did not reduce the stakes. Beginning in 1620, a series of shady palace squabbles over succession to the throne degenerated into a bloody struggle between a eunuch-minister named Wei Chung-hsien (1568–1627) and the Tung-lin group. Scholars were tortured and flogged, hounded to suicide, or murdered at Wei's instigation. When their friends and survivors convinced a new emperor, Ch'ung-chen (reign: 1628–44), of the eunuch's guilt, a counterpurge followed. The government was thus torn apart, year after year, by savage vendettas whose original causes seemed to have been long forgotten. Policy-makers were paralyzed, for all that an opponent had to do was to identify them—not their reform proposals—with one or the other of these two cliques, while the common weal was forgotten. By 1640, this long bureaucratic war had sapped the strength and dedication of most men of good will. Hundreds of high- and low-ranking officials began to plead illness or the death of a close relative as an excuse to withdraw entirely from government life and return to their home towns.

The Tung-lin struggles went on long after the fall of Peking. Ming loyalists were still fighting out these tragically absurd battles as Ch'ing forces besieged them in Yunnan. Seeing this, what conscientious Chinese scholar-official could help feeling that the Tung-lin affair had been a major cause of the Ming's decline? Later political thinkers found it hard to question the Ch'ing emperors' repeated warnings against the danger of cliques (that, too, was part of their rhetoric of conquest), for the Ch'ing had saved China from itself, from fratricide as well as rebellion. The very

[10] This was the title of the private academy that led the movement.

ease of the Manchus' initial victory over the Ming proved the correctness of K'ang-hsi's insistence that bureaucratic disputes weakened China. Of course, this stricture rigidly hampered serious policy debates, but was it not better to work for harmony and give up corporate representations than to risk clique formation? The scholar-officials would not be twice burned.

This abnegation may have been ambivalent, but it was complete enough to ensure that the Ming party experiment would not be repeated. The vertical system of rule was restored as thoroughly as the Imperial Palace itself. No more, promised the Ch'ing, would eunuchs bully officials. No more would the emperor arbitrarily neglect just and personal rule. But no more, in turn, must the gentry of China capriciously form political bodies to interfere in affairs of state. In fact, the academies themselves, once chambers for serious philosophical discussion, were to be transformed into vocational schools for the bureaucracy, and the balance of local power was to be subtly reversed.[11] Where the Ming had favored the interests of local notables against the power of magistrates, the Ch'ing threw their support behind district officials. After 1661, when the powerful households of the Yangtze valley were punished for tax evasion, the Ch'ing rulers took great pains to keep the gentry out of prominent local positions of influence.

Thus—to return for a moment to the architectural images of High Ch'ing—the state sheltered but also restrained. As much as the Summer Palace and Forbidden City differed in contour, they did share that one characteristic of enclosure: walls upon walls, everything in its place in this best of all possible Confucian worlds.

As the flow of eighteenth-century politics was perpendicular, so were cultural endeavors drawn up toward the figure of the emperor himself. It has often been said that the Ch'ing was a time of recapitulation rather than exploration. Its cultural hallmarks were the encyclopedia and the dictionary, not the seminal essay or the carefully penned philosophical treatise. Under K'ang-hsi the past was catalogued and preserved for the future and the emperor: In 1711 there appeared the *P'ei-wen yun-fu*, which indexed classical phrases into a glorified Bartlett's of incomparable value to literary and philosophical studies; then the sixteen-hundred-volume encyclopedia *Ku-chin t'u-shu chi-ch'eng;* and, in 1716, the authoritative K'ang-hsi dictionary itself. These were nothing, however, but a prelude to the collation of Ch'ien-lung's reign. In 1772, the emperor ordered that a "Complete library in the four branches of literature"

[11] See Frederic Wakeman, Jr., *Strangers at the Gate: Social Disorder in South China, 1839–1861* (Berkeley, Calif.: University of California Press, 1966), Appendix II.

(*Ssu-k'u ch'üan-shu*) be prepared. Scholars from all over the realm presented themselves in Peking to begin work on the massive task of editing over ten thousand different works collected from libraries and private homes. Of these, one-third were selected to be carefully recopied for the emperor's private library. A decade later, the first set of thirty-six thousand volumes was completed—an appropriate cultural monument to Ch'ien-lung.

Much has been made of the fact that this wholesale culling of the better private libraries of China was an opportunity for the Ch'ing authorities to censor their contents. Indeed, Ch'ien-lung himself devoted a great deal of effort to eradicating anti-Manchuism in the writings of an entire generation of Ming loyalists. Perhaps more important than this, though, was the way in which bibliographical pyramid-building monopolized the talents of literati. K'ang-hsi had consciously used compilation projects to entice many eremitic scholars out of political retirement and thereby to help gain their support for the new dynasty. Ch'ien-lung's *Ssu-k'u ch'üan-shu* was not so specifically designed, since Ming loyalism was no longer a serious problem, but the compilation did have a dampening effect of its own.

After the fall of the Ming, many Chinese political thinkers had begun to question the tenacity of Confucian thought. How effective was the Chinese *Tao* if their own dynasty had collapsed so dismally to Manchu barbarians? Men like Ku Yen-wu, Huang Tsung-hsi, Wang Fu-chih, and Chu Chih-yü, each in his own way, played variations on a shared theme. The tenor of their reevaluation of Chinese thought was that the "empty" metaphysical speculation of Neo-Confucian philosophy had diverted the attention of Ming statesmen from the world around them to cosmic conundrums. Instead of uselessly mulling over ontological riddles or adding yet another gloss to a fifteenth-century interpretation of an eleventh-century interpretation of a sixth-century version of a Han classic, these loyalists suggested, the scholar would do far better to engage in "practical learning." The world of phenomena and of current affairs had to be understood and mastered lest Confucianism become a useless creed.

This brave call for a new departure, for a turn from metaphysics to empiricism, held great potential for China. If theorists had stopped worrying about the relationship between a mysterious hexagram in the *Book of Changes* and an elusive phrase in the *Analects* and had instead become interested in hydraulics or the laws of motion, then Chinese civilization might have been better prepared to deal with modern technology in the nineteenth century. But somehow this call for "practical studies" was misinterpreted. One hundred years later, empiricism was ostensibly still an active, querying school of investigation; yet it found expression not in scientism but in scientific philology. Eighteenth-century scholars like Tai Chen (1724–77) radically reevaluated the Confucian canon by challenging the authenticity of certain texts through new philological techniques of refined quality and subtle rationality. As admirable as these techniques were, however, empiricism's range of investigable phenomena was still Classics-bound. Of course, it is easy for post-Keplerians to sneer at Ch'ing scholars who continued, like their Ming predecessors, to pick at the *pilpul*, the trivia, of Confucian book learning instead of sitting under an apple tree like Newton. But who, after all, is to say that Tai Chen's examination of the Classics was not as important a "contribution" as the invention of the steam engine, particularly within Tai Chen's own frame of reference? We can criticize only because we know, despite the adjuration at the beginning of this essay, what the Opium War (1839–42) is going to mean for Ch'ing China. We can see that intellectual enclosure will become a luxury the country cannot afford when it comes to feel that walls are for defense, not for museums. Naturally, if Tai Chen's work had been matched by researches of a similarly high quality into other subjects of human curiosity, then there would be no need to denigrate it at all. But he was only the best of many like him; and the startling fact about these philologists was that they believed their work to be in the best tradition of the loyalists' appeal for "practical studies."

There were several reasons for this misinterpretation, but one is directly related to the Ch'ien-lung Emperor's encyclopedia-gathering. The loyalists' disgust with philosophizing and concern with *engagement* made them value direct effort. Instead of reading about waterworks in an old text, a scholar should leave his studio and examine the dikes first-hand. Oddly enough, philological collation seemed to do justice to this concept. "Practical" and "concrete" were easily confused. To pick up a text, tactile and palpable, from the third century B.C. and read it directly, without using the prisms of generations of commentators, was to get at the real, the concrete, truths of Chinese civilization. Moreover, valuing effort for its own sake coincided with the gargantuan efforts of the Ch'ien-lung Emperor's compilation bureau. Methods and ends became confused. Certainly, it would be absurd to claim that editing the *Ssu-k'u ch'üan-shu* sapped the creative genius of an entire generation, but the great collections did somewhat more than reify the cataloguer's art and equate textual knowledge with philosophical perception. They employed men like Tai Chen for tens of years, invariably drawing skill and interest toward the seat of power and culture.

POLITICS were also in the shadow of Peking, and politics dominated economics. During the Ming, commerce grew within the interstices of the imperial purveying and transport systems. Outside this cadre, a money economy developed apace. Along the southeastern coast, a flourishing junk trade was carried on with Southeast Asia and Japan; coastal vessels hauled goods up and down the littoral whenever and wherever pirates permitted them to sail. Shansi bankers traveled the length and breadth of the country. Soochow and Sung-chiang developed important weaving industries. All of this, save the coastal commerce, was partially interrupted by the wars of the seventeenth century, but by 1700 the trend had resumed. Salt merchants prospered on the proceeds of their monopolies. Copper mines were opened. Petty consignment merchants carried tea and silk over the mountain passes south to Kwangtung. Cottage industry became more prevalent in the central part of the country. With taxes and labor services commutated, money continued to replace kind and corvée in the Chinese countryside.

Arguing from European parallels, economic historians have asked why this commercial growth and monetarization did not engender enough capital to create a class of entrepreneurs capable of helping China industrialize later on when it tried to catch up with Japan and the West. Wealth there certainly was. Howqua, the great Hong merchant of Canton, amassed a fortune of twenty-six million silver dollars from foreign trade in the early 1800's. Yet he and others like him seldom invested in anything other than land, pawnshops, and conspicuous consumption. Parvenu merchants patronized poets, commissioned painters, collected rare books or jade—adding to the cultural splendor of the eighteenth century but depriving the nineteenth of entrepreneurial skill and disposition. The tone of the 1700's encouraged extravagance. Capital was constantly dispersed as mercantilists tried their best to acquire refinement and learning. One bought a degree for his son or became a *bourgeois gentilhomme* by spending more on tea parties and courtesans than the wealthiest of provincial governors or ministry officials. The status rise may have been enjoyable, but it was usually short. Mercantile families seem to have risen and fallen as often as degree-holders: from shirtsleeves to shirtsleeves in the proverbial three generations.

It was not enough to be a mere bourgeois, perhaps because the *bourg* itself did not exist. Merchants had their guilds, of course, and called them *hang* (literally, "rows"). The name can be traced back to the T'ang period, when it was used to designate merchants who owned places of business along the same street. Since T'ang cities were divided into occupational quarters, the spatial organization coincided with shops of the same trade: butchers' *hang*, goldsmiths' *hang*, weavers' *hang* and so forth. At first glance, these *hang* seem quite like the municipal guilds of medieval Europe, but the differences between the two are more suggestive than the points of resemblance. European guilds grew organically as groups of merchants or craftsmen sought to gain monopolies and ensure the protection of their trade. The *hang* of T'ang China, on the other hand, were created by the government itself and imposed on businessmen or artisans as a mechanical controlling device. The guild syndics of the T'ang, Sung, Yuan, Ming, and Ch'ing did not sit in state, controlling their own municipal councils. Instead, the towns remained administrative capitals, where merchants lived on bureaucratic sufferance, constantly prey to official extortion. Even by the High Ch'ing, strict Confucianists continued to believe that commerce had to be controlled because it created a class of social parasites, attracting men and goods away from agriculture, which was the nation's economic "foundation." Moreover, trade bred crime and corruption—first, because its profits invited official embezzlement and, second, because it truly was associated with the underworld. This was especially true of maritime commerce. From 1500 on, the inhabitants of entire villages along the Fukienese coast became virtual caste-traders and pirates, switching easily and naturally from commerce to robbery and back again as circumstances decided. Inland, traveling consignment merchants (*k'o-shang*) were also intimately involved with criminal elements. Enough evidence has been accumulated to show that after 1800 such men often joined secret societies for credit and protection when they traveled away from their home towns and could not turn to friends or kinsmen for support. Naturally, an important guildsman eschewed such contacts; but even the most respectable merchant, by his very profession, exceeded the enclosures of an ideally settled agrarian empire. His physical mobility, the liquidity of his assets, even the way he linked autarchic and sealed economic units by bringing buyer and seller together, defied traditional notions of a fixed social and political order. The guilds, therefore, were used to turn merchants into hostages, controllable and always available. A bargain was struck. In exchange for being accessible to "squeeze" and official price manipulation, the guild merchant was granted monopoly rights to a portion of the trade. He was thereby guaranteed government backing to sell at *his* prices to all consumers but the government itself. As competition was curtailed, the monopoly merchant became concerned with cornering a market, not with developing new ones. The price of security was relative economic stagnation.

The imagery of imperial walls coincides with this collective division of merchants into manageable enclosures. The imagery of vertical relationships suggests yet another characteristic of commercial activity. Restraint of the *collective* profession of traders was seemingly mollified by society's willingness to allow *individual* merchants to escape guild bondage. This was much more characteristic of the High Ch'ing than of any other period. Just as the polity constantly disengaged the gentry from their locale, so did the state offer individual businessmen an ascent upward into elite status. By buying a degree for his son, or adopting a gentleman's way of life, the bourgeois could hope for social and political acceptance. This precious license made commerce attractive, not as an end in itself, but as a means of reaching the world of big villas, tea parties, poetry readings, and official circles. It did not, however, make *continued* pursuit of commerce either desirable or necessary for a single individual.

In ascriptive societies like medieval Europe or Japan, a trader's rank was fixed by a nobility that seldom opened its ranks to those below. This forced merchants to try to elevate their collective status by creating a new milieu of their own, like the urban culture of seventeenth-century Dutch burghers, or by stubbornly insisting, and later believing, that acquisition had its own special godliness not shared by a parasitic and useless aristocracy. But in China wealth, talent, and potential ideologues were siphoned out of mercantile circles, weakening those forces that eventually would have threatened traditional gentry society. The combined effect of collective security and individual mobility was the same in the economic as in the political sphere: commitment to Peking and the status quo.

PEKING was also, as someone once wrote, "a biological device for ruling the world." Any tribute-bearer (whether a chieftain from the Ryukyus or an ambassador from Holland) who had to walk those long approaches to the palace reception hall physically appreciated his own puniness before the majesty of Chinese rule. Gate after gate swept by, square after square, until the viewer grew dizzy, overcome with a growing sense of *déjà vu*. Sheer fatigue may have accounted for the trembling knees of some "barbarian" envoys, but there was a psychological set to this as well.

Since the Chinese tribute system has been described in most textbooks of Asian history, we need not linger here except to reiterate that the High Ch'ing limited diplomatic relations to a set of highly ritualized ceremonial exchanges designed to leave no doubt as to who was vassal and who was suzerain. "The ruler faces south, the minister north; the father sits, the son crouches," goes the commentary to the *Book of Changes*, which adds, "This Way is undeviating." Equality was out of the question, since both cosmically and politically there had to be divisions and hierarchy. Nor does the inadequacy of this method for accommodating modern Europeans need to be discussed in detail. China's premodern relations with Japan showed more than once that friction and even warfare resulted when another sovereign nation was unwilling to deal with the Central Kingdom on these terms.

Of course, tribute had its cultural aspects, too. In the Ch'ing scheme of things, political inferiority was accompanied by intellectual inferiority. All foreign imports, even if intangible artifacts of thought, were considered only barbarian curiosities. This frame of mind was entirely different from eighteenth-century Europeans' corresponding attitudes toward China.[12] To ambitious egalitarians of Europe, China was a civilization that valued merit, not birth. To deists, it was a country where even state-sponsored religion was rational and tolerant, permitting Jesuits to serve the emperor as easily as Buddhists or Confucians. To physiocrats, it was an immense agrarian empire where agriculture was valued above all other pursuits. To Englishmen watching dazzling tableaux on the London stage, China was an exotic and fascinating land where anything could happen. To rococo-loving Parisians, it was pastels and porcelain, delicate lines and variegated colors—a Watteau landscape with conical hats. Much of this was pure fantasy, but that was precisely why China was so important to the men of the Enlightenment. Like Montesquieu's Persians, the Chinese and their empire presented an ideal lens through which European faults and inadequacies could be more clearly seen. This did not necessarily mean that Western Europe was inherently more open to foreign influences than other cultures. Rather, Europe found itself ready for intrinsic change when China began to intrude upon its sensibilities after the 1680's. When Church and State were already being questioned, Confucius provided but another mode of instruction, another sort of caliper with which to plot out change.

The High Ch'ing showed none of this openness to change, mostly because of cultural self-satisfaction. We now dismiss those great encyclopedias as replays of old themes, but then they were vaunted highly. There was no fear of stagnancy in eighteenth-century China. And so, when European envoys brought elaborate clocks and fancy moving toys, the emperor and his courtiers admired their tick and tinkle and never thought to look through the curious intricacy of the mechanisms to wonder at the science behind them. This is all the more astonishing when it is realized that both the Ming and Ch'ing dynasties used European cannoniers against each other, or that the K'ang-hsi Emperor employed Europeans as court astronomers because their mathematics were so obviously superior to the native product. Of course, some Chinese scholars did realize that certain practical arts were made more highly developed in those strange, barbarian countries beyond the pale than in the Central Kingdom itself. Some even showed a sense of inadequacy when they argued defensively in the late seventeenth and early eighteenth centuries that China had absolutely nothing to learn from the West. But these doubts were rare. China, after all, had proved itself superior against weaponry and barbarians before. Better guns and more effective arithmetic might be important as techniques, but the foundation of cultural

[12] For an elegant analysis of this, see Louis Dermigny, *La Chine et l'occident; le commerce à Canton au XVIIIᵉ siècle, 1719–1833* (Paris: S.E.V.P.E.N., 1964), Vol. 1, pp. 11–80.

success was the Way of civil rule, evinced and explained in the very classics collected in those huge encyclopedias. These, and the *Tao* behind them, were superior to anything else that man had ever devised. Anything else was merely barbarian—sometimes interesting, sometimes amusing, sometimes even useful, but never crucial.

This Chinese rejection of the West between 1700 and 1850 was not entirely a result of self-satisfaction. It also reflected the general Ch'ing spirit of control and enclosure. Until the sixteenth century, China had remained reasonably open to foreign visitors. The men of the T'ang had been fascinated with exotic customs and goods. The Southern Sung (1127–1278) had strongly encouraged foreign merchants to come and trade with the Chinese by granting them official ranks and extraterritorial privileges. The Yuan dynasty (1280–1368) had opened up an overland trade route across Central Asia and had brought in thousands of foreign merchants like Marco Polo, even favoring them over native Chinese as emissaries and officials. Some scholars, in fact, believe that the Ming's severance of these contacts after the fifteenth century represented a conservative revulsion against this very foreignness of Mongol rule. Historical evidence now shows, though, that as of 1500 a new and vigorous maritime way of life was beginning to change the contours of Asian society. Resisting classification and control, this energetic stratum appeared among the entrepôts of Southeast Asia, in the Indonesian Archipelago and Indian Ocean, and along the coast of Northeast Asia. First composed of Chinese junkmen and Javanese sailors, Japanese pirates and Korean merchants, then enriched by Portuguese explorers and Spanish adventurers and finally by the Dutch and English, this new brotherhood of traders began to link together the ports of Asia much as these coasts are finally joined today by modern maritime power into an international world of trade and exchange. But—also a foretaste of the twentieth century—the inner reaches of China were barely affected, barely touched.

As pointed out earlier, trade and piracy went hand in hand. By the mid-sixteenth century, freebooters controlled entire stretches of the China coast. Since many of these pirates were Japanese *wakō* (a perjorative term meaning "dwarf bandits"), they shortly became associated by the Chinese with the same forces that prompted Hideyoshi's invasion of Korea in the 1590's. After 1645, this coastal world was even further blemished in Ch'ing eyes by its relationship to Ming loyalism. The ruler of Formosa, Koxinga (or Kuo-hsing-yeh), who was the son of a Chinese pirate and a Japanese mother, consorted with English traders, sent pirate fleets up and down the coast, and pretended to act in the name of the vanquished Ming. Since it was difficult to adapt a land army to maritime warfare, the Ch'ing simply carried the Ming prohibition of foreign trade one step farther by evacuating the population from the seacoast. A deserted ten-mile strip, running from Shantung to Kwangtung and sealed off by ditches and walls, separated China from the dreaded ocean. Thus did the empire defensively enclose itself, thereby forsaking the opportunity to experiment with sea power.

The wall image may by now seem complete, but enclosure was carried yet one more step, for China did not wish to deny itself the revenue advantages of a controlled foreign trade. When K'ang-hsi reopened trade relations after 1684, all overseas commerce was slowly squeezed down into the area around Canton. By 1757, when all other ports were formally closed to foreign merchants, the "Canton system," which combined collective guild-control mechanisms and hierarchical tributary restraints, had been elaborated. In strictly limiting trade to this one port, the High Ch'ing tried to keep the new maritime forces manageable and isolated. In their own way, the Thirteen Factories of Canton were thus very much like the *hang* quarters of the T'ang. But, judging from the history of native mercantilism, there had to be an opening somewhere to release the pressure of frustration. Since the tribute system had been combined with the guild mechanism, this opening was blocked. Foreigners could not even deal directly with Chinese officials but had to petition via the Cantonese hong merchants. Thus, there was no hope at all of moving back up that vertical line of authority, or up the perpendicular coast of China itself, to the source of it all: Peking. So fine a filter was bound to clog, and when it did all enclosures shattered.

THE *pax sinica* that the Manchus offered China demanded self-restraint —maintenance and consolidation rather than initiative and exploration. The implications of so implicit an arrangement—which was, of course, never consciously agreed to by either ruler or ruled—have been the subject of this essay. One other implication must therefore be mentioned: the reward of peace itself. Never have the Chinese enjoyed such general security as during the middle years of the eighteenth century, the great Indian summer of their traditional history. In a conclusive (and not merely suggestive) sense, this peace carried its own ruin within it. The introduction of European crops like maize and sweet potatoes made theretofore barren areas cultivable, and migrants began to settle the sparsely populated hill regions of the country where these new crops could be grown. Without wars and famine to check it, population rose sharply. During the course of the Ch'ing reign, the number of people in China more than doubled, reaching at least three hundred million by the early 1800's. The reward of peace was population pressure.

Once again traditional signs of dynastic decline appeared: rising costs of military expeditions, corruption in high places, declining waterworks. In the 1790's, "White Lotus" rebels—offshoots of a chiliastic Maitreyan sect—revolted in Central China. The government mounted a desperate campaign, at huge cost and effort, that finally pacified those provinces, but new catastrophes followed. The Yellow River flooded repeatedly. In fact, there were hints that officials charged with flood control were actually letting the dikes collapse so that they could "squeeze" money from local landowners when special assessments were made for repairs. In 1813, another group of rebels belonging to the *T'ien-li-chiao* arose near Peking and tried to assassinate the emperor. Pirates began to attack the southeastern coast once again. Aboriginal tribesmen in Kiangsi and Hunan, who had been pacified by Ch'ien-lung fifty years earlier, began to quarrel with the authorities, and finally revolted in 1832. Copper supplies began to run low, causing a dangerous inflationary trend throughout the country.

However, these were traditional omens of dynastic decay, and they began to seem anachronistic once the challenge of the West became obvious after 1842. Rebels and waterworks were still important enough, but to more and more Chinese the enemy was without, not within. The country needed saving from others far more than from itself. In 1860, Lord Elgin, who commanded a British military expedition that had taken Peking with the help of the French, decided to punish the Ch'ing ruling house for certain minor excesses committed against English prisoners-of-war. His behavior was righteous but atrocious—and far more of a despoliation than the seizure of the Parthenon's friezes (which were, after all, preserved). Wanting to strike at the dynasty where it would hurt the most, he bypassed the Imperial Palace—which could have belonged to *any* emperor —and loosed his men on the Manchus' Summer Palace. The gorgeous gardens and promenades, the high walls and decorated pavilions, were burned to cinders, and a pall of smoke hung west of Peking for days on end.

Over twenty-five years later, the Empress-Dowager Tz'u-hsi fulfilled her fondest dream when, at enormous cost, she began to rebuild that monument to the ruling family. But personification, so apt to the eighteenth century, when Ch'ien-lung was sheltered by the general acceptability of his rule, ill suited the 1890's. The walls might stand again, but their imagery had changed. At a time when Confucian standards had already begun to wane, personification now drew attention to the very Manchu-ness of Ch'ing governance. And even by traditional ideals Ts'u-hsi would have stood condemned, for the construction funds for those walls had been taken from the national defense budget, depriving the navy of supplies and ships. When China was ignominiously defeated by Japan four years after the building was completed, the Summer Palace came to be a symbol of Manchu selfishness and corruption. The ruling house, purveyor of a peace so many had wanted two hundred and fifty years before, was soon to be ushered out; and those scrolls, those books, those jade and gold personifications of the spirit of High Ch'ing left to mere curators' hands.

Selected Readings

Chang Hsin-pao. *Commissioner Lin and the Opium War*. Cambridge, Mass.: Harvard University Press, 1964. Tracing the career of Lin Tse-hsu, the imperial commissioner who closed down the opium traffic at Canton and precipitated war with England, this study meticulously details the steps that led to the conflict.

Ch'ü T'ung-tsu. *Local Government in China Under the Ch'ing*. Cambridge, Mass.: Harvard University Press, 1962. A carefully researched description of district government, emphasizing the role of clerks and yamen employees.

Dermigny, Louis. *La Chine et l'occident: le commerce à Canton au XVIIIᵉ siècle, 1719–1833*. 3 vols. Leiden, Netherlands: Brill, 1964. This is the best—though one of the longest—studies in any language on eighteenth-century Chinese foreign relations. At the very least, the first chapter of Volume 1 should be read for its eloquent account of China's view of the West and vice versa.

Fairbank, John K. *Trade and Diplomacy on the China Coast*. 2 vols. Cambridge, Mass.: Harvard University Press, 1953. By now a historical classic, Fairbank's study examines the political and diplomatic consequences of the Opium War for the Chinese nation.

Greenberg, Michael. *British Trade and the Opening of China, 1800–1842*. London: Cambridge University Press, 1951. This was the first close study, still to be superseded, of the "free traders" who challenged the Canton monopoly system, spread the opium traffic, and helped bring about the Opium War (1839–42).

Ho Ping-ti. *The Ladder of Success in Imperial China*. New York: Wiley, 1965. This is much more than what it purports to be—namely, a study of social mobility during the Ch'ing period. Thanks to background information, translated biographical materials, and incidental analysis, Professor Ho's study is one of the most exciting accounts in print of Ch'ing social history.

———. *Studies on the Population of China, 1368–1953*. Cambridge, Mass.: Harvard University Press, 1959. Again, one should not be misled by the title and leave this kind of reading to students of demography. Ho presents several important theses here—such as those on the importance of the introduction of new food crops and on the role of merchants in Chinese society—as well as giving a superb summary of Chinese economic history during the Ming and Ch'ing periods.

Hsiao Kung-ch'uan. *Rural China: Imperial Control in the Nineteenth*

Century. Seattle: University of Washington Press, 1960. This is not an easy book to read because of the voluminous materials on village government and rural social groups. For anyone wishing to get below the surface of rural China, however, it is a necessary supplement to Ch'ü T'ung-tsu's study.

Hucker, Charles. *China: A Critical Bibliography*. Tuscon, Ariz.: University of Arizona Press, 1962. Though slightly outdated, this is an excellent short bibliography with critical annotations for beginning and advanced students.

Levenson, Joseph R. *The Problem of Intellectual Continuity*. Vol. 1, *Confucian China and Its Modern Fate*. 3 vols. Berkeley, Calif.: University of California Press, 1958–65. This sensitive and enlightening study by a brilliant intellectual historian focuses on China's cultural malaise toward the end of the nineteenth century but also includes an extremely important thesis ("the amateur ideal") concerning earlier periods.

Michael, Franz. *The Origin of Manchu Rule in China*. Baltimore: Johns Hopkins Press, 1925. A short, analytic study of early Manchu institutions, stressing their emulation of Chinese administrative organs.

Nivison, David S. *The Life and Thought of Chang Hsueh-ch'eng*. Stanford, Calif.: Stanford University Press, 1965. One of the few studies in English of the intellectual history of eighteenth-century China, this book explores historiography and philosophy through the biography of a noted literatus.

Spence, Jonathan. *Ts'ao Yin and the K'ang-hsi Emperor*. New Haven, Conn.: Yale University Press, 1966. A brilliantly written account of one of the K'ang-hsi Emperor's personal bond-servants, whose grandson wrote *The Dream of the Red Chamber*. This study has much to say about both the K'ang-hsi Emperor and the institutional nature of the early Ch'ing.

Wakeman, Frederic, Jr. *Strangers at the Gate: Social Disorder in South China, 1839–1861*. Berkeley, Calif.: University of California Press, 1966. An account of the effects of the Opium War on rural society around Canton.

Waley, Arthur. *The Opium War Through Chinese Eyes*. London: Allen & Unwin, 1958. This book, by a famous Sinologist and translator, takes the reader inside China—looking out at the "barbarians"—via translated excerpts and summaries of Lin Tse-hsu's personal diary, gentry accounts, and battle records. Fascinating and enjoyable reading.

Ch'ing China:
Confrontation with the West,
1850–1900

PAUL A. COHEN

WESTERN reconstructions of Chinese history from the Opium War (1839–42) to the Boxer uprising (1899–1900) tend to lean heavily on the concepts of "Western impact" and "Chinese response." This conceptual framework rests on the assumption that the confrontation with the West was the most significant influence on events in China in the last half of the nineteenth century. A further assumption, implicit in the phrasing of the concepts, is that it was the West, rather than China, that initiated the confrontation.

The impact-response framework stands up tolerably well at a high level of historical generality. It becomes progressively less satisfactory, however, as we get closer to actual happenings. An analogy to the Newtonian explanation of the physical universe comes to mind. Developments in the field of physics over the past century have not "disproved" Newton's laws; they have merely shown that these laws have a limited range of applicability, that they are valid for large bodies only. So with the impact-response approach to late Ch'ing history: The task is not to demonstrate its falsity but to refine and improve on it so that a more complex historical reality can be accounted for.

Let us begin by indicating a few of the problems of this approach. Some are probably inherent difficulties; others might be better characterized as pitfalls that, though theoretically avoidable, are seldom avoided in practice.

The Prevailing Framework
of Interpretation: Some Problems

One problem is the tendency, when speaking of the "Western impact," to ignore the enigmatic and contradictory nature of the nineteenth-century

West. Most of us are properly humbled by the superficiality of our understanding of "non-Western" societies. Not so with the West, which is home
ground and which we take as a known quantity. Yet, "when we turn our
attention back to the modern West itself," as Benjamin Schwartz has
wisely observed,

> this deceptive clarity disappears. We are aware that the best minds of
> the nineteenth and twentieth centuries have been deeply divided in their
> agonizing efforts to grasp the inner meaning of modern Western de-
> velopment. . . . We undoubtedly "know" infinitely more about the West
> [than about any given non-Western society], but the West remains as
> problematic as ever.[1]

It is well to keep in mind too that the "total West" never had an impact
on other societies. Shanghai in the late nineteenth century seemed "Western" in contrast with an indubitably Chinese hinterland, but Shanghai
was no more a microcosmic version of Western culture than New York
City is of the culture of North America. Similarly, in viewing the first
half of the twentieth century, when virtually every strain of Western
thought at one time or another found an advocate in Chinese intellectual
circles, it would be absurd to think in terms of an impact of the total culture of the West. Even when Chinese talked of "all-out Westernization,"
what they really had in mind was not the mechanical substitution of
Western society for Chinese but the transformation of China in line with
a highly selective vision of what the West was all about.

The "West" that countries like China encountered was only part of a
whole. Even this part, moreover, was metamorphosed in the process of
encounter. A man who left the West to do missionary work in China in
the nineteenth century was probably not a very typical Westerner to begin with. After living in China for a while, he surely became even less
typical. In learning Chinese and adopting certain Chinese customs, he
interacted with his new environment, and a process of hybridization set
in. No longer a Westerner pure and simple, he became a Westerner-in-
China. Although the Chinese with whom he came in contact continued to
view him as a foreigner—which of course he still was—their perception of
his foreignness was colored by *his* response to *Chinese* foreignness. It is
not enough, therefore, to explain what took place simply in terms of a
Western impact and a Chinese response, for there was also a Western
response to a Chinese impact.

A similar hybridization occurred in the realm of ideas. Ideas, unlike
people, cannot actively respond to situations. But they are, at least in
part, defined by situations, for they have meaning only in the minds of

[1] *In Search of Wealth and Power: Yen Fu and the West* (Cambridge, Mass.:
Harvard University Press, 1964), pp. 1–2.

people, and the meaning a given idea has for a given person will be richly conditioned by the circumstances of its presentation. It makes little sense, then, to talk of direct Chinese responses to such Western ideas as national sovereignty, Christianity, and progress. Before these ideas could evoke responses, they had to be communicated, and they could be communicated only by being filtered through Chinese language and thought patterns. (The reference here, of course, is specifically to the nineteenth century, when it was still rare for Chinese to have direct access to Western languages.) Inevitably this resulted in distortion of the original ideas. (For example, "liberty" or "freedom" was translated as *tzu-yu*, which literally means "from the self" and has connotations of "license" or "lawlessness.") And it was to the distorted version rather than to the original that most Chinese responded.

The initial Western impact was subject to another sort of distortion when it was Chinese-carried. In some cases, as in the relationships between merchants and compradors or between missionaries and converts, the West's impact was more or less immediate and direct. But in others it was not. When Christianity was purveyed by Chinese rebels, or Western-style institutions were championed by Chinese reformers, the impact of the West was at one or more removes from its source. As this happened, it became hopelessly entangled in the sea of Chinese personalities and politics, and it is highly questionable whether, from this point on, the conventional impact-response framework of analysis remains useful. The Ch'ing government's response to the Taiping Rebellion and the responses of conservatives and moderate reformers to the reform movement of 1898 were elicited as much by traditional challenges of rebellion and reform as by the nontraditional challenge of the West. It would be extremely misleading to characterize them simply as responses to the West.

One more trap that is easily fallen into is the tendency to lapse into excessive abstraction in discussing the "Chinese response." There are really two problems here. One is the danger of reducing a great variety of responses to a few that are highly visible and easily labeled. The second is the temptation to regard responses as specifically *Chinese* when they may have been shaped in part by supracultural (that is, non-Chinese) factors. China, as a geographical entity, is continental in size and exhibits an incredible range of ethnic, linguistic, and regional variation. Within any given region there has always been a great gulf between the world view and life pattern of the elites and those of the masses. Even within an elite of one area, as in any grouping of human beings anywhere, attitudes and behavior have been governed by personality, character, age, sex, and the particular constellation of a given individual's social and political relationships, as well as by intrinsically Chinese qualities. The phrase "Chinese response," therefore, can serve at best as shorthand for a very complex historical situation. The fact is that in the nineteenth century, as in the twentieth, there were many Chinese responses, and not all of them were conditioned primarily by the Chineseness of the responders.

We can sum up by saying that Chinese in the last century seldom responded to the West in a simple and direct fashion. They responded to the total situations confronting them, of which the Western impact, decisive as it may have been in some of these situations, was only one ingredient. Once this is recognized, we can proceed with the task of defining and measuring this impact in different contexts. One way of going about this is to depart from a strictly chronological approach and focus instead on major modalities of Chinese behavior in the last half of the nineteenth century. Three such modalities, to be discussed in the following pages, were rebellion, reform, and reaction. Each of these was affected by a Western impact. Yet none of them can be understood merely as responses to such an impact and thus they suggest some of the limitations of a too rigid reliance on the impact-response framework.

Major Modalities of Chinese Behavior, 1850–1900

REBELLION

In terms of immediate effect on the position of China's ruling dynasty and the lives of tens of millions of ordinary Chinese subjects, the most newsworthy development in the middle of the last century was not the nettling behavior of small bands of Westerners pocketed here and there along the seacoast. Internal unrest was the big story, and it was very big indeed. Aside from numerous local revolts, there were four rebellions of major proportions: a Moslem rebellion in Yunnan (1855–73), another Moslem rebellion in the Northwest (1862–73), the Nien (1853–68), and the Taiping (1851–64). The causes of these upheavals were many and complex, ranging from official corruption, overtaxation, and excessive land rents—all typical manifestations of Chinese dynastic decline—to population explosion, official discrimination against minority groups, and economic dislocation induced by foreign trade.

By far the most serious of the rebellions—and the only one to be significantly affected by the intrusion of the West—was the Taiping. In human and physical destructiveness, the Taiping Rebellion has had few if any parallels in world history. Large portions of the Lower Yangtze region, rural and urban, were totally devastated. Both sides in the conflict, the imperialists even more than the rebels, treated human life with unbelievable abandon. In addition to the millions butchered, millions more fell victim to famine and epidemic. Contemporary foreign estimates placed the total of lives lost at between twenty and thirty million. Although these figures were arrived at by guesswork and are doubtless exaggerated, there is strong evidence that in individual districts substantial portions of the population were eliminated.

The spawning ground for the Taipings was South China, where conditions favorable to rebellion were probably riper than anyplace else in the empire. The South was the last part of China to be brought under Manchu rule in the seventeenth century, and it remained one of the least secure links in the Ch'ing power structure. By the end of the eighteenth century it was subject to severe pressures from overpopulation and tenancy. On top of all this, it was in South China that the disruptive effects of Sino-foreign trade and the Opium War were most pronounced. Changing trade patterns and the spread of piracy and smuggling into the interior encouraged social dislocation, while British defeat of the Manchus activated Cantonese xenophobia and helped to give it an anti-Manchu focus. Whatever may be said of the superficiality of the Western impact elsewhere in China prior to 1850, in the far south it was real and profound.

The man who was to become the founder and early leader of the Taiping movement, Hung Hsiu-ch'üan, was born in South China, about thirty miles from Canton, in 1814. Significantly, Hung belonged to an ethnic minority—the Hakkas, or "guests"—which, although it had migrated south centuries before, was still segregated from the surrounding society by its distinctive language and customs. The brightest in a family of five children, Hung was given enough schooling to permit him to compete in the government examinations held in Canton. Each time he took the examinations, however, he failed. Once, after this happened, he suffered an acute mental collapse and was confined to bed for forty days, during which time he later claimed to have had visions. In 1843, after failing the examinations once again, he read a Christian tract that had been given him some years before and for the first time understood the meaning of his visions. Hung became convinced that he was the younger brother of Jesus, that he had been divinely charged to rid the world of demons and idols and to institute on earth the Kingdom of Heaven.

Hung Hsiu-ch'üan and a friend, also an unsuccessful examination candidate, now began to lead idol-breaking forays in Kwangtung and Kwangsi. With their followers, who consisted mainly of discontented peasants and secret-society members, they formed a loose grouping known as the Society of God-Worshipers. By the late 1840's local unrest and famine forced the society to organize for military protection against banditry. They themselves, however, were not readily distinguishable from bandits, and, in the unsettled conditions then prevailing in South

China, they soon found themselves engaged in pitched battle with imperial troops. One thing led to another, and in 1851 they raised the standard of dynastic revolt, Hung taking the title of "Heavenly King" (*T'ien-wang*) and the new dynasty being christened "the Heavenly Kingdom of Great Peace" (*T'ai-p'ing t'ien-kuo*).

The Taiping rebels quickly pressed north, piling success on success against the hapless imperial forces, until they reached the Yangtze River. They then turned eastward and in March 1853 established their capital in Nanking, which remained the political center of the movement until its collapse in 1864. Although the main arena of Taiping control was in central China, in fifteen years of fighting sixteen of the eighteen provinces of China proper were affected. A northern expedition in the mid-1850's reached the environs of Peking before being turned back, and in the early 1860's, as the center of rebel strength shifted toward the coast, Shanghai was threatened on a number of occasions.

From the outset, accidental factors played an important part in shaping the Taiping story. It was perhaps no accident that the rebellion should have been initiated by a disaffected scholar. But this scholar need not have turned out to be as fanatic and psychologically unstable as Hung Hsiu-ch'üan. (A psychiatrist has tentatively described Hung's illness as hysterical in basis with a possible schizophrenic-paranoiac element.) Also, it was no accident that the early leaders of the Taiping movement, discriminated against as Hakkas and alienated from a Confucian inner sanctum to which they had failed to gain access, should have rallied to the banner of a messianic, non-Confucian ideology to seal their alienation. But it could hardly have been preordained that a major ingredient in this ideology would be Western Christianity.

The ideology of the Taipings was a bizarre alchemy of pseudo-Christianity, primitive communism, sexual puritanism, and Confucian utopianism. The Christian influence was derived from Protestant religious writings and the personal instruction Hung received for a brief period in 1847 from a Protestant missionary in Canton. Yet certain basic Christian teachings, such as Christ's Sermon on the Mount, seem to have made little impact on the rebels' religion, while other Christian precepts underwent considerable modification in the process of being borrowed. Moreover, some of the most important features of Taiping religion—the Ten Commandments, a militant iconoclasm, the concept of a single supreme God who intervened on the Taiping side in battle and established direct relationships with rebel leaders—were gleaned not from the New Testament but from the Old.

The advanced social and economic doctrines of the rebels were built around the idea of the brotherhood and equality of all men, a corollary to the belief in the fatherhood of God. Security and protection were to be provided for the aged, the handicapped, the widowed, and the orphaned. Women were to be treated as full equals of men, being permitted to fight in the army, take the government examinations (which were based on Christian rather than Confucian texts), and hold office. The feminism of the Taipings was further evidenced in their proscription of footbinding, prostitution, and polygamy and in their injunction that land be allotted equitably without distinction as to sex. All private property was abolished, and movable goods were supposed to be placed in common treasuries for redistribution on the basis of need.

The political goal of the Taipings was to overthrow the Ch'ing and establish a new dynasty—new in kind as well as in name. The model for their political-military organization was taken from the *Chou li* ("Rituals of Chou"), a Chinese classical text believed to describe the administrative system of the early Chou period. At the top of the rebels' political structure was the Heavenly King, Hung Hsiu-ch'üan, who, theoretically at least, was supreme in both the spiritual and temporal realms. (Actually, by the end of 1853 Hung seems to have become little more than a figurehead, with real power lodged principally in the hands of his chief lieutenant, Yang Hsiu-ch'ing.) Hung was surrounded initially by five other "kings" (*wang*), each of whom had full civil and military power within his territorial jurisdiction. Beneath the top leadership was a hierarchy of lesser military commanders, who served concurrently as the military officers, civil administrators, and religious leaders of their units. The resulting organization—which was largely the creation of Yang Hsiu-ch'ing—has been characterized by Franz Michael as "totalitarian" and, in Michael's view, provided for "a system of total control of all life by the state which had no parallel in Chinese history."[2]

Was the Taiping Rebellion just another in a long line of Chinese peasant rebellions, or was it a revolution? So stated, this question is not really answerable. What, for example, is meant by "peasant rebellion"? If we mean that most of the rebels were of peasant extraction and that the grievances that drove them to rebel were the sorts of grievances that normally afflict peasants, then we certainly can call the Taiping a peasant rebellion. But, if we define "peasant rebellion" as a rebellion whose conscious object is to *redress* peasant grievances, it becomes more difficult to categorize the Taipings. Some Chinese Communist historians claim that the Taiping Rebellion was a peasant movement in precisely this sense. Recent Western historians have leaned toward the opposite view. The rebellion, in Michael's opinion, "did not have as its goal an agrarian revolution that would give the peasant the use of his land. . . . Its leaders

[2] Franz Michael in collaboration with Chang Chung-li, *The Taiping Rebellion: History and Documents* (Seattle: University of Washington Press, 1966), Vol. 1, p. 84. See also pp. 190, 198–99.

aimed at a political system in which the . . . rewards . . . were rank and title and the good life for them and their descendants on this earth and happiness in heaven after death."[3] Vincent Shih agrees, adding that even among Taiping followers "there was no evidence of peasant consciousness . . . . At the time of joining, Taiping followers cast aside with unbounded joy their role as peasants . . . ."[4]

Joseph Levenson intones the next question: "Why was this rebellion different from all other rebellions?" Michael's answer: "The Taipings attacked not only the ruling dynasty—they attacked the traditional social order itself. And this wider attack gave their rebellion a character totally different from that of rebellious movements of the past."[5] Levenson's own reply: "In all other rebellions such non-Confucian doctrine as the rebels held, Taoist or Buddhist in overtones, was not really a positive challenge to Confucianism as the intelligence of society; but the pseudo-Christianity of the Taipings was just such a challenge." In particular, Levenson emphasizes the radically non-Confucian premises on which the Taiping concept of monarchy was built. The Taipings denied the Confucian ideal of immanent virtue and substituted for it the Christian ideal of transcendental power. *T'ien-ming*, for the rebels, no longer meant "Mandate of Heaven"; it meant "the Commandments of God."[6]

Levenson and Michael are persuaded that the Taiping Rebellion was a revolutionary movement. Shih, while granting that the Taipings were "vastly different from any rebel group before," adamantly rejects the "revolutionary" label: "The [Taiping] leaders merely wished to take over the reins of government and showed no real revolutionary spirit— no wish to introduce fundamental changes into their society, whether in the form of government or in the fundamental pattern of their mental outlook." Significantly, Shih also parts company with Levenson and Michael when he minimizes the importance of the Western influence on Taiping ideology:

> There were certain ideas borrowed from Christianity and the West which held a genuine possibility of bringing about a real revolution. But this possibility was nullified when . . . the Taipings were unable to perceive Christian ideas except through the colored glasses of traditional concepts. Indeed, the elements of Christianity they accepted seem to have been only those that they could anchor to Chinese concepts.[7]

[3] *Ibid.*, p. 84. See also p. 192.

[4] *The Taiping Ideology: Its Sources, Interpretations, and Influences* (Seattle: University of Washington Press, 1967), pp. xvi–xvii.

[5] Michael and Chang, *The Taiping Rebellion*, p. 4.

[6] Joseph Levenson, *The Problem of Monarchical Decay*, Vol. 2 of *Confucian China and Its Modern Fate*, 3 vols. (Berkeley, Calif.: University of California Press, 1964), pp. 87, 91, 101–03.

[7] Shih, *The Taiping Ideology*, pp. xv, xix.

In part, the confusion over how the Taiping Rebellion is to be characterized is semantic in basis. Uniform definitions of concepts like "revolution" and "peasant rebellion" simply do not exist. In part, too, the confusion derives from the primitive state of our knowledge of earlier Chinese rebellions. Levenson and Michael, unlike Shih, appear to operate on the supposition that a rebel movement with revolutionary ideas need not fully actualize these ideas in order to be considered a revolution. It is enough that it pose a revolutionary *challenge* to the existing social and political order. But if this is so—and I believe it is—how safe are we in assuming, as we look backward, that the long line of Chinese rebellions (most of which failed) really consisted merely of rebellions? What shall we do, for example, with the revolt of the Yellow Turbans, which broke out in 184 A.D.? In short, before we can make much headway in answering the question "Why was this rebellion different from all other rebellions?" we must learn a lot more than we now know about the other rebellions.

THE Taiping Rebellion would have been a very different affair were it not for the presence of the West. The Opium War and the disruptive influence of foreign trade in South China contributed to the general dislocation out of which the rebellion emerged. Western Christianity provided the rebellion's leadership with some of its more distinctive ideological precepts, and one of the top rebel leaders in the last years of the insurrection, Hung Jen-kan (d. 1864), was directly and deeply exposed to Western culture. Moreover, the suppression of the rebellion in the early 1860's was materially, if not decisively, assisted by Western troops and arms.

Yet, in spite of everything, the Taiping Rebellion cannot be viewed, in any significant sense, as a response to the West. Rather, it was a Western-influenced variation on a theme that was played in widely scattered parts of China from approximately 1850 to 1870 in response to conditions that by and large predated the impact of the West.

The rebellion did, on the other hand, exert an important influence on China's response to the West. First, the rebel link with Christianity and the inability of a disunited missionary movement to dissociate itself convincingly from the rebellion tarnished the Western religion's image in China. Second, the new sources of regional power that had to be brought into being to suppress the rebellion weakened the central power permanently and thereby hampered the dynasty's subsequent efforts to respond creatively to the Western presence. Finally—and this point has not been stressed enough—the sheer magnitude of the problems created by the Taiping and other mid-century rebellions, together with the seemingly traditional nature of these problems, compelled Chinese leaders to turn inward at the very moment that their Japanese counterparts were devoting full attention to the challenge of the West. The "slowness" of China's response, in other words, was due not only to the nature of Chinese society but to the extraordinary problems facing it in the middle of the last century. There was no time to respond to the West.

REFORM

In the middle decades of the nineteenth century, the major question facing Chinese leaders was "Whither the Ch'ing?" By 1900 it had become "Whither China?" The story of the reform efforts that were made in the intervening period can be told in terms of the transition from the first question to the second.

Reform-minded Chinese began to respond to the West as early as the Opium War. But it was not until the 1870's and 1880's that the problem of the West finally assumed paramount importance—and even then for only a tiny minority of scholars and officials. In the decade or so prior to the 1870's, the principal concern of most Chinese reformers was the problem of domestic rebellion. Indeed, it was widely supposed during the T'ung-chih period (1862–74) that if the ills that had made rebellion possible could be removed, the problem of the West would take care of itself. The West, after all, would never have become a problem to begin with if China's house had been in better order.

In the fall of 1860 things could not have looked bleaker for the Manchus. Foreign troops had destroyed the Summer Palace and occupied Peking. The Hsien-feng Emperor had fled to Jehol with his entourage. The great Taiping Rebellion, which had seemed in the late 1850's to be fading rapidly, had gained a new lease on life with the advent to power of such leaders as Li Hsiu-ch'eng and Hung Jen-kan. Everything considered, the Ch'ing dynasty appeared to be on the verge of collapse.

And yet, miraculously, it did not collapse. The death of the incompetent emperor in 1861 paved the way for a new era at court. Chinese and Manchus both rallied to the support of the throne, and the top posts in the bureaucracy were staffed in the ensuing decade with an unusually gifted array of officials. The foreigners, after forcing through a new set of treaties, evacuated the capital and returned south, demonstrating that they were not hungry for Chinese territory. Most important, and partly as a result of these other factors, the tide finally turned against the Taipings, and by 1862 the fate of the rebellion was sealed.

The T'ung-chih reign was classified by the Chinese as a restoration (chung-hsing), suggesting an eleventh-hour attempt by the dynasty to revitalize its severely shaken institutional foundations and regain popular and gentry support. There had been several other restorations in Chinese history. The novel feature of this one was the presence of the West, which forces us to consider the question: To what extent was the T'ung-chih Restoration a response to the West?

To answer this question, we must say something of the reforms proposed and implemented in the 1860's. By and large they were restorative rather than innovative in character. In the sphere of civil government, for example, while the importance of selecting men of talent for official posts was generally recognized, "talent" continued to be defined in its traditional sense as omnicompetence rather than specialized ability, and Chinese remained convinced that as long as the bureaucracy was staffed by men of talent, institutional changes would be unnecessary. Similarly, when it came to reviving a seriously disrupted examination system, the best that critics could offer was the conventional suggestion that more emphasis be placed on substance and less on calligraphy and style. Nothing was done to update the subject matter of the examinations to cover the various branches of Western learning.

In the economic field too, as Mary Wright has ably shown,[8] the overriding emphasis in the proposed reforms was on restoration of the traditional economy. In agriculture, efforts were made to reduce imperial expenditures, increase the area of land under cultivation, repair waterworks, and the like. But the growing problem of tenantry was left unheeded. Moreover, it was still taken for granted that agriculture was the only truly important sector of the economy, and no one objected to high taxation of such nonagricultural activities as commerce. Further evidence of the backward-looking orientation of Restoration economic thought was the great resistance to the introduction of railway and telegraph systems. No Chinese of any consequence shared the foreign view that an expansion of Sino-Western trade offered China her best hope of prosperity and growth. The very concept of economic growth eluded the understanding of Restoration leaders.

There were two important areas in which Restoration officials accepted the need for innovation along Western lines. The first was the reorganization of China's military. The Taiping Rebellion had bared the hopeless decay of the dynasty's regular military units, while the recent display of British and French power dramatically highlighted the benefits of Western military methods and technology. In response, Restoration leaders, with Western technical aid, founded modern arsenals and shipyards and made a significant effort to streamline China's fighting forces and introduce more modern methods of training. Thus began the "self-strengthening" (*tzu-ch'iang*) movement, the aim of which was to provide for China's long-term security. The trouble was that true military modernization could go only so far before it disturbed the equilibrium of the tradi-

[8] *The Last Stand of Chinese Conservatism: The T'ung-chih Restoration, 1862–1874* (Stanford, Calif.: Stanford University Press, 1957), Chapter 8.

tional society. "A modernized army with a competent officer corps," as Wright has pointed out, "would have disrupted the very social order the new arms were designed to protect."[9] (And the same could be said of T'ung-chih efforts in the field of educational modernization.)

The other important change made in the Restoration period was in the field of foreign relations. China's old system, based on tribute, was revived for dealing with Asian countries. But for the Western nations a new institution was created, the Tsungli Yamen. From its inception in 1861 the Tsungli Yamen had to grapple with enormous problems, for, in addition to shouldering the usual burdens of a foreign office, it had to master the intricacies of an entirely strange system of international relations and somehow justify its acquiescence in this system to a hostile Chinese public. Measured against its problems, the achievements of the Yamen by the end of the 1860's were considerable.

Significantly, in both areas of innovation just discussed there were extenuating circumstances that made the changes appear less drastic. Learning from the West in the military sphere was only a variation on a well-worn Chinese theme. At various points in their long history, the Chinese had been able to accept being tutored in the arts of war by "barbarians." The creation of a new institution for dealing with the Western countries was more genuinely innovative, but here also there was a catch—namely, that it was conceived only as a temporary step. Prince Kung and his associates, in their memorial requesting the establishment of the Tsungli Yamen, had clearly specified: "As soon as the military campaigns are concluded and the affairs of the various countries are simplified, the new office will be abolished and its functions will . . . revert to the Grand Council for management so as to accord with the old system."[10]

Thus, even in those areas in which the Restoration leaders innovated, the generally noninnovative character of the period was underscored. Chinese reformers were still far from the point where they could attach a positive valuation to fundamental change.

Mary Wright assesses the T'ung-chih Restoration in the following terms:

> This last of the great restorations of Chinese history was at the same time the first, and the most nearly successful, of a series of efforts to modify the Chinese state to a point where it could function effectively in the modern world without revolutionary changes in traditional Chinese values or in the institutions that embodied them.

[9] *Ibid.*, p. 220.

[10] Cited in Teng Ssu-yü and John K. Fairbank, *China's Response to the West: A Documentary Survey, 1839–1923* (Cambridge, Mass.: Harvard University Press, 1954), p. 48.

One of Wright's major theses is that "the Restoration failed because the requirements of modernization ran counter to the requirements of Confucian stability."[11]

Two questions may be raised with regard to this thesis. First, did the Restoration in fact fail? Second, assuming that it did, was it, as Wright suggests, because of the conflicting claims of modernization and Confucianism? These questions have an immediate bearing on the broader issue of the extent to which the Restoration reform program was a response to the West, for the areas in which it most clearly was—the diplomatic, the military, and the commercial—were just those areas where, in Wright's view, the Restoration was "the *most* and not the *least* successful."[12] On the other hand, the areas in which the T'ung-chih reformers were possibly least successful—the restoration of effective civil government, the reestablishment of local control, and the rehabilitation of the economy—were the very areas in which they were least concerned with the Western challenge. The frustration of Restoration efforts in the domestic arena, it could thus be argued, was due less to incompatibility between modernization and the establishment of a stable Confucian order—this generalization actually holds up much better for the last decades of the dynasty —than to the refusal (or inability) of Chinese reformers to see the *relevance* of modernization to what, in their eyes, were essentially traditional problems. The center of gravity of Chinese thinking in the 1860's still lay within.

It is sometimes maintained that one of the major reasons for the failure of the Taiping Rebellion, or, conversely, for the success of the imperial forces in vanquishing it, was the pseudo-Christian ideology of the rebels. Because of the anti-Confucian implications of this ideology, the argument runs, many Chinese scholars and officials who in other circumstances might have supported an uprising against the Manchus chose instead to cast their lot with the dynasty. The fate of Confucianism hung in the balance, and that was a much more important issue than Sino-Manchu intramural rivalry. The logical end product of this line of reasoning is that the whole Restoration effort to reestablish the foundations of Confucian society was precisely what, in the preceding paragraph, I suggested it was not: a massive (if negatively stated) response to the impact of the West.

This is a persuasive thesis and probably not one that could ever be conclusively refuted. It rests, however, on several assumptions that should be brought out clearly: first, that alienation of elite Chinese from their Manchu rulers was still a significant force two hundred years after the founding of the dynasty; second, that Chinese scholars, gentry, and

[11] Wright, *The Last Stand of Chinese Conservatism*, pp. 8, 9.
[12] *Ibid.*, p. 9.

officials, despite their vested interest in order and stability, would have flocked to the Taiping banner in sizable numbers had the ideology of the rebels been more in harmony with Confucian precepts (in passing it may be noted that in the last years of the rebellion there was actually a considerable degree of "re-Confucianization" of rebel ideology, partly owing to the efforts of Hung Jen-kan); and, third, that it was the Western origin of this ideology rather than its heterodox (non-Confucian) nature that was decisive. None of these assumptions have yet been proved. Until much more evidence is in, therefore, it would seem unwise to go too far in viewing Restoration behavior as having been principally conditioned by the challenge of the West.

TECHNICALLY, the T'ung-chih Restoration ended with the close of the T'ung-chih period in 1874. The time when it actually ended depends on what one believes it to have been in the first place. Mary Wright, assigning considerable weight to the Restoration effort to devise a viable framework for Sino-Western relations, feels that the Tientsin Massacre and the rejection of the Alcock Convention in 1870 marked the beginning of the end.[13] If, shifting the emphasis somewhat, one were to attach primary importance to the tone and character of the reform thought of the period —its inward- and backward-looking orientation—one could argue that "restorationism" as a response to China's difficulties continued to attract adherents well into the succeeding Kuang-hsü reign (1875–1908). As late as the 1890's there were still Chinese who minimized the Western threat and believed that China's problems could best be solved by the time-honored methods of the past.

Still, it was a measure of the change that had taken place that such persons were now viewed as obscurantists. Certainly, they no longer stood in the mainstream of Chinese reform thought. In the two decades from the end of the T'ung-chih period to the outbreak of the Sino-Japanese War (1894), China was free of major internal unrest. But the penetration of Westerners and of Western influence, instead of abating, became more intense than ever. In response to this, the central preoccupation of most Chinese reformers shifted to the challenge of the West, and there emerged among them a growing recognition of the need for true change—innovation, not just restoration.

The need for change was seen, but the acceptance of it as a positive good was slower in developing, and for some time Chinese reformers felt obliged to camouflage their advocacy of change in a variety of intellectual disguises designed to make the changes appear innocuous. How much this intellectual masking was dictated by the psychological require-

[13] *Ibid.*, p. 7.

ments of the reformers themselves and how much by the political need to deflect the criticism of their opponents is a puzzle intellectual historians are only beginning to work out.

Many of the most common justifications for reform were outgrowths of a kind of Chinese thinking known as *pen-mo: pen* (literally, "root") meaning the beginning, the fundamental, the essential; and *mo* (literally, "branch") meaning the end, the incidental, the nonessential. The best-known illustration of this was the *t'i-yung* formula, immortalized in the 1890's by Chang Chih-tung in the famous phrase *Chung-hsüeh wei t'i, Hsi-hsüeh wei yung* ("Chinese learning for the essential principles, Western learning for the practical applications"). The purpose of *t'i-yung* thinking was to justify the acceptance of "Western learning," with all its practical benefits, while at the same time reasserting the sanctity and ultimate inviolability of Chinese civilization. For *t'i* and *yung* some Chinese substituted *tao* (ultimate values) and *ch'i* (technical contrivances). But the meaning was at bottom the same. The dilemma inherent in all such thinking was that the area embraced by *yung* (or *ch'i*) underwent a qualitative change as well as a quantitative expansion as more and more of the Western "model" was accepted by Chinese reformers. As the content of *yung* expanded—from "ships and guns" to "science and mathematics," then to "industrialization," and finally to "modern schooling"—*t'i* (or *tao*) inevitably shrank, and the Chinese found themselves in the impossible position of trying to preserve a civilization by subjecting it to fundamental change.

Another justification for reform, which flourished in the period just before and after the reform movement of 1898, was the argument that Western learning originated in China. This was an updated version of the *hua-hu* thesis propounded by Chinese in the Period of Disunion as an apology for the acceptance of Buddhism. (Buddhism, it was maintained, was an Indianized form of Chinese Taoism and therefore could be followed by Chinese without shame.) It was widely believed, for example, that Western military technology, science, mathematics, and Christianity were originally derived from the writings of the Warring States philosopher Mo-tzu. (Even the contradiction between Mo-tzu's advocacy of universal love and his close attention to military matters was, in the opinion of one Chinese, reflected in Western attitudes.) The functions of this line of reasoning were several: First, it provided a sanction for Western-inspired changes without doing damage to Chinese cultural pride; second, it reassured the Chinese that, as a race, they were not intellectually inferior to the Westerners; and, third, it suited the general Chinese predilection for reviving antiquity.[14] On the other hand, the sud-

---

[14] Ch'üan Han-sheng, "Ch'ing-mo ti 'Hsi-hsüeh yüan ch'u Chung-kuo' shuo" [The late Ch'ing theory that 'Western learning originated in China'], in Li Ting-i *et al.,*

den respectability accorded the heterodox, non-Confucian Mo-tzu reflected a shift of the greatest importance that was taking place in the last years of the nineteenth century. Nationalism was replacing culturalism as the chief stimulus of Chinese reform thought—the key fact about Mo-tzu was that he was Chinese.

This same transition was mirrored in the evolution of yet another sanction for change: the goal of establishing a wealthy and powerful Chinese state. The preoccupation with wealth (*fu*) and power (*ch'iang*)—enshrined in the slogan "Enrich the state and strengthen its military power" (*fu-kuo ch'iang-ping*)—was a Legalist contribution to Chinese political thought and represented a distinct alternative to the usual Confucian (and Restoration) emphasis on frugal government and popular welfare. There was, however, a less orthodox strain of Chinese political economy which maintained that the goals of wealth and power were quite compatible with ultimate Confucian values. This train of thought began to appear with growing frequency in the 1870's and 1880's, as increasing numbers of Chinese became convinced that the Chinese state would have to be greatly strengthened if the Confucian values they cherished were to be saved from extinction. The danger of this kind of thinking was that the means—the creation of a wealthy and powerful China—would eventually supplant the end—the preservation of Confucian civilization. When wealth and power became goals to which all other values were subordinated, the ground was laid for a thoroughgoing nationalism. This was precisely the point reached, in the mid-1890's, by Yen Fu (1853–1921), the famous translator of Western social and political thought. And, in the ensuing decade, hundreds of other Chinese flocked to join Yen.

All the justifications for reform so far discussed were aimed at maintaining the Confucian order intact. None affirmed the possibility—not to mention desirability—of a fundamental change of this order. There was, however, one current of reform thought that did do this, by attempting to find sanctions for change within the Confucian tradition itself. As early as 1880, the pioneer journalist Wang T'ao (1828–97) wrote that if Confucius were alive in the nineteenth century he would unhesitatingly give his support not only to the introduction of Western technology and industry but to the general cause of reform. Wang's view of Confucius as a would-be reformer provided a justification for particular changes; implicitly, it also introduced into Confucianism an affirmative attitude toward change in general.

Much more influential and systematic than the ideas of Wang T'ao were those of K'ang Yu-wei (1858–1927), the leader of the reform move-

eds., *Chung-kuo chin-tai-shih lun-ts'ung* [Collected essays on modern Chinese history], 1st ser. (Taipei: 1956), Vol. 5, pp. 216–58.

ment of 1898. K'ang rejected as spurious the interpretations of the Classics then current and insisted that the only authentic interpretation was that of the "New Text" school. In the doctrines of this school he claimed to discover philosophical grounds not only for viewing Confucius as an architect of new institutions (in itself a revolutionary stand) but for treating history as an evolutionary process. Influenced by recent Western thought, K'ang pushed the New Text interpretation far beyond the limits of Confucian acceptability and ended up with nothing less than a full-dress presentation of the modern concept of progress.

Reinterpreting Confucianism in order to provide a positive sanction for innovation represented a definite advance over such negative sanctions as the *t'i-yung* formula. But it still failed to solve the basic problem of how China could become modern and remain Confucian at the same time. The other sanctions pretended that Confucianism need not be changed at all. The sanction developed by K'ang Yu-wei rested on the equally dubious premise that true Confucianism had always meant change. In either case, Confucianism as it had been known receded into the background. By 1900 the path had been cleared for an intellectual revolution of unprecedented scale.

To what extent did the late Ch'ing revolution in Chinese thought find expression in action? How much innovation was there in fact? As early as the T'ung-chih reign, a small number of reform-minded Chinese saw that "modernization" would have to go well beyond the level of "ships and guns." Feng Kuei-fen (1809–74), possibly the first modern writer to use the classical phrase *tzu-ch'iang* ("self-strengthening") in reference to the Western threat, recognized that foreign military superiority was rooted in the West's advanced knowledge of mathematics and urged that Chinese study both the mathematics and the natural sciences of the "barbarian." Feng's plea for the translation of Western books led to the founding of a translation bureau and foreign-languages school in Shanghai in the 1860's.

Wang T'ao was another writer who, at a relatively early date, perceived the difference between the new "barbarian" and the old. Appalled by the provincialism of China's knowledge of the rest of the world, he conceived a plan in the late 1860's to write a history of France. This book was completed in 1871 and was followed two years later by another on the Franco-Prussian War. Both Feng Kuei-fen and Wang T'ao, it may be noted, lived for varying periods of time in Shanghai (Wang T'ao also lived in Europe and Hong Kong), where direct exposure to Westerners and to Western ways helped them transcend the insularity of their contemporaries.

During the 1870's and 1880's much was done to improve the state of

China's knowledge of the West. More books were either written or translated (often by missionaries). Modern newspapers, with up-to-date coverage of world affairs, began publication in port cities like Shanghai and Hong Kong. Young Chinese were sent to the United States and Europe to study, and in 1876 China for the first time appointed diplomatic representatives to the major world capitals.

Reform efforts were also made in the economic and military fields. The modernization of China's army and navy, begun during the T'ung-chih period, went on apace. Mining, textile, and other new industrial enterprises were initiated, often with Western technical assistance. In 1881 the first telegraph line was opened between Shanghai and Tientsin, and a short railroad was completed.

The Chinese seemed to be making visible progress in the direction of "self-strengthening." Yet, if there was ever any real basis for optimism, it was cruelly shattered by China's humiliating defeat in the Sino-Japanese War of 1894–95 and the ensuing intensification of Western imperialist activity. Now, for the first time, an acute feeling of shame enveloped significant numbers of Chinese and stimulated them to contemplate a much more far-reaching reform effort. Between 1895 and 1898 reform-oriented newspapers and periodicals sprang up in many places, and societies for the discussion of reform were founded. When the Kuang-hsü Emperor himself became sympathetic to the goals of the more radical reformers (led by K'ang), the stage was set for the hectic, drama-filled summer months of 1898.

The reform movement of 1898 began on June 11, the date of the emperor's first reform degree. It ended abortively on September 21 with his imprisonment and the assumption of power by his aunt, the empress dowager. During this period, often referred to as the Hundred Days, reform decrees on a vast array of subjects were issued by the throne. With K'ang Yu-wei's prodding, the young emperor took as his models not the sage kings of Chinese antiquity but such reform-minded monarchs as the Meiji Emperor and Russia's Peter the Great. Orders were sent down for the remodeling of the examination system and the establishment of modern schools; the modernization of the army, navy, police, and postal systems; the revision of China's laws; the elimination of superfluous officials and posts from the bureaucracy; the promotion of commerce, agriculture, mining, and industry; and so forth.

Although most if not all of these reforms had been proposed at one time or another by Wang T'ao, Cheng Kuan-ying, and others, collectively considered they went far beyond all previous efforts. This was the first massive assault on China's outmoded institutional structure and, equally significant, the first time such an assault had been launched from the top.

And yet, when the dust had settled, it was clear that little had been accomplished. Only in the province of Hunan, which had a governor sympathetic to reform, was a serious attempt made to carry out the emperor's decrees. In the rest of the empire reactions ranged from passive bewilderment to stubborn resistance. Many officials who might have been willing to carry out the reforms did not understand them, and many who understood their import only too well vigorously resisted implementing them. Manchus were piqued at the fact that the reformers closest to the emperor were mostly Chinese. Conservatives were fearful of reform in general. And many in the bureaucracy, though perhaps not opposed to reform as such, were apprehensive lest this or that particular reform jeopardize their personal futures as bureaucrats. All in all, it can be said of the reformers of 1898 that if they were long on good intentions, they were abysmally short on the practical political wisdom and experience needed to put their good intentions into effect.

CHINESE reform efforts in the last three decades of the nineteenth century clearly were *related* to the impact of the West. But shall we view them simply and exclusively as *responses* to this impact? Or were they, to some extent, Western-influenced responses to internal Chinese situations?

Students of nineteenth-century Japanese history have shown that Japan's "response to the West" and Japanese responses to internal Japanese political conditions were subtly and inseparably linked. Thus, in the late *bakumatsu* period the *jōi* slogan, literally meaning "expel the barbarian," was used as "a stick to beat the bakufu (shogunate)" by young samurai who, it turned out, not only had no intention of expelling the barbarian but were actually quite receptive to certain kinds of Western influence.[15] Similarly, the efforts of Chōshū and Satsuma leaders, on the eve of the Meiji Restoration, to introduce Western science and weaponry into their respective han (feudal domains) were as much han responses to the impending struggle between the bakufu and the throne as Japanese responses to the West.

Recent studies suggest that a comparable phenomenon existed on the Chinese side. Stanley Spector, for example, compares the two great "regional" leaders, Tseng Kuo-fan and Li Hung-chang, in the following terms:

> While Tseng's protestations of loyalty to Confucian civilization and the Ch'ing dynasty may seem to indicate that he strengthened his own forces in order that he might better serve his imperial masters, the same cannot

[15] W. G. Beasley, ed., *Select Documents on Japanese Foreign Policy, 1853–1868* (London: Oxford University Press, 1955), Introduction.

be said for Li Hung-chang. When Li Hung-chang spoke of self-strength-ening, he discussed generalities; when he engaged in self-strength-ening, he was strengthening himself.[16]

In short, what seemed to be a simple response by Li to the Western challenge was also, at least in part, a response to internal Chinese power rivalries. Ultimately, the problem of the West may have been less impor-tant to Li Hung-chang than the problem of Li Hung-chang.

Were Chinese reform efforts in the late nineteenth century slow and ineffective? Did they fail? The obvious answer to both questions is, of course, yes. But there are also less obvious answers. Scholars, even while denouncing historical determinism, find it difficult to write history with-out implying the very thing they denounce. Thus, China loses to Japan in 1895, reform loses to reaction in 1898, and historians, ever uncom-fortable with immediate and accidental causes, seek long-term explana-tions for the two events. The more we seek, the more we find that there were grave shortcomings in the Chinese reform effort prior to the Sino-Japanese War. And the more these shortcomings come to monopolize our attention—as they must do, given the questions asked—the more the events of the 1890's appear inevitable. Of course, to gain some sense of the degree of distortion that can result from this kind of historical recon-struction, all we have to do—taboo for the professional, but all right for amateurs—is to imagine the sorts of questions we would be asking of the 1870's and 1880's if the events of the 1890's had taken a different turn.

Another potentially misleading perspective is the unavoidable compari-son with Japan. Such a comparison is invaluable in disclosing the more salient differences between Chinese and Japanese societies, but it can have the unfortunate side effect of masking over some very fundamental similarities. For example, the rate of literacy in Japan around the middle of the last century was higher than that in China by a wide margin, but in both countries the social benefits of literacy had long been universally recognized. Again, the government of Meiji Japan was much more effec-tive than that of late Ch'ing China in amassing state power; but both countries (China even more than Japan) enjoyed long experience with centralized bureaucratic rule, and both were able, partly for this very reason, to avoid being dominated politically by the West. The point is a simple one. If China and Japan alone are compared in respect to effec-tiveness and rapidity of response to the "challenge of modernity,"[17] Japan

[16] *Li Hung-chang and the Huai Army: A Study in Nineteenth-Century Chinese Regionalism* (Seattle: University of Washington Press, 1964), p. 153.

[17] The phrase is Cyril E. Black's. In his stimulating book *The Dynamics of Mod-ernization: A Study in Comparative History* (New York: Harper & Row, 1966), Black, adopting a worldwide perspective, argues for the existence of seven distinct

must necessarily come off well, China poorly. But, if the comparative perspective is considerably widened and the modernizing experiences of China and Japan are measured against those of the rest of the nations of the world, we are liable to find that both Japan *and* China come off relatively well. Scholars may even contend one day that China's response to the West in the late Ch'ing was reasonably effective.

REACTION

Reformism in late Ch'ing China, whether restorative or innovative in impulse, was basically an elitist phenomenon. Reaction—which is here taken to mean uncompromising resistance either to change or to the West—was, like rebellion, a form of behavior involving both the masses and the elites. In its quieter manifestations, reaction appeared as a prominent strain in the thought of China's educated strata. But it also had a more violent side, as dramatized by the endless succession of antimissionary outbreaks that punctuated the second half of the nineteenth century. When violence and disorder became sufficiently large-scale, as happened in the Boxer uprising of 1899–1900, distinctions between reaction and rebellion were in danger of being lost.

In the 1870's and 1880's, as we have seen, a significant effort was made by reform-oriented scholar-officials to meet the West on its own terms. Other scholar-officials during the same period, however, took an aggressively anti-Western stand, embodied most typically in the political force known as *ch'ing-i*. Literally meaning "pure discussion" and sometimes freely translated as "public opinion," the term *ch'ing-i* had been used in the Later Han dynasty to describe the criticisms of disenfranchised Confucian literati against a government increasingly dominated by eunuchs and empresses' relatives. It was used again during the Southern Sung, when China lay under threat of "barbarian" invasion, to characterize that segment of opinion which vehemently opposed a policy of appeasement. In all periods, *ch'ing-i* manifested itself as a militant defense of Confucian doctrinal and moral purity aimed at those power-holders whose actions in one way or another threatened to undermine the Confucian order.

Unlike public opinion in modern Western countries, the usual vehicles for the expression of *ch'ing-i* in the nineteenth century were not newspapers and public speeches but social gatherings, poems, folk songs, and above all official memorials.

In the 1870's and 1880's the main guns of *ch'ing-i* attack were trained on the growing trend toward limited accommodation of the West, as evi-

---

patterns of political modernization. Significantly, he views China and Japan as belonging to the same pattern (along with Russia, Iran, Turkey, Afghanistan, Ethopia, and Thailand).

denced in the activities of the self-strengthening movement and in the policy of yielding to foreign military pressure. A harbinger of things to come had been the denunciation and recall in 1851 of the Fukien governor, Hsü Chi-yü, whose book *Ying-huan chih-lüeh* ("A brief survey of the maritime circuit"), first published the year before, was one of the earliest Chinese attempts to gather together information on the West. Hsü was attacked because his relations with foreigners had been too intimate, though, ironically, his book revealed a considerable strain of antiforeign sentiment.

In the 1870's the most celebrated instance of *ch'ing-i* excoriation was the withering assault on Kuo Sung-tao (1818–91). Kuo, though deeply immersed in the Confucian tradition, was one of the first to recognize (in the early 1860's) the fundamental differences between the barbarian tribes China had previously encountered and the new barbarians from the West. Realizing the impossibility of defeating the Western countries militarily, he urged that Westerners be treated with fairness and sincerity and insisted on the need to resolve conflicts with the West through diplomatic rather than military means. Kuo's first run-in with *ch'ing-i* vitriol came as a result of his impeachment of the governor of Yunnan in connection with the Margary affair of 1875. Although his hidden intent was, by having the governor charged with the relatively minor offense of dereliction of duty, to prevent his being subject to the much graver accusation of connivance in the murder of a British consular officer, the literati failed to detect this and condemned Kuo as a traitor. The attack on Kuo was especially savage in his native city of Changsha, Hunan, where his impending voyage to England as the head of a Chinese apology mission was satirized in 1876 in the following pair of scrolls:

> Outstanding among his associates,
> Elevated above his peers,
> Yet ostracized in the nation of Yao and Shun.
>
> Unable to serve men,
> Why able to serve devils?
> Of what use to leave his fatherland and mother country![18]

Under unbearable social pressure, Kuo Sung-tao tried to beg off going to England. But the throne insisted, and he left Shanghai late in 1876. In England, where he was accredited as China's first envoy to the Court of St. James, Kuo continued to feel the sting of *ch'ing-i*. When the diary of his mission, in which he had some favorable things to say about the West, was published by the Tsungli Yamen, it aroused such savage criticism

[18] Cited in Immanuel C. Y. Hsü, *China's Entrance into the Family of Nations: The Diplomatic Phase, 1858–1880* (Cambridge, Mass.: Harvard University Press, 1960), p. 183.

that the court had to order its suppression. On finally returning to China, moreover, Kuo was so fearful of attack in Peking that he went straight home to Hunan, where, his public career in a shambles, he spent the rest of his life in self-imposed obscurity.

The proponents of *ch'ing-i* in the 1870's and 1880's did not stop at the vilification of those who saw some worth in Western civilization. Even the limited objective of adopting Western military technology was vehemently rejected by them. Reviving a tradition that had its roots in the Southern Sung and that Schwartz has described as "muscular Confucianism," they maintained that what was needed to expel the barbarian was not the cunning gadgetry of the West but an aroused Chinese population. As one *ch'ing-i* diehard put it, "The superiority of China over foreign lands lies not in reliance on equipment but in the steadfastness of the minds of the people."[19]

The natural corollary to *ch'ing-i* deprecation of Western military strength was *ch'ing-i* bellicosity in situations where war with the West threatened. In the summer of 1870, when the Tientsin Massacre brought China and France to the verge of warfare, Tseng Kuo-fan was so severely criticized by *ch'ing-i* stalwarts for his policy of accommodation that the throne had to transfer him from his post as Chihli governor-general. Again, during the Sino-Russian controversy over Ili in 1879–80 and the Sino-French conflict of 1884–85, the enunciators of *ch'ing-i* took militant prowar stands. Now it was the "appeasement" course of Li Hung-chang that came in for the brunt of the attack; but, as before, *ch'ing-i* proved itself a political force to be reckoned with.

Ch'ing-i opinion, in the period we are dealing with, was manifestly a response to the West. But it was also something more. The key point is that *ch'ing-i*, for all its surface concern with the West, was predominantly a Chinese phenomenon, involving the responses of certain Chinese to the actions and policies of other Chinese. By its very nature, *ch'ing-i* had to be intramural: One did not ask Confucian purity of barbarians; one asked it of Confucians.

Nor, it may be added, was *ch'ing-i* merely an expression of moral outrage. It was also a powerful political instrument. "Officials who attracted attention by their rigorous Confucianism," Lloyd Eastman writes, "were often promoted to higher posts. And charges that a political opponent had disregarded Confucian ritual, disrespected the emperor, or was a sycophant of the foreigners frequently sufficed to remove the object of attack from imperial favor."[20] Under these circumstances, there was always the temptation, especially among lower- and middle-level officials

---

[19] Schwartz, *In Search of Wealth and Power*, pp. 15–16.

[20] *Throne and Mandarins: China's Search for a Policy During the Sino-French Controversy, 1880–1885* (Cambridge, Mass.: Harvard University Press, 1967), p. 18.

with little administrative power, to use *ch'ing-i* to further what were essentially selfish and parochial interests. And, as Eastman shows, in the complex balance of political forces prevailing in China in the late nineteenth century, the throne too could manipulate the expression of *ch'ing-i* for the purpose of gaining political leverage against such powerful provincial officials as Li Hung-chang. Thus, it would appear that in at least one important respect *ch'ing-i* preoccupation with Western culture ran parallel to Taiping preoccupation with Western religion. For, in both instances, the West was made to serve as an unwitting accomplice in the playing out of dramas that would have been staged, in one form or another, even in the West's absence.

Another manifestation of Chinese reaction in the last century—the hostility to missionaries and converts—was more unequivocally a response to the Western presence, though even here some qualification is necessary. During the period from 1860 (the year in which missionaries were first permitted to reside and preach in the Chinese interior under treaty protection) to 1900, antimissionary activity in China was extremely widespread.[21] There were several hundred incidents important enough to need top-level diplomatic handling, while the number of cases that were settled locally probably ran into the thousands. (One Catholic missionary in eastern Chihli reported that in a single year his work was hampered by over two hundred minor cases of "persecution.") Moreover, aside from incidents as such—the burning down of churches, the destruction of missionary and convert homes, the killing and injuring of Christians both Chinese and foreign—there were times when the empire was virtually deluged with inflammatory anti-Christian pamphlets and handbills.

The sources of anti-Christian feeling were many and complex. On the more intangible side, there was general resentment against the unwanted intrusion of the Western countries; there was the understandable tendency to seek an external scapegoat for internal disorders that were only tangentially attributable to the West; and, perhaps most important, there was a virile tradition of ethnocentrism, which had been vented long before against Indian Buddhism and, since the seventeenth century, had been focused increasingly on Western Christianity. Thus, even before the missionary movement really got under way in the mid-nineteenth century, it was already at a disadvantage. After 1860, as missionary activity in the hinterland expanded, it quickly became apparent that in addition to the intangibles, there were numerous tangible grounds for Chinese hostility.

In part, the mere presence of the missionary made him an object of

[21] The ensuing discussion is partly based on Paul A. Cohen, *China and Christianity: The Missionary Movement and the Growth of Chinese Antiforeignism, 1860–1870* (Cambridge, Mass.: Harvard University Press, 1963).

attack. Missionaries were, after all, the first foreigners to leave the treaty ports and venture into the interior, and for a long time they were virtually the only foreigners whose day-to-day labors carried them to the farthest reaches of the Chinese empire. For many Chinese in the last century, therefore, the missionary stood as a uniquely visible symbol against which opposition to foreign intrusion could be directed.

In part, too, the missionary was attacked because the manner in which he made his presence felt after 1860 seemed almost calculated to offend. By indignantly waging battle against the notion that China was the sole fountainhead of civilization and, more particularly, by his assault on many facets of Chinese culture per se, the missionary directly undermined the cultural hegemony of the gentry class. Also, in countless ways, he posed a threat to the gentry's traditional monopoly of social leadership. Missionaries, especially Catholic ones, frequently assumed the garb of the Confucian literati. They were the only persons at the local level, aside from the gentry, who were permitted to communicate with the authorities as social equals. And they enjoyed an extraterritorial status in the interior that gave them greater immunity to Chinese laws than had ever been possessed by the gentry.

More important, perhaps, than any of these concrete invasions of the gentry's traditional prerogatives was the fact that the missionary was a teacher. He was educated, at least to the extent that he could read and write; he preached in public; and, especially if he was a Protestant missionary, he wrote and distributed a prodigious amount of literature. The effect of this on the literati was aptly summarized by a leading Protestant missionary:

> It is impossible not to displease them. To preach is to insult them, for in the very act you assume the position of a teacher. To publish a book on religion or science is to insult them, for in doing that you take for granted that China is not the depository of all truth and knowledge. . . . To propound progress is to insult them, for therein you intimate that China has not reached the very acme of civilisation, and that you stand on a higher platform than they.[22]

Although it was the avowed policy of the Chinese government after 1860 that the new treaties were to be strictly adhered to, this policy could be carried out in practice only with the wholehearted cooperation of the provincial authorities. Unfortunately, there is abundant evidence that, in relation to missionary activity, such cooperation was often somewhat less than wholehearted. Why did so many Chinese officials, especially lower-ranking ones, oppose the foreign missionary? The simplest and most direct answer is that all officials were, in the broadest sense, members of

[22] Cited in *ibid.*, p. 85.

the gentry class. Thus, to the extent that they shared the cultural and intellectual commitments of this class, it was natural that they would be vigorously opposed to the spread of Christianity. But to the extent that the officials took their responsibilities to the throne seriously, one might expect that they would do their best to overcome feelings of personal antipathy and make an earnest effort to implement the treaties. Such was the situation *in vacuo*. In actual practice, there were a number of factors that tended to encourage the natural opposition of the officials to Christianity and to discourage them from genuinely fulfilling their imperial obligations.

The most important of these, perhaps, was gentry opposition to the missionary enterprise. In a severely understaffed bureaucracy that ruled as much by persuasion as by force, the official, almost always a stranger in the locality in which he served, was highly dependent on the active cooperation of the local gentry class. If he energetically attempted to implement the treaty provisions concerning missionary activities, in direct defiance of gentry sentiment, he ran the risk of alienating this class and destroying his future effectiveness.

Another factor was the missionary's exploitation of his privileged legal status and the resulting challenge to the prestige and authority of the official. Sometimes this challenge was a direct consequence of the missionary's treaty rights, as when missionaries who suffered injury or property damage obtained satisfaction from the Chinese government. In other cases missionaries made their power felt on the local scene by abusing their treaty rights or by using them with a minimum of discretion. Both Catholics and Protestants regularly accepted the application of force on their behalf to obtain redress. Catholic missionaries often demanded excessively large indemnities for injuries. (In the province of Szechwan alone, between 1863 and 1869 they collected 260,000 taels in damages.) During the early 1860's Catholics took full advantage of the treaty provisions providing for the return of previously confiscated church properties, the Franciscan fathers even going so far as to request additional reimbursement for house and land rents collected over the preceding hundred-year period. Also in this connection, Catholic missionaries routinely demanded, as restitution for injuries suffered in antimissionary riots, buildings (such as literati halls and temples) that had been erected with public funds and were of symbolic importance to the Chinese.

Sometimes missionaries encroached on official authority even more directly. In the 1860's Kweichow Catholics pressed the French legation to obtain the transfer of two successive governors of that province. Catholics occasionally aroused the ire of the protocol-conscious Chinese government by employing improper forms of address in their correspondence. Finally, the most serious and widespread missionary abuse, in the view of almost all Chinese officials, was the tendency after 1860 to interfere in local official affairs, either on behalf of converts or in order to win converts.

Although many missionaries of the last century felt that the common people were not unalterably opposed to the spread of Christianity, the unpleasant truth is that the participants in, if not the instigators of, antimissionary riots were largely drawn from this class. Nor do we have to search far for reasons. Missionary attacks on ancestor worship and "idolatrous" folk festivals offended all Chinese, not merely the elites, and missionary demands for compensation following antimissionary outbreaks often had to be met by disgruntled commoners in the localities concerned. Ordinary Chinese were further irritated by the unsavory behavior many of their fellows exhibited after becoming converts, and they were bewildered and frightened by the strange ways of the foreigners in their midst.

Even when the populace of a given locale had concrete grievances against the Christians, however, these grievances usually had to be articulated before they could be translated into action. Often, antimissionary incidents were not spontaneous but were planned in advance and, to some extent, organized. Here the role of the gentry and official classes became all-important. The gentry, primarily through the distribution of inflammatory anti-Christian tracts and posters, were able, on the one hand, to create an explosive climate of rumor and suspicion concerning the activities of the foreigner and, on the other, to activate the suspicions, fears, and resentments that the non-Christian populace accumulated on its own through immediate contact with the missionary and his followers. In this way an interplay of forces was built up that, given the necessary spark, could and often did lead to violence.

The officials' part in this process sometimes paralleled the gentry's. But usually it was more indirect and passive. The officials gave the gentry almost complete liberty to carry on their propagandist and organizational activities and rarely took action against them when antimissionary incidents occurred. They thereby furnished the gentry with an operating framework relatively free of obstacles or risks.

Still, wherever the sympathies of officials may have lain, the fact remains that after 1860 antimissionary incidents were a source of acute embarrassment for the Chinese government at all levels. At the local and provincial levels, if the incidents were serious enough, officials could be demoted or otherwise punished. At the level of the central government, there was always the possibility that foreign force would be applied, resulting in humiliation and loss of prestige for the dynasty. This raises some nice questions: If antimissionary activity posed such grave problems for the Chinese authorities, how sure can we be that, in the period

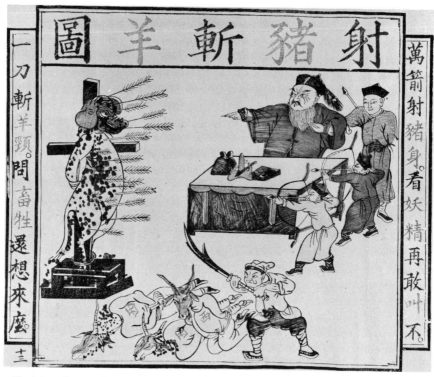

Shooting the Pig [Jesus] and Beheading the Goats [the Foreigners]

text on right: After we have pierced the pig's body with ten thousand arrows, will this monster again dare to grunt?

text on left: After we have beheaded the goats with one stroke of the sword, will these beasts still entertain thoughts of coming [to China]?

> Faintly inscribed on the body of the pig are the characters for "Jesus." The characters on the goats' bodies are those for "Westerner." Foreigners in Chinese anti-Christian posters are often represented as goats, the characters for "goat" and "foreigner" being homophonous. Jesus is frequently represented as a pig, the character for "pig" being partially homophonous with that for "Lord." The character for "grunt" is homophonous with that for "religion, teaching."

A poster from a pamphlet reproduced in "The Cause of the Riots in the Yangtse Valley: A 'Complete Picture Gallery' " (Hankow: 1891).

from 1860 to 1900, the primary motive for active opposition to the missionary was invariably antimissionary feeling and never antiofficial or antidynastic feeling? Was antiforeignism, to put it somewhat differently, always "authentic"? Or was it sometimes politically inspired? Certainly, there were more than enough grounds for the kindling of genuine antiforeign sentiment in nineteenth-century China. But this does not mean that, given the proper context, antiforeignism could not be manipulated for political purposes.

To illustrate, there is evidence that the anti-Christian riots of the early 1890's were fomented in part by secret-society members whose aim was not to do injury to the Christians but to bring down the dynasty by forcing it into conflict with the Western powers. The initial phase of the Boxer movement may have been guided by a similar goal; the original slogan of the Boxers early in 1899 was "Overthrow the Ch'ing, destroy the foreigner." Conversely, it appears that the authorities themselves, in some instances, intentionally identified with extreme antiforeign stands, not so much because they were extremely antiforeign, but because this was the only way to prevent popular antiforeign feeling from being turned against them. This happened in Canton in the 1840's, and it may also have been a factor in the official and dynastic responses to the Boxers. Clearly, the whole subject of politically motivated antiforeignism in the last decades of the nineteenth century deserves a great deal more attention than it has so far received.

POLITICAL antiforeignism was more directly a response to Chinese political conditions than to the West. What about authentic antiforeignism? This is a hard question to answer, for there were several varieties of Chinese antiforeignism in the second half of the nineteenth century, all equally authentic. First, there was the fear-centered antiforeignism of the uneducated masses, perhaps more properly described as xenophobia; second, there was the contempt-centered antiforeignism of the educated, based on their overwhelming sense of Chinese cultural superiority; and, finally, there was the shame-centered antiforeignism of a small but growing number of protonationalistic Chinese, who were more averse to Western political encroachment than cultural influence and tended to favor reform along Western lines over wholesale rejection of the West.

In the latter case, antiforeignism was manifestly one aspect of an overall Chinese response to problems posed by the West qua West. In the other two cases, however, the situation was more ambiguous. Contempt-centered antiforeignism (the sort generally evoked by *ch'ing-i*) was more a Chinese response to a non-Chinese (but not specifically Western) cultural threat, while popular xenophobia (of the kind vented in antimissionary disturbances) was at least in part a local response (Cantonese or

Hunanese, rather than Chinese) to the presence of strangers who just happened to be Western. Obviously, to lump all of these manifestations of antiforeignism together and label them simply as Chinese responses to the West does scant justice to the historical complexities involved. Aside from the distinction between "political" and "authentic" antiforeignism, at the very least an effort must be made to distinguish between varieties of antiforeignism that could have emerged at *any* juncture in Chinese history and varieties that were linked to a specifically *Western* impact.

Toward a Revised Framework of Interpretation

The Ch'ing dynasty is generally treated as two periods. Up to 1800 or thereabouts, it is still part of "the Great Tradition."[23] The questions asked of it in this earlier period could just as well be asked of the Ming or Yüan. The sources used, although more abundant, have a basic similarity to those used in the study of previous dynasties. Even the historians who work on it frequently have a greater affinity for pre-Ch'ing than for post-1800 Ch'ing studies. They are more concerned with "traditional China" than with the Sino-Western confrontation.

After 1800 we change gears rather abruptly, passing on to a fresh set of questions, different themes, new kinds of source materials, and, with few exceptions, a different corps of historians. The basic orientation of most nineteenth-century historians is less toward the eighteenth century than toward the twentieth. In their books and articles they supplement the use of Chinese documentation with extensive Western-language materials. Most important, their central preoccupation is not—to trade on a familiar book title—with Confucian China, but with its modern fate. The Sino-Western confrontation, the impact of the West and China's response, is not of peripheral concern to them—it is everything.

This picture is overdrawn. But it is not so severely overdrawn as to nullify a basic point, which is that nineteenth-century Chinese history, especially from the Opium War on, has been too much under the spell of questions prompted by the Sino-Western encounter. Because of this, much of the history of the period has suffered from distortion or neglect, and our comprehension of even the encounter itself has been gravely impaired.

What is to be done to remedy this imbalance? As a start, it might be profitable to think of Chinese history in the latter half of the nineteenth century in terms of a series of concentric spheres. The outermost sphere would consist of those facets of the period's history that were most clearly

[23] See Edwin O. Reischauer and John K. Fairbank, *East Asia: The Great Tradition*, Vol. 1, *A History of East Asian Civilization* (Boston: Houghton Mifflin, 1960).

and unambiguously responses to or consequences of the Western presence. In this sphere would be included such diverse phenomena as treaty ports, modern arsenals and shipyards, journalists like Wang T'ao, innovative reform activity, Christian converts, institutions like the Tsungli Yamen and the Maritime Customs Service, and the dispatch of Chinese students and envoys abroad. It is here that the conventional impact-response approach seems most clearly applicable. But it must be used with all caution. A Chinese might convert to Christianity as a result of his being convinced of that religion's superior worth—a clear response to the West. But he might also convert in order to gain leverage against an adversary in a lawsuit—not so clearly a response to the West.

Next, there would be several intermediate spheres embracing aspects of the period that were activated or given shape and direction, but were not actually brought into being, by the West. The Taiping Rebellion, the T'ung-chih Restoration, some self-strengthening efforts, bureaucratic and court politics, antiforeignism, and social and economic tensions between urban and rural China are the kinds of things that might be included here. Again, we have a very heterogeneous assortment. In some instances (expressions of shame-centered antiforeignism, for example), the impact-response framework of analysis may still work tolerably well. In other instances (such as politically inspired antiforeignism or self-strengthening activity undertaken to augment personal power), modes of behavior that appear to be simple responses to the West also turn out, on closer inspection, to be responses to internal political challenges. In still other cases (the Taiping Rebellion being the most notable), even the semblance of a response to the West is largely absent: The response is to a Chinese challenge—one sometimes, as in the case of population pressure, unprecedented in scope—and the West's role is largely confined to that of an influencing agent. These examples all seem to suggest that in a Chinese setting a "pure" response to the West was virtually an impossibility. Perhaps it would be safer and more productive to think in terms of Western-influenced responses to Western-influenced situations, the degree of Western influence at both ends varying from case to case.

Finally, the innermost sphere of our model would be comprised of those facets of late Ch'ing culture and society that not only were not products of the Western presence but were, for the longest time period and to the highest degree, left undisturbed by this presence. Alongside such relatively immutable items as language and writing, we would find in this sphere traditional forms of intellectual, religious, and artistic expression; the style and pattern of life in agrarian China; and time-honored social, economic, and political conventions and institutions. These areas of Chinese life can in no way be construed as responses to the West. Yet they did constitute a major part of the environment in which such responses were nurtured. Therefore they must be studied carefully, even by scholars whose primary interest is in the Sino-Western encounter.

The contents of these spheres were fluid, and among the spheres there was constant interaction. The relative importance of any given sphere, moreover, changed significantly over time. In particular, the outermost sphere grew in importance between 1850 and 1900, while the innermost sphere was subjected to increasing pressure and erosion. The central problem for the student of the Sino-Western encounter is to identify these shifts and to explain how they came about. The concept of a "Western impact" conveys nicely the sense of an initial collision, but says little about the complex chain of effects set in motion by the collision. Conversely, the concept of a "Chinese response" will not take us very far if we insist on linking it too closely to an initial Western impact. If we are going to retain these concepts, therefore, it is imperative that we address ourselves to a much more elaborate web of impacts and responses—Chinese *and* Western in each instance—than has hitherto been the case. Only then will we arrive at a surer understanding of the transformations that overtook China in the latter half of the nineteenth century and the role of the West in effecting these transformations.

Selected Readings

Cohen, Paul A. *China and Christianity: The Missionary Movement and the Growth of Chinese Antiforeignism, 1860–1870.* Cambridge, Mass.: Harvard University Press, 1963. An exploration of negative Chinese responses to the Christian missionary enterprise in the 1860's.

de Bary, William T., Jr., *et al.,* eds. *Sources of Chinese Tradition.* 2 vols. New York: Columbia University Press, 1964. Volume 2 contains translated excerpts of representative Chinese writings of the nineteenth and twentieth centuries; background material provided by the editor.

Eastman, Lloyd E. *Throne and Mandarins: China's Search for a Policy During the Sino-French Controversy, 1880–1885.* Cambridge, Mass.: Harvard University Press, 1967. A pioneer analysis of the forces influencing Chinese government policy during the Sino-French War.

Fairbank, John K., Reischauer, Edwin O., and Craig, Albert M. *East Asia: The Modern Transformation.* Vol. 2, *A History of East Asian Civilization.* Boston: Houghton Mifflin, 1965. The fullest and most stimulating text treatment of late Ch'ing history.

Feuerwerker, Albert. *China's Early Industrialization: Sheng Hsuan-huai (1844–1916) and Mandarin Enterprise.* Cambridge, Mass.: Harvard University Press, 1958. A study of early modern Chinese industrial enterprise through the career of a leading participant.

Hsü, Immanuel C. Y. *China's Entrance into the Family of Nations: The Diplomatic Phase, 1858–1880.* Cambridge, Mass.: Harvard University Press, 1960. An account of the changes made in China's conduct of foreign relations as a result of Western influence.

Levenson, Joseph R. *Confucian China and Its Modern Fate.* Berkeley, Calif.: University of California Press, 1958–65. Volume 1, *The Problem of Intellectual Continuity* (1958); Volume 2, *The Problem of Monarchical Decay* (1964); Volume 3, *The Problem of Historical Significance* (1965). A perceptive, far-ranging analysis of intellectual transition in modern China.

————. *Liang Ch'i-ch'ao and the Mind of Modern China.* Cambridge, Mass.: Harvard University Press, 1959. A suggestive study of the tensions in modern Chinese intellectual development, focusing on a leading reformer-publicist of the late Ch'ing.

Michael, Franz, in collaboration with Chang Chung-li. *The Taiping Rebellion: History and Documents.* Seattle: University of Washington Press, 1966. Vol. 1. The best and most up-to-date general account of the Taiping Rebellion; to be joined eventually by two volumes of translations of Taiping writings.

Schwartz, Benjamin. *In Search of Wealth and Power: Yen Fu and the West.* Cambridge, Mass.: Harvard University Press, 1964. Through a close study of Yen Fu's translations of works by Western political and social thinkers, the author provides a penetrating analysis of one of the most pervasive sanctions for change in late Ch'ing China.

Spector, Stanley. *Li Hung-chang and the Huai Army: A Study in Nineteenth-Century Chinese Regionalism.* Seattle: University of Washington Press, 1964. A study in depth of one aspect of the career of the most powerful official of the late Ch'ing period.

Teng Ssu-yü and John K. Fairbank. *China's Response to the West: A Documentary Survey, 1839–1923.* Cambridge, Mass.: Harvard University Press, 1954. The evolution of China's response to the West, as revealed in Chinese writings; background material provided by the editors.

Wright, Mary C. *The Last Stand of Chinese Conservatism: The T'ung-chih Restoration, 1862–1874.* Stanford, Calif.: Stanford University Press, 1957. A seminal work on the Restoration period, comprehensive in coverage and provocative in approach.

Tokugawa Japan: 1800–1853

JOHN WHITNEY HALL

JAPAN in 1800 was not much in the eye of the rest of the world. Standing at the farthest reach of the sea routes of that time, its frontiers closed for more than a century to all but the most carefully controlled foreign contact, the island country had largely escaped the active interest of the other people of the world. Certainly it was not within the wildest stretch of the imagination of either the Chinese or the Europeans that behind the mists of seclusion lived a people who within a hundred years would have dealt China a decisive military defeat and would be on the way toward building a modern empire on the Western model. Nor, in fact, could many Japanese have imagined such a possibility. For in 1800 they lay secure in the grip of the Great Peace created by the Tokugawa House two centuries earlier. The outside world seemed remote and unessential to a Japan that was content in its way, or at least preoccupied with its own thoughts and problems.

For us today, looking back upon Tokugawa Japan, it is difficult to disengage current preconception from past reality. Tokugawa has become background, a set of explanations for what came after 1868. For some, Tokugawa nourished the roots of a remarkable capacity for modernization; others find in its "feudal" and "restrictive" society traits that were to lead to political absolutism and "fascism" in the twentieth century. Modern historians have by and large given Tokugawa Japan a bad image. Writing with the pattern of European history before them, they have blamed the "retrogressive policies" of the Tokugawa regime, particularly the seclusion policy, for having slowed Japan's normal process of historical development. Closure, they claim, led to social and political regimentation and eventually to cultural stagnation. Japan faced the modern world technologically retarded and politically on the defensive.

Modernization came only as the result of pressure from the West. The process was defensive and forced; it was consequently distorted and lacked the saving political qualities that would have given the Japanese people freer participation in their government and avoided the tragic march toward "fascism" and disastrous war in the 1940's. For the Japanese historian who lived through the war years, recognition of Japan's "successful" modernization is colored by the sense of its failure to achieve modern goals smoothly, humanely, and in a manner less imitative of the West. For him the Tokugawa period has remained a dark age, a breeding place for "feudal elements" that depressed the Japanese ability to modernize democratically and in its own way.

Yet for all the negativism that can be mustered by historians convinced that Japan should have reached its present state of world eminence and economic affluence by some different route, the fact remains that by most scales of measurement the country made its transformation into a modern nation-state with unusual speed and completeness. And, if the Tokugawa period is looked upon in strictly negative terms, it becomes difficult to account for this transformation other than as a miracle or as the product of an excessive willingness to imitate an alien civilization. Obviously there was more to Japan in 1800 than a set of negative preconditions for its impending confrontation with the West. And the nineteenth-century Chinese intellectual who watched Japan forge ahead of his country in the business of modern "nation building" would have been the first to admit it.

Japan in 1800

As of 1800 Japan could muster a set of quite respectable national statistics. In a country of slightly over thirty million persons, the administrative capital, Edo, had a population of close to a million, making it larger than London or Paris. Two other cities, Osaka and Kyoto, numbered from three to four hundred thousand inhabitants. Although predominantly agrarian, the country's economy was tightly organized and highly developed technically by comparison with all economies but the more advanced European ones. A unified currency and a national market structure knit the country together. Paper currencies and centralized financial-exchange facilities had been developed. Agriculture was probably more efficient and productive than in any other part of East Asia. Literacy rates approximated those of contemporary England. Consumer goods of silk, cotton, lacquer, porcelain, and metal were produced with great artistry and in considerable profusion. The intellectual and artistic life of the people was self-contained and satisfying. Knowing whence they had come—that is, from the destructive civil wars of the sixteenth century—and what alternative ways of life were available to them (the model of China provided the main comparison), the Japanese of the mid-Tokugawa period were not inclined to exchange their lot for any other. Fifty years later, English and American observers found the Japanese for the most part happy and well fed, though living in a land that could boast little of grandeur in the work of either man or nature.

Japan in 1800 was a narrow island, a tight island, and to a large extent a proud island. It could reflect upon past exploits: Only two centuries before, its armies had overrun Korea and faced the Ming forces on the Yalu. Japanese ships had once plied the China seas. Bands of Japanese freebooters had plagued both the Ming and Ch'ing dynasties, forcing the Manchus to the desperate expedient of evacuating populations inland along the entire coast of China from Shantung to Kwangtung. The Tokugawa policy of restricting trade to the port of Nagasaki and of interdicting Christianity had been an act of strength, a means of forcing foreign trade under the monopoly control of the Tokugawa House and of securing the loyalty of people who were in danger of beguilement by an alien and subversive religion. The Spanish and Portuguese had been expelled, leaving the Catholic Church to mourn an estimated three thousand martyrs. The uprising near Nagasaki at Shimabara in 1637, which had taken on Christian overtones, had been put down with the slaughter of twenty thousand persons. After 1640 the Chinese could trade at Nagasaki only on Japanese terms, and the Dutch were obliged to engage in a style of tributary homage to maintain their slender privileges on the prison-like island of Deshima. Japan's frontiers were under control and seemed secure, for as of 1800 only the first uncertain hints of the coming of the Russians and English had reached Japan. Within these frontiers subversion had been rooted out, and peace had reigned for nearly two centuries.

Yet, if the Japanese could take pride in the condition of their country, they permitted themselves little complacency. Unlike the Chinese or the Europeans, they knew their land was not the totality of the civilized world. It may have been all that mattered to them, but there was always China to be reckoned with, and they could not ignore the maps from Europe, which placed Japan on the edge of the world. While a Yamaga Sokō could claim that the Japanese state was more virtuous than the Chinese, his countrymen refused to indulge in the easy ethnocentrism that made barbarians out of all visitors to Nagasaki. Foreigners could be ridiculed, certainly—the Chinese for their bumbling ways and the Dutch for their long noses and red faces—but they were also respected for their achievements. Pride, then, was in what Japan had achieved within its own sphere as a people working together against odds. And here, despite the views of modern Japanese historians, pride was justified.

Perhaps the outstanding feature of Japanese institutional history was its linear development. Historically, Japanese state and society had shown little of the cyclical return to established models; the process of political and social change was continuous and evolutionary. The Tokugawa political system was a new creation in its time. The cities that grew up to dominate its life, except for Kyoto, had existed only as villages in 1550, and the style of urban life, which embraced all the ruling class and a significant portion of the commoners, had come into existence only in the seventeenth century. In terms of its own historical development, then, Japan in 1800 had come a long way from the conditions of the 1550's, when the polity was still decentralized, civil wars still ravaged the land, and foreign missionaries wandered freely about.

Unification and the Rise of the Tokugawa

It was the destiny of the Tokugawa House to fashion a lasting unity for Japan, bringing to maturity a style of government and a form of local control that had been in the making for several centuries. The sixteenth century was a major watershed in Japanese institutional development. The imperial system of government adopted from China in the eighth century, whereby the country had been divided into provinces and administered by officials sent out from the capital, had long ago been replaced by the rule of local military lords (daimyo) who served only loosely under a military hegemon (shogun). Yet remnants of the influence of the imperial court and of the Buddhist and Shinto religious organizations had continued into the fourteenth and fifteenth centuries, as did the old proprietary (*shōen*) system of family inheritance. It took the great civil wars of the sixteenth century to destroy all evidence of the *shōen* system and to put into the hands of the feudal magnates all superior rights to land and government. Kyoto remained the city of the emperor, in whom a slender portion of residual sovereignty rested. But the country became divided into a hundred or more autonomous military domains, each dominated by the towered castle of its military lord, each ruled and defended by the lord's men, his two-sworded retainers of samurai status. There was a sturdiness in the way these provincial rulers governed their territories that impressed the European travelers who caught their first glimpse of Japan at about this time. Jesuit missionaries and Portuguese traders who had braved the long journey to the end of the Orient found Japan a land of militant princes, impregnable fortresses, brave and even arrogant warriors—a land, they wrote, comparable in all but morality with the Europe they had left.

It was upon this extreme political and military decentralization that unification began to be imposed. Portuguese musket and cannon hastened the military consolidation; in region after region powerful leaders emerged at the heads of clusters of daimyo, until, eventually, one of these regional groups asserted its hegemony over the rest of the nation. The final stages of the process took roughly the forty years between 1560 and 1600. This consolidation was the work of a powerful military coalition that drove out of east-central Japan under the successive direction of three military geniuses, who beat the daimyo into submission and imposed a rough unity upon the land. Oda Nobunaga (1534–82) first took possession of imperial Kyoto and with great brutality destroyed once and for all the military and economic power of the Buddhist establishment. Toyotomi Hideyoshi (1536–98) completed the conquest of the great daimyo and went on to send his forces into Korea toward China. After Hideyoshi's death, Tokugawa Ieyasu (1542–1616) grasped the hegemony when, at the great Battle of Sekigahara in 1600, he and his allies defeated a coalition of daimyo who had remained loyal to Hideyoshi's infant heir. In 1603 he took the title of shogun and in 1615, at the Battle of Osaka Castle, exterminated the last adherents to the Toyotomi memory. Japan was ripe for peace, and it was to accept, until 1867, the hegemony of the Tokugawa House and its right to rule Japan.

The manner of Tokugawa Ieyasu's rise to power set the style of the administration he established at his castle headquarters at Edo. The scion of a middling daimyo house in the province of Mikawa, he had skillfully extended his territories while allied first with Nobunaga, then with Hideyoshi. Victory in border wars gained him new territories and an expanding retinue of military followers. By 1590 he stood next to Hideyoshi, the largest single daimyo in Japan, and it was Hideyoshi who moved him out of his ancestral territories in central Japan to the broad eastern plain of Kantō, into territories just wrested from the Hōjō coalition. There, at the little village of Edo, Ieyasu built a new central castle, strategically placing his vassal daimyo into the captured defenses of the Hōjō. Before long his hold over the eight eastern provinces was secure; he was master of one-eighth of the territory of the Japanese islands.

The method of administration Ieyasu used to hold the Kantō laid the pattern for the national hegemony that emerged ten years later. The system of authority was feudal, its character military. The eight provinces were divided between the lord's land (tenryō), about half of the total, and the domains of vassals. Administration was decentralized, but the lord's lands were managed directly by intendants, and power was concentrated in Ieyasu's hands through his group of thirty-eight castellans of daimyo size. This was the beginning of Ieyasu's band of house daimyo (the fudai), who later, numbering over a hundred and forty, became the backbone of shogunal administration.

After Hideyoshi's death, Ieyasu's final push toward national hegemony proceeded rapidly. Pledges of loyalty from Hideyoshi's former vassals flowed to him, voluntarily at first, then by submission after their defeat at Sekigahara. These were enlisted as "allies" (*tozama*) and added to the Tokugawa roll of vassal daimyo. Confiscation of the territories of nearly ninety daimyo defeated at Sekigahara and further seizures thereafter permitted Ieyasu to expand his own direct holdings and to increase the number of his house daimyo. With his acquisition of the title of shogun, Ieyasu gained legitimization of his miltiary hegemony. By then, and particularly after 1615, when Osaka Castle lay in ruins, all daimyo were his pledged vassals. There was now but one sovereign, the emperor in Kyoto, and one authority, the shogun at Edo. And, while local administration continued to be decentralized among some two hundred and fifty daimyo, the Tokugawa House, through its legal position as shogun, its direct control of nearly one-fourth of the land of the realm, its control of all the major commercial cities, and its overwhelming military might, possessed a preponderance of power that remained uncontested for two and a half centuries.

The Tokugawa polity was new to Japan, yet it represented a logical maturation of two political institutions that had been evolving since the decline of the imperial system: the shogunate as a national authority and the daimyo as regional rulers. Historians have asked why unification was not "carried to conclusion" by the elimination of the daimyo and the creation of a unitary state under a monarchal shogun. Yet a review of the stages by which the Tokugawa House had come to power provides its own answer. From beginning to end, Ieyasu rode to national hegemony on the shoulders of his band of daimyo adherents. He was as much of their making as they were of his. The Tokugawa system was neither a feudal throwback nor a bit of unfinished historical business; it was a major achievement in statecraft. And it is this fact that is recognized in the term "baku-han," by which modern historians refer to it. The composite term indicates that the system was based upon the shogunate (bakufu) and the daimyo domains (han). Other historians have used the term "centralized feudalism." Certainly, the underlying force of authority within it was feudal; the daimyo were bound to the shogun by sworn oath and written pledges. But within the administrative subparts of the system, in the individual governments of the shogun and the daimyo, authority was increasingly exerted through appointed officials and according to codified legal norms. Feudalism colored only selective aspects of Tokugawa government.

But was Tokugawa Japan something more than a loose cluster of independent domains? Was it in any sense a nation? The political map of seventeenth-century Japan shows a crazy patchwork of several thousand political divisions. Not even the territories of the two hundred and fifty or more daimyo were fully unified; some consisted of several separate pieces. The shogun's enfeoffed retainers with territories of less than daimyo size numbered about five thousand, and beyond these were many hundreds of small but separate holdings of temples and shrines. The shogun's own territory (the *tenryō*) meandered in and out among these independently administered units. Yet somehow all this was pulled together. Between shogun and emperor, an acceptable conception of sovereignty and legitimacy had been established. There emanated from the shogunate a reasonably strong pressure toward uniformity in basic administrative practices. And, above all, a sense of unity joined the ruling class, the samurai, who served by hereditary right as officials throughout the land. However much the samurai were individually pledged as retainers of the shogun or of one or another of the daimyo, they comprised a national elite conscious of its primary loyalty to its class mission and to the Japanese homeland.

Crucial to Japan's consciousness of itself as a political entity was the continued existence of the emperor. The Western diplomats who visited Japan after 1850 were mystified by the existence of what they could comprehend only as a dual sovereignty. To them the shogun (Tycoon) was the temporal ruler and the emperor (Mikado) the spiritual. Their explanation was reasonable enough. To the Japanese of the Tokugawa period, however, explanations seemed less necessary; tradition accounted for the existence of both the "heavenly emperor" (*Tennō*) and his delegate, the shogun. The question of conflicting sovereignties was raised only at the end of the regime, when the Tokugawa House was under attack.

The persistence of the imperial house at the apex of the political hierarchy has been one of the remarkable constancies of Japanese political history. The emperor had once combined military power with political authority and had served, like the shogun of later times, as a real hegemon over subservient military houses. Declining political power had been buttressed from the seventh through the ninth centuries by the adoption of institutions of centralized imperial rule borrowed from China. The emperor of Japan served for several centuries as a true monarch, ruling a far-flung bureaucracy from his capital city of Nara, then Kyoto. Thereafter the emperor lost his political influence, first to members of a civil aristocracy and then to a military aristocracy. His "spiritual" authority remained by hereditary right, and his economic supports continued to be adequate to maintain a certain pomp in his style of living down through the fifteenth century. Thereafter the political decentralization that accompanied the rise of the daimyo left the emperor destitute and momentarily forgotten—forgotten, but never desecrated or replaced. For no one questioned the prerogative of the imperial house to retain the hereditary title of *Tennō* or disputed that the *Tennō* was the descendant of the Sun Goddess, the supreme deity of the Japanese homeland.

The sixteenth-century unification movement refocused attention upon the emperor as the ultimate source of political sanction, for, no matter how powerful a daimyo's military capacity, the backing of some claim to legitimacy was a useful asset in the struggle against military competitors. Nobunaga entered Kyoto posing as protector of the imperial house. Hideyoshi used the symbol of the emperor to back his demand for absolute loyalty from his vassals. The Tokugawa shoguns pursued the dual policy of playing up the prestige of the sovereign, while making sure that they controlled access to him. The emperor and the group of court families surrounding him were given sustenance lands and were assisted in rebuilding their palaces and sacred shrines. Yet in practice they were carefully controlled and removed from free participation in the affairs of state. A shogunal military governor (*Kyōto shoshidai*) and his garrison of troops presided over the imperial city.

Yet, for all his remoteness, the emperor, standing by tradition above the shogun and daimyo, symbolized the oneness of the Japanese polity. It was a symbol in which both shogun and daimyo could take pride, for, as the Confucian-trained scholars of the Tokugawa period so frequently pointed out, not even China could claim an imperial line unchanged by time, or a nation of faithful officials whose loyalty had never permitted a dynastic overturn. Separation between emperor as national symbol and shogun as ruling power seemed reasonable enough. It was also ultimately to prove a blessing. For after 1853, in the political turmoil that followed the abandonment of seclusion in response to the threat of Commodore Perry's "black ships," the nation could turn against its Tokugawa rulers and yet cling to the emperor as symbol of Japan's abiding national unity.

For most of the Tokugawa period, however, the Tokugawa House itself possessed sufficient prestige and military strength to enforce a supreme authority upon the daimyo. Tokugawa hegemony was based upon a tight and carefully contrived balance of power. The shogun's military establishment was itself massive and impressive. Edo Castle, rising on the edge of Edo Bay, encircled by ring after ring of wide moats and protective walls, surrounded by the residences of vassal daimyo and the garrison quarters of officer retainers, was an eloquent expression of transcending military capacity. Besides Edo the Tokugawa holdings included the great castle at Sumpu, used as a secondary capital; Osaka Castle, rebuilt after its destruction in 1615, when its siege had cost Ieyasu over thirty thousand lives; and Nijō Castle, from which the shogun's agent guarded the imperial city. Beyond this the shogun could count on a force of twenty-three thousand direct retainers, his bannermen (*hatamoto*) and housemen (*gokenin*). The latter, when mustered for battle, were considered capable of putting sixty thousand men in the field.

Tokugawa power stretched out from Edo into the castled headquarters of vassal daimyo through an intricate network of loyalties. Ieyasu had set out the heads of his collateral branches at strategically significant locations: Mito to the north, Nagoya to the west, and Wakayama, south of Osaka. His house daimyo guarded the major cities and occupied strategic locations extending into Kyushu. Only in the far west, where great *tozama* daimyo who had reluctantly submitted to Ieyasu after Sekigahara were thickly clustered, did the Tokugawa hold remain somewhat precarious.

Over the daimyo the shogun asserted the powers of direct overlordship, extracting from them oaths of loyalty and granting them their patents of investiture as gifts of benefice. Over them he held the provisions of the Code of the Military Houses (*Buke sho-hatto*), which made their military establishments, their successions, their marriages, and even their manner of dress and travel subject to his regulation and interference. Coloring the whole relationship between daimyo and shogun was the practice of "alternate attendance" (*sankin-kōtai*), whereby all daimyo were obliged to build residences in the shadow of Edo Castle from which to pay regular homage to the shogun. Edo thus became the permanent residence of the wives and children of the daimyo, who became in effect hostages in the shogun's capital. The daimyo themselves were permitted to alternate their residence between Edo and their own castle headquarters, usually on an annual basis. No better system could have been devised to assure the continued loyalty of the daimyo.

Beyond this, the *sankin-kōtai* system made Edo a true center of government, a congregating place for the daimyo of the realm. As the daimyo assembled periodically at Edo Castle, each going to an assigned hall according to his status, the national political hierarchy was ritually reaffirmed. And, in the frequent confrontations between shogunal and daimyo officials, the policies of the realm were directly communicated to the ends of the land. The Japanese islands never seemed so large that the affairs of government could not be handled directly on a face-to-face basis. Although tensions were eventually to build up between the daimyo and shogun, the system of residence in Edo created a single body out of the high military aristocracy.

Administration

In a modest way, the holders of political power in Japan proved themselves more successful in maintaining effective government than in creating visible monuments to power and wealth. If anything, Tokugawa

Japan was "overgoverned."⌉The large size of the samurai class and the proliferation of political divisions assured a density of administrative supervision that few peoples have ever matched. The baku-han system proved a remarkably vigorous and comprehensive form of government at both the national and local levels. The daimyo, of course, differed greatly in the size of their domains and the specifics of their administrations. The domain of the Maeda House, for instance, covered three provinces and had a population of more than a million inhabitants. Twenty-two "great daimyo" had territories roughly equivalent to a province, with populations of from 250,000 to 800,000 persons. But most daimyo held territories of smaller size, whose inhabitants might number no more than ten or fifteen thousand.

Daimyo administration showed certain commonalities, however, and in sum provided the basis of local government for the entire country. Han governmᵉnt radiated outward from a central castle town that dominated the domain politically and economically. Over his territory the daimyo exercised full rights of governance as prescribed in the shogunal grant. Specifically, he was given rights of exploitation and the responsibility to protect and govern "the land and the people" of his domain. For this purpose the daimyo relied on his band of retainers, his *kashin*, the members of which were individually tied to him by oath and enrolled on his "register of men." They were organized by military rank, depending on size of fief or amount of stipend, assembled at the castle headquarters, and assigned residences or quarters according to precedence.

The highest rank of retainers, generally referred to as "elders" (*karō*), were often enfeoffed vassals of independent stature. As a group they formed a council of advisers and staffed a board of high policy. In wartime they served as generals in the field. Next in rank was a more numerous body of retainers who served as heads of units in the daimyo's army or of the major divisions of the daimyo's civil administration. They commanded units of the han guards and superintended the offices devoted to local administration, taxation, finance, security, and liaison with the shogunate. Middle-rank retainers performed specific administrative functions, serving as magistrates of the castle town, village intendants, superintendents of temples and shrines, heads of civil police, procurement officers, managers of the daimyo's household, instructors in the domain schools, physicians, protocol officers, and the like. The lower levels of samurai retainers filled out the ranks of foot soldiers, pages, clerks, and policemen and performed a host of routine or menial tasks. An important characteristic of all these officials was that (except for the *karō* class) they were stipended and possessed no land of their own. Even those who held fiefs did not "own land" but merely held precarious rights of taxation.

The common people of the domain were considered wards of the daimyo, whose responsibility it was to govern with compassion. An office of rural affairs administered the villages (*mura*) through a corps of intendants (*daikan*). The magistrate of the castle town superintended the wards (*machi*) of the nonsamurai sections of the castle town. Below the level of the daimyo's administration, the farmers and merchants lived in self-governing units (villages or wards) under the regulation of their own headmen.

The *mura* had become increasingly autonomous as the samurai class had been withdrawn from the land. So-called village self-government came into being after the completion of the nationwide cadastral survey begun by Hideyoshi in 1582 and repeated several times by the Tokugawa. Hideyoshi's agents had begun a veritable revolution in land administration, whereby each piece of arable land was surveyed, graded according to productivity, and recorded against the name of its cultivator, who thereby became officially responsible for its dues. Taxpaying cultivators were thus made secure in their tenures, forming in the process a new peasant class, the *hyakushō;* but they were bound by the cadastral register and prevented from disposing freely of their lands. The surveys of Hideyoshi and of the early Tokugawa period virtually transformed the country at the village level. The land registers of a given area, brought together in the name of a single village, became the basic documents that defined the land area, the peasant membership, and the tax assessment of the village. For the daimyo the village became in essence a tax unit. Village administration—that is, the collection of taxes for delivery to the daimyo's intendant, the settling of village disputes, the assignment of internal duties—became the responsibility of the headman (*nanushi* or *shōya*). The village households themselves were divided into mutually responsible groups of about ten families each, known as "five-man units" (*gonin-gumi*), for further regulation.

The system of control was tight and applied to all. Above the line of local autonomy, the daimyo's force of samurai officials was inscribed on the daimyo's rolls and held to a rigorous and never abundant salary scale. Villagers and townspeople were also each inscribed on the registers of their locality, restricted from change of domicile except by special permission and from travel except by passport. Police scrutiny and mutual surveillance were close and severe. On top of this were the requirements of religious investigation adopted as a means of suppressing Christianity. Each year the head of every family, whether samurai or commoner, was obliged to go to his temple of family registry and sign for the members of his family, swearing that there was no Christian among them. So rigorously was this investigation carried out that the registries of religious investigation (the *shūmon aratame-chō*) were to provide the most accurate population figures available for most of Japan.

The organs of shogunal administration (the *bakufu*) were for the most part simply those of the Tokugawa daimyo house written large. The most important consequence of this was that, although the shogun's authority extended over all daimyo and over the entire country, he depended for his administrative officials only upon his house daimyo (*fudai*) and direct retainers, and for his income only upon the dues from his own lands. Relying first upon his *fudai* of greatest size, the shogun organized his retainer-officials into two boards. The senior councilors (*rōjū*, literally "elders") made up a supreme administrative council and were given authority over matters of national scope, such as supervision of the imperial court and the daimyo, foreign affairs, military affairs, taxation, currency, the distribution of lands and honors, and the regulation of religious bodies. A second board of junior councilors (*wakadoshiyori*, or "younger elders") supervised the shogun's bannermen and housemen and directed the shogun's military forces and disciplinary officers.

It was under the board of senior councilors that the prime functional offices were placed: magistrates of major cities such as Edo, Osaka, Nagasaki; the finance officer; superintendents of construction, roads, mines; the governor-general of Kyoto; the keeper of Osaka Castle; and members of the High Court of Justice. Below these, a vast assemblage of military and civil officials tended the shogun's military establishment and administered his far-flung territories. Together the shogun's house daimyo and retainers staffed a bureaucracy that effectively asserted the shogun's powers as national hegemon and administered as well the nearly one-quarter of the country that was the shogunal domain.

The Samurai Aristocracy

If emperor, shogun, and daimyo provided the superstructure of legitimacy and the apparatus of government for the Tokugawa system, the samurai as an aristocratic ruling class provided the broadest base of commonality in the ethos of the Tokugawa state. Government in Tokugawa Japan rested on the simple but fundamental fact that above the level of the self-governing villages and town wards, all superior legal and administrative rights resided with the military estate. Over the Tokugawa countryside the towers of the daimyo castles signified both military and civil authority. Civil government was administered entirely by a professional military class. Legal authority, the authority to govern, was thus the prerogative of the samurai estate by virtue of professional training maintained on a hereditary basis. And, since civil authority evolved out of military, it weighed with a heavy authoritarian hand upon all it touched.

Among the various elite types produced by the several cultures of East

Asia, the samurai of Japan was certainly unique. In contrast with the Chinese literatus, he regarded military training and service as his prime reason for being; scholarly erudition was a secondary matter. By tradition the samurai cultivated military skills (handling the sword and the bow—the musket that was once used to win the wars of consolidation fell into disuse). He admired bravery and took pride in his adherence to a code of honor, loyalty, and obedience to authority. Readiness to die for a cause became his fetish. And to prove it he made sure that his "way out"—*seppuku,* or cutting of the belly—was no easy one; it could keep one hovering between life and death for hours. Stern visage, resoluteness in action, physical toughness—these were the qualities most admired by the samurai class.

Originating in the eleventh century as the armed estate-managers of the civil court aristocracy, the samurai had become more and more a hereditary class of military officers serving the daimyo. During the sixteenth century they were still for the most part located on the soil, managing the fiefs assigned to them by their overlords. In the great battles that preceded the final unification of the daimyo, as potential hegemons like Nobunaga and Hideyoshi mustered armies numbering upwards of two hundred thousand men and as musket and cannon required the building of great protective fortresses defended by far-flung moats and stone battlements, the samurai were drawn into the castled headquarters of the daimyo to serve as permanent garrison forces and to staff the extensive administrative networks required to manage territories of increasing size. By Tokugawa times, then, the samurai, amounting to some seven percent of the population, had become a homogeneous caste concentrated in the environs of the castle headquarters of the shogun and daimyo. Once the civil wars were ended, access to the caste became closed to those not born into it, and the Tokugawa made every effort to maintain the boundaries between the samurai, the peasantry, and the commercial class.

As a military aristocracy, therefore, the samurai asserted both social and legal prerogatives when they carried out their administrative duties. Their badges of distinction—surname, court rank, long and short sword—were tokens of unquestioned authority to govern the lesser classes. In theory, a samurai had the right, indeed the responsibility, to draw his sword summarily upon a wrongdoing commoner. Writing in the early eighteenth century, Arai Hakuseki, the closest to a model Confucian adviser any Tokugawa shogun was to have, mentioned with special pride a sword, treasured by his family, that was called the "bowl cutter," so named because when his grandfather had used it to cut in half a disrespectful servant, the servant had been carrying a bronze bowl that was sliced in two in the process.

Critics of the Tokugawa period have claimed that the perpetuation, even the exaltation, of the samurai caste ranked along with the failure to eliminate the daimyo as a major retrogressive aspect of Tokugawa policy. No evaluation of Tokugawa government, of course, can ignore the rigidity of the system of social stratification, the oppressive regulatory machinery, the sumptuary laws, and the petty restraints imposed by samurai officialdom. But the samurai was as hard on himself as he was on the commoners. The social policies of Hideyoshi and Ieyasu, described by some as unnatural and outmoded, represented rather the culmination of lengthy social trends and widespread efforts at social control by which the daimyo had sought to regulate their territories. Hideyoshi's sword hunt (*katana gari*), which disarmed the peasantry, and his cadastral survey, which laid the basis for the separation of samurai from the land, had been anticipated for many decades. His ability to carry these measures through merely indicated that it was not until the end of the sixteenth century that the daimyo had the power to assert full control over the manpower and the tax production of their domains. Far from being a conservative throwback, the policies brought to perfection new forms of political control by powerful military leaders who were nevertheless sensitive to the pressure points of the society they wished to rule. They reflected, on the one hand, a society in which occupations were becoming more specialized and functionally differentiated and, on the other, the development of new techniques of administration and legal control.

Looked at in terms of the long evolution of government and legal institutions in Japan, the baku-han system constituted a major achievement in the formulation of a systematic philosophy of government and in its application through law to the people. Under the rule of the Tokugawa shogun the country again achieved, after nearly eight centuries, something of a unified polity, enunciated through public laws and based on general principles. The long period of decay following the eighth-century attempt at legal codification using Chinese models had led increasingly toward feudal privatization. Not until the end of the sixteenth century was this current finally reversed in the administrative procedures adopted first by some of the great daimyo and then by the national hegemons Hideyoshi and Ieyasu. This is not to say that the Tokugawa rulers attempted to create a systematic legal structure for all Japan. But the vast quantity of laws, injunctions, and regulations that flowed from Edo and the han headquarters indicated, if nothing else, that a new and conscious effort was being made to bring order to government and to provide guidelines for a well-regulated society.

The samurai's military origins meant that his style of administration was authoritarian and his method of enforcement rigorous. Yet it would be unjust to characterize his laws as unnaturally reactionary or to assume that they were imposed upon a reluctant country simply to safeguard an anachronistic political and social system. By Tokugawa times Japanese law had come to rest on certain broad principles that gave to it a universality quite different from the localized rule of custom by which the samurai had once managed their fiefs. Here was the beginning of "natural law" premised on the existence of a natural order. Assuming that society by nature formed a hierarchy of classes, the Tokugawa legal system sought first to clarify fundamental social divisions and then to devise rules of conduct appropriate to each division. The result could be described as "rule by status." In Tokugawa society, the individual was bound to a particular status in life, but within that status he was treated the same as his peers. To this extent public law had taken the place of custom privately enforced.

Early Tokugawa legislation was directed principally toward the clarification of class boundaries and the definition of behavior appropriate to each class. Perhaps the effort was overdone. Natural striations had begun to appear in the society of the day; a military aristocracy, a peasantry, an urban merchant-artisan class had each begun to separate out and take on its distinctive style of life. By making social categories hereditary and by imposing the Chinese four-class theory upon them, the Tokugawa rulers may well have added unnecessary restraints to the evolving social law. Yet rule by status was for its time a clear advance in legal philosophy, a step in the direction of impersonal rule by law. Above all it made for a tidy society, and this to the samurai was a major virtue.

If Tokugawa law was broadened through systematization, it was deepened by the absorption of Confucian ethical principles. By Tokugawa times Japanese society coincided more clearly with the Chinese model than ever before, and the relevance of Chinese thought was apparent as never before. A new surge of interest in Confucian philosophy thus went hand in hand with the evolution of the baku-han political order. Confucian literature, filled with words of wisdom on government and the achievement of social harmony, became suddenly attractive to the Tokugawa rulers, for, in the early seventeenth century, shogun and daimyo faced acute problems of social engineering in their effort to bring order out of military turmoil. The shift from a feudal society toward one of large classes, the shift from military to civil rule, required the formulation of new and more general principles of government, the elaboration of new laws and administrative institutions. Confucian writings, particularly those of Chu Hsi and his school, appeared especially pertinent. As the shogun and daimyo filled out their responsibilities toward their territories, as they became more the "complete rulers," their dependence on Confucian theory increased proportionately.

Confucian political thought by and large gave rational support to the form military government had taken under the baku-han system. It buttressed the idea of a social hierarchy in which the individual lived to fulfill the mission of his allotted station. But it did more. It set before the Tokugawa rulers a moral order as well, one that stood above human society and regulated the conduct of both ruler and subject. It placed shogun and daimyo under the responsibility to rule for the benefit of the people—to provide a benevolent administration and to instruct the samurai in the way of the scholar-administrator. Before long, the samurai had adopted for himself the designation of literatus (*shih*). Military government justified itself as purveyor of universal social virtues, protector of a harmoniously regulated civil state. It had begun to acquire a sense of social responsibility.

Life Under the Tokugawa

The most abiding product of Ieyasu's legacy was domestic peace and stability. By 1800 the Tokugawa regime had given Japan a breathing space of nearly two hundred years. Within the limitations of the baku-han system the country had prospered. Bakufu and han institutions had settled down to a secure routine. Life for the several classes had become easier and more culturally rewarding. Arts and letters flourished. Among the indices of growth, the most immediately apparent was the increase in productivity of the land. Officially assessed at 18.5 million *koku* (the standard Japanese measure for grain, roughly five bushels) in 1597, production had grown to an assessment of 25.8 million *koku* by 1700. Thereafter the rate of increase dropped off considerably, but the total had nonetheless reached 30.4 million *koku* by 1832.. These figures give evidence first of all of the return to normalcy in the countryside, but they also reflect the new attention given by the shogun and daimyo to river control, irrigation, and land reclamation. Little was done dramatically, but the sum total of the efforts of each territory made for a dramatic aggregate. Assessment figures, moreover, were only a partial measure of the growth in the agricultural base. Improved farming methods—better tools and more effective fertilizers, particularly the use of night soil gathered from city privies—made more of the soil and extended the areas of double cropping. Cereal production probably doubled between 1600 and 1730. On top of this, production of cotton, tea, sugar, silk, and other consumer products was encouraged. Silk became a particular symbol. In 1600 it was the prime import from China through Nagasaki, but by 1800 the trade in Chinese silk had nearly disappeared—the Japanese farmer had taken over.

Population increase accompanied growth in agricultural production, but not at the fantastic rate that made it a major affliction for China. Population may well have grown by fifty percent between 1600 and 1721. By 1800 the total national figure was just over thirty million. But this was only a million or so more than it had been a hundred years before. And it was not to increase much more before the 1850's. In general therefore we must assume, and not without evidence, that the standard of living had improved for all classes. But the improvement was not necessarily distributed uniformly, and this was the rub. There were backward areas in the north and south and in the mountainous provinces. There were obvious inequities between wealthy and landless villagers and between prosperous merchants and the urban poor. However, on the whole the signs of improvement—evidence of better housing, clothing, food, education, and entertainment—were impressive and widely shared.

After the middle of the sixteenth century a major change occurred in the Japanese style of life, without plan and almost without notice, as the city became a dominant cultural factor. At the beginning of the sixteenth century, other than Kyoto there were only a few commercial cities (Hakata, Sakai, Muro) worthy of the name and, in addition, a few towns built around religious centers (Nara, Ishiyama) or the headquarters of some of the leading daimyo (Kagoshima, Yamaguchi). The main highways supported numerous wayside towns, and each region had its market towns and centers of craft production, but such towns were not much differentiated from the villages that adjoined them. True bourgeois life was a rare phenomenon. Then suddenly, following the consolidation of the larger daimyo domains in the latter half of the sixteenth century, Japan's urban topography was revolutionized. [From one end of Japan to the other, daimyo castle headquarters became centers around which thriving commercial quarters developed.] Castle cities sprang up overnight, many in locations where not even a village had existed before, for strategic considerations came first. But the new castles were by and large well placed at the economic centers of their domains. [Once they had drawn the samurai into residence around their castles, the daimyo were confronted with the necessity of acquiring military supplies and satisfying the daily needs of their establishments and retainers.] Commercial quarters were added and merchants brought in by offer of special privileges or by force. Thus most of the new cities that were to house the samurai class during the Tokugawa period were constructed at great expense of labor and material by the regional daimyo in the short span of years between 1580 and 1610.

The distinctive feature of these cities was that their size depended in no way upon their distance from Edo or Kyoto or from the traditional trade routes; they were the immediate reflection of the wealth and power of their daimyo creators. Sendai in the north became a city of sixty thousand; Kanazawa on the Japan Sea side may have reached one hundred thousand; Kagoshima at the extreme south grew to over seventy thousand. Edo, Osaka, and Kyoto, giants among the cities of Tokugawa Japan, took on special characteristics of the central metropolis and led the way in creating an urban culture peculiar to the Tokugawa age. But the castle towns that dotted the Japanese countryside shared this culture. The steady flow of traffic between Edo and the provinces, as the daimyo and their retinues performed their *sankin-kōtai* duties, linked the capital to the remotest town and made tastes cultivated at the center the model for life in the provinces.

One suspects that the Tokugawa rulers never quite acknowledged and never fully planned for the drastic shift in the way of life that followed the move to the castle town. The samurai considered themselves products of a landed economy and carried into their new environment a deep commitment to an agrarian philosophy. Yet the realities soon belied their theories. By the end of the seventeenth century the samurai were out of touch with the countryside, for cities and towns had become their domicile. All told, perhaps ten percent of the population of Japan was living an urban style of life in cities with a population of ten thousand or over.

THE combination of peace, urbanization, and civil service thus transformed the everyday lives of the samurai. The battlefield was now remembered only in stories told of an earlier, more rugged generation. The possibility of advancement through military exploits was denied. Skill at weapons could not be tested other than in games, and the display of courage was no longer rewarded with titles and lands. [The samurai, living now in houses provided by the daimyo and on rice stipends received at the daimyo's granaries, had but one outlet for their ambitions: service in the line of administrative duty.] So the good samurai became the capable official, trained as an administrator, educated and cultivated in the aristocratic arts. Education was no longer a luxury or something to be left to weaklings; it became a means of advancement or at least of preserving self-respect in the new environment. The arts were no longer the province of only the highest levels of the ruling class; security and leisure gave even the lower samurai access to cultural pastimes.

Tokugawa samurai society has never gained great recognition for its cultural achievements. In the arts and literature it is the products of plebeian life—the plays of Chikamatsu or the prints of Hiroshige—that have won the acclaim of later generations. The Tokugawa samurai, either as artist or as patron, was more derivative than creative. The shrine to Ieyasu at Nikko, with its gaudy and ornate buildings, was only later saved aesthetically by the growth of evergreens, which enclosed it in a mass of towering green. Daimyo patronage produced miles of painted gold screens, great quantities of multicolored Imari and Kutani porcelain, lacquered chests, and chiseled ironwork. There was a comfortable affluence and a tendency toward conspicuous display. Every daimyo could aspire to the image of the aristocratic life. But, though the products of the past were avidly collected, earlier models were never surpassed; connoisseurship became acquisitive.

Nevertheless, the Tokugawa elite made its contribution to cultural development, though in a way less obvious and less easily appreciated by succeeding generations or outsiders to Japan. Its province was scholarship, in classical studies, history, philosophy, and the laws. The mood was serious and scholastic, but the product moved Japan forward intellectually. It was not simply peace and leisure that encouraged the spread of education after 1600. The ability to read and write, knowledge of the historic texts—skills that had been left to the priesthood during the years of active warfare—now became part of the mark of the well-trained samurai official. Shogun and daimyo encouraged scholarship. The Code of the Military Houses enjoined the samurai to cultivate *both* learning and military training, and it put learning first. Ieyasu began his patronage of the Hayashi family as Confucian advisers and instructors in the classics soon after becoming shogun. By 1630, the beginnings of a bakufu college had been established at Edo. The daimyo followed suit, vying for the services of well-known Confucian scholars and establishing han schools and colleges. By 1800 hardly a daimyo domain was without its school for the training of youthful retainers, and no samurai worth his salt could admit to ignorance of the basic Confucian texts. The encouragement of learning went deeper still, for education was no longer monopolized by the aristocratic few or a captive priesthood. The sons of merchants and peasants were provided for, particularly those destined to become headmen. For them the so-called temple-schools (*terakoya*), small private elementary schools, sprang up by the thousands in the cities and villages. Japan by 1700 was already on the way toward becoming a basically literate society. By 1800 the Japanese male population was from forty- to fifty-percent literate.

[It was the written word, then, that became the most distinguished product of Tokugawa samurai society.] The areas that the mind of the samurai scholar probed started with the practical and turned later to the historical and literary. By "practical studies" was meant, of course, investigation of the metaphysical and historical texts, the guides to proper conduct and to good administration. In this sphere, from the early works of the Hayashi School to the practical treatises on agriculture and trade of the mid-nineteenth century, the output was enormous. Every shogun had his advisers, whether by design or by sufferance, and so did the several daimyo. Ex-samurai scholars made their living by setting up academies in Kyoto or Edo or by writing free-lance memorials on state policy. Shogun and daimyo established boards of historians to compile histories of Japan, or of the several provinces, and to prepare guides to ritual and official precedence.

The bulk of this work was derivative or simply archival; but the treatises were often saved from banality by their practicality and freedom from reliance on formula. Here were the beginnings of a literature of political economy that was able to cut itself off from Confucian dogma to minister to problems peculiar to Japan. There was little in these works to make them pertinent reading today, for the philosophy was not deep and the policy statements were too speculative. Once Western science and education touched Japan, the works of the Tokugawa scholars were quickly forgotten. But for its age the Tokugawa scholarly product was impressive, and the thrust it gave to the samurai mind was profoundly significant. Above all, it developed a vocabulary of political and social concepts capable of dealing with complex problems of state and society, capable even of some flexibility of approach to such problems.

THE spread of urbanized samurai life was paralleled by yet another profound change in the composition of Tokugawa society. With cities came merchants, and the country thereby faced another troublesome anomaly. If the growth of cities had been an unexpected by-product of the establishment of military headquarters by the daimyo, the proliferation of a merchant class was not only unprepared for but was actually considered undesirable. From beginning to end, the Tokugawa samurai official held to a theory of economy that denigrated commerce at the expense of agriculture; yet it was the commercial sector of the economy that was most stimulated by the new urban emphasis.

The position of the merchant in Tokugawa society reflected the failure of the commercial estate to achieve independence under either Confucian theory or Japanese law. The Tokugawa polity from the outset denied the merchant free access to foreign trade and placed him under severe government control in the production and distribution of key commodities. The hand of government monopoly control extended far and deep. Foreign trade was considered a shogunal monopoly, and the several daimyo sought to monopolize commodities produced in their domains, working the economy of their local territory against the larger national market. In the castle town, merchants, though protected, were regulated and restricted in their activities. And above all there was no thought that the merchant, any more than the peasant, should have a voice in the affairs of government. Confucian theory regarded the merchant as simply a mover of goods and placed him at the bottom of the social hierarchy. Tokugawa law subscribed to the same theory.

[While the samurai scorned the merchant's way of life, he had in fact, long before 1800, become deeply dependent upon the latter's services.] Living, as one contemporary writer put it, "as though in an inn" in his castle towns, the samurai was forced to rely upon the merchants to bridge the economic separation between town and country. In the new castle towns, merchant quarters were laid out under the walls of the daimyo's castle. And here the merchant class came to rest, encouraged to serve the needs of the samurai, yet segregated by official decree and rigidly excluded from participation in the political affairs of the domain. The position had some advantages, to be sure, for the merchant was never taxed by the authorities as fully as he might have been had the economic bases of his wealth been better understood; and, since commerce was denigrated, the merchant was left alone in his own realm. Few merchant communities elsewhere in the Far East managed to acquire as vital a place in the national economy or to remain as secure in that place.

But, since the Tokugawa merchants were never really free, they were obliged to make their way as handlers and agents for the samurai class. Thus, in actual practice, something of an alliance of interests grew up between the merchants and the authorities. Guilds and protective associations, once abolished by the daimyo in an effort to lure merchants to their castle towns, were again recognized by the shogunate in its effort to control commercial activity in its major cities. Shogunal monopolies of precious metals, silk thread, copper, lime, and vegetable oils were part of the effort to regulate the national economy. Private protective organizations and wholesale guilds were licensed after 1721 in response to the expansion of commercial activity and as a means of stabilizing prices and assuring adequate distribution. By making annual payments of "thank money" (myōga-kin), merchants in the great cities obtained government backing for their own monopoly efforts.

The interdependence of the samurai and merchant communities became particularly complex in regard to the fiscal operations of the shogunate and the daimyo domains. In the countryside, rural wholesalers bought up commodities from the villages for sale in the castle towns or in the national entrepôts of Osaka and Edo. In the castle towns some merchants took over the handling of goods and rice for shipment to the daimyo's Edo residence or to Osaka for sale. Soon the volume of han financial dealings in the exchange centers led to the establishment of daimyo warehouses superintended by hired financial agents. Increasingly, such agents were selected from among wealthy and financially influential business houses. [Under the administrative supervision of samurai officials, then, the commercial class organized a network of commercial and financial operations linking the han capitals with Edo or Osaka.] What has been called the "feudal-merchant alliance" was made complete.

Well before the beginning of the nineteenth century, commercial activity within the country had shaped itself into a national market centering in Osaka and Edo. Here were the great exchange houses and commodity markets. The Osaka rice exchange at Dojima dealt in futures and acquired the ability to influence the price of rice on a national scale. By 1750, Osaka had over one hundred and thirty domain warehouse offices, and the annual flow of rice into its docks is said to have approached five million bushels. It was here that the economic heart of the nation beat, despite the political power wielded by the samurai class. Increasingly, in fact, samurai government and the samurai as a class became dependent upon merchant handlers and financial agents. Since taxes were collected in grain and stipends paid out in units of rice, and since the necessities of life were bought in cash, there was no escape from the rice exchange. Once the samurai's desires passed beyond his income, once samurai government was pushed in its responsibilities beyond its revenues, the pressure to borrow from the commercial agents or to float loans as paper currency became irresistible. Before long the samurai's alliance with the merchants had been further deepened by a vast amount of indebtedness. As holders of credit and as active agents in the fiscal and commodity transactions of the shogunate and han, the merchant class became an economic power of unexpected strength.

[Commercial wealth gave rise to a bourgeois society with its own identity.] The urban class—the *chōnin,* as it was called—had its merchant princes in the great cities. By 1800 the houses that were to persist into modern times to become the heads of the zaibatsu cartels had already appeared. Mitsui, which had started in the seventeenth century as a simple sake brewer, had become financial agent to shogun and emperor. Its operations included a network of dry-goods wholesalers, a rapid-runner service between Edo and Osaka, and money-exchange houses in the three major cities. Kōnoike, also starting as a sake brewer, had gone into shipping and moneylending in Osaka, there to become financial agent and warehouse-keeper for over forty daimyo houses. Sumitomo, starting as drug and iron-goods merchants, had gone into copper refining and ended up as the bakufu agents for the monopoly production and minting of copper.

Yet the remarkable thing about the merchant leaders of the Tokugawa period was that for all their wealth they showed no inclination to use their economic resources to break into positions of political influence. The first head of the Mitsui House advised his successors to stay clear of involvement in samurai affairs. The favor of shogunal officials and of daimyo was too fickle a thing to set store by. And the government still had the power to ruin a merchant and confiscate his hard-won wealth. [Thus the commercial estate put no pressure on samurai government for a say in policy or for representation in councils of state. Tokugawa society produced no movement toward the formation of a parliament.]

Wealthy merchants thus were confined to their own bourgeois world. An individual Mitsui might enter the samurai world by adoption, but the Mitsui "house" remained forever within the *chōnin* status. Nor could the purchase of land bring with it a rise in status, for land was not a mark of aristocratic distinction. So the *chōnin* cultivated his own community and created his own world of social and cultural activity, vulgar by comparison with the life of the samurai, but robust and relevant.

Out of the mercantile quarters, first of Kyoto and Osaka, then of Edo, came the arts and pastimes of the *ukiyo*, the floating world of the theatre and geisha quarters. Before the seventeenth century was out, *chōnin* had added to the Japanese cultural tradition the bawdy tales of Saikaku, the kabuki plays of Chikamatsu, the woodblock prints of Moronobu, and the great poetic essays and *haiku* perfections of Bashō. If samurai arts were formal and derivative, these were fresh and creative. Samurai and *chōnin*, kept apart by the class-based legal concepts and the separate living quarters that divided the castle cities, thus lived in different worlds. Yet the *chōnin*'s world was more of the city in which the samurai now lived; and it was the *chōnin* who transformed the samurai's traditions into a contemporary and living vernacular. Thus, increasingly, the two worlds drew together.] Samurai left their swords at home to "pass" in the off-limits streets of the licensed quarters, while merchant scholars gained recognition for their studies in mathematics and finance.]

Intellectual Ferment and the Sense of Crisis

Japan had obviously grown under the Tokugawa peace, adding new dimensions to its economic and social life. But it had acquired problems as well. Some were simply the product of the passage of time. Government had settled into a routine, even a lethargy. The samurai class was obviously too numerous for what was required of it; the manpower needs of warfare had been more demanding than those of peace, yet the class had grown rather than diminished since 1600. And, while the revenues of the daimyo had expanded somewhat, expenditures for public works and the general rise in the standard of living had put the samurai in an acute economic squeeze. Stipends were being reduced, if not in absolute terms at least in terms of purchasing power, well before 1800. Meanwhile the rising level of needs and wants clashed with the sense of ennui that came with too much honor to maintain and too little work to do. Moralists were quick to point out that the samurai had grown flabby; living in luxury, neglecting military training, he had become a disgrace to the memory of the spartan swordsmen who had won the peace for Ieyasu.

Overstaffed bureaucracies added to the sluggishness of the political process. The creative acts of the early shogun and first-generation daimyo became precedents that later generations dared not modify. Policy was not made; it was adhered to. System took over where men had once commanded. Shoguns and daimyo became faceless figures presiding over ritualized routine. Meanwhile the financial conditions of the shogunate and daimyo domains deteriorated. The debts of the samurai class and of samurai government to the merchant houses of Osaka and Edo mounted. And among the common people inequalities of wealth and the periodic ravages of famine and natural disaster incited uprisings in the villages and violence in the towns.

Yet, if there were problems in 1800, there were those who acknowledged them. The polity was sensitive. Corruption there was, perhaps, but the scale was small—a questionable appointment here, a commercial privilege granted surreptitiously there. There was no space for a grand pillage of the national treasury or the massive acquisition of tax-free land. The system was tight, and it was remarkably moral. Rumors that Tanuma Okitsugu, the tenth shogun's favored minister, had taken a bribe in the form of a dancing girl or that his subordinates had indulged in rowdy parties had shaken the bakufu. No famine persisted but that the government came to the support of the people with relief rice.

There was no lack of advice from official and self-appointed critics of the regime on what to do about the economic and social ills of the times. From the hard-line Confucianists came the expected chant: Breakdown of agrarian self-sufficiency, increase in money economy, and desire for luxuries had destroyed the foundations of the ideal economy. Even so practical-minded a thinker as Ogyū Sorai advocated strict control of the merchant class, curtailment of "luxuries," renewed attention to military preparedness, and, most essential of all, return of the samurai to the villages. There in his natural habitat, close to the soil, the samurai, he believed, would regain his manly vigor and live the spartan life that was his heritage.

Samurai government was especially sensitive to the problems of the land. The shogunate and han governments sought periodically to effect "reforms." The prototype of shogunal reform had come some eighty years before, when the eighth shogun, Yoshimune, had taken a firm hand at the bakufu helm. His policies of agrarianism, hard money, retrenchment of expenditures, protection for indebted samurai, sumptuary regulations, and control of merchant economy were essentially traditional. Their effects were invigorating for a time but brought no lasting solution.

Yoshimune had exemplified the standard military response to a baffling problem—firm disciplinary action and an effort to get back to first military principles.

Yet when it came to the everyday operations of government, the trend of the times was more pragmatic and flexible than the purists would have wished. Officials in the finance office had to roll with the commercial tide and cooperate with the world of the *chōnin*. The path was one of least resistance. But it was also difficult to legitimize, and it was the saving quality of the Japanese scholar-adviser of the nineteenth century that there were those bold enough to advocate policies of mercantilism and commercial development in defiance of accepted Confucian theory.

By the beginning of the eighteenth century many members of the Japanese intellectual world had abandoned their strict reliance on Chu Hsi Neo-Confucianism when it came to writing about problems specific to Japan. Whether by influence from Ch'ing China or on their own initiative, a turn to "practical studies" and rationalism within the body of Confucian orthodoxy produced scholars of singular individuality. Realists faced the growing commercialization of the Japanese economy frankly and sought ways of taking advantage of it. A writer such as Dazai Shundai (1680–1747) considered a money economy a fact of life and urged the government to think in terms of capital accumulation. Kaibo Seiryō (1755–1818) argued that the samurai, being obliged to sell portions of his rice stipend for cash, was no different from a *chōnin;* and the merchant was no different from the samurai, for profit from trade was in essence a kind of stipend. Why should the samurai disdain profit, he asked, when the king of Holland actively patronizes commercial ventures? Honda Toshiaki (1744–1821) studied what he could of world geography and concluded that Japan's seclusion policy was misguided. Japan, he said, should strike out across the seas as a maritime power. Satō Nobuhiro (1768–1850) spent a vigorous life traveling about Japan advising daimyo on agricultural improvements, new mining techniques, the development of natural resources, and the latest methods of national defense.

Mercantilist policies of the kinds advocated by these nineteenth-century thinkers were most successfully applied to the daimyo domain. The domains were smaller than the shogunal territories and had less complicated economies; moreover, the daimyo found it possible to work their local economies against the national market by dealing in the controlled production and sale of special products. Thus it was sugar that pulled Satsuma out of financial trouble, and silk served a similar purpose in a number of the northeastern domains. The shogunate had a harder time of it, for with foreign trade curtailed it had no markets outside its own territory to exploit. Debasement of coinage was one of its only expedients, and, though the bakufu officials realized full well that this had a depressing effect upon the economy as a whole, they constantly resorted to it. Other measures—cautious encouragement of foreign trade (as a shogunal monopoly), development of sponsored commercial ventures, sale of monopoly licenses—never gained full support, largely because of the bad name given to such techniques by Tanuma Okitsugu toward the end of the eighteenth century. The bakufu continued to drift or to engage periodically in unsuccessful reforms of the Yoshimune type.

But the encouragement of technological improvement was safe, particularly so long as there was no question of denying the official orthodoxy. Yoshimune had had the courage to admit the existence of a superior science in the books of the Hollanders at Deshima and had encouraged his official scholars to learn what they could of Western systems of astronomy, agronomy, military technology, and geography. By the end of the century the private study of Dutch language and medical science had begun to spread, and men like Hiraga Gennai had toyed with electricity. Practical studies, it was expected, could be controlled, for the religion and political philosophy of the West was still scrupulously censored at Nagasaki. But the new science of the West, with its Copernican foundation, let loose in Tokugawa Japan conceptions that undermined the cosmology of Confucianism as surely as they had struck at the foundations of Christian dogma in Europe. The Tokugawa Japanese played with the knowledge that trickled in from the West at his own risk and at the risk of the Confucian world view to which he subscribed. Yet he did so, and avidly; and it is perhaps this that differentiated him most clearly from the Chinese of his day.

Confucianism was still the basis of the samurai's education and his moral and political outlook on life, but he was not so wedded to what was still to him a Chinese import that he could not admit of something better. To him it was the system—the shogunate, the han, the samurai world—that mattered most and had to be protected. Philosophy or technology, things from outside the system, could be appropriated freely or discarded, and this applied to Confucianism. Perhaps the most deeply revealing quality of the early nineteenth-century samurai critic was that he was capable of being intellectually acquisitive. In an effort to meet practical problems with rational means, he could use the fragments of knowledge that came to him, often in imperfect form. Technology and political economy could be made to solve real problems and create a future better than the past. Knowledge for him could be for the improvement, not simply the preservation and protection, of an honored tradition. He was, in other words, on the threshold of thinking scientifically.

IF there was intellectual ferment in the air of the early nineteenth century, there was also a deepening sense of crisis and alarm that problems were not being solved. This, more than anything else, was the mark of the Tokugawa political system—its sensitivity to tremors in the structure. And by the 1830's a sufficient number of things seemed to be wrong with the country to warrant the serious concern of its leaders. In an economy still overwhelmingly agrarian, natural calamities such as disease and crop failure could have profound effects. Japan was plagued with natural disaster after 1800. Crop failures were widespread from 1824 to 1832. A severe famine struck northern Japan in 1833, and in 1836 there was a nationwide famine. By the mid-1830's the countryside was seething with displaced peasants, and the cities were choked with villagers seeking employment. The shogunate and the affected daimyo opened relief stations, but this provided only temporary assistance. The poor were driven to desperation. Outbreaks of violence became common in the villages, and the establishments of rice merchants were broken into in the cities.

Then suddenly there occurred the incident that dramatized the seriousness of the state of affairs and gave evidence to some that drastic measures were needed. The incident was Ōshio Heihachirō's abortive uprising in Osaka in 1837—a minor flare-up to be sure, put down in all but a day, yet it was a sign of the nervousness of samurai officialdom and of its concern for the general welfare that 1837 became something of a domestic turning point.

Ōshio, a minor official in the bakufu's Osaka city administration and an amateur scholar, had taken to heart the plight of the rural and urban poor. When his official superiors failed to do enough on their behalf, Ōshio plotted direct action. He called upon the peasants of the four provinces around Osaka to rise up and kill "the heartless officials and the luxury living merchants who profited while the poor starved." He planned to capture Osaka Castle and distribute the wealth of the city to those who needed it. There was a day of violence. The bakufu could well be ashamed of the ineptness of its police forces, but Ōshio's uprising was quickly surpressed.

This event made a deep impression on the Tokugawa shogunate, whose authority had been challenged. Tokugawa Nariaki (1800–60), head of the Mito branch of the house, predicted dire results if the bakufu did not "undertake reforms" immediately by working for the good of the country. The bakufu, he claimed, had put its own interests ahead of the nation's, which he saw embodied in the concept of an all-concerned emperor. In a moment of crisis the name of the emperor had been raised in its transcendental sense. Bakufu reforms did follow in 1841 under Chief Councilor Mizuno. But the effort was ill conceived and antagonized more than it satisfied the critics of Tokugawa policy. The domestic crisis of the Tempō era, as it is generally known, remained unresolved.

But domestic events proved to be only half the reason that Tokugawa leadership was troubled. For there was the lurking knowledge that the country was facing a new foreign crisis as well. The foreign issue was not to come to a head until 1853, with the arrival of the Perry mission, but the country had been reacting with increasing unease to evidence of Western activity in its waters since before the turn of the nineteenth century. It was another measure of the sensitivity of samurai government that contact with foreigners outside the provisions of seclusion law, no matter how casual, rapidly became a matter of official concern.

The original seclusion policy had been enacted against the old colonial powers and had been maintained with little difficulty for well over a century. By the end of the eighteenth century, however, the Japanese came to realize that a whole new group of European powers was at its doors. How powerful these new nations were and how persistent their demands for free access to the Japanese homeland would be was soon apparent as well. The initial alarm had been raised by the approach of the Russians from the north down the Kuril chain. Laxman's bold effort in 1792 to gain trading concessions from the daimyo of Matsumae, the only authority at the time in Hokkaido, had been communicated to Edo. The reaction had been nervous and positive. The bakufu clamped a censorship on the spread of news about the "new foreign peril." An immediate effort to map and develop Hokkaido was put under way, and by 1802 the northern island, so far little known to the Edo authorities, had been taken over by the bakufu. The daimyo of Matsumae was moved to Honshu, and a bakufu commissioner was placed at Hakodate with responsibility for defense and colonization. Russian probes continued to give the bakufu officials concern. Rezanov's attempt, as director of the new Russo-American Trading Company, to break into the Nagasaki trade in 1804 was thwarted, but the Russians took out their frustration in a number of retaliatory raids on Japanese outposts in the north. The sense of danger increased.

Meanwhile, the British had begun to probe Japanese coastal waters. In 1808 the English frigate *Phaeton* entered Nagasaki under a Dutch flag and obtained supplies by threat of bombardment. Although the *Phaeton* was ultimately driven off, the sense of disgrace at having permitted a violation of the seclusion policy caused the magistrate of Nagasaki, himself a daimyo, to commit suicide. Administration might have been sluggishly performed, but honor, particularly national honor, could not be taken lightly.

By the 1820's British whalers had entered the North Pacific, and their efforts to secure supplies from the Japanese gave rise to a new series of incidents involving the inhabitants of coastal territories, many of them outside bakufu jurisdiction. The possibility of clandestine intercourse with the foreigner now became a danger, and in 1825 the shogun issued his order to local authorities that all foreign vessels should be driven away without prior contact.

More worrisome to the bakufu authorities than these relatively minor incidents was the growing knowledge that Japan was coming under the pressure of a general phenomenon that was affecting the rest of East Asia as well. The Dutch at Nagasaki now proved useful. They were required to submit annual reports on the state of the world, and these confirmed the bakufu's worst fears. News of the Opium War in China and its outcome sent a tremor through the inner circles of samurai officialdom. For Tokugawa Nariaki this news, together with the shame of the Ōshio uprising, became the final proof of crisis. Japan, he believed, was at a turning point. Never in its history had the need been greater for samurai leadership to fulfill its destiny. Fifteen years later, when Perry stood at Japan's doors, Nariaki expressed the gut reactions of the tough-minded samurai administrator. The issue was simple: To open the country was to shame the sacred memory of Ieyasu and to defy the national policy of seclusion. The question was clearly one of war or peace, and Japan must take the course of war, even in expectation of immediate defeat. For war would bring mobilization; it would jar the samurai out of his lethargy, regenerate in him the martial spirit that once had made him capable of coping with any emergency. With resolution and with a show of solidarity around the emperor, the samurai could meet this new crisis. In an extremity, the Japanese official was quick to put his hand to his sword, whether to turn it on a foe or against his own person.

The foreign crisis of the 1830's and 1840's, provoked by minor incidents along the Japanese frontier of seclusion, reflected the tenseness of samurai society. Before the issue of seclusion was fully forced, in fact, the foreign question had been picked up by the samurai intellectual. The issue was not just one of whether to defend or relax a sacred policy of seclusion; the question was fundamental. Where did Japan stand in the world now that the world itself had begun to change before the eyes of the Japanese? The issue was one of national identity more than of shogunal policy. The stranger at the door forced a rethinking of the samurai world view, but the process had been in operation well before the final confrontation with the West.

By the nineteenth century, Japanese writers in almost any field were being influenced, whether they realized it or not, by knowledge of Western sciences and fear of Western encroachment. The necessity of confronting new and strange ideas from abroad cut many ways. Most were impelled simply to rejection and a retreat into formalism, others to an eclecticism that tried to have it both ways. A Yamagata Bantō (1748–1821), for instance, might try to integrate Western heliocentric theory with Confucian cosmology and find an equivalence between science and the Neo-Confucian concept of reason. Still others took the lonely path of prophet for the coming of the West, pointing out Japan's weakness and calling for a change in the seclusion policy, an opening of the ports and minds of the Japanese to the outside world. From practical knowledge of Western technology to political criticism was a hazardous step, as men such as Takano Chōei (1804–50) and Watanabe Kazan (1793–1841) were to discover. Their call for the abandonment of seclusion in 1838 following the visit of the American ship *Morrison* to Japan resulted in imprisonment and eventually death. The open advocacy of Westernization was still unpopular and could be dangerous.

But the alternative for the Japanese intellectual was not necessarily submission to Confucian orthodoxy. For him there was a way out of the Sinocentric bind into which the West had put him, and it lay in the direction of his own past, in a rediscovery of his own national individuality. A strong nationalistic element had run through the writings of the Tokugawa Confucian school from its inception. Hayashi Razan had used Confucian ideas to enrich the significance of the imperial symbols of sovereignty. Yamaga Sokō's doctrine of *bushidō* had elevated the samurai to the rank of virtuous rulers. Yamazaki Ansai (1618–82) had found in Shinto doctrine an ancient Japanese "way of the gods," which matched the way of the Sage Kings. Revived interest in Shinto and classical Japanese history and literature led ultimately to a school of indigenous studies based on a body of "Japanese classics." "National learning" (*kokugaku*), as against Chinese learning (*Kangaku*), became a recognized field of study by the early eighteenth century. Beginning as an effort to recover a Japanese literary and historical heritage, it had become by the nineteenth century a movement dedicated to an intellectual return to Japan's national origins.

There is no denying the Confucian foundations of the *kokugaku* movement. Kada Azumamaro (1668–1736), one of its earliest advocates, had openly sought a Japanese "way of the ancients." Motoori Norinaga (1730–1801), who more than any other gave prominence to the movement, devoted his life to a study of the *Kojiki* (presumably written in 712) in an effort to rediscover Japan's "original sources." What he claimed to find was a uniquely Japanese "ancient way," a state of natural goodness exemplified in the age of the gods (*kami*). Motoori came to the conclusion that Japan's problems stemmed from the contamination of this utopian age by Buddhist and Confucian influence. Confucianism was a clever gloss that had corrupted the vision of Japan's leaders, and he urged his countrymen to leave off their slavish reliance on Chinese thought.

After 1800 *kokugaku* attracted many minds to the serious study of Japanese literature and to renewed inquiry into the theological aspects

of Shinto. The violently nationalistic and antiforeign Hirata Atsutane
(1766–1843) called strenuously for a revival of Shinto beliefs. It was
time the Japanese recognized their unique position in world history, he
wrote, for theirs was a nation created by the Sun Goddess, a nation distinguished by its unbroken imperial line, a nation superior to all others,
including China, India, Russia, and Holland. His claims were both irrational and exaggerated, but he had struck a deep chord of emotional
attachment to the homeland in a time of crisis. And he was reacting to
the new geography that was forcing the Japanese to rethink their position in the world. His reaction was half bravado, but it sought to accentu-
ate Japan's traditional sense of advantage. If the West claimed the sun
was the center of the universe, was this not to the credit of "the nation of
the sun"? Hirata and his colleagues had shown the way to the acquisition
of a new sense of identity built around symbols peculiar to Japanese history: the national deities of Shinto and the emperor. It provided a singu-
larly Japanese answer to the challenge of the West.

An Assessment

The crisis of the 1830's was compounded of many factors, domestic and
foreign, but the foreign element proved decisive. The crisis was not, of
course, to be fully resolved until after 1868, when the shogunate had been
torn down and the seclusion policy long since abandoned. It is only by
hindsight that we can look upon the shogunate as a doomed institution
by the mid-nineteenth century, or imagine that samurai government was
in its last stages. Certainly it was inconceivable to contemporary Japanese
that within a generation the Tokugawa edifice would be destroyed. And
it is difficult to imagine from our knowledge of the domestic power the
bakufu had at its disposal that it could not have retained its position of
superiority in the crisis of national defense that the West forced upon
Japan. Yet by the 1850's bakufu leadership clearly experienced a loss of
nerve. The nation was now more than shogunate, and it was to the
credit of shogunal and daimyo leadership that this conflict of interest was
acknowledged and that it elicited no die-hard effort to defend the old
regime at all costs. The internal power struggle that took place between
1853 and 1868 was intense, to be sure, but it was characterized by one
thing: acute awareness of the pressure of the Western powers and of
the jeopardy in which this placed the Japanese as a people. The final
legacy of the Tokugawa system to the new Japan came in these years, for
in the moment of crisis the samurai estate rose to the occasion. Appealing
to the transcendent sovereignty of the emperor, to a new vision of
national identity, reform-minded leaders were able to liquidate the sho-

gunate without disrupting the political structure. The emperor was salvaged from obscurity to become the symbol of the new sense of national purpose with which Japan would confront the world.

Selected Readings

Bellah, Robert N. *Tokugawa Religion: The Values of Pre-industrial Japan.* Glencoe, Ill.: Free Press, 1957. An effort to apply the ideas of Tolcott Parsons and Max Weber to the political behavior of the Tokugawa samurai and commercial classes.

Crawcour, E. S. "Changes in Japanese Commerce in the Tokugawa Period." *Journal of Asian Studies,* Vol. 22, No. 4 (August 1963), pp. 387–400. An important interpretive article on the nature of commercial development in Tokugawa Japan.

de Bary, William T., Jr., *et al.,* eds. *Sources of the Japanese Tradition.* 2 vols. New York: Columbia University Press, 1958. Part IV of this anthology provides excellent insight into Tokugawa intellectual movements.

Dore, Ronald P. *Education in Tokugawa Japan.* Berkeley, Calif.: University of California Press, 1964. A very broad treatment of the development of educational facilities and the spread of literacy as background for Japan's modern intellectual development.

Hall, John W. "The Confucian Teacher in Tokugawa Japan," in David S. Nivison and Arthur F. Wright, eds., *Confucianism in Action.* Stanford, Calif.: Stanford University Press, 1959. An attempt to assess the role of Confucian thought in the political and social life of the Tokugawa Japanese.

———. *Government and Local Power in Japan, 500–1700: A Study Based on Bizen Province.* Princeton, N.J.: Princeton University Press, 1965. A detailed study of the development of the local political and economic institutions that gave rise to the shogunate and the daimyo of Tokugawa times.

Hall, John W., and Jansen, Marius B., eds. *Studies in the Institutional History of Early Modern Japan.* Princeton, N.J.: Princeton University Press, 1968. A collection of twenty-one basic articles covering the development of local government in Tokugawa Japan, the nature of urban and village society, and various evidences of social and political change in the late Tokugawa period.

Keene, Donald. *The Japanese Discovery of Europe.* Stanford, Calif.: Stanford University Press, 1969. A fascinating treatment of the efforts of a Japanese scholar to comprehend the significance of the West in an isolated Japan.

Sansom, G. B. *The Western World and Japan.* Stanford, Calif.: Stanford University Press, 1959. A scholarly inquiry into the effects of social and economic change on Japan in the eighteenth and nineteenth centuries.

Smith, Thomas C. *The Agrarian Origins of Modern Japan.* Stanford, Calif.: Stanford University Press, 1959. An important study of the economic development of the agrarian sector of Tokugawa Japan, placing special emphasis on the commercialization of agriculture and its social implications.

Totman, Conrad. *Politics in the Tokugawa Bakufu, 1600–1843.* Cambridge, Mass.: Harvard University Press, 1967. A good source for understanding the structure and operation of the Tokugawa shogunate.

Tsukahira, Toshio G. *Feudal Control in Tokugawa Japan.* Cambridge, Mass.: Harvard University Press, 1966. A study of the *sankin-kōtai* system that also contains a good description of daimyo life in Tokugawa Japan.

Webb, Herschel. *The Japanese Imperial Institution in the Tokugawa Period.* New York: Columbia University Press, 1968. A thorough study of the position of the emperor and the ideological structure that grew up around the imperial court prior to the Meiji Restoration.

The Meiji State: 1868–1912

MARIUS B. JANSEN

IN January 1868 an imperial rescript announced that "the Shogun Tokugawa Keiki has abdicated his administrative power. Henceforth all administration will be carried out under Our direct control, and all public affairs will be executed under the name of Emperor, instead of Taikun, as it has been hitherto. Further, special officials will be appointed for intercourse with foreign countries." A few weeks later the shogun, charging that the court had been manipulated by his enemies into a breach of the understandings under which he had resigned his powers, made an unsuccessful attempt to regain military ascendancy at the imperial capital. After his efforts failed, he himself made no great effort to defend his patrimony, but sporadic resistance from his closest vassals led to a civil war with the new "imperial government" that extended into the early summer of 1869.

In April 1868, long before the issue was decided, the imperial government made an important bid for national support with a five-point pledge. This Charter Oath promised that the government would provide the opportunity for "all classes" to achieve their "just aspirations," give attention to the general will by establishing a council chamber, conduct a search for wisdom "throughout the world," and abolish "absurd customs of the past," in order to establish firmly "the foundations of the Empire."

This combination of military force and political and psychological appeal brought the new government steady gains over its less united opponents, and by the fall of 1868 it was ready for a symbolic act that inaugurated the Meiji period. On October 23 the young emperor Mutsuhito, in a Shinto ceremony, selected a slip of paper that bore the Chinese characters "bright" and "rule," pieced together from a quotation in the *Book of Changes*. The combined characters read "Meiji," thus designating the era that would extend until the emperor's death in 1912. The announcement of the era of "enlightened rule" was joined with the statement that henceforth there would be only one era name per sovereign. History was to unfold in emperor-sized units, instead of being divided into eras at the discretion of the government in accordance with numerological wisdom. Thus, a development that had begun in China with the Ming dynasty in 1368, one that signified the final stage of imperial absolutism there, came to Japan at the beginning of the modern era.

A few weeks earlier the court had renamed Edo, the shogun's capital, as Tokyo, or "Eastern Capital." And in November the boy emperor set out on a visit to his new city. A procession of three thousand men surrounded his great palanquin, which was topped by a phoenix and carried by a host of yellow-robed bearers. Having watched the approach of the strange conveyance, which was carried a full six feet above the ground, a reporter wrote that

> a great silence fell upon the people. Far as the eye could see on either side, the roadsides were densely packed with the crouching populace. And as the phoenix car with its halo of glittering attendants came on . . . the people without order or signal turned their faces to the earth. No man moved or spoke for a space, and all seemed to hold their breath for very awe, as the mysterious presence, on whom few are privileged to look and live, was passing by.[1]

Thus the symbolism of a hallowed past, one recently revived by the fervor of the leaders of the national cult, was utilized to sanctify the changes that the discovery of Japan's inability to deal with the outside world had shown to be necessary. And the children of the uncomprehending commoners who crouched in the dust by the roadside as the procession passed were to learn as schoolboys that their rise to equality within Japanese society, like Japan's rise to equality in the world at large, had its origins in the will and virtue of the silent occupant of that Phoenix-topped palanquin.

The Meiji Restoration

The Meiji Restoration represents a remarkable combination of fact and fiction that puts it in a special category among the turning points in the history of the modern world. Viewed as a symbol of Japan's rise to modernity, it can be seen as the product of the interaction of external pressures with the long-range development of Tokugawa thought and

[1] Cited in F. V. Dickins and Stanley Lane-Poole, *The Life of Sir Harry Parkes* (London: Macmillan, 1894), Vol. 2, p. 98.

society. The economic strains within the Tokugawa system had produced increasingly difficult problems for shogunal administrators and reformers, and the intellectual currents of the eighteenth century had substituted for the neat, hierarchical structure of official Confucianism a dynamic mixture of voluntarism and practicality, emotive national affirmation, and curiosity about the learning of the West. The arrival of the West in the middle of the nineteenth century made impossible a preservation of the delicate balance of centralization and decentralization, custom and reason, status and ambition, that had characterized late feudal society. And the discovery of the inadequacy of their society and political system in safeguarding the national integrity against the threat of the West, the sudden realization of Japan's weakness and inferiority, led a generation of Japanese to remarkable efforts to correct these failings. The Restoration was thus nothing less than the opening of a political system that had been closed for more than two centuries. Though the Restoration began as a movement within a small sector of the old elite, and though it was later surrounded with emperor-centered mystique, the need of the Japanese government to attract a broad response in the face of national danger and disunity led it to make the Restoration a national renovation.

The opening of the country had been prepared for by an opening of minds. Late Tokugawa Japan had seen a growing interest in the knowledge of the West. In the early decades of the nineteenth century the shogunate, as well as a number of important domains, made efforts to encourage and also to control, channel, and utilize the information about medicine, war, and technology that could be found in Western books. By the late 1830's some conservatives were beginning to doubt the advisability and safety of such potential subversion of the traditional wisdom, but the shattering intelligence of Britain's defeat of China in the Opium War made it a matter of urgent necessity to intensify efforts to learn about the West. Shortly after the coming of Commodore Perry, the shogunate responded affirmatively to memoranda proposing the establishment of centers for instruction, training, and translation, and in 1857 the Bansho Shirabesho, an "Institute for the Investigation of Barbarian Books," was opened near Edo Castle with a staff that had been selected in a national search for qualified specialists.

It was in good measure the Japanese awareness of the impossibility of resisting the West, an awareness prepared through Nagasaki and underscored by the failure of China's resistance, that produced the opening of the ports to Westerners in the half-decade between the Treaty of Kanagawa, negotiated by Perry in March 1854, and the arrival of consuls and merchants in 1859 under terms of the treaty that Townsend Harris had worked out the previous year. With this beginning, a pattern of unequal treaties, like those worked out earlier with China, began to take form.

Treaty ports were set for Nagasaki, Hakodate, and Yokohama, then Niigata and Kobe. More important still, Osaka and Edo were to be opened in 1862 and 1863. Foreign ministers and consuls were given legal jurisdiction over their countrymen, customs duties were fixed, and the "most favored nation" clause made the system operate to the perpetual and increasing advantage of the outside powers. This was the more certain as a virulent antiforeignism, the product of samurai extremism and economic hardships exacerbated by foreign trade, began to take its toll of foreign lives—and tempers. Outrage led to indemnity and, in two instances, reprisal, in the course of which Japanese inability to withstand the guns of Western ships was made apparent.

The pressures connected with the opening of the ports also produced openings in Japanese politics. The shogunate's first reaction to the problem of Perry's request for a treaty had been to issue a request for the opinion of its vassals; and, since its options were limited by its strength, the shogunate inevitably went on to alienate and antagonize its supporters in the course of accommodating its rivals.

The agreement with Townsend Harris had been made in haste, in fear of new foreign dangers, and in confidence of ability to secure the approval of the imperial court. But this approval proved elusive in fact, and efforts by the shogunate to secure it showed that events of the 1850's had served to activate court nobles as well as daimyo to a new interest in national policies. Conservative Tokugawa collaterals, who disapproved of the agreement with Harris, seized the opportunity to intrigue with Kyoto nobles. They tried to tie reform of the bakufu with approval of the treaty. Since the reforms they proposed included innovation in succession procedures to ensure the choice of a mature and "able" shogun, they provided startling evidence of the way the outside threat had produced reverberations in the center of what had always been the private concerns of Tokugawa house policy. For a brief period the emergence of a strong-willed Tokugawa vassal, Ii Naosuke, as chief administrator in the Edo councils produced reaffirmation of shogunal prerogatives. The succession issue was dealt with according to tradition to thwart the hopes of innovators. The innovators, who included collateral Tokugawa vassals as well as reform-minded outside lords, were dealt with firmly to discourage further efforts at interference. Their retainers were dismissed, and in some cases executed, to emphasize the arbitrariness of bakufu power. From carrying out this "Ansei purge," as it became known, Ii Naosuke then turned to wringing approval of the Harris treaty from a now reluctant imperial court. It was granted in February 1859.

These Tokugawa "victories" proved expensive. Foreign policy and accommodation to the West's demands had now been lodged at the center of Japanese feudal rivalry and politics. Thereafter they were to be associated with Tokugawa policy, while the leadership of the antiforeign cause would be out of Tokugawa hands and outside its domains—although it did not pass there without a final drama in which Ii himself lost his life. On a snowy day late in March 1860, at the very gate of the shogun's castle, he was cut down by a small party of samurai, most of them from the vassal domain of Mito (whose daimyo he had disciplined). Their manifesto associated resistance to foreigners with the Imperial Will and invoked the sanction of the Sun Goddess to rebuke the bakufu's first minister. The murder of the regent in 1860 revealed the strength and intensity of opposition to the new diplomatic moves and inaugurated years of loyalist energy that marked the border between Tokugawa and Meiji Japan.

The political issues of the 1860's in Japan defy neat categorization. The Western world, to the degree that it was not consumed with its own problems, was fortunately engrossed by the tumultuous upheavals of the Taiping insurrection in China. The result was that Japan had the better part of the decade to work out the greatest crisis and disunity it had experienced since the sixteenth century.

The alternatives were not a simple acceptance or repulsion of the West, although this is the way they were phrased by the catch-slogan of the day, *kaikoku/jōi* ("Open the country/Drive out the barbarians"). These alternatives were complicated by advocacy of reconciliation between court and shogun (*kōbu gattai*) and simply phrased insistence on reverence for the emperor (*sonnō*). In these amuletic phrases political and philosophical discourse was structured to produce, or as often to conceal, a steadily growing emphasis on the prerogatives of the imperial court at the expense of the Edo bakufu.

The logical sponsors of the court in national politics were the great domains of southwestern Japan. Satsuma and Choshu had known defeat by the Tokugawa armies in 1600, and both came through the Tokugawa centuries reduced in land and wealth as a result. Cut off from office or influence in the bakufu, they were nevertheless more autonomous, more proud, and more military in their internal structure than most of central Japan. They were remote from the great Tokugawa cities and less involved in their problems. More integrated and sizable as domains, they were also more capable of internal, local reform and economic controls than were the great majority of fiefs. In both Satsuma and Choshu resentment of Tokugawa dominance had survived. They were sufficiently remote from Tokugawa control to be able to import Western small arms by way of the newly opened ports, and both areas experimented with military resistance to the West—Choshu in the shelling of foreign ships in the straits of Shimonoseki, and Satsuma in the effort to resist British demands for punishment of an antiforeign outrage. Neither effort succeeded; the

British shelled Kagoshima in 1863, and a Western flotilla shelled Shimonoseki in 1864. Both areas also sponsored efforts to learn directly of the West—Satsuma through the education of students sent to London in the 1860's and Choshu through the experiences of Itō Hirobumi and Inoue Kaoru, two of the Meiji leaders, in Europe. By the second half of the decade, many Japanese were looking to these baronies. As a contemporary loyalist put it, "Satsuma and Choshu are the two han that will be able to stir the realm in the future; . . . anyone can see that we will all be following the orders of these two domains."[2]

Cooperation between them, however, was hindered by a jealousy and distrust that were as great as the suspicion they both bore the bakufu. During the early 1860's they competed in posing as sponsors of the court in advancing a series of plans for restructuring the bakufu-court relationship. These efforts were not without result, and in 1863 a new and reformist group in the bakufu came to the forefront. But revolutionary discontent among the samurai outran the concessions made to them, and each concession was inadequate by the time it was made. What was necessary constantly turned out to be more than what was politically possible. Gradually the "reformist" schemes began to hide intentions of overthrow.

These developments came gradually and at different speeds for differing groups and areas, but within this process two developments were of critical importance. The first was the politicization of large numbers of samurai. The conviction of imminent crisis from foreign danger, domestic treachery, and personal distress as foreign trade altered long-standing patterns of distribution and resources affected the warrior elite profoundly. Significant numbers of young men left their homes and their immediate loyalties in the name of a higher, national loyalty. The excitement of participation in the political maelstrom of antiforeignism resulted in a wave of terrorist violence that brought home to many more the instability and crisis of the times.

A second development was the readiness of groups of men in several domains, but especially in Choshu, to stand sponsor to zealots from other areas and to challenge their regular authorities for control of the direction of han policy. The extremist stand taken by Choshu leaders led to their being driven out of Kyoto in 1863 through the cooperation of Tokugawa and Satsuma units, and to their defeat by a Tokugawa-led coalition in 1864. But shortly afterward the Choshu loyalists rose again, deposed their samurai superiors, and manipulated their daimyo in a flagrant rejection of Tokugawa authority.

The bakufu had alarmed many of its erstwhile supporters by a vigor-

[2] Cited in Marius B. Jansen, *Sakamoto Ryōma and the Meiji Restoration* (Princeton, N.J.: Princeton University Press, 1961), p. 210.

ous reform program. A new group of able leaders seemed bent on increasing traditional Tokugawa dominance and utilizing French support to create a centralized Tokugawa state. They first tried to crush Choshu. In February 1866 Satsuma and Choshu reached an agreement to cooperate. The bakufu's effort to chastise Choshu in battle failed miserably.

When it seemed that Japan was slipping into full-scale violence and international danger, moderates who had ties to Satsuma and Choshu as well as to the bakufu introduced ideas of compromise. The daimyo of Tosa proposed to the shogun that he resign his powers and agree to stand as but one, though still the greatest, feudal lord in a new national structure headed by the emperor. The present disunity, he argued, was "a great disaster to us and of great happiness to the foreigners. This is exactly what they have been hoping for." What was needed was a government "for which no shame need be felt before future generations of foreign countries." This proposal was agreed to by the shogun, who petitioned the court to accept return of his political powers on November 9, 1867.

The court, however, was soon in the hands of Satsuma and Choshu leaders, who secured an edict directing the shogun to surrender his lands as well. The Tokugawa, as has been noted, resisted, but not to the death. The outcome had indeed been foreshadowed by a document the shogun had addressed to the foreign representatives in January. "As to who is the sovereign of Japan," he admitted, "it is a question on which no one in Japan can entertain a doubt. The Mikado is the Sovereign."[3] As a result, the former Tokugawa head, despite his protests, accepted deposition from his rule over country and house and retired to Shizuoka, while his vassals to the north were still resisting the Satsuma, Choshu, and Tosa (now officially termed the "Imperial") armies.

As of 1868, the year of the Charter Oath and the emperor's procession to Tokyo, the Meiji Restoration had not gone beyond a coup within the ruling class. The appearance of the West had shown the need for drastic changes in Japan's state structure. It was clear that greater unity was the country's most immediate need and equally clear that unity could best be achieved under the aegis of the emperor. But the way this should be done was still to be worked out.

Yet the events of the Restoration did change Japan permanently. They produced a clean break in Japan's political continuity and offered the opportunity for equally striking institutional innovations. Scarcely less important, the Restoration achieved symbolic importance as a breakthrough made possible through the individual commitment of its leaders. One of the most interesting and colorful aspects of the Restoration struggle was its legacy of national heroes. The "men of high purpose"

[3] U.S. Minister R. B. van Valkenburgh to Secretary of State William Seward, enclosure in dispatch of January 16, 1868.

(shishi), the young activists who had put the national purpose ahead of traditional family and feudal claims, gave the decade much of its color and its life. They became the ethical ideals for later times and models for later revolutionaries of both left and right, men who saw in their courage, individualism, and determination examples of what times of crisis demanded of committed youth.

The Meiji Revolution

Tokugawa resistance ended with the surrender of the shogunate's naval units to the national government in the early summer of 1869. Political power was now in the hands of the Satsuma-Choshu forces and their allies in the fief of Tosa. The court nobles who had worked with them and the young emperor they served held promise of legitimacy of rule. But these forces held chiefly their own domains and those of the Tokugawa lords whose armies they had defeated or outmaneuvered. Few thought they had seen an end to the fighting. The Tosa leaders, who expected a new war between Satsuma and Choshu, worked out an alliance with their Shikoku neighbors and made plans for a quick dash to rescue the emperor once fighting broke out. Yet somehow things held together. By the time the new leaders were seriously challenged a few years later they were ready for the contest, and by then their plans for fundamental reform were already well under way.

How was this possible? Clearly, the patterns of Tokugawa decentralization helped the new leaders at first. Their limited geographical control also limited the political and economic responsibilities they inherited. Moreover, their strongest foes, the Tokugawa vassals, had just accepted defeat and imperial admonition. Most of the other lords maintained a cautious inaction. Samurai in the southwestern fiefs like Satsuma and Choshu still had heroic expectations of importance in the new order. The Satsuma-Choshu-Tosa leaders recruited further support from the domain of Saga (or Hizen), thereby tapping the considerable knowledge of Western technology that that domain, with its access to Nagasaki, had built up. The four-way partnership of power, Satsuma-Choshu-Hizen-Tosa, that would characterize the Meiji political picture was now in being.[4]

Perhaps most important for the early Meiji transition, the leaders of the new regime had time to experiment and plan because there was no revolution from below. The peasants who crouched with foreheads to the ground as the imperial procession passed in 1868 were seldom a problem.

---

[4] It would return, at least in memory, as late as the 1930's, when an anti-Choshu faction in the Imperial Army sought to build a factional alternative by promoting men from Tosa and Saga.

Since, as Thomas Smith has pointed out,[5] there was so little pressure from below, since administration went on as before in so many parts of the country, those at the center had an invaluable period of time in which they could think about problems and priorities and consolidate their power.

The most important consensus of Restoration days was that Japan needed more unity. Feudal decentralization was badly out of place in the international society of the nineteenth century, and Japanese leaders were determined to build a political order for which their descendants would "know no shame," one that could stand up to external pressure. Their anxiety to end every cause of shameful weakness was conspicuous throughout the memorializing of 1868. The Charter Oath of that year spoke of ending "uncivilized customs" of the past. It soon became clear that these customs included the divisions of feudalism that had made so difficult any effective response to the threat of Western imperialism. Like their Tokugawa predecessors, the Meiji leaders realized that new provisions had to be made for external defense and internal security, but unlike their predecessors, they no longer had to keep the stability of the existing political structure in mind in planning their steps. The Tokugawa fall had already interrupted political continuity. Not only were the existing feudal principalities a limitation on the power of government to lead, but as individuals the principal architects of the Meiji state were themselves in a position of inferiority to higher feudal authority and dependent on personal and factional favor for political opportunity. Thus they had as much interest in ending the feudal structure in Satsuma and Choshu as in Japan at large.

Although their personal situation was different from that of the Meiji leaders, the great majority of daimyo do not seem to have seen things very differently. The routine and ritual of daimyo life produced few figures of ability and initiative in the 1860's. Also, in the hectic politics of pre-Restoration decades the daimyo had been the object of constant pressure and criticism from their underlings, for whom the domain had long ago come to outweigh the person as primary focus of consideration. Moreover, few daimyo had realms that were in any sense profitable or economically viable. Repeated economic crises and attempted solutions had found them unable to adapt an archaic tax structure based upon subsistence agriculture to the expenses of rearmament and reform of their times. Nor, in any event, were their realms truly their own personal property. According to Tokugawa feudal theory, founded on the memory of an overwhelmingly powerful bakufu that had moved daimyo almost at will during the seventeenth century, domains were merely held in trust

---

[5] "Japan's Aristocratic Revolution," *Yale Review*, Vol. 50 (Spring 1961), pp. 370–83.

from the shogunate and administered in accordance with broadly phrased directives that came from it. And, as will be recalled, daimyo life in Edo, like samurai life in castle towns, had long tended to separate the fief-holder from his land. All these factors combined to suggest retrocession of the fiefs. The first petition from a daimyo to the new government requesting permission to return his lands, in fact, cited financial difficulties as the reason.

The new government had already established its control over the Tokugawa realms, which included the economic heartland of the country, in the Restoration wars. The baronies of the southwest, which had led in the Restoration, were the second most powerful group, after the Tokugawa core. When the daimyo of these baronies, at the behest of their young advisers, petitioned the imperial government to accept the return of their land registers in 1869, the remainder of the feudal lords were sure to follow, lest, as laggards, they seem less loyal.

In March 1869, before the surrender of the last Tokugawa holdouts, the lords of Satsuma, Choshu, Tosa, and Saga petitioned the court:

> Now that a new regime is being sought, the great Polity and the great Authority should not be delegated. The abode where we dwell is the Sovereign's land; the people over whom we rule are his people. Why should we privately own them? Now, therefore, we respectfully restore our domains to the Sovereign.

They went on to ask that

> the domains of all the han be reorganized, and also that all the regulations, from the ordering of laws, institutions, and military affairs, even to the fashioning of uniforms and instruments, issue from the Imperial Government, [and that the] conduct of all the affairs of the realm, whether great or small, be placed under unified control. Then only, name and reality complementing each other, the Empire can stand beside the foreign powers.

The court accepted the petition. It bridged the transition by appointing the former daimyo as governors of their realms. Within the year orders were issued simplifying the numerous degrees of status. Court nobles and daimyo were now one rank, upper samurai a second, ordinary samurai a third, and everybody else was "commoner," including the former pariah class. Now the government leaders began to give meaning to their talk of bringing society and customs into line with world standards. Some of the new leaders returned to Choshu, Satsuma, and Tosa and set in motion sweeping changes that struck at the system of official and social status that earlier had hampered their own rise to power. These reforms proceeded in tandem with plans for national change. In August 1871 the new government announced the abolition of feudalism and the assumption of central control over the former han, which were now redivided into larger, more rationally structured prefectures. Successive changes reduced the two hundred and fifty or so han into some seventy-five prefectural units of administration, a number that was later reduced by another third.

These jurisdictional changes were accompanied by sweeping instructions from the center to abolish legal distinctions between classes. Restrictions on occupation, cropping, and residence were removed, and commoners received the long-desired dignity of family names. Now that it finally had responsibility for administration and power to tax, the new government inaugurated land surveys in 1873 to prepare for a predictable tax income that would permit budgetary planning. The new land tax was set at three percent of the assessed value of the land, and with it came certificates of land ownership for farmers. The removal of feudal restrictions on peasant farmers represented the abandonment of the old efforts to increase revenue by extracting a greater yield from subsistence agriculture. It was a process that had begun in late Tokugawa times, as the shogunate and han struggled to find bases for taxation in money instead of in kind. With the Meiji changes, commercial agriculture had become the basis of the government's income and, by extension, the basis of Japan's emerging capitalist economy.

It was now necessary to educate and activate the commoners to serve their country. The task could no longer be left to the privileged classes of Tokugawa feudalism. Here also, changes represented in part a continuation of developments in the Tokugawa period. The Tokugawa emphasis on education had brought Japan into the Meiji period with one of the highest literacy rates of any nonindustrial society. What was needed was the utilization of this education for national purposes. Nothing more impressed Japanese travelers to the West than what they learned about popular patriotism, the more so in view of the contrast it offered to the relative indifference of the Japanese masses. For just as the commoners had bowed, impassive, as the imperial procession passed in 1868, they had watched, unparticipating, as English gunners dismantled Shimonoseki fortifications and Tosa armies stormed the defenses of Tokugawa vassals in northern Japan. Thus, education of the masses, in the arts of peace and of war, seemed essential to national safety. Japanese returned from Europe convinced, as one put it, that public education was the essential "foundation for a strong army," and a leading educational bureaucrat argued that the way to bring Japan to "the leading position among all countries of the world" was to "lay the foundations of elementary education." Few were prepared to dispute the contention of the Fundamental Law of Education, which appeared in 1872, that "education is the key to success in life, and no man can afford to neglect it." The goal announced by the law was that there should be "no community with an illiterate family, and no family with an illiterate person."[6]

The military extension of this attitude was the conscription law of 1873. The decision to abandon Japan's long-standing reliance upon the warrior class was not made without difficulty, but the combination of Western example and recent performance of the nonsamurai units in the Restoration fighting settled the issue. In addition, of course, the disestablishment of the samurai provided the most obvious source for government savings. If the samurai were no longer to rule the land, it made no sense to support them in idleness. And so their privileges disappeared. They were first permitted, and then ordered, to give up their swords; their distinctions of dress and their special status under law disappeared, and with these their incomes. Sharply reduced salaries gave way to pensions and those in turn to interest-bearing bonds. No doubt most of the leading figures in most walks of life were former samurai, but the number of those who could be accommodated with dignity in the new structure was limited. Far larger was the number of those who were soon in difficult straits, their pensions and bonds squandered or swallowed by inflation. Yet in some sense even these steps were only a continuation of the progressive attenuation of samurai income that had accompanied their separation from the land and their conversion into salaried bureaucrats during late Tokugawa times. The impoverished samurai had long been a stock figure of Tokugawa storytelling. In the Meiji period, with his special airs, dress, and punctilio, his pension slipping through his fingers, he became the perfect example of waste of human and material resources in an age of efficient, businesslike reconstruction. The former daimyo were in time absorbed into the new nobility that was set up in 1884 and retired to moderate affluence and prestige. Having long been symbols rather than wielders of power, they were well suited to lives of ceremonial inactivity. Life was harder for the samurai.

Changes of these dimensions could hardly be announced without stirring opposition. The substitution of new for familiar forms of rule produced sporadic distress and nearly two hundred local rebellions or protests within the first ten years of the Meiji period. Some were the result of groundless fears, some were based on resistance to change, and some were responses to specific local outrages. By and large, however, the commoners forebore; their expectations were modest, and the changes they experienced were sufficiently gradual to provide at least some appearance of continuity. The practical applications of decrees for conscription and education and taxation were some time in coming home to

[6] Cited in Herbert Passin, ed., *Society and Education in Japan* (New York: Teachers College Press, 1965), p. 69.

farmers, and they did so at different times in different parts of the country.

Revolution and dissent came from the samurai whose expectations had been highest, especially from those within the leading southwestern fiefs, whose military force had won the Restoration wars. The discovery that the freewheeling activism in which they had gloried in the 1860's was at an end must have come as a shock to many. Now that all policies were to come from the center, said a government statement ostensibly designed to praise them for their valor, "it is hoped that those who had previously left their han will return to their original prefectures, properly registered, abide with faith and justice, mind their conduct, and cooperate with and assist the Government." That took care of the individualists. But the problem came with members of the leadership who took strong exception to the priorities that had been set.

An inviting issue that presented itself concerned policy toward Korea. The peninsula state, most conservative of the East Asian respondents to the Western challenge, rejected Japanese attempts to modernize and regularize the traditional, tribute-style trade that had gone on between the two during the Tokugawa period and scornfully grouped the Meiji Japanese with the Western barbarians as beyond the pale of civilization. Meiji samurai, smarting from their inability to avenge Western insult, desired a solution that would combine domestic and foreign objectives; an expedition to "punish Korea," they held, would occupy and reward the increasingly impoverished samurai class. When these counsels were rejected by those who held that an adventurous foreign policy would benefit only the waiting European imperialists, important members of the leadership left the government. A compensatory agreement made in 1874 to punish aboriginal tribes in Taiwan for the murder of Okinawan sailors satisfied no one. Rebellions broke out in Choshu, then in Saga, and in 1877 in Satsuma, where the new government met its severest test in a rebellion led by the Restoration hero Saigō Takamori. After the failure of this uprising, the Meiji government had for the first time complete freedom of action at home. It also had a new leadership, for the suicide of Saigō was preceded by the death of the Choshu leader Kido Kōin and followed by the murder of the Satsuma figure Ōkubo Toshimichi. The three leading figures of the first decade of the Meiji state were gone.

Despite the flurry of edicts, the chief accomplishment of the first ten years of the Meiji period had been the demolition of the old order. Much of the work required for the creation of a new infrastructure for modernization still lay ahead. The significance of what had happened, it can now be seen, was that a modernizing elite had emerged, a group firmly committed to making their backward country a modern nation-state. Their goals were expressed in terms of the models of which they had knowledge: the capitalist, representative, dynamic, industrial, and maritime powers of the Atlantic world. Those goals were further fixed by the misfortunes of their immediate neighbors in China, where resistance to change had brought humiliation and defeat. And, since a new idea is always easier to explain in terms of an old one, their thoughts of strength and unity had instinctively formed around the imperial symbol.

As the Meiji period went on, the surviving members of this leadership group, who were of restricted numbers and had common origins and much shared experience, had also developed an unusual ability to work, and disagree, and nevertheless cooperate, with one another. Many of them had gone abroad for eighteen months in 1871–73 and had returned to find their jobs waiting for them. They respected one another's feelings in defeat and concealed their own exultation in success. Having shared goals, they tended also to share power. In the more visible posts there was and continued to be a good deal of rotation to bring balance between factions, which helped to institutionalize and smooth the rivalry inevitable among them. Perhaps most important and remarkable, the modernizing oligarchy—which is what it became—made no attempt to perpetuate itself or to seat its heirs in posts of power. This is worth noting, for the men sprang from a patriarchal, hereditary class. It is true that the modern world of which they had knowledge was moving in the opposite direction (though perhaps most slowly in the Germany they admired); but the Meiji leaders performed a great service by failing to provide powerful progeny, and the abolition of the peerage after World War II ended even ceremonial honors for a group that was already past its service to the country. The development of the Meiji state was thus dominated by concerns for succession and legitimacy, problems that centered around the court and for which solutions were sought through the preparation of the Meiji Constitution.

The Meiji State

Not all who broke with the leadership over the issue of Korea were conservative in inclination, and not all had recourse to arms. A group led by Itagaki Taisuke from Tosa, which included most of the Tosa men in the central government, resigned and issued a statement (in which they were joined by a group of Saga men who later rose in revolt) calling for an elected assembly in order to avoid further violations of "public opinion." Future decisions, they argued, would then reflect the will of the people, and national unity could be perfected. The Itagaki document showed the influence of recent Japanese familiarization with European constitutional thought, but it also related to the assumptions put forth in the original 1867 Tosa petition to the shogun asking him to resign his powers. The Tosa men saw representative government as the only possible alternative to domination by the Satsuma-Choshu clique. Initially their ideas of popular will were undoubtedly restricted to the consultation of samurai elite like themselves; but the points they made, and their own subsequent descent from office, gave their arguments a broader significance and application. The government needed all the support it could get in the years of crisis that followed 1874, and Itagaki was briefly persuaded to return to office in 1875; but he soon returned to the task of organizing his followers, first in Tosa and then nationally. By 1881 he had made the beginnings of a national structure for the Liberal party (Jiyūtō), the ancestor of Japan's presently ruling conservative party. Widespread enthusiasm resulted in rapid growth of the organization. Initially a group of ex-samurai, it soon extended its influence to rural leaders, and by the mid-1880's, years of deflation and agricultural depression, the Jiyūtō was becoming an important and vocal force in politics.

The Meiji government had in fact become committed to the idea of a representative structure even before Itagaki's demand. The Charter Oath of 1868 had promised the creation of public councils. Experimentation with crudely representative bodies had been incorporated in the first political structures of 1868 and then given up. First-hand experience with the West had helped convince the Meiji leaders of the advantages of broadening the base of popular support for government, and their own recent discontent with the Tokugawa despotism was fresh in mind. Gaining support greater than that evoked by their old institutions clearly would require some sort of popular participation. The large party of government leaders that toured the Western world under the leadership of Prince Iwakura between 1871 and 1873 returned convinced by the lessons they had learned. Kido Kōin of Choshu used the tragic fate of Poland to argue that "laws and constitutions" that prevented arbitrary action by governments in the pursuit of selfish ends were the only guarantee of national survival. In addition to these truths, it was painfully evident that Japanese ability to escape from the humiliations and handicaps of the unequal treaties—an escape equally essential to economic development and to national independence—would depend on a measure of conformity to what the West considered adequate guarantees for regularity of administration. As Ōkuma Shigenobu put it years later,

> It was perceived that in order to attain an equal footing with the Powers, it was necessary to change the national institutions, learning and education. Hence, the replacement of clans by prefectures took place as well as

coinage reform, enforcement of the conscription law, revisions of various other laws and promulgation of new ones, establishment of local assemblies, and the granting of local self-government—a step that led at length to the promulgation of the Constitution.[7]

In the 1870's an early, unsuccessful "senate" was charged with preparation of a draft constitution. The government felt that the proposals of this constitution would lead to the establishment of a parliament with excessive powers, and thus called for individual drafts from all government leaders by the end of that decade. These varied widely in degree of liberality, but the process was speeded by Ōkuma, a Saga man who had remained with the government after the departure of many of his fellow provincials in 1874. His draft, which he submitted directly to the emperor in 1881, proposed a basically English system of government by political parties and suggested that an elected parliament be convened the following year. The Satsuma-Choshu leaders, together with Iwakura, now forced Ōkuma's resignation from the government and simultaneously had the Meiji emperor promise that a parliament would be convened in 1890. Gradualism had now been accepted as government policy, and a clear commitment to constitutionalism had been made.

Ōkuma, in private life, now organized a "Reform party," which became, with Itagaki's, the progenitor of modern Japanese bourgeois politics. For the next few years the two political parties battled each other as vigorously as they did the government, which was able to hamper their activities through restrictive press and association laws. They disbanded for several years and re-formed at the end of the decade to resume work in the new parliamentary structure. Throughout the 1880's newspapers, magazines, and political novels were full of speculation and debate about the kind of state structure that Japan should develop.

The adoption of a Western-, especially Prussian-style, constitution was by no means the simple operation that some who write of Japan's "Westernization" have suggested. The "West" was, after all, a complex cultural phenomenon. For a time the Meiji Japanese saw it as a unit in which the railroads, guns, and Bibles were all interrelated, but by the late 1880's greater familiarity with the West made it clear to them that distinctions were possible and in fact necessary. Okakura Kakuzō (who worked out his own equally misleading characterization of "Asia is one") put it well on a return to Japan in 1887:

> Where is the essence of the West in the countries of Europe and America? All these countries have different systems; what is right in one country is wrong in the next; religion, customs, morals—there is no

---

[7] Cited in Joseph Pittau, S.J., *Political Thought in Early Meiji Japan, 1868–1889* (Cambridge, Mass.: Harvard University Press, 1967), p. 39.

common agreement on any of these. Europe is discussed in a general way; and this sounds splendid. The question remains, however, where in reality does what is called Europe exist?[8]

The debate over constitutional structure was carried on in terms of Western theory and example, with arguments drawn from Anglo-French and German sources, but it was essentially concerned with traditional predispositions, each of which could be clothed in Western dress. The advocates of popular sovereignty and political party responsibility found Rousseau and English practice, respectively, congenial to them; but their advocacy of these preferences was full of Confucian overtones phrased in terms of Mencius' emphasis on the importance of the people. Nakae Chōmin's evocation of Rousseau owes as great a debt to Mencius as to Rousseau, and the same can be said of his disciple (and pioneer anarchist) Kōtoku Shūsui. A generation later the Taisho political philosopher Yoshino Sakuzō used some of these same themes in his elaboration of democracy under imperial aegis, which he defined as "people based" (*mimponshugi*). The Meiji "radicals" moreover shared with their opponents a belief in the importance of national unity, and they often reached instinctively to the totalist implications of Rousseau's "general will." "How is the government to be made strong?" Itagaki's document had asked in 1874, and it had answered, "It is by the people of the empire becoming of one mind." And a council chamber was the means for having government and people "mutually unite into one body. Then and only then will the country become strong."[9] The goal, in other words, was still a truly perfect unity in which groups would find no need to organize.

The government leaders, for their part, saw theories of natural rights as dangerous to national unity, and they were convinced that the nation could best be built through reliance upon the authority of the imperial institution. In this they inevitably made contact with the currents of historicism that underlay the thinking of their German constitutional advisers, who thought of the state as a historic, living entity. Party cabinets, they thought, would be divisive. In the absence of an agreed-upon code of religion with political utility like Christianity, Japan should instead make the most of its indigenous cult of a sacred emperor. "The one institution in our country which can become the cornerstone of our constitution is the Imperial House," Itō Hirobumi argued. "Because the imperial sovereignty is the cornerstone of our constitution, our system is not based on European ideas of separation of powers or on the principle . . . of

[8] *Ibid.*, p. 128; quoted from Masaaki Kosaka, *Japanese Thought in the Meiji Period*, trans. D. Abosch (Baltimore: Johns Hopkins Press, 1958), p. 220.

[9] Cited in Nobutaka Ike, *The Beginnings of Political Democracy in Japan* (Baltimore: Johns Hopkins Press, 1950), p. 57.

joint rule of king and people."[10] The constitutional debate thus became an important vehicle for the articulation of views of national conscious- ness and identity, and its solutions channeled and gave form to what was permissible in that debate until midway into the twentieth century.

Itō Hirobumi played the principal public role in the creation of the constitution. He returned from a study mission to Europe in 1883; created a European-style peerage (with an upper house in the Diet in mind) the following year; headed the first modern cabinet in 1885, its seats evenly divided between Satsuma and Choshu men; submitted his draft of the constitution in 1888; and then chaired the Privy Council that considered the document before it was approved. After its promulgation in 1889, he showed his relief upon hearing of Western approbation of the document: "Now for the first time," he wrote, "I feel relieved. . . . There was doubt in my mind whether Europe and America would accept Japan, with a constitution conforming to Japanese national polity and history and yet containing substantial constitutional elements, as a mem- ber of the family of Western constitutional states."[11]

The Meiji Constitution took the form of a gracious grant by the em- peror and began with an affirmation of the unbroken imperial line. The imperial oath that was prepared for the promulgation put it clearly:

> In view of the progressive tendency of human affairs and the advance of civilization, it has been incumbent upon Us . . . to establish fundamental laws and clearly explain their provisions . . . the Imperial House Law and the Constitution . . . We solemnly regard as merely *a reiteration in Our own day of the grand precepts of government that have been handed down by the Imperial Founder of Our House and by Our other Imperial Ancestors to their descendants.*[12]

The constitution's provisions were couched in general terms. Effective power lay with the executive, which was not closely defined lest it ob- scure the emperor's majesty. The emperor was "sacred and inviolable"; he commanded the armed services (which consequently had separate access to him), he made war and peace, and he dissolved the lower house at will. Yet the constitution also represented very solid gains. Private property was inviolate, and the freedoms the constitution granted, even though most were qualified by the phrase "within the limits of the law," were greater than any the Japanese had known before. The lower house had the power to initiate legislation. The Diet had to approve the annual budget, but in the event it refused to do so the previous year's could be

[10] Cited in Pittau, *Political Thought in Early Meiji Japan*, p. 178.

[11] Cited in George Akita, *Foundations of Constitutional Government in Modern Japan, 1868–1900* (Cambridge, Mass.: Harvard University Press, 1967), p. 13.

[12] Cited in R. Ishii, *Japanese Legislation in the Meiji Era*, translated by W. J. Chambliss (Tokyo: 1958), p. 386.

followed. Yet even the budgetary arrangements meant that the Diet had to approve budget increases, the perennial needs of any administration. And, while the initial voting laws, which set a fifteen-yen direct-tax restriction, limited the electorate to less than five hundred thousand voters, that tax qualification was lowered in 1900 and again in 1920 and finally removed altogether in 1925. Government leaders began with the hope that they could, as representatives of the emperor, stay above all factional disputes, but within a decade their difficulties in getting the cooperation of the lower house were sufficiently great to stir Itō Hirobumi himself to organize his own political party. The constitution thus allowed for steady growth in political participation. But because it, and its sacred emperor, were inviolate, the gains scored under it in practice were never consolidated institutionally or admitted in theory. In consequence they could, in the 1930's, be modified again, still without alteration in the durable Meiji Constitution.

The year 1890, in which the constitution went into effect, was also important for the issuance of the Imperial Rescript on Education. That document, the product of a long dispute between conservatives and modernizers in the oligarchy, represented an attempt to lay down a code of behavior and belief for the newly participating citizenry. Experiments with a "National Teaching" had been carried on very early in the Meiji period, but during the apogee of institutional reform and enthusiasm for Westernization in the 1880's the idea of Japanese national essence or individuality seemed to some conservatives to be in danger. The builders of the educational system also became concerned about the need to inculcate patriotism in the commoners, who would man the new instruments of state power, and by the late 1880's a course in public morality had become the center of the compulsory education curriculum. With the Rescript on Education the pattern for citizens' beliefs was deemed complete. Schoolchildren memorized and recited the rescript's praise of "loyalty and filial piety" as "the glory of the fundamental character of Our Empire, and . . . the source of Our Education." They were to be filial, harmonious, and true and were told to "advance public good and promote common interests; always respect the Constitution and observe the laws; should emergency arise, offer yourselves courageously to the State, and thus guard and maintain the prosperity of Our Imperial Throne coeval with heaven and earth."

The emperor system, which seemed to the Meiji leaders their best hope for channeling patriotism and loyalty in a largely secular society, became in time the focus of a mystic faith for the commoners. In the 1880's newspapers still felt called upon to explain Japan's good fortune in having an emperor and chided their readers for not knowing more about him. Within little more than a decade the diffusion of the ideology of the modern state made this quite unnecessary. The emperor-idea thus began as a force for modernization in the early Meiji period; in later years, its application began to seem a block to further enlightenment. As with symbol, so with presence; the Meiji Emperor himself was a participant in the power circle made up of his trusted ministers; his immediate successors, without that shared experience or personal ascendancy, became more mysterious and distant, more spoken for than speaking.

The 1880's, so important in the shaping of political and educational institutions, were equally definitive for the development of other important supports of the modern state. Tokyo University became the training ground for the modern bureaucracy, and its graduates quickly became the central figures in the new, specialized ministries. Yamagata Aritomo organized both bureaucracy and military, introduced the German general-staff system, and secured imperial rescripts to soldiers and sailors that provided the core of their indoctrination. Perhaps more important still was the series of careful steps whereby Matsukata Masayoshi, finance minister for more than sixteen years, turned back the inflation that the Satsuma rebellion had generated and instituted a reliable, convertible currency. Despite the outcries caused by his policies of austerity and deflation, he managed, by cutting government expenses to the bone, to save more than one-quarter of the current revenue, thereby providing a solid beginning for capital accumulation and the industrial growth that followed. During his years at the helm, earlier government ventures in pilot plants and mines were discontinued. The bulk of these earlier enterprises ended up in the hands of a few great family combines that later came to be denounced as "money cliques" (zaibatsu). The truly significant economic growth of the Meiji period, economists suggest, began after 1886; Matsukata had provided the setting for it.

Through all this the slogans—Meiji Japan, like modernizing China, was urged on by slogans—continued to point toward economic strength as a corollary to military strength. *Fukoku-kyōhei* ("rich country–strong military") were paired. Institutional reform was prerequisite to the willingness of Western imperialist powers to loosen their hold on Japanese tariffs, trade, and jurisdiction; and changes in those sectors were prerequisite to effective economic nationalism. It was clear to the leaders that Japan had to be patient, avoid adventurism, and concentrate on the main business at hand. Foreign Minister Inoue Kaoru put it succinctly in 1887: "What we have to do," he wrote, "is to transform our empire and our people, and make the empire like the countries of Europe and our people like the people of Europe. To put it differently, we have to establish a new, European-style empire on the edge of Asia."[13] For him and his

[13] Cited in Marius B. Jansen, "Modernization and Foreign Policy in Meiji Japan," in Robert E. Ward, ed., *Political Development in Modern Japan* (Princeton, N.J.: Princeton University Press, 1968), p. 174.

contemporaries, affiliation with the West necessarily meant taking care to keep the West from mistaking Japan for her less progressive neighbors. As the educator-publicist Fukuzawa Yukichi put it:

> When judgments of China and Korea are applied to our country it hurts our foreign policy. We do not have time to wait for neighboring countries to develop and then to join them in the revival of Asia. We ought instead to get away from them and join the company of Western, civilized nations. If we keep bad company we will only get a bad name.[14]

In the setting of the nineteenth century these judgments were shrewd, and the policies to which they led were successful. The implementation of a constitution and codes of modern law made it possible in 1894 to renegotiate the unequal treaties. Although full tariff autonomy would come only in 1911, Japan was now a full member of the family of nations. The following year a victory over Manchu China enabled the Meiji government to join the circle of China's uninvited guests by exacting both the usual concessions and some additional ones from the prostrate Manchus, to claim Taiwan, and, for a fleeting moment, to gain a foothold in South Manchuria as well. Territory for expansion, indemnity for investment, and gratification in achievement all rewarded the end of a caution that had lasted a quarter-century. The road to power, empire, and prestige in the international order was now open.

Some Meiji Values

No recital of policies in Meiji times should end without some indication of the color and the motivations of Japan in this striking period of world history. Meiji Japan was, after all, the first, and in some respects is still the only, latecomer to modernization to make a successful bridge between indigenous institutions and values and imported technology and techniques. The resulting combination of old and new, native and import, was of particular interest for the marks it left on a generation that experienced a rapid erosion and virtual overturn of its views of self and world. China, so long the source of civilization, was for a time decried as a symbol of backwardness. In 1868 the Japanese government still found it useful to remind its people that foreigners were not, as some had it, to be grouped with "wild barbarians, dogs, and sheep"; instead, it warned, "we must work out arrangements to show that they are to be considered

[14] Marius B. Jansen, "Japanese Views of China During the Meiji Period," in Albert Feuerwerker, Rhodes Murphey, and Mary C. Wright, eds., *Approaches to Modern Chinese History* (Berkeley, Calif.: University of California Press, 1967), pp. 172–73. See also Kimitada Miwa, "Fukuzawa Yukichi's 'Departure from Asia': A Prelude to the Sino-Japanese War," in E. Skrzypczak, ed., *Japan's Modern Century* (Tokyo: Sophia University and Charles E. Tuttle, 1968), p. 17.

on the same level as Chinese." But by the end of the Meiji period those same foreigners were well above the Chinese in the scale of Japanese esteem and treatment. Because it seemed somehow feudal and backward, Buddhism, so long the creed of Japan, was the object of a furious assault in the early Meiji years that resulted in the destruction of many temples and much art. Confucianism, however basic to the code of most educated Japanese, was also roundly attacked as unprogressive. During its first years in power the Meiji government continued the Tokugawa persecution of Christians, but the Iwakura Mission's view of the West changed all that, and soon skeptics like Fukuzawa seriously proposed declaring Japan a Christian country so that it could qualify for the related boons of modernization. But then, in the 1890's, the currents once again ran differently. A suitably nationalized blend of Confucianism and Shinto was seen as basic to the national polity (*kokutai*). Confucian studies again found sponsors, and Christianity, no longer essential to the modern state, became the object of discrimination in education out of fear that its converts would deny support to the national cult and hence weaken patriotism.

These judgments about the outside world were instrumental rather than basic to the values of the Meiji Japanese. Their first and strongest urge was certainly that of nationalism. Throughout most of the Meiji period the leadership in most walks of life, and certainly the tone of public life and discourse, were provided by members of the samurai class. A self-confident, committed group, educated to lead and schooled in the primacy of the collectivity of the political unit, the samurai provided Japan with single-minded, nation-directed leadership. The phrase *kuni no tame* ("for the sake of the country") was a constant in political discussions, but it is more striking to find authors using it as a rationale in their determination to build a modern literature, create an epic poetry, and develop new schools of painting and areas of scholarship. Here, no less than in the state structure, there was agreement that something should be built for which "future generations would feel no shame."

The main current of youthful ambition was political, although those who lacked contacts were likely to find their ambitions frustrated. For the Meiji generation the Restoration activists had set the style, and any red-blooded young man was expected to want to be a minister of state. Even those who rejected this goal as old-fashioned subservience to authority—Fukuzawa Yukichi, with his call for independence and autonomy, or Shibusawa Eiichi, with his determination to build a private banking system—formed their objections within this community of discourse; the argument was not whether the nation needed building, but how it could be built most rapidly and effectively.

These things are reflected with particular clarity in the values of the business class. Its leading representatives contrasted the patriotic role of industrialist, to which they aspired, with the selfish, nonproductive role of the traditional merchant, and they did their best to wrap themselves in the borrowed garb of samurai values. Adam Smith's "invisible hand," which pictured the common good as being advanced by private ambition, went quite the other way in Meiji thinking; here entrepreneurs accumulated great wealth by accident while working for the national interest. Shibusawa Eiichi, who built one of the great Meiji fortunes (and incidentally became a patron of Confucian studies), assured his countrymen that "never for a moment did I aim at my own profit." In turn, one writer had it that "just as the samurai gathered behind Minamoto to follow him into the battle of war, so now the younger generation gathers around Shibusawa to follow him into the battle of enterprise."[15] Some of this logic was of course self-serving and disingenuous. But the public posture, and the assumption of its necessity, remain significant.

Closely related to the goal of national service were themes of ambition and achievement. *Risshin shusse* ("Make something of yourself!") was a slogan that typified the tone of much of the Meiji period until at least the 1890's, when government conservatives began to fear that private goals were beginning to infringe on public ones. Samuel Smiles' *Self-Help*, first translated in 1871, set the style for journals and novels in which the ideals of ambition and success were lauded. Itagaki's first political organization, formed when he left the government in 1874, was called the Self-Help Society (Risshisha). And it was typical of Meiji times that many of these ideas, conceived for the individual, were applied to national purposes and needs. It seems clear that many readers of Smiles came to view Japan as a poor apprentice in the family of nations, a country that would have to scrimp and sacrifice with a view to future affluence and power. Much of the literature of economic individualism of the nineteenth-century West could with little adjustment be translated to conform to the political priorities of Meiji Japan. At the same time, of course, the intense striving for success and honor that distinguished official and popular culture in Tokugawa Japan provided a strong basis for this further reinforcement from the nineteenth-century West.

The slogan "Civilization and enlightenment!" (*bummei kaika*) expressed in terms of inevitable progress the requirements of cultural advancement for a Japan in the process of change. At home, it could be invoked in applying for a bank charter, as when Osaka merchants petitioned that:

> As we live presently in the era of civilization and enlightenment, we feel ashamed to follow the old foolish practices of each one considering noth-

15 Byron K. Marshall, *Capitalism and Nationalism in Prewar Japan: The Ideology of the Business Elite, 1868–1941* (Stanford, Calif.: Stanford University Press, 1967), p. 47.

ing but his own profit. . . . We have been cherishing . . . the desire to shoulder our share, as far as our weakness permits, of the burden to promote the progress of civilization . . . enlightened by the banking act, we shall immediately work for the establishment of a bank. . . .[16]

Abroad it merged smoothly with the traditional tendency to erect a hierarchic ranking of nations, one that was now justified in terms of Herbert Spencer's science. For Fukuzawa Yukichi, aborigines, nomads, undeveloped (Asian) states, and civilized (Western) states indicated a smooth progression that would lead in time to equality with Europe and America. Mori Arinori, minister of education, could hold out the even higher hope that through effort, education, and perseverance Japan could come to hold the leading position among all countries. Every urge of patriotic effort or personal ambition, and every thought of history or international affairs, seemed to contribute to a congruent view of Japan's goals and problems.

Meiji successes owed much to the stability of leadership, which provided the time in which to work things out. The time it took was greater than it seems. Returns for the effort expended began to come only in the 1890's, and a recent authority notes that "in a number of important respects the amount of time required for the political modernization of Japan has not been much shorter than that required in the classic Western cases."[17] Yet without the consensus on goals, without the agreement on the urgency of addressing all efforts to attaining equality with the West, that same stability of leadership would not have been possible.

By the 1890's there were signs that the consensus was beginning to weaken. A new generation was coming to the fore—one that had not personally experienced the weaknesses and fears of Restoration disunity, that was less securely rooted in Confucian values than its fathers had been, and that was impatient with the frustrations of Meiji nation-building. No longer satisfied with catching up, it sought areas in which to excel. What was Japan, and what could it do supremely well? In a world increasingly dominated by the maritime imperialist powers and the civilizations of the Atlantic world, where could Japan still find a mission? The late 1880's saw a new affirmation of nationalism: Journals like *Nihonjin* and newspapers like *Nihon* examined the questions of national essence and goals and wondered how Japan could be kept Japanese. In the arts the native styles, temporarily threatened by the wave of Westernization, were being restored to favor, and in religion Christianity, briefly on the rise in the early 1880's, never again seemed a viable candidate for a national faith.

[16] Johannes Hirschmeier, S.V.D., *The Origins of Entrepreneurship in Meiji Japan* (Cambridge, Mass.: Harvard University Press, 1964), p. 37.

[17] Ward, *Political Development in Modern Japan*, p. 589.

It was in this mixed setting of doubt and affirmation, in this search for definition and destiny, that the constitution and Rescript on Education had their meaning and effect. Within a few years after they were issued, the opportunity to take assertive steps at last made Japan the victor over Manchu China. Fukuzawa spoke for millions when he editorialized in his newspaper that "we intend only to develop world civilization and to defeat those who obstruct it. . . . Therefore this is not a war between people and people and country and country, but a kind of religious war." And Tokutomi Sohō, a popular journalist, rhapsodized that at last "the true nature of our country, our national character, will emerge like the sun breaking through a dense fog."[18]

The new day was to bring new problems, frustrations, and burdens. Imperialism would dismay a few and tax the many. New military burdens and strategic responsibilities would also lead to heavy industry and to the great industrial development of twentieth-century Japan. The Meiji Restoration and revolution were at an end, and imperial Japan was ready to join the circle of the great powers it had learned to emulate.

Selected Readings

Akita, George. *Foundations of Constitutional Government in Modern Japan, 1868–1900*. Cambridge, Mass.: Harvard University Press, 1967. A perceptive study of the introduction and implementation of constitutionalism in Meiji Japan, emphasizing the degree to which the Meiji Constitution represented a genuine sharing of power.

Beasley, W. G. *Select Documents on Japanese Foreign Policy, 1853–1868*. London: Oxford University Press, 1955. A full translation of major documents and memoranda during the period between Perry and the Restoration. A masterful introduction summarizes the history of those decades to place the documents in proper perspective.

Craig, Albert M. *Chōshū in the Meiji Restoration*. Cambridge, Mass.: Harvard University Press, 1961. The social, intellectual, and political roots of the emergence of this great southwestern barony into one of the two great power centers of Meiji Japan. Basic to all discussions of "lower samurai" leadership in its careful distinctions of class role in the politics of the Restoration.

Hirschmeier, Johannes, S.V.D. *The Origins of Entrepreneurship in Meiji Japan*. Cambridge, Mass.: Harvard University Press, 1964. An important and interesting examination of the changes in values and leadership in the firms that bridged the Tokugawa-Meiji transition and of the social origins of reprsentative entrepreneurs in the early Meiji.

[18] Cited in Kenneth B. Pyle, *The New Generation in Meiji Japan: Problems of Cultural Identity, 1885–1895* (Stanford, Calif.: Stanford University Press, 1969), p. 173.

Jansen, Marius B. *Sakamoto Ryōma and the Meiji Restoration*. Princeton, N.J.: Princeton University Press, 1961. Biography of a Restoration activist, based upon his letters and set against the tubulent politics of his Tosa fief and the late Tokugawa struggles for opening and reform.

————, ed. *Changing Japanese Attitudes Toward Modernization*. Princeton, N.J.: Princeton University Press, 1965. A collection of studies tracing changes in values and perceptions in late Tokugawa and Meiji intellectual life.

Lockwood, William W. *The Economic Development of Japan: Growth and Structural Change, 1868–1938*. Princeton, N.J.: Princeton University Press, 1955. The standard analysis of economic growth in modern Japan.

Marshall, Byron K. *Capitalism and Nationalism in Prewar Japan: The Ideology of the Business Elite, 1868–1941*. Stanford, Calif.: Stanford University Press, 1967. A study of national and "samurai" motivation and self-image on the part of the modern entrepreneurs, emphasizing their failure to develop an explicitly merchant or capitalist apologia. Since, the author suggests, industrialists emphasized their service to the nation, they could defend themselves only poorly against later attacks by military and nationalist critics who denounced capitalist selfishness.

Najita, Tetsuo. *Hara Kei in the Politics of Compromise, 1905–1915*. Cambridge, Mass.: Harvard University Press, 1967. A fine study of the way Japan's first successful political-party leader developed a national base of support for his party through patronage and practical benefits while retaining the confidence of the oligarchic elements at the center of the decision process.

Nakamura, James I. *Agricultural Production and the Economic Development of Japan, 1873–1922*. Princeton, N.J.: Princeton University Press, 1966. An important examination of the significance of the land and taxation policies that provided the bulk of the Meiji government's income during its formative decades.

Norman, E. Herbert. *Japan's Emergence as a Modern State*. New York: Institute of Pacific Relations, 1946. A pioneering synthesis of Japanese studies of the Meiji transformation. Though dated in its sources and misleading without parallel reference to authors like Craig and Nakamura, it remains an important milestone in the interpretation of modern Japan.

Passin, Herbert. *Society and Education in Japan*. New York: Teachers College Press, 1965. A thoughtful and cogent presentation of the role of educational developments in modern Japan.

Pittau, Joseph, S.J. *Political Thought in Early Meiji Japan, 1868–1889*. Cambridge, Mass.: Harvard University Press, 1967. An important reassessment of the Meiji Constitution, which sees it less as a reluctant concession wrung from a despotic government than as a conscious, albeit hesitant, grant of powers by a regime that realized the necessity of power-sharing for stability and strength.

Pyle, Kenneth B. *The New Generation in Meiji Japan: Problems of Cultural Identity, 1885–1895*. Stanford, Calif.: Stanford University Press, 1969. A thoughtful study of the reaffirmation of Japanese national goals in the 1880's.

Sansom, George B. *The Western World and Japan: A Study in the Interaction of European and Asiatic Cultures*. New York: Knopf, 1950. A brilliant survey of Restoration and Meiji letters, thought, and politics, emphasizing the selective nature of Japan's Westernization and the tenacity of traditional patterns and outlooks.

Scalapino, Robert. *Democracy and the Party Movement in Prewar Japan: The Failure of the First Attempt*. Berkeley, Calif.: University of California Press, 1953. A fine survey of modern Japanese politics that has set a pattern for later reinterpretations of Akita, Najita, and Pittau.

Smith, Thomas C. *Political Change and Industrial Development in Japan: Government Enterprise, 1868–1880*. Stanford, Calif.: Stanford University Press, 1955. An important study of the industrial policies of the Meiji government and the emergence of the zaibatsu firms.

Ward, Robert E., ed. *Political Development in Modern Japan*. Princeton, N.J.: Princeton University Press, 1968. A collection of essays covering many aspects of the political development of modern Japan.

Imperialism in East Asia

AKIRA IRIYE

"I MPERIALISM" is a word no student of East Asian history can avoid. Sooner or later he has to come to grips with it and satisfy himself as to its meaning and its location in his understanding of modern history. This is not an easy task. Although the word is used in historical literature so frequently and indiscriminately as to render it almost meaningless, few works exist that analyze imperialism in East Asia in frontal fashion. Several recent studies of imperialism, while excellent, all but ignore the region and are much more concerned with Africa, the Middle East, and Oceania.[1] At the same time, most works on East Asian international relations refuse to use the concept in an analytical way. Western writers usually describe what happened and then either call the sum of these events "imperialism" or avoid the term altogether. East Asian historians go back to the Opium War to locate the origins of Western imperialism, but few have tried to trace the changing connotations of imperialism during the following decades. After all, a half-century elapsed between the Opium War and the "age of imperialism" at the end of the century, and to group the developments of all the intervening decades under the blanket term "imperialism" is to state nothing meaningful.

Thus there exists a serious gap between specialists in imperial history and those in East Asian history. The former are generally concerned with such topics as the making of imperialistic foreign policy, colonial administration, and commonwealth affairs. Here impressive progress can be

[1] Richard Koebner and Helmut Dan Schmidt, *Imperialism: The Story and Significance of a Political Word, 1840–1960* (New York: Cambridge University Press, 1964); A. P. Thornton, *The Imperial Idea and Its Enemies* (London: Macmillan, 1963); A. P. Thornton, *Doctrines of Imperialism* (New York: Wiley, 1965); and D. K. Fieldhouse, *The Colonial Empires*, English ed. (London: Weidenfeld & Nicolson, 1966).

seen—as, for instance, in the massive volume *The Historiography of the British Empire-Commonwealth.*[2] Imperial historians, however, have not turned their scholarly attention to East Asia, a seat of relatively "informal" imperialism.[3] Few, if any, of them can read Chinese, Japanese, or Korean; and among those who can, few have studied imperial history as their primary concern. For instance, American scholarship on East Asian history has advanced impressively in recent decades, but most American specialists have been interested in domestic politics, industrialization, or intellectual developments rather than in foreign relations. American "imperialism" has been a subject of lively debate among historians, but they have tended to be obsessed with the uniqueness of American imperialism and generally have failed to put it in a comparative framework.[4] Writers on American-Asian relations have all but ignored advances in European imperial history and have produced little fruitful discourse on imperialism in East Asia.

Unless some attempt is made to close the gap between imperial historians who pay little attention to East Asia and East Asian historians who are ignorant of incessant reinterpretations of imperialism, there will be no satisfactory understanding of modern East Asian history. This essay is an attempt at a synthesis; it tries to take note of some pervasive forces in world history at the end of the nineteenth century that, at one level, crystalized in Western imperialism and, at another, produced specific responses in East Asia.

The Imperialists

Who were the imperialists? Since there can be no imperialism without imperialists, theories of the former have been essentially generalizations about the latter, either as individuals or groups. Different authors have put forward their candidates for late nineteenth-century imperialists. They range from the bourgeoisie (Parker T. Moon) and the finance capitalists (V. I. Lenin) to aristocrats (Joseph Schumpeter), from officials (Ronald Robinson and John Gallagher) to the masses (D. K. Fieldhouse).[5]

[2] Edited by Robin W. Winks (Durham, N.C.: Duke University Press, 1966).

[3] For a discussion of "informal empire," see Charles R. Fay, *Imperial Economy and Its Place in the Foundation of Economic Doctrine, 1600–1932* (London: Oxford University Press, 1934).

[4] For a convincing and comprehensive critique of American theories of imperialism, see Ernest R. May, *American Imperialism: A Speculative Essay* (New York: Atheneum, 1968).

[5] Parker T. Moon, *Imperialism and World Politics* (New York: Macmillan, 1926); V. I. Lenin, *Imperialism: The Highest Stage of Capitalism* (1916), trans. J. T. Kozlowski (Detroit: Marxian Educational Society, 1924); Joseph R. Schumpeter, *Imperialism*

Some of these alleged imperialists are pictured as responding rationally to certain clearly defined needs, such as for overseas markets and national security, whereas others are described as victims of blind, psychic, and irrational urges. Lenin's imperialists would be seen as motivated by the sole purpose of exporting surplus capital, whereas Schumpeter's would represent a dying class, an echo from the past, wanting to expand for no practical purposes. And there have been as many interpretations of the anti-imperialists.

Not all anti-imperialists were against expansion, and not all expansionists were imperialists. This distinction is vital if we are to avoid dealing in semantic ambiguities. One could call for peaceful and more or less universalistic forms of expansion, such as free trade and emigration, without becoming an advocate of "imperialism," a term that connotes a more particularistic type of expansion aimed at control and involving nationalistic symbols. This essay is primarily concerned with the latter phenomenon.

The common denominator uniting all imperialists and anti-imperialists is that they lived in the last decades of the nineteenth century. There must have been certain forces at that time, to which men responded, that led some to espouse imperialism and others to reject it. To understand these forces it becomes necessary to look at the world at large, not just at a single country. Only the global approach will enable us to compare different characteristics of imperialists in various countries, and only through a comparative study shall we be able to generalize about imperialism. This, however, is a formidable task. As John S. Galbraith has written,

> though the actions of each state were in part attributable to conditions peculiar to itself, they were also the result of forces affecting Europe generally. Perhaps eventually there will emerge scholars of European expansion in the nineteenth century. At this stage, when so few monographic studies have appeared on the policies of individual nations, the prospect of such broad interpretations seem remote.[6]

If it is difficult to develop broad interpretations of European expansion, it will be nearly impossible to generalize about extra-European societies. Yet an attempt must be made, for the forces pervading Europe in the

and Social Classes (1919; reprinted, London: Oxford University Press, 1951); Ronald Robinson and John Gallagher, Africa and the Victorians: The Official Mind of Imperialism (London: Macmillan, 1961); and D. K. Fieldhouse, "'Imperialism': An Historiographical Revision," Economic History Review, 2nd ser., Vol. 14 (December 1961), pp. 187–209. For more evaluations, consult the recent anthology The "New Imperialism": Analysis of Late Nineteenth-Century Expansion, edited by Harrison M. Wright (Boston: Heath, 1961), and D. K. Fieldhouse, The Theory of Capitalist Imperialism (New York: Barnes & Noble, 1967).

[6] "The Empire Since 1783," in Winks, The Historiography of the British Empire-Commonwealth, p. 67.

last decade of the nineteenth century were not peculiar to that region. They were also affecting the United States and evoking responses in the rest of the world. It is indeed by taking such a global view that one may hope to bridge the gap between imperial history narrowly defined and the history of modern East Asia. These two must be viewed as aspects of world history, and imperialists in the West as well as the Asians on the receiving end of Western expansionism must be seen as products of the same age, members of the same world going through a particular stage of history.

What the forces were that characterized the late nineteenth century and gave rise to imperialism is a subject of continuing debate among historians. According to Lenin, the most fundamental phenomenon of the age was that the Western economies were entering the stage of monopoly capitalism. Thus he saw the politics of imperialism as "capitalism in that phase of its development in which the domination of monopolies and finance-capital has established itself." John A. Hobson and others had already noted the correlation between finance interests and overseas expansionism, but they had not considered imperialism an inevitable phase of history; they thought that there was something artificial, unnatural, and immoral about imperialism that could be eradicated without destroying capitalistic society itself. Lenin, on the other hand, saw imperialism as an external but integral aspect of monopoly capitalism, which, according to him, was emerging at the end of the nineteenth century. His major contribution to contemporary history lay in his ability to see that there existed societies at different stages of economic development and that therefore not all of them would go through the phase of finance capitalism. Thanks to the interaction between advanced Western economies and colonial societies, the development of capitalism in the latter would take a nationalistic form and serve to hasten the downfall of monopoly capitalism in the former.

Lenin introduced the novel concept of nationalism developing in the colonial areas. But he had difficulty accounting for the intense nationalistic rivalry in the West. Instead he emphasized "international capitalist monopolies" and "international trusts" as the driving forces behind imperialism. However, late nineteenth-century history would be incomprehensible without reference to intense power rivalries among nations. Hobson pointed out in his *Imperialism: A Study* (1902) that the imperialists of the time were characterized by their competitiveness, nationalistic particularism, and mutual suspicion. An American writer, Paul S. Reinsch, noted in 1900 that the new imperialism of the time was "national imperialism," an expression of modern Western nationalism.[7] Others, like Earle Winslow, have tended to deny that nationalism leads to imperialism;

[7] *World Politics at the End of the Nineteenth Century, as Influenced by the Oriental Situation* (New York: Macmillan, 1900).

on the contrary, they argue, the two represent fundamentally divergent principles.[8]

The fact remains that at the end of the last century nationalism and imperialism both existed. Whether they embodied the same or contrary forces, their juxtaposition must somehow be explained. Walt W. Rostow, in his well-known *Stages of Economic Growth*, has argued that "the competition for colonies in the late nineteenth century was conducted for reasons that were unilaterally rational on neither economic nor military grounds: the competition occurred essentially because competitive nationalism was the rule of the world arena."[9] This still leaves unanswered the question of why at that particular time "competitive nationalism was the rule of the world arena." C. E. Black, one of the foremost students of comparative history, argues that modern imperialism was "an attempt on the part of more modern societies to enhance their security by extending their sovereignty over less modern societies and thereby gaining control over their resources and skills."[10] Thus modernization provides the clue to the simultaneous development of nationalism and imperialism; modernization entailed the strengthening of political authority at the national level and also the incorporation of underdeveloped societies as integral elements of policy.

All these interpretations make it clear that there were certain radical changes in national and international life in the last years of the nineteenth century and that these changes were related to the phenomenon of imperialism, at both its giving and receiving ends. Since, however, the perception of change may have as great an effect on behavior as the change itself, it will be useful to examine briefly how the imperialists were conceptualizing it and establishing a connection between change and expansionism. As Winslow has noted, late nineteenth-century imperialism was extremely self-conscious.[11] It imagined that it had constantly to justify itself, and this defensiveness was nowhere better revealed than in the imperialists' view of world transformation.

There was virtual consensus among imperialist tracts that physical distances between nations were shortening and the nature of international relations were being radically redefined. Technological advances were outmoding traditional concepts and methods of warfare, familiar notions about man and society were becoming obsolescent, and man's spiritual

---

[8] *The Pattern of Imperialism: A Study in the Theories of Power* (New York: Columbia University Press, 1948).

[9] *Stages of Economic Growth: A Non-Communist Manifesto* (Durham, N.C.: Duke University Press, 1960), pp. 110–11.

[10] *Dynamics of Modernization: A Study in Comparative History* (New York: Harper & Row, 1966), p. 133.

[11] Winslow, *The Pattern of Imperialism*, p. 13.

autonomy was being eroded by materialistic progress. Above all, diffusion of technology and knowledge was stirring the world beyond Europe. A great upheaval in the relationship between the West and the non-West could be anticipated. Experiences seemed to indicate that the natives in Asia and the Middle East were educable, that they could be taught Western techniques of administration, warfare, and manufacturing. Colonial armies were, in fact, manned by natives. The vast masses of the non-Western world had been touched by modern civilization, and the old fabric of government was everywhere disintegrating. Once change was set in motion, there was no knowing what shape and course it would take. The ancient order and stability seemed to be passing, and there appeared an imminence of motion, chaos, and disorder. These were matters for grave concern because, as was noted time and again, steam and electricity had made the world smaller. Disturbances in one part of the globe could have immediate repercussions in the rest.

The imperialists responded to these perceived developments forcefully and particularistically. In the words of Lord Rosebery, who articulated the imperialist sentiment the more clearly because he was a Liberal, it was Britain's mission "to take care that the world, as far as it can be moulded by us, shall receive the Anglo-Saxon and not another character." The idea was not so much aggressive as preventive and defensive—to see to it that changes in the world would not disrupt but confirm Anglo-Saxon supremacy. As Rosebery said, "We should in my opinion grossly fail in the task that has been laid upon us did we shrink from responsibilities and decline to take our share in a partition of the world which we have not forced on, but which has been forced upon us."[12] British law and administration should so restrain the impulses of non-Western peoples that the latter would not produce conditions of chaos and disorder conducive to the disruption of world order. To civilize natives meant to control them. They must be protected from the evils of superficial Westernization by adequate instruction and authority.

It may be seen that the imperialists, while narrowly nationalistic and parochial, were also concerned with the continued power and supremacy of Western civilization. As A. P. Thornton has aptly put it, late nineteenth-century imperialism had "the official stamp of European culture upon it"[13]—and, he might have added, the official seal of approval of America, for Americans were as much concerned as Europeans with the course of Western civilization. They both perceived a threat from forces in the non-Western world. Rudyard Kipling's exhortation to Americans to "take up the White Man's burden" expressed a community of feeling across the

[12] Cited in George Bennett, ed., *The Concept of Empire: Burke to Attlee, 1744–1947* (London: Black, 1962), p. 311.

[13] Thornton, *The Imperial Idea and Its Enemies*, p. 68.

Atlantic. The poem was a reaffirmation of faith in an age of uncertainty, a faith in the West's strength and duty even while it was confronted with the likelihood that "sloth and heathen Folly" might "bring all your hopes to naught."

What one sees in these expressions is an element of uncertainty, a sense of instability and insecurity in the frameworks through which men looked at the world in transformation. The imperialists, from such a point of view, were those who perceived radical changes and sought to control the forces of change to prevent disintegration and chaos. It was reassuring to be an imperialist and to feel that unfamiliar, threatening changes had been or could be contained. Such psychological observations emphasize the fact that the imperialists were human beings and that, in the final analysis, one must study their minds. O. Mannoni, in his *Prospero and Caliban: The Psychology of Colonization*,[14] has dealt admirably with the psychological needs of colonizer and colonized, which he sees as complementary. Until we have more such empirical studies, it will be dangerous to generalize about the mind of the imperialist. But it is worth noting that Western imperialism in the late nineteenth century was not, as is often claimed, so much an expression of exuberant self-confidence and energy as of uncertainty and even of insecurity. Whereas earlier self-confidence had dictated an attitude of liberal, universalistic expansionism, insecurity gave rise to particularistic, imperialistic responses.

The Imperialists in East Asia

The imperialists were never able to colonize the whole of East Asia. Though France established political control over Indochina, Britain over Tibet, and Russia over the Maritime Province and eventually Mongolia, China proper avoided the fates of India, Egypt, and Africa. China was perhaps a "semicolony" but never a formal colony. Japan and Siam remained independent. In short, there was an East Asian civilization that proved remarkably resilient.

The failure of Western imperialism to establish total hegemony over East Asia is one of the most interesting phenomena of modern history. The explanation for it lies in certain peculiarities of East Asia as well as in the West's view of them, and these peculiarities produced a story of imperialism in East Asia that was unique and pregnant with historical significance. It may be said that late nineteenth-century imperialism took the form it did partially because East Asia provided the spatial context for it, and also that Western imperialism entered a distinctive phase

[14] English ed. (New York: Praeger, 1956).

when it encountered challenges and opportunities, agonies and frustrations, in East Asia.

First of all, East Asia was traditionally a land of empires. This does not make the region unique—as Robert G. Wesson has noted anew in a recent book, "Empires are much more easily made than state systems."[15] (The rise and coexistence of sovereign nation-states in post-Renaissance Europe has been an exceptional phenomenon in world history, which had elsewhere been characterized by the rise and fall of empires.) But the longevity of the Chinese imperial order distinguished East Asia from the rest of the world. Empire as a political concept was synonymous with civilization as a way of life, for Confucian doctrine mediated the two. The Confucian empire was universalistic and legitimized itself by its very existence; it was not dependent on specific individuals.

The Chinese empire, then, defined an international order for the vast spaces of East Asia for two thousand years, while in the West, Roman imperial unity continued more in memory than in fact. What is sometimes forgotten, however, is that China's imperial order had been preceded by centuries of disorder and rivalries among semi-independent states. Scholars in preimperial China had sought to define acceptable codes of behavior among states and had developed a notion of international law applicable to "all under heaven." This was an equivalent of the Western concept *magna civitas,* which jurists postulated when nation-states emerged in post-Renaissance Europe. The idea of universal order and the experience of empire were very deeply rooted in East Asia.

China did not, however, remain the only empire. In modern times the East Asian order was defined as a juxtaposition of several empires, a situation vastly different from both post-Renaissance Europe and the single universal empire of Rome. To the north the Russian empire expanded into the immense space of Siberia, and in the south European colonies were established. These various empires had met long before the age of imperialism. After the 1840's the unequal treaty system had defined their relationship—a sort of multilateral imperialism in which the West extended its notions of international law and commercial practice to the Chinese empire, while the latter refused to transform itself into a modern nation-state but continued to concern itself with the affairs of Korea, Annam, and other traditional tributary states. Then, when aggressive nationalism in the West drove it to particularistic imperialism, East Asia was both ready and unprepared for the new situation; it was accustomed to the plurality of empires, but it had also a tradition of universalistic reign.

The second peculiarity of the East Asian scene was that Japan did not

[15] *The Imperial Order* (Berkeley, Calif.: University of California Press, 1967), p. 1.

become a colony but joined the ranks of imperialists as a full-fledged member—the first non-Western country to become an imperialist power. The implications of this fact were enormous, as will be seen. No account of late nineteenth-century imperialism that leaves out the Japanese empire is adequate, and certainly no interpretation of imperialism in Asia can ignore the rise of that empire.

Third, American policy affected the shape of imperialism in East Asia. The United States played a much more active role in the diplomacy of East Asia than elsewhere in the world, with the possible exception of Central America. American involvement was negligible in Africa, the Middle East, and South Asia, but it was a significant factor in East Asia and the Pacific even before the 1890's. At least as a subjective reality, the United States had always been an Asian power. Not only were Americans constantly conscious of their relationships with China and Japan, but Chinese and Japanese considered America one of the three or four major powers of the West. Since the United States had always been closely involved in East Asia, its emergence as a particularistic, insular empire in the 1890's caused little surprise. All the same, the European imperialists could not regard their rivalries in East Asia as merely an extension of the European state system. They had to reckon with the United States, a Western and Atlantic, but also an Asian and Pacific, power.[16]

Finally, to say that Western imperialism expanded into but never completely dominated East Asia is to note the phenomenon of cultural confrontation. For Western-Asian relations in the age of imperialism were not simply military and economic. At the bottom they were cultural, ideological, and psychological. The minds of Asia and the West met and reacted to one another to an extent never before witnessed. Asians became Westernized, but the process was never unidirectional. As Paul Cohen's earlier chapter demonstrates, China's "response to the West" was never a simplistic phenomenon. What is equally significant is that the West, too, responded to Asia in the process of encounter with it. Europeans and Americans became intensively conscious of the non-West for perhaps the first time, and they grappled with the problems that the encounter seemed to be presenting. If it can be said that Asians somehow "responded" to the challenge of the West, it is equally plausible to argue that the West, too, responded to Asia in the age of imperialism. In fact, some of the ideological and psychological roots of Western imperialism can be traced to the West's view of a changing East Asia.

East Asia played two conflicting roles in the development of Western imperialism in the late nineteenth century. On the one hand, it impressed many as the area where the future of the world's power politics

[16] For a general discussion of the United States as an Asian power, see Akira Iriye, "American Power—Asian Reality," *Interplay*, Vol. 2, No. 1 (June–July 1968), pp. 11–14.

was likely to be determined. Only by extending influence to this region, it appeared, could Western powers succeed in their rivalry. The fierce competition for power in Europe could be solved in Asia. The noted French traveler, Prince Henri d'Orient, wrote in 1894, "It is in Asia once more that will be decided the destinies of the world. In Asia will be founded and will increase great empires, and whoever succeeds in making his voice heard in the Far East will be able also to speak in dominating accents to Europe. . . . *Be Asiatic, there lies the future!*"[17] This view of East Asia served further to divide the Western imperialists. Fabulous as the potential economic wealth of that area seemed, it could be exploited only by the energetic few. According to Brooks Adams, "Eastern Asia is the prize for which all the energetic nations are grasping. . . . Our geographical position, our wealth, and our energy preeminently fit us to enter upon the development of Eastern Asia and to reduce it to part of our own economic system."[18] On the other hand, Western imperialists were becoming acutely conscious of the changing relations between Asia and the West. East Asia seemed suddenly very near and of crucial relevance to the future of Western civilization. In responding to this perceived change, the imperialists often, if only momentarily, forgot their rivalry and sought ways of effecting joint strategy.

"Would it be possible," remarked Emile Zola, "to have a revolution from within our old race corrupted by monarchism? Would we not need a new race? It would be a race of barbarians . . . perhaps the Chinese if we waited long enough and if they threw themselves upon us."[19] Such an idea expressed the uncertainty and malaise shared by many observers in the last years of the nineteenth century. Part of this was the usual *fin de siècle* sentiment, but there was more to it than that. According to an American writer, Hiram Stanley, "It is perfect folly for us to ignore that our civilization is in the most vital parts of its decadence, and unless some effective measures are soon adopted and strictly enforced, our cause will be irremediable." The concern with the future of "our cause" was genuine and serious, for many Westerners envisioned a seemingly imminent rise of the barbarians. In 1896 Charles Eliot Norton wrote, "And thus are we brought face to face with the grave problem which the next century is to solve—whether our civilization can maintain itself, and make advance, against the pressure of ignorant and barbaric multitudes."[20] Hith-

[17] Cited in Henry Norman, *The Peoples and Politics of the Far East* (London: Allen & Unwin, 1895), p. 599.

[18] Brooks Adams, *America's Economic Supremacy* (New York: Harper & Row, 1900), p. 221.

[19] *Les Rougon-Macquart,* Edition Pléiade (Paris: Gallimard, 1966), Vol. 4, p. 1599.

[20] Cited in Akira Iriye, *Across the Pacific: An Inner History of American–East Asian Relations* (New York: Harcourt, Brace & World, 1967), p. 58.

erto, Western supremacy and superiority had been taken for granted. Norton expressed the feeling that such optimism was no longer warranted. A few, like Zola, thought a new barbarian invasion might be a healthy and good thing, but most writers refused to be so fatalistic. As John W. Burgess wrote, "It is in the interest of the world's civilization that law and order and the true liberty consistent therewith shall reign everywhere upon the globe." Once civilization was threatened from without by chaotic and disruptive forces in the non-West, it was incumbent upon all the nations of the West to stand together to preserve order and stability. Their internecine struggle must be subordinated to this supreme goal, said the German historian Max Lenz.[21]

If a barbaric uprising was to be checked, it did not follow that Westernization of the world was the answer. If barbaric Chinese masses were a menace, civilized Chinese might be even more so. As Charles H. Pearson's influential *National Life and Character* pointed out:

> The Chinese would be less dangerous than they are if they were as warlike as the Turks in the sixteenth and seventeenth centuries, because, in that case, they would waste their reproductive forces in arms. . . . With civilization equally diffused, the most populous country must ultimately be the most powerful; and the preponderance of China over any rival— even over the United States of America—is likely to be overwhelming.[22]

Similarly, Max von Brandt, German minister to China, wrote that "an industrialist struggle will develop between Europe and Eastern Asia, which will be the more violent and the more detrimental to the former according to the financial aid which Europe puts at the disposal of Asia for its campaign against European industry."[23] The prominent anti-imperialist John A. Hobson noted the same possibility:

> It is at least conceivable that China might so turn the tables upon the Western industrial nations, and, either by adopting their capital and organizers, or as is more probable, by substituting her own, might flood their markets with her cheaper manufactures, and refusing their imports in exchange might take her payments in liens upon their capital, reversing the earlier process of investment until she gradually obtained financial control over her quondam patrons and civilizers.[24]

Hobson was concerned with the impact of such a development upon the well-being of workers and farmers in the West, whose livelihood and

[21] Cited in Julius W. Pratt, *Expansionists of 1898* (Baltimore: Johns Hopkins Press, 1936), p. 9, and in Ludwig Dehio, *Germany and World Politics in the Twentieth Century* (New York: Knopf, 1959), pp. 45–46.

[22] *National Life and Character: A Forecast* (London: Macmillan, 1893), pp. 95–96, 130.

[23] Cited in William L. Langer, *The Diplomacy of Imperialism, 1890–1902*, 2nd ed. (New York: Knopf, 1951), p. 389.

[24] *Imperialism: A Study* (London: Allen & Unwin, 1954), p. 309.

liberty would be menaced by "yellow workmen . . . yellow mercenary troops . . . [and] staple foods and manufactures flowing in as tribute from Asia and Africa." But the economic threat was only one aspect of the "yellow peril." Other writers were asking more fundamental questions about the implications of the changes that Western diplomacy, trade, and missionary activities were bringing about in East Asia. Alfred Thayer Mahan's article, "A Twentieth Century Outlook," which was published in *Harper's* in 1897, provides a good example. Asia, Mahan said, "is rapidly appreciating the material advantages and the political traditions which have united to confer power upon the West." This had initially been the West's doing, for "the history of the present century has been that of a constant increasing pressure of our own civilization" upon other peoples, so that "civilizations on different planes of material prosperity and progress, with different spiritual ideals, and with very different political capabilities, are fast closing together." But differences between East and West would remain, for, "Our own civilization less its spiritual element is barbarism; and barbarism will be the civilization of those who assimilate its material progress without imbibing the indwelling spirit." Thus, said Mahan, "we stand at the opening of a period when the question is to be settled decisively . . . whether Eastern or Western civilization is to dominate throughout the earth and to control its future." Mahan was not very confident that the West would win. In a frank expression of desperation that contradicted his view of the nobility of Western civilization, he concluded that "the great armies and the blind outward impulses of the European peoples are the assurance that generations must elapse ere the barriers can be overcome behind which rests the citadel of Christian civilization."

The rise of the masses of Asia might still have seemed a distant prospect in the 1890's. But in one country, Japan, could be seen the first example of successful Westernization brought about in Asia. As such, the Japanese experience aroused an intense curiosity among Western observers. Most of them willingly accepted Japan to the ranks of imperialists, but they held radically different views of changes, actual and potential, in that country. The differences, as will be seen, reflected uncertainty about the role of the West in Asia at that time. Western imperialism entered a new phase when it interacted with Japanese imperialism, and the field of that encounter was the world's oldest and longest-lasting empire.

Japan as an Imperialist

How different was Japanese from Western imperialism? There are historians who find little difference; they write as though Japanese behavior was much the same as that of the Western powers. Some apply economic interpretations to both forms of imperialism. Since, however, it is all but impossible to ascribe monopoly capitalism to Japan in the 1890's, economic determinists see a preventive imperialism in this instance; Japanese overseas expansion was undertaken, it is maintained, in order to reserve certain areas for future capitalistic exploitation. Others seeking analogies between Japan and the West have looked for subtler factors. Thorstein Veblen, whose theories are much like Joseph Schumpeter's interpretation of Western imperialism, popularized the view that Japanese imperialism was more an outgrowth of feudalism than of capitalism; it was an indication that the nation had not totally departed from its feudal past. The samurai-type will to power, urge to expand, and pursuit of fame have been noted by other writers. In these views Japanese imperialism owed its source to feudal ethos and its agents were imbued with an atavistic spirit.

On the other hand, there have been writers who stress differences between Japanese and Western imperialism. Many Japanese have considered their country's expansionism less tinged with cupidity and materialism than Western imperialism; they have stressed the nobler impulses and self-sacrificing zeal of the Japanese imperialists. Non-Japanese authors, in contrast, have often considered the Japanese version of imperialism far more ruthlessly oppressive, aggressive, and sinister than their own. Thus self-conscious interpretations of differences between the two at times became part of the vocabulary of imperialism in both Japan and the West.

No matter what the differences or similarities between them, the fact remains that Western and Japanese imperialism existed side by side in East Asia in the late nineteenth century and left upon it a distinct imprint. Obviously, the two were products of the same forces—those making up the environment of the age of imperialism.

This is not to say, however, that Japanese expansionism was a new phenomenon, emerging solely in response to those forces. Japan had a tradition of expansionism that had retained its appeal even during the Tokugawa period. There was also a vast literature on colonialism, and, after the late eighteenth century, writers called for expansion both northward to Ezo, Sakhalin, and Kamchatka and southward toward the Philippines, Java, and the South Sea islands.[25] Little evidence exists that these writings were prompted much by an intimate knowledge of Western colonialism and an urge to do the same thing. Most expansionist ideas remained abstract. Namekawa Tenmin advocated territorial aggrandizement so as to turn "Great Japan" into "Great Great Japan"; Hayashi Shihei would spread civilization to the unenlightened natives of Ezo; Baba Masamichi had a vision of a vast, mercantilistic empire under Japanese

[25] See Kuroda Ken'ichi, *Nihon shokumin shisō-shi* [History of Japanese ideas of colonialism] (Tokyo: Kōbundō, 1942).

control; and Sato Shin'en proposed a global imperialism in which all countries would come under Japan's Shinto influence. In propounding these ideas, the Japanese did not have to study Western colonialist literature; their Shinto background, coupled with the practical experiences of government, enabled them to perpetuate expansionist consciousness.

This tradition, however, must be distinguished from late Meiji imperialism. Earlier ideas had been largely abstract speculations that were not translated into specific action, and they existed in Tokugawa Japan alongside just as persistent a tradition of nonexpansionism. Not until the Japanese came into direct contact with the West and saw the world as Westerners were viewing it did a new Japanese imperialism develop.

In Japan, as in the West, a feeling of uncertainty and insecurity characterized expansionist thinking and behavior. Early Meiji Japan has been described as a period of buoyant self-confidence and belief in the human capacity to achieve change. If one looks at the psychology of the leaders, however, it becomes apparent that underlying Japanese behavior throughout the Meiji era there was what might be termed a functional equivalent of the sense of insecurity that was developing in the West. Its roots were traceable in part to the feudal past, to a tradition of shifting loyalties as well as of self-alienating elitism sustained by the philosophy of Wang Yang-ming, but more immediately to the rapid transformation of national life after the 1850's. This feeling of insecurity was not, however, articulated in sophisticated language until the Japanese learned and adopted Western political vocabulary, nor did it necessarily lead to imperialism. In fact, it made the Japanese government extremely cautious and unwilling to undertake overseas adventures.

As to the imperialists themselves, however, there is no doubt that whatever traditional urge to expand the Japanese already had was reinforced by a sense of desperation and uncertainty to provide the language of expansionism during the early years of the Meiji era. Kirino Toshiaki wrote around 1875:

> The situation in the world today is such that nations swallow up one another, some rise, others fall, and all struggle for greater power. Our country is isolated in the Eastern ocean, driven by the inertia of 2,500 years, ignorant of conditions in the world, devoid of national energy, weak in armament, unsupported by strong public opinion, and in danger of losing its independence.

Such an image of Japan led Kirino to advocate an aggressive foreign policy so that Japan would expand into Asia and Europe and vie with the greatest powers for influence and supremacy.[26] Similar quotations can be cited to show the thinking of the early imperialists, especially those

[26] Kokuryūkai, ed., *Tōa senkaku shishi kiden* [Biographies of pioneers in East Asia] (1935; reissued, Tokyo: Hara Shobō, 1966), Vol. 1, pp. 48–49.

connected with the movements for strong policy toward Korea and the rest of Asia.

This does not mean that Meiji expansionism was always imperialistic. In Japan, as in the West, there were those who advocated liberal, universalistic forms of expansion such as trade, emigration, and peaceful activities abroad. As we have said, however, this essay is primarily concerned with the more particularistic type of imperialism, the rationalization for which could be readily found and couched in the language of contemporary Western imperialism. (The ideological underpinning of universalistic expansionism, too, was derived from Western notions.) In short, Japan's imperialists found little difficulty in appropriating Western vocabulary to verbalize their own needs.

Note, for instance, the famous letter written by Enomoto Takeaki, minister to Russia, in 1876:

> I think that Korea, because of its geographical position and political conditions, is intimately connected with our rights and interests vis-à-vis our neighbors in Asia. It is, therefore, a crucial factor in our "policy" to initiate steps so as to extend our influence to it. . . . Although little actual economic profit can be expected from our dealings with Korea, there are important "political" and "strategic" factors involved.[27]

Enomoto's diplomatic mission abroad had taught him how to phrase imperialistic sentiment. The process of education in imperialism continued through the 1880's, when former foreign minister Soejima Taneomi, a leader of continental expansionists, declared that the nation's security needs dictated the acquisition of territories on the continent of Asia, especially Korea and China. It was nonsense, he said, to talk of preserving Korea's independence, as that country was destined sooner or later to be absorbed by a foreign power. The principle of the balance of power alone justified the Japanese seizure of Korea, and the strengthening of the nation through wars was a legitimate means of securing and preserving its independence.[28] Yamagata Aritomo's famous memorandum of 1888, which represented official thinking on the subject, noted that Asia seemed destined to be an arena for fierce conflict among Western nations, in particular Russia and Britain. India, China, and Korea would be involved in war. The involvement of Korea was especially to be feared, as conflict in the peninsula could drag Japan into war. It was therefore incumbent upon Japan to seek Korea's "independence" so that it would not come under the control of a strong Western power. Two years later, Yamagata defined the Korean peninsula as Japan's "line of interests"—as

---

[27] Cited in Yamabe Kentarō, *Nik-Kan heigō shōshi* [A brief history of the Japanese annexation of Korea] (Tokyo: Iwanami shoten, 1966), pp. 37–38.

[28] Cited in Kokuryūkai, *Tōa senkaku shishi kiden,* pp. 88–90.

distinct from its "line of sovereignty," which designated the home islands. It was accepted international practice and absolutely essential to national security, he said, to eject potentially dangerous powers from the "line of interests."[29]

It would be a futile exercise in tautology to try to find the causes of Japanese imperialism in these ideas expressed by the Japanese themselves. Historians have seldom gone beyond reproducing them, as though they felt words alone were a sufficient explanation for action. One must go a step farther and examine the way in which the Japanese came to adopt the Western way of viewing international politics. The hypothesis here is that the Western vocabulary and psychology of imperialism were the more easily picked up by Japanese imperialists because the Japanese already had developed a sense of insecurity. It was as though universalizing their feelings of insecurity made them feel more certain and confident. They would express their ideas and emotions in the same way as Westerners, and they would pattern their behavior after the nations of the West. In short, they would become imperialists.

Since this was so, it is easy to see that at least in language Japanese imperialism was little different from Western. The Sino-Japanese War provides a good example. It was as a result of the war that Japan emerged as a full-fledged imperialist. From the Japanese point of view, the war was no different from other wars and incidents in the annals of Western expansionism. Foreign Minister Mutsu Munemitsu wrote on the eve of the war, "We have carried out our real diplomacy and foreign policy for the first time since the opening of the country." The diplomacy consisted of dispatching Japanese troops to Korea with the clear intention of provoking Chinese retaliation. To do so, Mutsu reasoned, had been necessary in order to entrench Japanese power in Korea. If some tangible material benefits were not obtained, however, public opinion at home might oppose such military action. For this reason it was desirable to acquire railway, telegraph, mining, and other concessions in Korea so that these would impress the Japanese as fruits of imperialism even though, Mutsu wrote, "in fact they might bring no substantial benefit at all."[30] Mutsu also justified Japanese action as being in the interest of civilization. As he said, "The origin of this war was certainly the clash between new European culture and old East Asian culture." This may have been simply a propaganda device to please Westerners, but such an appeal to civilization was an important aspect of Japanese psychology at that time. The Japanese were trying to universalize their experience and

[29] Cited in Kokusai Seiji Gakkai, ed., *Nihon gaikōshi kenkyū* [Studies in Japanese diplomatic history] (Tokyo: Yūhikaku, 1957), pp. 186–95.
[30] Yamabe, *Nik-Kan heigō shōshi*, pp. 101–05.

were borrowing from the vocabulary of imperialism in the West in order to describe and justify the adventure on the Asian continent.

As a result of the Sino-Japanese War, Japan emerged as an imperialist, in terms not only of power but of national self-image. In official thinking, at least, the distance between Japan and the advanced countries of the West was shortened. Paradoxically, this very fact made both Japanese and Westerners conscious of their differences.

Just as the coming of Perry had wrought a chain reaction of events in domestic politics leading to the overthrow of the Tokugawa regime, so the Sino-Japanese War and its aftermath had a profound impact upon subsequent history, an impact whose repercussions were felt down to the 1940's. As a result of the Treaty of Shimonoseki, Japan emerged as an empire, possessing Taiwan and the Pescadores. It obtained Korean "independence" and became involved in schemes and intrigues in the peninsular kingdom. Securing firm control over Korea became the cardinal goal of Japan's foreign policy. The army and navy had to be expanded to defend the new empire and prepare for contingencies in the Korean question. The Sino-Japanese War also brought in an indemnity payment from China that not only paid for the cost of the war but enabled Japan to start heavy industrialization and adopt a gold standard. Above all, the Japanese viewed their country as an imperialist, a member of the select group of strong powers. For them this meant that the nation could behave as a civilized power, as a respectable participant in the game of imperialist politics.

Japan and the West in China

The Sino-Japanese War had the effect of embroiling China in imperialist politics and the Western powers in East Asian affairs. Though the war had involved only the two combatants, its aftermath concerned other powers. Russia, France, and Germany directly influenced the shape of the peace when they objected to Japan's acquisition of the Liaotung Peninsula and forced it to renounce that territory in return for an increase in China's reparations payment. This tripartite intervention revealed the interrelatedness of European and Asian politics. Russia feared that Japan's foothold on the continent would menace its own designs in the Maritime Province, Korea, and Manchuria. Germany was interested in promoting Russian intervention in East Asia so as to divert the latter's attention from Europe. France acted with Russia to show solidarity with its ally. Britain did not act, as it was immobilized by pressures from the three powers to join them and from Japan to repudiate them. All in all, the episode heralded the coming of the age of imperialist politics in East

Asia and also indicated that Japan was emerging as a power whose behavior would have repercussions among other imperialists.

The postwar years also saw the political dismemberment of the Chinese empire. Germany, France, and Russia sought, and in time received, rewards from China for the tripartite intervention. France extended its control from northern Indochina to South China, including the lease of Kwangchow Bay. Germany established itself in the Shantung Peninsula and obtained the lease of Kiaochow Bay. Russia acquired the very territory from which Japan had been repulsed, the Liaotung Peninsula. Britain, in its turn, obtained the lease of Weihaiwei to balance Russia and secured some Chinese territory bordering on Burma to offset French gains. Even Italy, aspiring to join the ranks of the great imperialist powers, sought to obtain a naval base, and had the distinction of being the only Western nation that met a rebuff by the Chinese.

Political control was buttressed by economic control. Russia and France extended loans to China to finance its indemnity payment to Japan and in return obtained railway and mining concessions. Britain and Germany followed suit, and within a few years after the Sino-Japanese War as many as nineteen railroads, totaling 6,420 miles in combined length, had been contracted away in return for hundreds of millions of dollars in loans. Usually each power sought to define a sphere of influence in China within which it would have an option to build railways and engage in exploration, mining, and other activities. France regarded South China as its special preserve, and Britain claimed it had preponderant interests in the Yangtze region, which it tried to perpetuate by means of a nonalienation agreement with China. The Chinese empire thus was carved up into several segments, in each of which a foreign imperialist predominated.

Why the "scramble for concessions" should have taken place just at this juncture is a fascinating but difficult question. For one thing, China represented an immense pocket of inaction in a time when the waves of industrialization were sweeping across northern Eurasia. China lagged far behind Japan and the West, and there was a temptation for the latter to fill the vacuum in order to prevent the radical shift in power balance that would result if China were disintegrated or dominated by a single nation. More specifically, Japan's defeat of China made Western powers realize the potentialities as well as the dangers of expanding into China. They felt potentialities could be realized and dangers avoided through development of a particularistic diplomacy of imperialism.

The new system of diplomacy was particularistic in that each power sought to extend its own influence by means of leases, spheres of influence, concessions, and loans. The rights and interests obtained were as a rule not made available to all but were held for exclusive use of the particular country's designees. However, these particularistic arrangements were often guaranteed by means of bilateral agreements between imperialists, with or without China's knowledge. For instance, a French-British agreement recognized their respective spheres of influence in China, and a German-British agreement assigned Shantung as Germany's sphere of interests and the Yangtze as Britain's, while a Russian-British pact defined the mutual limits of railway concessions in North China. Thus the very multiplicity of the imperialists and their interests in East Asia limited the extent of their power. An imperialist could not extend its power too far without infringing upon the prerogatives of another. There was an inherent mechanism for preserving the status quo, backed up by a series of agreements on respective spheres of influence.

In contrast to its detachment elsewhere on the globe, the United States was deeply involved in East Asian imperialist politics. But its role was sometimes that of imperialist and at other times that of anti-imperialist, and this fact contributed to the peculiarities of the East Asian scene in the 1890's. America's emergence as an Asian imperialist has provoked fierce historical debate, the end of which is not in sight. Some have seen in the expansion to Hawaii and the Philippines a mere extension of the continental expansionism that had characterized American history before 1890.[31] Another school of thought has stressed the economic factor, interpreting the new empire in the Pacific as a territorial base from which the United States could penetrate the Asian markets.[32] Some writers have stressed the spread of expansionist ideology among middle-class Americans, while still others have called attention to a psychic crisis of the 1890's that caused the American people to "retreat from reality" and welcome overseas adventures.[33] More recently, Ernest May has suggested that the short-lived territorial aggrandizement of 1898–1900 was brought about by an abdication of responsibility by those members of the opinion-making elite who had ordinarily presented a coherent consensus on the side of anti-imperialism.[34]

Undoubtedly these interpretations are all relevant, but most of them tend to focus on domestic factors. While no blind application to the

---

[31] Charles Vevier, "American Continentalism: The History of an Idea, 1845–1910," *American Historical Review*, Vol. 65, No. 2 (January 1960), pp. 323–35.

[32] Walter LaFeber, *The New Empire: An Interpretation of American Expansion, 1860–1898* (Ithaca, N.Y.: Cornell University Press, 1963), and Thomas J. McCormick, *China Market: America's Quest for Informal Empire, 1893–1901* (Chicago: Quadrangle Books, 1967).

[33] Pratt, *Expansionists of 1898*, and Richard Hofstadter, "Manifest Destiny and the Philippines," in Daniel Aaron, ed., *America in Crisis* (New York: Knopf, 1952), pp. 173–200. See also Richard Hofstadter, *The Paranoid Style in American Politics* (New York: Knopf, 1966).

[34] May, *American Imperialism*, Chapter 9.

United States of an abstract formula of "imperialism" will do, one must also guard against excessive parochialism in discussing American expansion to Asia. As was noted earlier, there were forces in the world that transcended particular nations and had an impact upon all of them. The sense of uncertainty and insecurity that produced the self-conscious espousal of imperialism was not a monopoly of Europeans. Americans, too, looked at the world in a similar way, and they read European imperialist literature such as James Anthony Froude's *Oceana* and J. R. Seeley's *The Expansion of England.* The feeling of insecurity was reinforced in the United States by the influx of immigrants from eastern and southern Europe, who were regarded by self-conscious "Anglo-Saxons" as a threat to free institutions. To preserve freedom and civilization, and to save the nation from stagnation and decay, aggressive expansionism seemed the only course.[35]

No matter what the causes, the fact remains that the United States did become an Asian imperialist in 1898, with new territories in the Philippines, Hawaii, Guam, and Wake Island. The taking of these islands prompted another imperialist, Germany, to obtain the cession of the Caroline and Marianas islands from Spain, while Britain welcomed the United States to the ranks of the imperialists as a counterweight to Germany. The great powers henceforth expected as a matter of course that America would act like an imperialist. Within the United States, Alfred Thayer Mahan, in his *Problems of Asia* (1900), urged that the nation act together with Britain and Japan against Russia and France in the contest for control of Asia. Charles Conant argued that the United States should obtain exclusive mining and other rights in China to take care of the nation's surplus capital. The American minister to Peking, Edwin Conger, recommended in November 1898 that the United States take possession of a good port in China "from which we can potently assert our rights and effectively wield our influence." Several months later he suggested establishing an American sphere of influence in Chihli province. The Navy Department's Bureau of Equipment recommended the taking of Chusan Island, an idea warmly seconded by Navy Secretary John D. Long. In 1900, during the Boxer uprising, American soldiers marched

[35] May's *American Imperialism* is very useful in suggesting links between European and American thinking on world affairs. For the growth of anti-immigration movements, see John Higham, *Strangers in the Land: Patterns of American Nativism, 1860–1925* (New Brunswick, N.J.: Rutgers University Press, 1955). It should be noted, however, that expansionists and anti-expansionists had many ideas in common, as revealed, for instance, in Robert L. Beisner, *Twelve Against Empire: The Anti-Imperialists, 1898–1900* (New York: McGraw-Hill, 1968). The differences between them, which often seemed very minor but were of crucial significance, indicated varying degrees of acceptance of the particularistic thinking then current among European imperialists.

side by side with those of other imperialist powers to rescue the legations in Peking, and the State Department considered obtaining a lease at Samsah Bay in Fukien province.[36]

On the other hand, American behavior in East Asia was not totally identifiable with that of the other imperialists. While the latter were busily engaged in carving up China into spheres of influence and entering into particularistic arrangements to uphold the status quo, American policy stressed the equality of commercial opportunity and, eventually, China's "territorial and administrative entity." The policy came to be known as the Open Door policy after Secretary of State John Hay's notes of September 1899 and circular of July 1900. In the context of the present discussion of imperialism in East Asia, the Open Door principle may be taken as negative evidence that the United States would not be like other imperialists insofar as policy in China was concerned. America would in fact pursue an anti-imperialist policy, insisting on equal treatment of all foreigners in China and opposing the disintegration of the Chinese empire. Such a policy, however, could still be viewed as imperialistic, and William A. Williams and others have termed it "open-door imperialism."[37] But even they would not deny the different orientation of American from European expansionism in East Asia. While both were rooted in the awareness of changing forces in the world, American imperialism had, paradoxically, an anti-imperialistic element in it. This fact was to become crucially significant in the twentieth century.

American-European differences, however, pale in significance when contrasted with the enormously complex problems raised by Japan's rise as an imperialist. After the Sino-Japanese War the Japanese did their best to fit into the developing system in East Asia and retain their newly won status. The humiliating tripartite intervention made them keenly aware of their military and material inferiority vis-à-vis the Western imperialists, and the Japanese resolved to close the gap through massive exertion. Efforts were made to obtain concessions and spheres of influence in China not because Japan was ready to make use of them but because they were considered to be symbols of Japan's imperialist status. As Kurino Shin'ichirō, minister to France, wrote in 1897, Japan should extend loans to China, obtain railway concessions, and invest in China's industrial development. Strictly speaking, Japan could not afford to export capital, but for this very reason it was imperative to establish close connections with parts of China. Otherwise the whole of China would be

---

[36] See Marilyn B. Young, *The Rhetoric of Empire: America's China Policy, 1895–1901* (Cambridge, Mass.: Harvard University Press, 1968), and William R. Braisted, *The American Navy in the Pacific, 1897–1907* (Austin, Tex.: University of Texas Press, 1958).

[37] *The Tragedy of American Diplomacy*, rev. ed. (New York: Knopf, 1962).

subdivided into Western spheres of influence, and there would be little chance for Japan to join the game.[38] Ōkuma Shigenobu likewise expressed a common attitude when he declared, in 1898, that through the new treaty with China, granting Japan most-favored-nation treatment and other privileges, the nation had attained the position already enjoyed by Western powers. Now it must exert every effort to maintain its position and compete in the Chinese trade.[39]

It was awareness of this new status as an imperialist that was behind the numerous agreements Japan entered into with Western powers to define their mutual spheres. Thus, instead of protesting against the Russian occupation of Port Arthur in 1898, the Japanese government made this an occasion for obtaining Russian recognition of Japan's position in Korea. Again, just as the powers were defining their spheres of influence in China, Japan pressed the Manchu government to recognize Fukien as part of the Japanese sphere through a nonalienation agreement. Fukien lay opposite the island of Taiwan, and it was hoped that through the foothold in Taiwan Japanese influences might penetrate Fukien, Chekiang, and the adjoining provinces. When the United States sought to obtain a naval base on Samsah Bay, in Fukien province, Japan vehemently protested. For its part, the latter assured the United States that it had no designs on the Philippines. The Japanese government discouraged any support of Emilio Aguinaldo, which some private citizens were contemplating. In other words, Japan's leaders sought to have their nation recognized as a respectable imperialist in East Asia.

In this task they were mostly successful. Europeans began talking of Japan as a power and a potential ally. The idea of an Anglo-Japanese alliance was afloat already in the late 1890's. The Western powers entered into agreements with Japan just as they did with one another, clarifying their respective spheres of influence in Korea and China. The allied expedition to Peking during the Boxer uprising was a symbolic event in which soldiers from Japan and the West marched side by side to punish the Chinese. Secretary Hay addressed his Open Door notes to Japan as well as to the other imperialists (but not to China).

Japan was not just another imperialist, however; it was an Asian imperialist. Beneath the surface drama of power politics, new currents of thought and patterns of international relations were developing, all related to this phenomenon. How Westerners, Chinese, and Japanese reacted to the emergence of Japanese imperialism provides a key to the understanding of the 1890's. To be sure, imperialism was not the only

[38] Hiratsuka Atsushi, *Shishaku Kurino Shin'ichirō den* [The Life of Count Kurino Shin'ichirō] (Tokyo: 1942), pp. 216–21.

[39] Sumiya Mikio, *Dainihon teikoku no shiren* [The Japanese empire on trial] (Tokyo: Chūōkōron-sha, 1966), pp. 136–39.

aspect of Japanese modernization, but it was the one most often noted by foreign observers, many of whom viewed Japan's economic transformation in terms of its far-reaching consequences now that the country was an empire.

The cultural implications of the emergence of the Japanese empire were also noted by many Westerners. For example, some imagined that the Japanese were imbued with the spirit of "Asia for Asians" and would use their power to drive Western influence out of Asia. Such a view would follow rather naturally from the premise, shared by numerous observers, that Japan was still an Asian nation despite its veneer of Westernization. It should be recalled that Western readers were already familiar with different interpretations of modern Japan and that in the 1890's fairly sophisticated accounts of Japanese life and culture were written by first-hand reporters. For instance, Lafcadio Hearn's *Kokoro: Hints and Echoes of Japanese Inner Life* was published in 1896. Written just after the Sino-Japanese War, the book sought to examine the Japanese *kokoro* ("inner life"). Hearn remained convinced that "the so-called 'adoption of Western civilization' within a time of thirty years cannot mean the addition to the Japanese brain of any organs or powers previously absent from it. [It] cannot mean any sudden change in the mental or moral character of the race." The mental readjustments that had accompanied Westernization had occurred "only along directions in which the race had always shown capacities of special kinds," and never "in directions foreign to the national genius."[40] Similarly, George Trumbull Ladd pointed out that despite some important changes taking place in Japanese life, "so far as the great social, political, ethical, and religious principles, in which modern civilization has its very life, are concerned, and even so far as the scientific view of nature which has led to the triumphs of applied science is important—all this is as yet almost wholly foreign to the Japanese mind."[41] Thus it followed that Japan remained an outsider to the West. There could be no true understanding between the two. In Lafcadio Hearn's words, "We may sympathize to the same degree that we understand. One may imagine that he sympathizes with a Japanese or a Chinese; but the sympathy can never be real to more than a small extent outside of the simplest phases of common emotional life. . . . For converse reasons, the Japanese cannot, even though they would, give Europeans their best sympathy."[42]

For those predisposed to suspect the deep-rooted antagonism of the

[40] *Kokoro: Hints and Echoes of Japanese Inner Life* (New York: Houghton Mifflin, 1896), pp. 8–10.
[41] "Mental Characteristics of the Japanese," *Scribner's Monthly*, Vol. 17, No. 1 (January 1895), pp. 80–81.
[42] Hearn, *Kokoro*, pp. 11–12.

non-West toward the West, these observations reinforced the argument that Japan was waiting to seize an opportunity to rally the Asian masses and drive Westerners from Asia. The greatest fear was the possibility that Japan might combine with China and deny the West its opportunities in East Asia. As a British newspaper noted during the Sino-Japanese War:

> Consider what a Japan-governed China would be. Think what the Chinese are; think of their powers of silent endurance under suffering and cruelty; think of their frugality; think of their patient perseverance, their slow, dogged persistence, their recklessness of life. Fancy this people ruled by a nation of born organizers, who, half-allied to them, would understand their temperament and their habits. The Oriental, with his power of retaining health under conditions under which no European could live, with his savage daring when roused, with his inborn cunning, lacks only the superior knowledge of civilization to be the equal of the European in warfare as well as in industry. Under the Japanese emperor the dreams of the supremacy of the Yellow Race in Europe, Asia, and even Africa . . . would be no longer mere nightmares. Instead of speculating as to whether England or Germany or Russia is to be the next world's ruler, we might have to learn that Japan was on its way to that position.[43]

Such remarks, which reflect the then prevalent notions of racial and cultural differences, seem to have been typical of the period. Even those who admired and accepted as genuine Japan's modern achievements echoed similar sentiments. Henry Norman's widely read *The Peoples and Politics of the Far East* (1895), while noting with wonder the Westernization of Japan during the preceding quarter-century, believed there was a secret design for establishing a Monroe Doctrine for East Asia. The pan-Asianist movement, he wrote, foretold the coming of "the most momentous events in the relationship of nations since Napoleon Bonaparte was exiled to St. Helena." But Norman's belief was based on no more solid evidence than the fact, as he stated it, that "Englishman, American, Frenchman, or German is one kind of human being, and Japanese is another. Between them stands, and will stand forever, the sacred and ineradicable distinction of race."[44]

Whether pan-Asianism was more than a figment of Western imagination, a product of fear, whether it was a source as well as an explanation for the Western sense of insecurity, is a fascinating question. As an active movement, pan-Asianism was quite insignificant in Japan and China before the Russo-Japanese War. Certainly the Japanese had some romantic notions about kinship with their continental neighbors, but Japanese im-

[43] Cited in Norman, *The Peoples and Politics of the Far East*, pp. 398–99.
[44] *Ibid.*, pp. 394–97.

perialism did not have as its aim the idea of Asia for Asians. It is well to recall that some of the earliest ideological exponents of pan-Asianism, like Nakae Chōmin, were ardent anti-imperialists. But the imperialists, ranging from governmental leaders to opinion-makers such as Fukuzawa Yukichi, had little use for the concept of solidarity with the Chinese. "Those who call for a Japanese-Chinese alliance to protect Asia's interests," wrote Fukuzawa, referring to idealistic pan-Asianists,

> seem to suggest that the two peoples should cooperate together to civilize Asia, strengthen it militarily, and cope with the West. It is like saying that Japan and China, as two doctors, should jointly treat the sick man that is East Asia. But how can such cooperation work when one is a Chinese medicine man and the other a civilized and scholarly physician?

The two countries, despite their common cultural roots, were by the 1890's as different as dog and elephant, and it was nonsense to say they could act together against the West.[45]

Pan-Asianism was essentially a Western idea, an expression of what Westerners feared Asians were secretly promoting. It had the same psychological roots as the notion of the "yellow peril" and exemplified the way the West responded to changes, real and imagined, in the East. It must be noted, however, that there were Asians who were receptive to the ideas of cultural dichotomy and racial diversity then current in the West. The Japanese government on the whole reacted to the yellow-peril concept by dissociating itself from any pan-Asianist movement. As Minister Kurino wrote, any idea of working against Western imperialists through cooperation with the Chinese was dangerous and doomed to failure, given Western superiority. If Japan was to maintain its status as a power, it must join the league of European nations and act as one of their number. There were others, however, who responded to Western suspicions about Asian solidarity by promoting it. "Asia exists for the sake of Asia," declared Konoe Atsumaro, and only Asians had the right to determine the fate of Asia.[46] Such a remark should perhaps be taken as a defensive response to the yellow-peril concept. If the West should continue to regard Japan as an Asian nation and group it with China and others, then the Japanese should not hesitate to assert their identity and rights as Asians. They would act as Westerners expected them to behave.

There was one area where mutual animosity between Westerners and Japanese was quite real. This was their confrontation in China. Japanese

[45] Somura Yasunobu, "Tairiku seisaku ni okeru imeiji no tenkan" [Changing images in Japan's continental policy], in Shinohara Hajime and Mitani Taichirō, eds., *Kindai Nihon no seiji shidō* [Political leadership in modern Japan] (Tokyo: University of Tokyo Press, 1965), pp. 261–62.

[46] *Ibid.*, p. 260.

merchants who went to China became immediately aware of the presence of Westerners, who seemed to enjoy a predominant position of power and influence in the Chinese economy. Japanese traders and consuls thus began a concerted drive to compete with Westerners, especially in the export of cotton fabrics. Buddhist missionaries were sent to the coastal provinces of China to proselytize among Chinese and undermine the efforts of Christian missionaries. A handful of Japanese in China were eager to promote the cause of reform in the Manchu empire. Still, most of these activities were an expression of a desire to compete with Western influence in China and not of a deep-seated plot to effect a pan-Asian union. The methods the Japanese imperialists used in China were essentially the same as those of their Western rivals.

In one sense Japanese imperialism may be said to have been distinguished from Western—that is, in the Chinese perception of the two. This again is a subject that has hardly been studied. What evidence there is indicates that the Chinese at this time were much more concerned with Western imperialism. It is well to recall that the 1890's saw the beginning of serious reformist and revolutionary movements in China, buttressed by the founding of numerous modern schools and newspapers. Young students were asserting themselves more and more loudly and forming associations to study current affairs. There was little they could do to check foreign encroachment, but through educational and journalistic activities they were laying groundwork for the emergence of nationalistic public opinion. Their views after the Sino-Japanese War were very alarmist vis-à-vis Western imperialism but hardly concerned with Japanese imperialism. By 1900 "imperialism" had become a familiar word to young Chinese nationalists, and they read economic and racial connotations into the term. Liang Ch'i-ch'ao, the most prolific and influential writer on the subject, repeatedly discussed the demographic and ethnic factors behind the West's territorial expansionism and predicted that the twentieth century would be a century of struggle between forces of independence and imperialism. As for Japan, he wrote that it was "simply following trends in Europe."[47] The Boxers adopted the slogans "Help China and punish the Western religion" and "Restore China and destroy the West." They did not say "destroy the Japanese also," although they attacked and killed Japanese as well as Westerners.

However, their anti-imperialism did not lead many Chinese to seek alliance with Japan against the West. Sun Yat-sen was developing his pan-Asianist thought at this time; as he confided to his Japanese friends, the two peoples should cooperate to save China's four hundred millions and efface the humiliations suffered by the yellow race. His followers

[47] Chang Nan, ed., *Hsin-hai ko-ming ch'ien shih-nien-chien shih-lun hsüan-chi* [Essays on current affairs during 1901–1911] (Peking: San-lien shu-tien, 1960), Vol 1, No. 1, pp. 53–58.

were encouraged to go to Japan. But the notion of utilizing Japanese assistance to attack Western influence was never consistently upheld. There was no thought of turning to Japan as an antithesis of the West. Japanese Buddhist missionaries, for instance, were uniformly unsuccessful in their endeavor in China. Reformers and revolutionaries were not ideological pan-Asianists. They were pragmatists, and sought to strengthen the country by adopting Western ideas and institutions. They would learn from the West how to regain national autonomy and power, and Japan would be useful as a transmitter of Western ideas and technology, not as an ally in an anti-Western crusade.

The significance of imperialism in East Asia in the late nineteenth century lies in the fact that at this time world history was becoming international history, that developments in Asia and the West were interacting and being intertwined with each other to an extent never before witnessed. It was not simply that Asian politics affected world politics or that Asia was putting an end to the near-autonomy of the European state system. It was not merely that the Japanese economy became related to the world economy and that China began attracting the West's surplus and nonsurplus capital. Most fundamentally, Asia was becoming part of the Western consciousness, and the problems of Asian-Western relations were fascinating Asians and Westerners alike. They were encountering one another in growing numbers and were asking serious questions about that encounter. Western civilization in Asia was no longer represented by a handful of missionaries, traders, and sailors, existing mostly in isolation from the mass of native populations. It was now coming face to face with Japanese imperialism and involving itself more and more deeply in the potential transformation of China.

The questions being asked, then, were ultimately related to the future shape of East Asia. What was to be the relationship between Western imperialism and Asian industrialization? What political expression was Asian modernization to take? No one questioned that the West would continue to exert its political and economic influence in East Asia, but few believed that Western supremacy would last forever. Specifically where and how, then, would the West fit into the emerging new East? Could there develop an international order in Asia with its own mechanisms for maintaining peace and regional stability without its constantly being affected by European developments? Could Westerners help promote a new, nonimperialistic definition of Asian-Western relations?

Unfortunately, the new century was to show that there were no neat and peaceful solutions to these issues. The first years of the twentieth century, in particular, demonstrated how difficult it was to define a new international system in East Asia in which forces of nationalism and imperialism, East and West, power politics and economic interdependence, could be reconciled. Even in the 1960's, the political map and economic shape of East Asia were ill defined, and the fundamental question of the nature of Western involvement was being fought out on the battlefield.

The history of modern East Asia is a history of interaction between Westerners, Chinese, Japanese, and other Asians. One can evaluate the significance of the East Asian phase of imperialism only by looking at what happened to Asians and Westerners as a result of their encounter. How did it affect them, their patterns of behavior and thought? How did the Asian experience transform Western life, and what did imperialism bring to Asia? These questions can be fully answered only after empirical studies are accumulated and methodological ambiguities inherent in the study of imperialism are squarely faced. This essay has dealt chiefly with the ideological-psychological aspect of imperialism. For at bottom what happened to the minds of Asians and Westerners as a result of their direct and indirect contact is the crucial legacy of the age of imperialism. It may be said that the vocabulary of Asian-Western confrontation was enriched through the experiences of the 1890's. Both Asians and Westerners learned to ask new questions about interracial and intercultural association and about the future of human civilization.

If it is true, as seems clear, that modern Asia has been a land not only of Asians but of Westerners and that their relationship, mostly one-sided and resented by the former, nevertheless provided experiences in intercultural confrontation, then the age of imperialism may be said to have been a crucial stage in the history of mankind as a whole, in which the awareness of human unity has been fostered through the consciousness of diversity. Some of the more sophisticated minds in the age of imperialism grappled with serious and fundamental questions about the future of civilization and of mankind as they pondered the implications of the diffusion of Western knowledge to the non-West. It is significant that Charles Pearson's above-mentioned book, usually considered a yellow-perilist tract par excellence, was at the same time a magnificent analysis of what happened to man as a result of the spread of modernization. This is precisely the central question we are asking today as we study East Asian history.

Selected Readings

In addition to those titles cited in the text and footnotes, the following books are recommended for further reading on the subject of imperialism in East Asia:

Brunschwig, Henry. *French Colonialism: Myths and Realities*. London: Pall Mall Press, 1966. A recent, balanced account.

Conroy, Hilary. *The Japanese Seizure of Korea, 1868–1910*. Philadelphia: University of Pennsylvania Press, 1960. An insightful discussion of the theories for Japanese expansion toward Korea.

Eastman, Lloyd E. *Throne and Mandarins: China's Search for a Policy During the Sino-French Controversy, 1880–1885*. Cambridge, Mass.: Harvard University Press, 1967. One of the few accounts examining China's reaction to imperialism.

Jansen, Marius B. *Changing Japanese Attitudes toward Modernization*. Princeton, N.J.: Princeton University Press, 1965. A collection of essays on modern Japan, some of which offer stimulating discussions of Japanese attitudes toward external affairs.

————. *The Japanese and Sun Yat-sen*. Cambridge, Mass.: Harvard University Press, 1954. A good study of pan-Asianist thought.

Kelley, Robert. *The Transatlantic Persuasion: The Liberal-Democratic Mind in the Age of Gladstone*. New York: Knopf, 1969. A fascinating comparative discussion of British and American anti-imperialism.

Lowe, Cedric J. *The Reluctant Imperialists*. London: Routledge & Kegan Paul, 1967. A systematic treatment of British imperialism in various parts of the world, including East Asia.

May, Ernest R. *Imperial Democracy: The Emergence of America as a Great Power*. New York: Harcourt, Brace & World, 1961. The best study of American imperialism as an aspect of international politics in the years 1895–98.

Nish, Ian H. *The Anglo-Japanese Alliance: The Diplomacy of Two Island Empires, 1894–1907*. London: University of London Press, 1967. A meticulous study tracing the interaction between British and Japanese policies and attitudes.

Pearl, Ceryl. *Morison of China*. Sydney: Angus & Robertson, 1967. A fascinating account of an Australian doctor-journalist-adventurer who was active during the height of imperialism in China.

Pelcovits, Nathan A. *Old China Hands and the Foreign Office*. New York: Octagon, 1967. An informative study of the influence (and lack of influence) of the "old China hands" upon British policy.

Sun, E-Tsu Zen. *Chinese Railways and British Interests, 1898–1911*. New York: Columbia University Press, 1954. A factual monograph dealing with specific instances of imperialism.

Tan, Chester C. *The Boxer Catastrophe*. New York: Columbia University Press, 1955. The best account of the Boxer incident in its Chinese and international contexts.

Nationalism, Reform, and Republican Revolution: China in the Early Twentieth Century

ERNEST P. YOUNG

THE men who dominated Chinese politics in the first two decades of the twentieth century were marked by their agreement that China had failed. They were the first generation that was forced, no matter what other assumptions they might bring to their understanding of current problems, to recognize that "tradition" would not provide the answers. What in the nineteenth century had been a prophetic warning was now an accepted cliché: Only radical departures from the old ways could save the very existence of China. Beliefs that had been the foundation of the political system for millennia no longer carried conviction; they survived only as empty rites or symbols useful for manipulating the uneducated. The "Confucian state" in its last decade, before it was finally overthrown in the 1911 revolution, was merely an evocation of the past, not its continuation.

Only virtual unanimity among leaders could have produced such unruffled assent to the conspicuous dismantling of the old structure. In 1905 the examination system—for centuries the main path toward superior status and the legitimizing agent for a whole class—was abolished, and there was no serious protest. In 1911 Chinese of all sorts and conditions joined to oust the last full-fledged monarch of China and in the process committed to oblivion the imperial system of government. The dissent from this action among Chinese was marginal. Such events betray the extent to which the country's leadership had forsaken the politics of the past.

The men whose leadership characterized these decades were not, of course, all members of one clique or one movement. They nevertheless shared an outlook that can perhaps be summed up in four main points. (1) The well-being, even the survival, of China was critically endangered

151

by the power and encroachment of the West and Japan, and the main task of government was to restore and protect China's national sovereignty. (2) The lessons of the past, the "tradition" and the precedents of the Ch'ing and earlier dynasties, were in no way an adequate guide (though there was no need to attack inherited ethical values per se). (3) Basic institutional changes, following modern Western and Japanese models, were urgently required in the political sphere. Finally, (4) China's problems were not severe in the social sphere, where preventive measures against future distortions would be largely sufficient. This particular set of attitudes had had a brief, partially disguised expression in the 1898 reform movement, but after 1900 it became the property of all active political movements. Only in the 1920's did it give way to a growing concern on the part of some intellectuals and politicians with existing social inequities, as well as to a disposition on the part of others to rediscover the lessons of the past.

Although movements in the early twentieth century were implicitly in agreement on the above four points, they differed about how to act on them. Three main styles of political behavior can be distinguished conveniently by the names of their most famous practitioners: Yuan Shih-k'ai, the reforming mandarin and man of power; Liang Ch'i-ch'ao, the Westernizing reformist intellectual; and Sun Yat-sen, the revolutionary spokesman. These names are signposts for the major divisions in the Chinese political world, though they should not be taken as fully representative of the broad movements to which they were attached.

China's leadership was divided over several questions, and they were important ones. For example, could the existing government (in the various forms it took in those years) check the foreigner and establish new institutions? Until faced with an irresistible revolt, officials, like Yuan Shih-k'ai, said yes. Revolutionaries, like Sun Yat-sen, generally said no, except during short periods of accommodation. A large middle group, including Liang Ch'i-ch'ao, vacillated, depending on the character of the government at the moment and their frustrations with it. Could reform best be achieved by a strong centralized government that reigned supreme over China as a whole? Or should power be decentralized, with there being large amounts of regional autonomy? Men of mandarin background generally supported centralization; revolutionaries and reformers were often divided on this issue. And, of course, there was always conflict, not just over how to bring about reform, but over who should do it.

Despite conflict, however, agreement on basic attitudes was extraordinarily profound. Virtually all politically active components of the elite were engaged in a search for new political forms with which to quench the spreading dissatisfaction with the present. The apparently high incidence of people transferring from one group to another or associating with more than one group at a time is a measure not only of uncertainty but of common assumptions. T'ang Shao-i, who was prime minister after the 1911 revolution, had been an official of the Manchus and Yuan Shih-k'ai's protégé but evolved during the revolution into an ally of Sun Yat-sen. There were many others who took similar routes. Meanwhile, the revolutionary movement lost men to the Ch'ing reform programs, to Liang Ch'i-ch'ao, and to Yuan Shih-k'ai. A prominent example was Liu Shih-p'ei, a leading anti-Manchu revolutionary, attracted to socialist and anarchist ideas, who in 1909 abandoned revolution, became an aide to a reformist Manchu governor-general, and in 1915 promoted Yuan's attempt to make himself emperor. Some were able to participate simultaneously in a variety of movements without diminution of their political seriousness. Wu Lu-chen, a military officer, served in different ways the court, the constitutional reformers, and the revolutionaries. Toward the beginning of his short career and at the end of it, he secretly participated in revolts against the Peking government (an abortive Yangtze valley rising in 1900 and the 1911 revolution). In between, he rose to the rank of general and divisional commander in recognition of his contributions to the dynasty's modern army. At the time of his assassination in November 1911, he was involved in a complicated conspiracy that included allies from all three categories. Even such exceedingly eminent and respectable people as Chang Chien, the scholarly industrialist, seemed able to straddle all groups, leaning toward one or another as events dictated.

Despite considerable and sometimes bloody conflict among the main contenders for leadership, there persisted, then, a commonality of outlook. The explanation for this lies, perhaps, in two large facts: common experience and common social ties.

The common experience that was so overwhelming for Chinese of this generation was the onslaught of imperialism. Western encroachment in one form or another on China was not new, but its intensity had increased dramatically in the last decade of the nineteenth century. Moreover, the ranks of imperialists had been joined by an ambitious and newly powerful neighbor, Japan. Though Japan was considered more a model and potential ally than a threat in the years immediately following the Sino-Japanese War, admiration turned to concern in the early years of the twentieth century. The new century opened, in fact, in the aftermath of the Boxer Rebellion, with troops of the major powers dictating a settlement to an apparently helpless China. The Boxer affair was further evidence of the West's superior force and a lesson in the futility of old-style, obscurantist antiforeignism. The legacy of the incident was the achievement of consensus among politicized Chinese that the main task was to develop sophisticated responses to the imperialist danger. Anti-imperialism as a broad, modern movement was born, and it was common property.

There is a touch of irony in its birth date, for, just as Chinese attitudes about imperialism reached a new level of understanding and concern, the more blatant forms of Western expansionism were about to pass their peak. Not only was a sort of equilibrium achieved in China (with Britain overseeing the balance), but outright conquest of foreign peoples was losing its glamour in consequence of the Boer War and American suppression of the Philippine insurrection. Nonetheless, there was realism in the new intensity of Chinese concern. Talk of partition was still common among Western diplomats in Peking. Even if few favored it, many anticipated it. There would surely have been another scramble for slices of the Chinese melon if somehow the fragile mechanisms for preventing complete colonialization had faltered. The Japanese in particular were increasingly difficult to restrain, and Japanese imperialism had by no means reached its high tide. In any case, it was part of the new sophistication about the foreign threat to view the growing economic position of the powers in China as at least as dangerous as the possibility of political partition.

The most vivid aspect of Western and Japanese imperialism in China in the first two decades of the twentieth century was its autonomous growth. It had struck roots in Chinese soil, as it were, and no longer needed special nourishment from London, Paris, Washington, St. Petersburg, Berlin, or Tokyo. During the 1911 revolution and in the first years of the republic, despite the lack of any actual conspiracy to extend foreign control, Chinese sovereignty was diminished in the handling of maritime customs funds, in the ownership of the major iron and steel plant in the country, in the control of the salt monopoly, and in the administration of justice in Shanghai. Foreign power seemed to be present everywhere and to fill all the vacuums left by internal disruption. For a Chinese to be obsessed with imperialism was not paranoiac.

The last five or six years of the nineteenth century, then, climaxed by the Boxer fiasco, had given to Chinese (and Manchu) a common experience of the apparently inexorable march of imperialism—an experience that broke down the last barriers to unanimity on the primary importance of this threat. The obscurantists, who helped destroy the 1898 reform movement, either were converted, fell silent, or were largely ignored. The empress dowager herself turned around to lead an official movement of radical institutional reform in an effort to stem the imperialist tide. As a Japanese diplomat in China reported to his government in 1904, "Nationalistic thought in connection with foreign rights has permeated the entire land of China, and all classes of people have been affected by the currents of the new thought."[1]

We may surmise that "all classes" referred to groups with which a

[1] Quoted in Akira Iriye, "Public Opinion and Foreign Policy: The Case of Late Ch'ing China," in *Approaches to Modern Chinese History*, Albert Feuerwerker *et al.*, eds. (Berkeley, Calif.: University of California Press, 1967), p. 229.

foreign consul was likely to have meaningful communications: officials of the government, the landed gentry, merchants, and students. Artisans and the small number of modern factory workers—and unemployed, urban aspirants to these categories—would for several years be drawn into the nationalist movement only peripherally, making almost no contribution of their own to the leadership. Peasants, even more remote from the movement, usually joined only when they had ceased to be peasants: They might come in touch with the new currents as laborers on railway projects or in the new industries; they might join the army and become exposed to surreptitious revolutionary propaganda; or, even more tenuously, they might participate through secret-society alliances with revolutionary organizations. It is possible that nationalist ideology penetrated the peasant village through such temporary coalitions, but the extent in time and place of that penetration seems to have been quite limited. A fortunate few, like Mao Tse-tung, acquired sufficient education to take part in modern movements as intellectuals, but their emergence as leaders occurred only during and after the May Fourth movement. By and large, the major political movements of the early twentieth century had limited social bases. It is this social homogeneity that is the second element behind the similarity of outlook.

Statements about Chinese social strata, not to mention self-conscious, politically awakened classes, in nineteenth- and twentieth-century China are at worst impressionistic, at best open to argument. Especially is this true of the period around the 1911 revolution, before the advent of sociological surveys but after great changes had begun in the traditional patterns of the late empire. Nevertheless, we cannot neglect this aspect of our subject and must proceed with hypotheses in the hope of stimulating further research and analysis.

Entrance into the elite—the small group at the top of both national and local political hierarchies—had become more fluid in the last half of the nineteenth century. More men who had not gone through the full discipline of the examination system were attaining high office and were reaping the corresponding rewards. A successful military career was increasingly endowed with the superior benefits of civil office. Men of landed or commercial wealth were purchasing status and official position in greater numbers than ever before. By the end of the century, wealth generated by merchant activity or even modern industry figured conspicuously in definitions of local leadership, especially as respectable gentry engaged publicly in such enterprises themselves.

Despite these developments, however, gentry (or literati) culture still predominated among the elite. Until 1900 an intensive classical education, acquired in the expectation of climbing the examination ladder, was, with few exceptions, an ordinary requirement for playing any considerable leadership role. As a result, an overwhelming proportion of mature political leaders in the first two decades of the twentieth century—whether official, reformist, or revolutionary—had imbibed gentry culture. Either they had been born to it, in families where close relatives were degree-holders or where there was a substantial scholarly tradition, or they were moving upward in the society themselves as candidates for the degrees that eventually qualified one for office under the emperor.

Around 1900 there appeared numerous breaks in the traditional pattern of advancement. Some men entered the new, Western-oriented schools and abandoned intensive classical studies. Some went abroad, with the same results. Some entered the military, out of patriotic as much as careerist motives. Although common among men who became revolutionaries, such breaks were not confined to them. Many official careers took the same turn. Nevertheless, all these men shared a common educational grounding in traditional classical studies undertaken before the break. More often than not, men undertaking these studies (as well as the few women striving for their emancipation through Western-style education) already had a social background quite removed from that of the peasant or laboring masses. If they did not, the acquisition of the education itself effected the removal.

There were exceptions. The most famous was Sun Yat-sen himself. He can be taken as representative of a new elite group whose status rested on the achievements of the overseas Chinese communities. Sun, though born and raised until age twelve in a village near Canton, was one of a number who at this time entered the Chinese political world with the support of their Chinese friends and relatives residing abroad. Sun combined overseas Chinese support with a foreign education and a highly persuasive personality to forge a revolutionary career. By no means all Chinese who entered politics via the overseas communities chose the revolutionary road, but, like Sun, unless they acquired a conventional Chinese education, they suffered from only partial acceptance by the more numerous literati elite. Throughout this period, in fact, Sun was something of an outsider in his own revolutionary movement. This was an advantage when it lifted him above factions and made him an obvious compromise candidate, but the shallowness of his support made it difficult for him to maintain his hold over any organization.

The result of the considerable social homogeneity of the newly nationalist elite was a lack of profound questioning of the existing social structure. Reformers, revolutionaries, and officials could agree about the need to reform social abuses that were not essential to the system as a whole and were particular objects of Western scorn (for example, opium smoking and footbinding), but they did not commonly direct their attention to the peasant mass or the urban poor except in a spirit of traditional paternalism. When revolutionaries wrote of social revolution, their emphasis was on *preventing* social distortions deriving from the operations of emerging capitalism rather than on overturning the existing structure, which was considered benign. In general, traditional political principles, supportive of the Confucian state and empire, were the conspicuous casualties of these years. Social issues were at most a muted and secondary theme, and this neglect was to prove costly.

Official Nationalism and Reform at the End of the Ch'ing

The most underestimated feature of the twentieth-century revolution in Chinese values and institutions is the impact of the official reform movement of the first decade. Because the government was opposed by nationalist revolutionaries, one is inclined to assume that the government was reactionary or passive, that it merely refurbished the inadequate reforms of the nineteenth century. On the contrary, official measures set in motion or gave a major impetus to much of what was to follow.

The reforms initiated by the imperial government in its last decade (1901–11) are to be distinguished from previous efforts by their remarkable encroachment upon the traditional political order. Before 1900, programs for "self-strengthening" and modernization were generally additions to an unchanging core of administration. Schools for teaching foreign languages and Western learning were established, but recruitment into the civil service continued to be dominated by the old examination system. New institutions, such as the Imperial Maritime Customs Service and the Tsungli Yamen, were tacked onto the existing administrative structure. They demanded room from older organs but did not replace them or even amalgamate with them. Most programs of industrialization (railroads, cotton mills, arsenals, the telegraph, and so forth) were segregated from the continuing traditional responsibilities of government. They were often supported from new and separate sources of funds. There was, so to speak, a small modernizing enclave, walled off from the rest of government activities like the carrier of some dread and contagious disease. After 1900, the wall was taken down.[2]

The changes in educational institutions are a model of the way in which reforms after 1900 cleared the ground and prepared for the reconstruction of politics on new bases. They illustrate the motives for the

---

[2] This theme has been argued and documented in detail in Esther Morrison, "The Modernization of the Confucian Bureaucracy: An Historical Study of Public Administration" (Ph.D. diss., Radcliffe College, 1959).

reforms, the effects on the government and on the society, and the resulting changes in the relationship between government and people.

Beginning in 1901, the examination system was dismantled in a series
of rapid moves. It was ruled that the selection of the official elite was to
be accomplished through a comprehensive system of new schools (which
was still being established when the old examinations ended in 1905) and
through study abroad (which was soon flourishing). The effect was revolutionary—but not in the sense that a social class was forthwith dispos-
sessed, for the same families that had been successful in producing
degree-earning sons could now adapt their training to the new requirements. And this they did in large numbers. There was a great spurt in
the creation of modern schools on local as well as central initiative (often
using Buddhist temples or existing traditional schools as a short cut to getting started), and thousands went abroad for study, especially to Japan.

The real revolution accompanying the abolition of the examination
system was in the realm of political attitudes and values. It was an abandonment of the centuries-old belief that only years spent with the Confucian classics truly qualified one for political leadership. It was a blow
against government by virtue acquired from Confucian discipline. The
study of classics was not abandoned, but it was consciously diluted. The
government was looking now for special skills and knowledge derived
from the West, and the reason was clear: Only a people endowed with
such talents could handle the imperialist threat. The culturally refined
literatus who had dominated for a millennium was recognized as anachronistic. Now children must learn mathematics, geography, science, and
above all nationalism. The textbooks published between 1903 and 1906
for the new school system stressed China's territorial losses in the nineteenth century, the unequal treaties, the free wanderings of missionaries
in the interior, the humiliation of the Boxer affair, the importance of racial
conflict and competition, and the virtue of military valor.[3] By 1909 the
new schools had over a million and a half students, all presumably being
nurtured on at least some portion of this heady diet. It was a far cry from
years spent with Chu Hsi's commentaries.

Of course, not all these students in the new schools could become officials. An auxiliary intention of the schools was to achieve "the dissemination of knowledge among the people . . . so that all may receive a universal education. . . ."[4] Although not opposed to the education of any
loyal subject, and kindly disposed toward private or local educational

[3] Cyrus Peake, *Nationalism and Education in Modern China* (New York: Columbia
University Press, 1932), pp. 180–81, 190–91.

[4] Quoted in Wolfgang Franke, *The Reform and Abolition of the Traditional Chinese Examination System* (Cambridge, Mass.: Harvard University Press, 1960), pp.
69–70.

programs, the imperial government of the past had not counted among its responsibilities that of providing formal schooling for the whole population. The government in Peking now took on this task, albeit without impressive statistical success for several decades. Gains were made, but probably more in the diversion of young men (and some women) from classical education into the modern curriculum than in a marked absolute increase in literacy.

What mattered was that the government was training specialists in modern knowledge and was invoking patriotic sentiment in an effort to rally the population to meet the external threat. In this case, internal reform and foreign problems were inextricably intertwined—or, rather, the reform found its origin and purpose in nationalistic concerns. Furthermore, the new commitment to universal popular education in this context implied new relations between government and people. If everyone should be educated, not just in Confucian homilies but in nationalism and the tools for the defense of the motherland, then by implication the population was invited to participate in the nation's politics. The government was seeking support, but in the process it opened the way for private groups to undertake political roles beyond the merely local.

Another consequence of the educational reforms at the end of the Ch'ing was a degree of social change. The immediate effect was not a social revolution, and certainly nothing could have been farther from the intent of the official reformers. But, for all the continuity of the gentry class in the early twentieth century, there was a loosening of requirements for entry into the elite. This change was too gradual for there to be any dramatic reflection of it before the May Fourth movement, but certainly the special advantages of a scholarly, gentry family background were diminished as the definition of educational achievement shifted. Government scholarships accentuated this shift. Hence, a facility in Japanese acquired in Tokyo at Chinese government expense was at least as useful as a talent for elegant imitation of classical essay styles. The difficulty of reaching the point where one might qualify for the limited number of government scholarships still operated to exclude from the elite all but the most exceptional offspring of the manual laborer or peasant. But there was greater opportunity for those from the lower reaches of the gentry or from merchant families. As in the Meiji Restoration in Japan, the leadership ranks were expanded (in that case, to samurai of relatively low status within their class) without immediate change in the dominance of the traditionally elite group. Gentry culture continued in China, but both its content and the social range of its leading participants were somewhat altered.

The pattern of effects arising from the educational reforms was largely repeated in the case of some of the other programs of the late Ch'ing.

One of the most important was the creation of a "New Army," based on Western and Japanese styles of military organization as they had developed in the nineteenth century. Experiments had been made with Western military technology ever since the Taiping Rebellion, but it was not until the Sino-Japanese War that the first fully Western-style troops were trained. These new troops amounted to only a few thousand before the Boxer affair, but after 1900 greater effort was put into the attempt to create an army that could meet a Western or Japanese invasion on its own terms. Yuan Shih-k'ai was prominent in the development of the first modern troops, and national troops trained in or near the capital area were largely in his charge until 1906 (after which he gradually lost control and was in fact dismissed from all offices in January 1909, not to return until November 1911). Meanwhile, a program initiated in 1904 to develop New Army brigades in all provinces, added to the few existing provincially based modern troops, soon resulted in a more complex arrangement than a military establishment dominated by Yuan Shih-k'ai.[5]

Like the educational reforms, the creation of the New Army reflected a new ranking of priorities. The older military organization, inherited from the developments of the mid-nineteenth century, was adequate for dealing with internal disturbances. The effort and expense put into building a truly modern army could be justified only in terms of defense against external enemies. As the citizens of most countries have discovered at one time or another, a military establishment designed for national defense can easily be adapted for use against the population it is supposed to protect, and this happened in China. But the stress in the late Ch'ing was on the nationalistic purposes of the New Army, and the program was not abandoned even as evidence mounted that the new troops were becoming a rebellious hazard to the dynasty.

The popular response to the military reforms contained in turn a degree of nationalism. Although there is probably no way to arrive at statistically significant figures, one cannot help but be struck by the number of New Army officers who convincingly claimed nationalistic motivation for joining. Among those entering military service before 1895, there seems always to have been a background of either military tradition in the family, poverty, or failure at the civil-service examinations. After 1900, young men often interrupted otherwise promising civilian careers to seek

---

[5] The goal had been to form 36 modern divisions by 1912. When revolution broke out in 1911, this goal had not been reached, but there were perhaps 200,000 New Army troops. Expressed in units, this was 14 divisions and 20 brigades, not necessarily at full strength. This total amounted to something approaching one-third of all effective troops at the time. These estimates are derived from a range of figures in Ralph L. Powell, *The Rise of Chinese Military Power, 1895–1912* (Princeton, N.J.: Princeton University Press, 1955), pp. 288–89, 298.

entry into the Westernized military units. Military drills became part of the curriculum even at ordinary civilian schools, and in 1903 volunteer brigades were formed among nonmilitary Chinese students in both Tokyo and Shanghai as a contribution to government resistance against the Russians in Manchuria. The government, of course, was not universally pleased with all forms of this enthusiasm for military service, and it sought to control the entry of Chinese into military schools in Japan as it did at home. Nevertheless, in this environment of unprecedented approbation for military service, the New Army acquired numbers of nationalistically motivated officers. These officers, in turn, were in a position to communicate their nationalism to the ordinary soldier, who, because of the high standards of recruitment in the New Army, was more likely than in past armies to be literate. The ideological ferment was considerable.

With respect to the level of centralized power, the New Army was an ambiguous institution. Its earlier history followed in part the regional character of the armies of Tseng Kuo-fan, Li Hung-chang, and Tso Tsung-t'ang. As the financing and control of the important early divisions were assumed by the central government, the national character of the new troops became more explicit. But, in the absence of a truly centralized fiscal system, the expansion contemplated could not be borne by Peking's coffers alone. Provinces were ordered to proceed with establishing modern units locally—on central models but at local expense. There were efforts to bind these units into a national system, through placing representatives of the Ministry of War on provincial New Army staffs and through national conferences of divisional commanders. But the real bond was common nationalist purposes, and Peking's control was only as strong as the conviction of New Army members that Peking was adequately pursuing these purposes or allowing others to pursue them. It was the drastic weakening of this conviction that caused the mass defection of provincial New Army units in 1911. The modernized army, then, was an expression of central initiative but an imperfect instrument for central control.

Like the educational reforms, the New Army produced social change without social upheaval. It contributed to a widening of the social background of the elite, giving lower elements of the gentry another channel for entry into areas of leadership. (This channel was less original, however, than the educational one, since the military route to political position had already been established via the regional armies of the nineteenth century.) More important, as nationalist aspirations spread, a career in the New Army, which expressed these aspirations, acquired a prestige all its own and not merely as a steppingstone to high civil posts. The government, unofficial reformers, and revolutionaries all joined in extolling military service to the country. With the added stimulus of excellent pay, the new military could attract the able and the socially exalted (sons of Manchu princes and Chinese governors-general) into its officer corps. The gentry were still in charge, but in yet another way their values were undergoing change.

This brief schematic presentation of two late Ch'ing reform programs has passed over the difficulties and struggles, as well as some of the limitations, encountered in their implementation. There was much accomplished, but it was not achieved smoothly. The efforts in this period at judicial reforms illustrate the complexities facing the reformers.

It is hard to imagine anything more resistant to radical institutional change than a society's legal structure, for it touches intimately upon formal ethics, more subtle moral feelings, and inherited social relationships. In Meiji Japan, no reform was more difficult to effect than adoption and adaptation of Western styles of judicial codes and procedures. Parts of the new code were not enacted until 1898, and even then the resulting legal structure was far from integrated with Japanese society at large. That is to say, social behavior only gradually approached conformity with the norms assumed by the Western-style codes.[6]

The initial impetus for judicial reform in China, as in Japan, came not from a sense of the inadequacy of existing legal processes but rather as a technique for abolishing foreign extraterritoriality. Hope that this might be accomplished was stimulated by Britain's promise in 1902 that it was prepared to forego the legal immunity of her subjects when it was "satisfied that the state of the Chinese laws, the arrangements for their administration and other considerations warrant her in so doing." Shen Chia-pen, the chief architect of Chinese legal modernization, memorialized in 1904 that, instead of "clinging to conservative regulations," which provided the foreigner with excuses for rejecting obedience to the law of the land, China should adopt the law of Western countries in order to obtain "complete control of our territory."[7] There may have been some who saw intrinsic merit in reform of the laws and their application, but no major reform would have occurred had that been the only reason. Anti-imperialist nationalism was again at the root of it all.

As a first step, existing legal practice was touched up according to contemporary Western sensitivities without changing its fundamentals, and in 1910 a moderately revised traditional code was enacted. For example, all corporal punishments were abolished (in theory, with some effect on practice). The collective responsibility of the family in criminal matters was ended. All provisions of criminal law discriminating between

[6] Dan Fenno Henderson, "Law and Political Modernization in Japan," in *Political Development in Modern Japan,* Robert E. Ward, ed. (Princeton, N.J.: Princeton University Press, 1968), pp. 434–37.

[7] Quoted in Marinus Johan Meijer, *The Introduction of Modern Criminal Law in China* (Jakarta, Indonesia: De Unie, 1950), p. 13.

Manchu and Chinese were eliminated in 1908, and in 1909 slavery (not a major institution) was legally abolished. Meanwhile, the ground was being laid for more basic borrowings from the contemporary West, since it was believed that the chanceries of Europe and their representatives in China would be satisfied with nothing less. A law school was established in Peking in 1905. A new system of courts, for the first time separated at the lower levels from administrative offices, was decreed in 1907. There was a new Ministry of Justice in Peking replacing the Board of Punishments. And a thoroughly new criminal code was drafted, discussed, revised, and imperially approved before the revolution.

The cultural distance between the old code and the new, as it was originally drafted, was immense. Behind the older conception of law lay the theory of a necessary balance in the natural order—an order that was moral and in which human society was an integral element. Any heinous moral breach endangered society as a whole, and it was urgent that the balance be redressed. This ancient idea was reflected in late imperial law by the effort to design punishments meticulously proportional to the moral violation involved in the crime. The legal codes, therefore, reflected the intricacies of the moral and social systems. This could be done only by incredibly detailed penal prescriptions. When the variety of experience and the ingenuity of turpitude outran the range of the code, the official sitting in judgment would resort to applications of punishments prescribed for some other, but analogous, offense. And there was an open-ended provision for punishment of any wrongdoings not otherwise covered in the code—presumably for the judge-administrator whose powers of analogical reasoning were feeble.

Shen Chia-pen, the reformer, without spelling out his premises, chose instead to regard the law as a set of rules determined by the state (rather than nature) whose purpose was to keep order and deter by punishment acts contrary to minimum social standards. Therefore, the new code was as comprehensive as the old but without the same detail. It denied a legal basis to the mitigation of punishment on the grounds of the superior position of the offender. It began with the premise of the equal position before criminal law of husband and wife. Disobedience to parents was no longer a punishable offense. Immoral behavior was not in itself sufficient grounds for punishment. And it was explicitly stated that an act not specified in the laws and ordinances could not constitute a crime. The direction of Shen Chia-pen's draft penal code—the product of imperially appointed commissions—obviously conflicted with traditional social and family morality. These official efforts are a generally neglected background to the attacks by intellectuals on the oppressiveness of the Chinese family—attacks that began before the 1911 revolution and reached a peak in the May Fourth movement.

The adverse reaction to these unfamiliar ideas was considerable when the new code was presented for discussion in 1907. Perhaps the surprising fact—and an indication of the disposition within the government to accept radical change—was the mere survival of the code through the general official scrutiny it underwent. The attack was many-sided. It was observed that the proposed laws ignored the *li*, the Confucian prescriptions for proper behavior. The critics unanimously deprecated the granting of a significant degree of equality in family relationships so that the central relationship in the social structure, that of father and son, was undermined. The new code, it was charged, was antifamily. Nor did it uphold the balance between crime and punishment, since, with the abolition of varieties of capital punishment, the retribution for assassinating one's sovereign was the same as that for murdering a commoner. And there was a telling practical criticism: Despite British promises, the promulgation of Western-style legal codes was not likely to achieve its objective of the abolition of foreign extraterritorial privileges. The hope was childish, said one censor, since the only path to recovery of rights was military strengthening.

Shen Chia-pen had to retreat before these protests, which came both from the provinces and from the officials of the ministries of education and justice themselves. He had not, of course, written laws *prohibiting* behavior according to traditional lights. He had only neglected to give particular force in penal law to the operation of filial piety or of deference to one's senior relatives. In a revised draft Shen made a number of minor concessions to these old moral distinctions. And, "lest [the people] might think that the old standards should be rejected," the Ministry of Justice added five "Provisional Regulations," which revived gradations of punishment according to one's status relationship to the victim.[8] In this form, the new criminal code was formally published in early 1911 to allow study and further discussion before its scheduled enactment in 1913.

The defeat was not total. Although efforts to produce an acceptable Western-based *civil* code proved abortive until the 1930's, Shen and his fellow reformers had not compromised everything in the revisions of their draft criminal code (for example, analogical sentencing remained excluded). And, when the revolution came, the new criminal code suddenly became law. It was not substantially revised until 1928.

The resulting court system and its codes represented not a vital part of the society but only a potentiality, operating at the fringes. Acceptance never came in China. As was the case with so many other reforms, the inadequate fiscal structure starved the system of funds, and the network of courts reaching down to the districts was not completed. There also

[8] Marinus Johan Meijer, *The Introduction of Modern Criminal Law in China*, pp. 110–11.

was popular resistance. The new courts soon gained a reputation for the same corruption that had burdened the old administrative channels in handling legal cases at the local level. It was, after all, a charade for the sake of inveigling the foreigners into accepting Chinese legal protection. Without constant and firm government backing, there seemed little reason for the ordinary Chinese to take the new system seriously. And the foreigners, accustomed to their old privileges and insistent upon them, were not taking the bait. In sum, the legal reforms were an impressive intellectual achievement and a sign of movement, but they failed utterly to change the norms of Chinese life. The gradual shift of social attitudes toward correspondence with the assumptions of a modernized law, as occurred in twentieth-century Japan, was not repeated in China.

The contrast between the general enthusiasm for the military and educational reforms and the hostility or indifference to legal reform is instructive. In each case the program was inspired by large national purposes, but the manner in which it was related to these purposes was crucial. The New Army seemed to stand heroically on the breastwork and, moreover, offered remunerative and politically promising careers to many. The new schools and the expanded educational opportunities abroad were means of studying the fundamental questions about China's failure and the secrets of Western and Japanese successes. And they were clearly avenues to a commanding position in the new order that was emerging. The judicial reforms could stand only in indirect relation to a national goal (they were not the struggle itself but merely a precondition to a struggle that would come later, on terms determined by other developments). They offered no broad political rewards to their advocates, and they seemed curiously antinational in their implied criticism of the common moral perspectives of virtually all Chinese. Very few people connected China's political problems with the hierarchical rigidities of family life. People were ready, even anxious, to dispense with the political expressions of the Confucian ideology (for example, the rapid extinction of the Board of Rites), since politics had so obviously failed; but there was not the same persuasive evidence that Confucian morality in the family was similarly culpable.

The Revolution of 1911

It is often said that the Manchu monarchy dug its own grave with the reform movement of the first decade of the century. It could not move fast enough to satisfy expectations, but the faster it moved, the more did revolutionaries thrive in the interstices of the reform programs. Certainly there was danger in a ruling ethnic minority encouraging the development of nationalist sentiment. The fact that it did so at all (and there were many reluctant moments) is perhaps best explained by the thorough integration of Chinese and Manchu at the top of the bureaucracy and by the compelling nature of the call to defend China.

The monarchy did not exactly fall of its own weight, even if the final abdication in February 1912 was extraordinarily unresisting. The Ch'ing dynasty was toppled by the intersection of two movements: a swelling gentry surge for participation in politics and the emergence of a body of revolutionaries who raised the issue of Manchu legitimacy and kept it raised.

The politicization of the gentry is perhaps the outstanding feature of the early twentieth century. The process began before 1900, but it cannot be said to have constituted a movement much before that date. The gentry as individuals had always been potential participants in politics as officials: they were the pool from which the imperial government drew its small bureaucracy. But, as Frederic Wakeman points out (see Chapter 1, pp. 13–15), in the traditional system the gentry did not constitute a corporate body, organizing itself politically outside the bureaucracy. There was no basis for conscious class activity or solidarity. Though they were leaders locally, the gentry engaged in empire-wide or even regional issues only by proxy, through the civil service, whose representative character was compromised by ideological and functional commitments to the interests of the throne. In the two decades before the May Fourth movement, all this was to change.

Many events conspired to stimulate gentry self-consciousness and political interest. In the background were the challenges to their social status presented first by the massive Taiping Rebellion and then by the spreading Western missionary establishment. As the largest portion of the literate population, the gentry were well informed about foreign imperialist encroachments and likely to be sensitive to Peking's failures to counter them. They were the class most exposed to the new ideology of nationalism, brought to them by the translations of Yen Fu and the prolific pamphleteering of Liang Ch'i-ch'ao, as well as by hosts of secondary versions in the burgeoning Chinese press. At this stage, it is already difficult to separate cause from effect, since the pamphlets and the newspapers were themselves responses to new gentry interests. Instead of trying to suppress these interests, the Ch'ing government tried to conscript the new movement where it was not openly seditious, and in the process encouraged it. The new schools, which the gentry took to enthusiastically, themselves augmented nationalist fervor through the curriculum. National economic rights were at stake in the arrangements to build railways, so the gentry (and their merchant allies) undertook in some provinces to construct the lines using local Chinese money and retaining Chinese control. In this they received considerable official cooperation.

The climax of the politicization of the gentry occurred in the development of elected-representative institutions. Gradually, from 1904 to a peak in 1913, a network of representative bodies chosen through a limited franchise blossomed at the town, district, provincial, and national levels. Even though the franchise was eventually broadened to a point where other elements, chiefly lesser merchants, could participate, gentry interest fostered the growth of the system, and the gentry dominated its activities. The system was a vehicle for the mobilization of gentry self-consciousness and concern about its interests. And the system was also an instrument for the expression of these interests to the government. It was characteristic of the time that private bodies (guilds, chambers of commerce, educational associations, and so forth) addressed directly, with letters and telegrams, the highest government organs.[9] The representative bodies institutionalized and systematically exploited this new openness to public opinion, and the bureaucrats' virtual monopoly on political communication with the throne was broken. In yet another way, the relationship between government and people was revised.[10]

Government and gentry constructed this system together. Each had its own reasons, but these reasons overlapped sufficiently to produce initial cooperation. An experiment with gentry community organization, conducted in Shansi by the imperial governor in 1904, was followed by suggestions to introduce elements of Western-style local self-government. In 1905 a pilot project of this sort was inaugurated in Chihli under Governor-General Yuan Shih-k'ai. Meanwhile, imperially appointed constitutional commissions gave attention to the organization of national representative government and studied foreign models on trips abroad. In 1908 a grand plan for the gradual adoption of constitutional government was announced. Provincial assemblies were formed in 1909, and in 1910 a partially elected consultative assembly gathered in Peking. The government wished to secure greater support from the people (that is, the unofficial local elite) by allowing them direct participation in the political process. The gentry responded favorably, since it could reasonably hope that the support would be used for nationalist purposes and since it could use the new institutions to expand its own power.

Of course gentry and government interests were not identical. The

[9] This point is made in Akira Iriye, "Public Opinion and Foreign Policy," p. 223.

[10] This aspect of the meaning of the elected assemblies has been explored by John Fincher, "Political Provincialism and the National Revolution," in *China in Revolution: The First Phase, 1900–1913,* Mary Clabaugh Wright, ed. (New Haven, Conn.: Yale University Press, 1968), pp. 185–226.

empire's stability had rested for centuries on a balanced tension between the satisfaction of gentry interests, to gain local acquiescence to central rule, and the restraint of these interests, out of concern for a larger social and political unity that served the dynasty. The question posed by the opening wedge granted representative government at the end of the Ch'ing was whether the centripetal force of patriotic support of authority through participation could contain the centrifugal force of greater opportunity to pursue particular local and class interests. In the end it could not, in large part because the central government could not produce satisfactory results in stemming Western imperialism. The price of patriotic support was achievement in nationalist terms by the government —this was true both before and after the 1911 revolution. When achievement could not be demonstrated (indeed, there was much that suggested further deterioration, both in the last years of the Ch'ing and in the early republic), the energies mobilized through the representative system turned against the government. At that point, nationalistic sentiment and particularistic self-interest among the gentry were powerfully combined.

There was no unified national organization of gentry. Liang Ch'i-ch'ao could not claim sole leadership of the gentry movement, although he was perhaps the main ideologue in its nationalistic aspects and was the organizational center of one important faction. One can nevertheless take his attitude toward the Manchu monarchy as emblematic of a new gentry attitude toward the state. In polemical debates with republican revolutionaries, Liang defended the continuation of the monarchy (even though he was personally exiled from it). But his support of the monarchy had nothing to do with the traditional Confucian and cosmological notions that had been the ideology of empire. (Indeed, the court's realization that these traditional supports were no longer firm after 1900, and that in any case even greater support was needed for the special tasks of reform, led to the search for new sorts of legitimacy in constitutional programs.) Liang's monarchism was pragmatic, not Confucian, based on modern needs, not ancient world views. Monarchy was useful, he felt, in preserving the unity and order that were the necessary accompaniment of thorough reform. From a loyalist viewpoint, however, the difficulty with the pragmatic approach to the Ch'ing emperor was that it was easy to abandon him once one was convinced that he was no longer useful. The apparent nonchalance with which many thousands of gentry and officials deserted the monarchy in 1911 and 1912 can be partly explained by the general atrophy of traditional commitments and the spread of political pragmatism of the Liang Ch'i-ch'ao strain. In any case, almost all the gentry-dominated provincial assemblies readily joined the revolution, once it had started, and embraced republicanism. Liang himself took several months to give up hope in the possible continuing usefulness of the Manchu monarch. But once he abandoned monarchy he did so permanently and refused to follow either Yuan Shih-k'ai or his teacher K'ang Yu-wei in subsequent monarchical efforts.

Despite the contribution from the constitutionalist gentry, it took revolutionaries to launch the revolution. Of all the subjects touched upon in this essay, none has received a fraction of the attention given the revolutionary movement. The volume of study has not, however, led to a consensus about the nature of the movement. Much recent opinion is disposed to disparage the importance or effectiveness of the revolutionaries. One reason for these unfavorable interpretations is that, with the exception of the 1911 revolution itself and perhaps the immediate aftermath, the decades before the May Fourth movement witnessed a series of military and political failures on the part of the revolutionary leadership. But more important, investigation of their programs and pronouncements leaves the nagging doubt that they themselves were not sure of their direction and had discovered no method of relating to Chinese society and building a broad base of support in the population. There were dramatic issues aplenty, and the revolutionary societies had important functions as catalytic agents. But, after the rhetoric was pared off, it was not clear what the revolutionary party offered that differed significantly from other nationalist programs of the time—that is, except for one issue, anti-Manchuism, which didn't survive the revolution.

How, then, did one become an anti-Manchu revolutionary in the years before the 1911 revolution? A few were disposed to revolution by a family tradition of anti-Manchuism, pockets of which had survived the centuries of Manchu rule and had been stimulated by the Taiping and other risings in the mid-nineteenth century. At the end of the century, it was natural that among the better educated the addition of nationalism would make such a tradition combustible. Then there were others who were truly alienated from imperial China and for whom the Manchus and the queue were an embarrassment. In particular, Chinese overseas were likely to look favorably on any radical reform in their homeland so that they could stand more confidently proud in their adopted countries and, more than incidentally, hope for greater protection from the government in Peking. Sun Yat-sen's early advocacy of an anti-Manchu republican revolution seems to have stemmed from a combination of these two influences.

Numerically much more important than traditional anti-Manchuism or cultural deracination in producing revolutionary activists was the experience of new styles of education in the first years of the twentieth century. A special fervor characterized the launching of Western educational patterns in the aftermath of the Boxer Rebellion (or, more significantly, of its brutal suppression by Western troops). Those who rushed to

Tokyo and Shanghai for the new schooling, even before it was clear that the government would favor the graduates, were presumably self-selected for the intensity of their nationalism. Tokyo and Shanghai, plus a few lesser centers, became incubators of radical politics. Until things settled down after 1905, the schools were frequently in turmoil over intramural issues—an index of the exposed emotions of the students.

One event in particular induced large numbers of students (of various ages) to take a revolutionary position. In the spring of 1903, Russian troops, present in Manchuria since the Boxer affair, were scheduled by agreement to evacuate the area. The news broke in April that instead of withdrawing, the Russians were pressing additional demands on Peking. The Russians were notorious for their indiscriminate slaughter of Chinese during the suppression of the Boxers, and this new development brought to a boil the heated nationalism of Chinese students and their like-minded elders in Tokyo and Shanghai. In both cities, volunteer brigades were organized in a gesture of extreme defiance of Russian treachery. Some actual drilling was done, and the volunteers were offered to the Peking government to assist its resistance against the Russians. The offer was rejected, and Peking distrustfully moved to dissolve the "student army." This spurning of a passionate concern to "save the country" (chiu-kuo) created at once a dedicated body of anti-Manchu revolutionaries. As more students came into the resulting radical atmosphere, especially in Tokyo, more revolutionaries were made. When they returned home, they spread the message across the country. This critical incident illustrates the nationalistic impetus behind the main current of the revolutionary movement. The Manchu government had to be overthrown, not so much for what it had done but for what it had not done—that is, led the people in a militant struggle of national salvation.

Once committed to violent tactics for solving the immediate political problem, the young revolutionary was likely to consider a whole range of Western radical thought. Socialism and anarchism, Marx and Kropotkin, "equal land rights" and the single tax, female suffrage and individual emancipation from family authoritarianism—these and more were discussed in revolutionary journals. But the discussions failed to produce any substantial social analysis of the Chinese scene—or even a consistent concern for existing social inequities. Occasionally an individual showed a penetrating understanding of a particular social problem (T'ao Ch'eng-chang on the need to rid the countryside of landlordism, Chu Chih-hsin on the heavy burdens of land rent as compared with land taxes, Tai Chi-t'ao on the hardship of peasant life). And during the great proliferation of political groups in the first year of the republic, a socialist party (which refrained from actual political struggle) acquired an estimated two hundred thousand members under a program that included strictures on the system of inheritance.[11] In general, however, despite a vague sympathy for the disadvantaged and an interest in tactical alliances with the socially disreputable secret societies, the revolutionaries were optimistic that the social order was not basically flawed. They spoke of social revolution, but they meant that the social distortions consequent to industrialism in the West should not be repeated in China. They saw no bar to the unity of all Chinese in a movement of revolutionary nationalism.

There was, after all, no great social divide between the revolutionaries and the leaders of either the gentry constitutional movement or the government. With few exceptions, they were all gentry in a largely preindustrial society. This fact facilitated the cooperation that occurred everywhere in 1911 between revolutionaries and the provincial assemblies. And it eased the sacrifice involved in turning the presidency of the republic over to Yuan Shih-k'ai, who had engineered the abdication. There were differences of style, temperament, tactics, and ideas among these groups, but the differences were not substantial enough to prevent periodic collaboration. The overthrow of the Manchu dynasty was itself the product of cooperation among all three groups.

The Early Republic

The revolution came and went, but the political stage still featured almost the same cast of characters. Most Manchus had retired to the wings, and a number of Chinese officials were too loyal to the Manchu emperor to play a role in the republic. But the reforming governor-general Yuan Shih-k'ai was again center stage, this time as the reforming president. Sun Yat-sen, briefly director of railway planning, had reverted by the summer of 1913 to his guise as a leader of revolution, although his following had thinned considerably. The various reforming constitutionalists and leaders of the gentry movement of the late Ch'ing generally found positions in either the national or the provincial governments of the republic—as did many revolutionaries until 1913. Large numbers of reforming officials in the old regime were now reforming officials in the new one.

It was not just the players that were holdovers; the script itself seemed to have changed only slightly. The most urgent theme remained the defense of national integrity. As had been predicted before 1911 by reformist opponents of Sun Yat-sen, the revolution produced setbacks—in increased foreign influence on domestic institutions and in the loss of territory (Outer Mongolia and Tibet) considered to belong to China. Al-

---

[11] Martin Bernal, "The Tzu-yu Tang and Tai Chi-t'ao, 1912–13," *Modern Asian Studies*, Vol. 1, Part 2 (April 1967), p. 147, and "Chinese Socialism to 1913" (Ph.D. diss., University of Cambridge, 1966), pp. 222–24, 314, 319, 330.

though World War I relieved the pressure from the European powers, it also made Japan feel freer to work its will. The result was the Twenty-One Demands. At worst, it appeared that a Chinese government was *inferior* to a Manchu one in protecting Chinese interests; at best, it appeared that the new government could not check the inherited trend of deterioration.

Continuity also marked a considerable portion of the reform programs. More new schools were established, and the student population grew. The new judiciary was further expanded and consolidated (though it was still superficial with respect to the country as a whole). A campaign to eradicate the domestic production of opium (simultaneous with negotiation of an international agreement to taper off opium imports) had been launched in 1906. Disruption during the revolution set back the campaign's splendid achievements in the last years of the Ch'ing, but soon the program was revived with its former vigor and with the full participation of most provincial governments. By the last year of Yuan's presidency, domestic production had been sufficiently reduced so that the terms of the international agreement were considered fulfilled, and legal opium importation ceased.

The weaknesses of the late Ch'ing reform programs were also perpetuated, sometimes in exaggerated form. During the last two years of the Ch'ing, an attempt had been made to lay the groundwork for a fiscal overhaul—through a national budget, a clarification of tax sources and channels for the flow of funds, and an increase in central control over the local collection and dispensing of tax monies. Once Yuan's presidency had acquired some administrative control over the whole country (that is, after the summer of 1913), attention turned again to these matters. But, as in the Ch'ing, the results were mixed and fiscal improvement paltry compared to the reforming ambitions of the regime. Afflicted with the temporary breakdown of the revenue flow from the provinces to Peking during and directly after the revolution, and with the drying up of foreign financial markets upon the advent of World War I, the Peking government under Yuan was unable even to maintain the momentum of the Ch'ing reform programs. Although the commitment to eventual universal mass education remained, some schools closed or were thrown totally onto local resources even as new ones opened up. The new and still unpopular court system underwent retrenchment in 1914 before it had been completed. The great spurt of railway construction during the late Ch'ing subsided. The search for a political system that could mobilize the people and their resources behind an effective reform program still eluded the men who sat in council in Peking.

The search had not become noticeably easier, even with the establishment of a new form of government. The departure of the Manchus removed the onus of non-Chinese contamination in an increasingly nationalistic atmosphere. However, the Manchus also took with them the emperorship, together with the accumulated habits of deference that it evoked. This traditional authority had not been enough in the last years of the Ch'ing, and the government had attempted to reinforce it with more modern props (a constitution, elected assemblies, patriotism). But in a transitional environment the Manchu regime could still draw on the awe shown the dragon throne. Yuan Shih-k'ai could not—as he learned when he tried in 1915 and 1916. With the 1911 revolution, China had decisively entered the era of popular sovereignty, where legitimacy rests on claims to embody popular will (whether expressed in elections, manipulated plebiscites, or an assertion of preestablished harmony between government and people). Even as Yuan tried to borrow the magic of an imperial tradition of two millennia, he recognized the irreversible change in the nature of political legitimacy: He had himself *elected* as monarch. But the attempt to straddle two ages left Yuan stranded between the two. By the end he had alienated almost everyone.

Yuan had other troubles. Provincial separatism and local particularism had been dramatically unleashed in the 1911 revolution. An interest in provincial autonomy had grown astonishingly since the 1890's and was, ironically, reinforced by and even integrated with nationalist sentiments. Provinces, it was felt by many, could best run themselves and in so doing could better contribute to national strengthening and salvation. The formal structure of the 1911 revolution was the successive declarations of provincial independence by the revolutionary provinces. Beyond that, localism within the province expressed itself in an indifference to higher authority and a resistance by the local elite to paying taxes to anyone. This was the opportunity for gentry class consciousness, assisted into being by the network of representative assemblies established in the late Ch'ing, to turn itself into gentry power. In large parts of China, the wraps were off, and local notables moved to take all authority, and its economic benefits, into their own hands. Peasant resistance to gentry encroachment, though not well documented, certainly occurred. Local gentry-dominated councils—part of the late Ch'ing electoral system—were direct objects of peasant demonstrations before and after the revolution. Unrest was at this stage muted, but this was not the last round.[12]

For the central government, committed to ambitious reform schemes and measured in the public mind by them, the situation presented a profound challenge. In 1912, Yuan Shih-k'ai presided over only the loosest sort of federation. He lacked the power to appoint officials of any impor-

[12] For an extended discussion of the phenomenon of gentry seizure of local power, see Chūzō Ichiko, "The Role of the Gentry: An Hypothesis," in *China in Revolution: The First Phase, 1900–1913*, Mary Clabaugh Wright, ed., pp. 297–313.

tance in most provinces, and he could not compel financial contributions to the central government. Resentment at his efforts to reassert Peking's authority was compounded by the assassination of a revolutionary leader (Sung Chiao-jen), for which Yuan seemed responsible, and by his cavalier treatment of the newly elected national assembly in concluding a foreign loan without its approval. The resulting conflict was the so-called Second Revolution, in the summer of 1913. His complete victory over this rising in the lower Yangtze region, which was led by associates of Sun Yat-sen and set off sympathetic movements in Kwangtung and Szechwan, provided Yuan for the first time with real authority over most of the country. He proceeded to use that authority in a program of centralization along the lines of what had been planned by the late Ch'ing government. Finances at the local level were to be brought more directly under Peking's control. A national currency was to be established. Representatives of the several ministries would operate at the provincial level and below as agents of the central government rather than as aides to provincial governors. The military structure was to be reorganized to clarify the separation of civil and military authority and to eliminate the political independence of regional military leaders.

Yuan struck also at the citadels of gentry power—the various elected assemblies, national, provincial, and local. Just as his attack on provincial autonomy was intertwined with (but not exclusively defined by) his conflict with Sun Yat-sen's associates, so too his dismantling of the representative assemblies was in part a blow at Sun Yat-sen's party, the Kuomintang, which had done well with the gentry electorate. (The Kuomintang in the early republic was a broad alliance of factions in which Sun Yat-sen loyalists and other radicals proved to be only a minority.) But there was more to it than that. As officials argued at the time, local assemblies had been instruments of social and economic abuse.[13] Yuan's plan was to re-create the system of assemblies more slowly, with greater attention to restraints on the local elite.

Neither his centralizing subordination of provincial power nor his subversion of the constitutional inheritance of the late Ch'ing won Yuan friends among the politicized gentry. If he could have shown solid achievement in handling foreign encroachment, much might have been forgiven. Broad support was offered him on the occasion of two foreign-policy crises: with the Russians over Mongolia and with the Japanese over the Twenty-One Demands. A vigorous negotiator, Yuan nevertheless faltered, settled for compromises rather than risk the country in war, and lost his constituency. In 1916, he was brought down by a tacit alliance (which enjoyed Japanese support) among the three groups that had de-

[13] Pai Chiao, *Yuan Shih-k'ai yü Chung-hua Min-kuo* [Yuan Shih-k'ai and the Republic of China] (Shanghai: Jen-wen yueh-k'an ts'ung-shu, 1936), pp. 120–22.

fined themselves in the first decade of the century: reformers (friends of Liang Ch'i-ch'ao as well as Liang himself), revolutionaries (Sun's group as well as others by this time only distantly affiliated with Sun), and officials (both military and civilian, whom Yuan had brought with him from his years as a reforming governor-general under the Ch'ing but who defected from him in large numbers when he presumed to call himself emperor). Only illness and death in June 1916 saved him from the degradation of expulsion from Peking.

Disintegration After Yuan Shih-k'ai and the Emerging Social Crisis

Yuan, perhaps by accident of training and circumstance, had taken on all challengers: the Manchu monarchy, the revolutionaries, the gentry movement, and eventually even his own generals as he tried to curtail their power and autonomy. All but the Manchus gained something from his demise. As central power disintegrated, generals, mostly Yuan's own, inherited power in the several regions that now made up a *de facto* Chinese confederation. Revolutionaries were able to gain footholds in the new, decentralized environment (Sun Yat-sen found military and parliamentary allies in Kwangtung in 1917 and 1918). And gentry were able to strike bargains with regional satraps rather than having to fend off the much more formidable overseer of a central government. Such were the general features of the warlord period.

While politics at Peking became increasingly disorganized, corrupt, and irrelevant, social and intellectual movements quietly under way since the end of the nineteenth century were begining to have visible influence. Industrial growth was still small as a proportion of the national economy, but a significant spurt under the favorable circumstances created by World War I had produced an urban working class of sufficient size to play some political role. Although we have no definitive quantitative measure, it seems that in some areas the conditions of peasant existence were suffering deterioration. The special burdens of the reform programs (which in some cases gave new powers to the peasants' potential exploiters, the gentry) were followed by the escalating and often arbitrary exactions of local military rulers.[14] And a radical critique of Chinese so-

rise of industry

[14] For the country as a whole, the economic benefits secured by the gentry during these decades at the expense of the peasantry can be only a matter of impression and speculation. But for one concrete local study of gentry income in these years, which is consistent with the argument presented here, see Muramatsu Yuji, "A Documentary Study of Chinese Landlordism in the Late Ch'ing and the Early Republican Kiangnan," *Bulletin of the School of Oriental and African Studies, University of London,* Vol. 29, Part 3 (1966), pp. 566–99.

cial norms was gaining currency among the growing class of Westernized intellectuals.

Against this background, the May Fourth movement emerged, and marked the end of an era. In one sense, the main theme of the movement was a recapitulation of the two decades that had preceded it. Anti-imperialist nationalism was the keynote, as it had been since the Boxer Rebellion. Some, like Sun Yat-sen or Ch'en Tu-hsiu (Peking University professor, critic of Chinese society, advocate of science and democracy, editor of the influential journal *New Youth*), had muted this theme—for tactical reasons (anti-Manchuism), or because they had confidence in the basically good intentions of the Western nations and Japan, or because they blamed China itself for its predicament. Most of the leadership, including close associates of Sun and Ch'en, had been strongly motivated by their keen awareness of the foreign danger and their concern to confront it forcefully. In the May Fourth movement, the minority among the leadership who had been disposed to tolerate Western behavior were also induced to raise the anti-imperialist banner.

It was not a beginning but rather a climax of nationalism. Anti-imperialism would continue and grow, but it was never again to be so simple. In the May Fourth period, any Chinese could curse the imperialist in the happy belief that his voice spoke for a unitary movement in which potentially all Chinese had equal and harmonious membership. There were later attempts to re-create this uncomplicated atmosphere, but one could not henceforth ignore the intrusion of class conflict and the apparent diversity of interests among Chinese, even as they faced the external enemy.

Questions of social structure had heretofore been slighted by the various nationalist leaders at a price. The price was a social problem that, from the early 1920's on, kept exploding in their faces—or rather, in their successors' faces, since it was not long before new persons representing a new generation emerged in positions of prominence. At first the center of ferment seemed to be the urban workers, some of whom participated tentatively in the May Fourth demonstrations and who attracted much attention in the urban turbulence of the early 1920's. But this proved to be a false start; the urban worker, let alone the factory worker, was still too small an element in the society to have great leverage or to endanger the inherited social order. It was rather the peasant and his discontents that were to overturn the present and produce an entirely different future. By the mid-1920's there were already men who had discovered the explosive potential of the countryside and had fired it experimentally, with striking results.[15]

[15] For a discussion of early peasant organizing, see Shinkichi Etō, "Hai-lu-feng— The First Chinese Soviet Government," *China Quarterly*, No. 8 (October–December 1961), pp. 160–83, and No. 9 (January–March 1962), pp. 149–81.

The pattern of Mao Tse-tung's life in these decades conveniently illustrates the evolution of social attitudes. His father was a peasant who had improved the family fortune through modest landholding and trading. There was sufficient surplus for Mao to intersperse working for his father with some classical education in a village school. In 1910, at the age of sixteen or seventeen, he took the decisive step of entering a district higher-primary school, part of the new educational network, where he read Liang Ch'i-ch'ao. As he was expanding outward intellectually, he was moving upward socially. His fellow students were from landlord families, and Mao had abandoned a life of manual labor or petty trading for participation in the world of gentry culture—or so it seemed at the time. In 1911 he consolidated this new status by admission to the next rung on the new academic ladder, the middle school in Hunan's capital. In the general enthusiasm for the 1911 revolution, Mao joined the ranks of the revolutionary army, but he betrayed his self-consciousness as a recent arrival in the elite by using his pay to avoid physical chores. He soon returned to his studies and spent five years at a Hunan equivalent of a college, the First Normal School. In these years, Mao was exposed to both traditional and Western thought, to nationalism and bits of socialist theory. Like so many others in the previous decade, he became intensely interested in military strength as an instrument for national salvation. But it was not until the May Fourth movement, in which Mao was a local leader, that his attention turned to the masses, to the political role of workers and peasants in the making of the new China.[16] For both Mao and China, the May Fourth movement was indeed the end of one era and the beginning of another.

It was the beginning of the end for the landed gentry class, the rural elite for centuries of imperial Chinese history. The early twentieth century had been a particularly eventful and active period for them. For the first time in the Ch'ing period (there are perhaps parallels with the end of the Ming), unofficial gentry as organized groups entered into politics. Nationalism was the prevalent ideology, and the general concern for national strengthening gave them their opportunity. New schools, industrial projects, railway building, representative assemblies—all came into being on behalf of nationalism, and all invited, even required, participation by those leaders of the society who were not in office. In coalition with a less numerous wealthy merchant group, the gentry responded with enthusiasm.

Nationalism brought the gentry into politics—and they in turn used nationalism to deliver to the central authority the *coup de grâce*. Neither the reforming Ch'ing administration nor the Yuan Shih-k'ai presidency could produce the results in internal reforms and external triumphs that

[16] This account follows Stuart Schram, *Mao Tse-tung*, rev. ed. (New York: Penguin, 1967), pp. 19–54.

could have channeled the new gentry political involvement into support of central authority.

But the gentry were not prepared to build an alternative edifice. They in effect destroyed themselves by their excessive accretions of power. The classical system had provided restraints, a sort of balance between gentry and officialdom, where the acquisitiveness of the landed class was compromised with the dynasty's interest in stability. With their new power of political organization after 1900 (and perhaps also with their increased numbers, resulting from more fluid standards for elite status), the gentry seems to have overindulged itself in self-serving schemes.

The nationalist leaders of the day were not sufficiently alive to the social dangers inherent in what was happening. Some radicals, including Sun Yat-sen, spoke of programs to contain the distorting consequences of economic development. But they were generally warning against the future effects of industry and capitalism, while behind their backs their gentry brothers were wreaking social havoc. The first round of the Chinese revolution led logically to its later phases after the May Fourth movement.

Selected Readings

Boorman, Howard L., and Howard, Richard C., eds. *Biographical Dictionary of Republican China.* New York: Columbia University Press, 1967–68. Vols. 1 and 2 (further volumes to be published). Although the social history of the period awaits study, a good way to gain a sense of the character and variety of the avenues to leadership is to browse through the ample entries in these volumes.

Cameron, Meribeth E. *The Reform Movement in China, 1898–1912.* Stanford, Calif.: Stanford University Press, 1931. Now somewhat out of date, but still informative and the only comprehensive account of the official reform movement of the late Ch'ing that has so far been published.

Ch'en, Jerome. *Yuan Shih-k'ai (1859–1916): Brutus Assumes the Purple.* London: Allen & Unwin, 1961. The only general study of the life of this critical figure in modern Chinese history.

Feuerwerker, Albert. *The Chinese Economy, 1912–1949,* and *The Chinese Economy, ca. 1870–1911.* Chinese Studies nos. 1 and 5. Ann Arbor, Mich.: University of Michigan Center for Chinese Studies, 1968 and 1969. These two works present a clear and succinct analysis of the structure and movement of the Chinese economy.

Hsüeh Chün-tu. *Huang Hsing and the Chinese Revolution.* Stanford, Calif.: Stanford University Press, 1961. Provides organizational details of the republican revolutionary movement as reflected in the life of a major leader.

Levenson, Joseph R. *Confucian China and Its Modern Fate.* Single vol. ed. Berkeley, Calif.: University of California Press, 1968. A stimulating collection of essays, many of which touch on the early twentieth century.

————. *Liang Ch'i-ch'ao and the Mind of Modern China.* Cambridge, Mass.: Harvard University Press, 1953. A pioneering study of the emergence of nationalistic attitudes in China, as seen in the development of the period's leading intellectual.

Schiffrin, Harold Z. *Sun Yat-sen and the Origins of the Chinese Revolution.* Berkeley, Calif.: University of California Press, 1968. A great contribution to our understanding of the republican revolutionary movement, although it takes us only to 1905.

Schwartz, Benjamin I. *In Search of Wealth and Power: Yen Fu and the West.* Cambridge, Mass.: Harvard University Press, 1964. A brilliant treatment of the main themes, as well as the intricacies, of the new intellectual tendencies of the time, as expressed in the writings of a most influential interpreter of the West to China.

Sharman, Lyon. *Sun Yat-sen: His Life and Its Meaning.* 1934; reprinted, Stanford, Calif.: Stanford University Press, 1968. A comprehensive account of Sun's life that is still rewarding reading.

Wright, Mary C., ed. *China in Revolution: The First Phase, 1900–1913.* New Haven, Conn.: Yale University Press, 1968. Although no full-scale interpretive work has yet appeared that weaves together the various strands of the period, the studies in this book are the first to give serious attention to many important themes.

The Era of Party Rule:
Japan, 1905–1932

PETER DUUS

THE opening of the Imperial Diet in 1890 was one of the boldest political experiments of the Meiji government. Less than a generation
before, the country had been ruled by an authoritarian regime that kept
most major political decisions in the hands of a tiny minority. Public
opposition to constituted authority had been tantamount to sedition, and
the idea of public political debate was so alien that one early Japanese
observer of the American Congress could only liken its deliberations to a
fish market back home. Despite the suddenness of the plunge into parliamentary politics, however, the experiment produced results. Public elections and public debates on policy issues became commonplace by the
1920's. Even more striking, the political parties in the House of Representatives established themselves as the dominant force in national politics. From 1905 until 1932 no government was organized without some
party support in the Diet, and after 1918 party leaders headed governments with increasing frequency. By the late 1920's, many Japanese regarded "normal constitutional government" as fully established.

The significance of party rule has been the subject of much historical
debate. Some historians, looking at the period through the dark glass of
the 1930's, point out that party hegemony lasted little more than a generation. And they regard party rule as a failure because the parties were
unable to check the rising political influence of the military. Other historians take a more positive view. They argue that the long experience of
the Japanese with representative government made possible the quick
revival of parliamentary politics after 1945. Had there been no native
roots for the American policy of democratization, it might have had little
effect. Instead of stressing the failures of party rule, these historians
stress its successes. Neither interpretation is entirely satisfactory. The

debate over whether the parties "failed" or "succeeded" is very much the argument between the optimist and the pessimist over whether a glass of water is half full or half empty. Both views are correct, but each reflects a different perspective.

Any convincing appraisal of the era of party rule has to recognize that the ascendancy of the parties rested on a peculiar balance of tactical strengths and strategic weaknesses. The parties enjoyed three decades of sustained growth by catering to key interest groups in Japanese society and by striking compromises with nonparty elements in the political elite. They proved highly effective in acquiring and using political power. These successes, however, were pragmatic, not ideological. Although the majority of the people accepted party rule as a matter of course, just as they had accepted oligarchic rule during the Meiji period, the parties were never able to cloak themselves in the mantle of legitimacy. Many had lingering doubts about the propriety of party rule, whose emphasis on open political conflict, partisan sentiment, and political log-rolling challenged deeply rooted social attitudes. Other, more radical elements in society, particularly in the army, were inimical to the very idea of parliamentary process. When the army created a moment of national crisis in 1931, the parties lacked the moral strength to sustain their pragmatic hold on the government. The result was the swift demise of party hegemony, although not of the parties themselves.

The Rise to Power, 1905–1925

THE BREAKDOWN OF CLIQUE GOVERNMENT

The rise of party hegemony was made possible by the failure of the Meiji Constitution to work as the oligarchs hoped it would. Like most written constitutions, it was an ambiguous document that permitted the development of a variety of political arrangements. Legally it vested all the powers of the state in the hands of the emperor, but in practice decisions about the exercise of these powers were made by the cabinet, the chief policy-making organ of government. The constitution, however, provided no clear-cut mechanism for deciding who was to organize the cabinet or how power was to be transferred from one government to the next. Selection of the premier and his ministers was placed in the hands of the emperor, but during the first three decades of the constitutional government he invariably followed the advice of the oligarchs in their role of genro, or elder statesmen. During the 1890's the genro had simply nominated one another for head of the government and had likewise monopolized most of the ministerial posts in the cabinet. But by the early 1900's they had begun to step aside from the forefront of national politics to occupy influential extracabinet posts in the Privy Council or the imperial-household bureaucracy.

In place of direct oligarchic domination of the cabinet, the genro substituted government by remote control, or "clique government," as it was known at the time. They relied on the loose web of personal connections that most of them, especially the politically tenacious Yamagata Aritomo, had built up since the middle of the Meiji period. By the early 1900's most of the key posts in the civil and military bureaucracies were held by men who had helped the oligarchs during the hectic days of building the Meiji state. The Privy Council and the House of Peers were also under the sway of the oligarchs' lieutenants. Knit to the older leaders by ties of friendship, patronage, and even marriage, they were a highly talented group of men, most of whom had been among the vanguard of Meiji youth exposed to the "new knowledge" of the West. The oligarchs doubtless expected that these personal protégés would be their heirs as leaders of the nation and, to assure this, had advanced them to the top positions in government.

Clique government functioned well enough before the Russo-Japanese War, but it was not a viable long-run solution to the problem of national leadership. For one thing, it was not very popular. Many journalists, politicians, and intellectuals felt that the oligarchic cliques stood in the way of "true constitutional government." Those who fell heir to the liberalism of the Meiji period complained that the oligarchs and their protégés prevented the achievement of responsible party cabinets. Others were moved by the vaguer notion, perhaps ultimately Confucian in origin, that the oligarchs and their satellites were "bad ministers" who prevented the harmonizing of the imperial will with popular aspirations. In either case, clique government seemed arbitrary, irresponsible, and willful. The oligarchs had no convincing answer to counter these charges. They protested their loyalty to the emperor and the state, but their obvious reluctance to retire from politics called this into question. To much of the educated and articulate public, the oligarchs looked less like dedicated servants of the emperor than like power-hungry despots anxious to maintain their personal influence at all costs. There were many, like the youthful Takayama Chogyū, who felt that "the new Japan should bid farewell to the decrepit genro."

Even more important, clique government suffered from internal difficulties. The cliques of the oligarchs were not like the autonomous, self-perpetuating elites in countries like the Soviet Union, where new generations of leadership are recruited through the mechanism of a totalitarian political party. Rather, clique government was a highly personal affair that depended on the prestige and personality of the oligarchs rather than on a stable organizational base. As the oligarchs grew older, the internal cohesion of the oligarchic cliques began to weaken.

By the end of the Russo-Japanese War there were unmistakable signs that the oligarchs were losing their hold on their followers. Many of their loyal lieutenants regarded their mentors as officious and superannuated old men who should relinquish their power to the younger generation. In 1901, Itō Miyoji, a protégé of Itō Hirobumi who had helped draft the constitution, noted in his diary that, although "the glow of their great achievement" lingered on, the people were growing tired of the genro. At the same time, the followers of the oligarchs did not always see eye to eye with one another on matters of policy. Just as there had been rifts between oligarchs like Itō and Yamagata in the 1890's, there appeared similar rifts in the ranks of their protégés. Particularly striking was the annual struggle between the army and the navy over the size of military appropriations during the years following the Russo-Japanese War. Both the higher civil service and the officer corps were also being infused with new blood. Young officers and bureaucrats who had been recruited through the military academies or the national universities rather than through oligarchic patronage were moving into positions of responsibility. By 1910, for example, nearly a third of the bureau chiefs in the civil bureaucracy were products of the examination system, and in 1912 many examination-recruited officials had reached the rank of vice minister. Factions or cliques within the bureaucracy were based less on personal loyalty to the oligarchs or their protégés than on ties between university classmates or between members of a particular bureau or ministry. Taken in combination, these rifts weakened clique government considerably, and it was through these rifts that the parties slowly marched to power.

THE POLITICS OF COMPROMISE

The shift of power into the hands of the parties was the result of a long and gradual process. Ever since the opening of the Diet in 1890, the political parties had been fighting for and winning a larger voice in the determination of national policy. The parliamentary struggles between the oligarchic cabinets and the pugnacious, party-dominated Diet had proved that, despite the considerable constitutional limitations on the House of Representatives, a majority party or even a plurality party could exercise considerable leverage over the cabinet. By refusing to approve the cabinet's budget proposals, the House could force the cabinet to fall back on the previous year's budget. In view of the growing level of government expenditure from 1895 to 1905, especially on armaments, most of the cabinets of the 1890's tried to avoid this alternative. The House could also obstruct other government legislation. Although this difficulty could sometimes be circumvented by the issuance of imperial ordinances, it was far less easy to deal with vituperative oratorical attacks on the floor of the Diet or with the passage of no-confidence resolutions there.

As a result of the constant pressure, the oligarchic premiers finally realized that cooperation with the parties was essential to the smooth operation of the constitutional machinery. From the close of the Sino-Japanese War on, men like Matsukata Masayoshi, Itō, and Yamagata tried to woo at least temporary Diet support for their governments by giving party leaders ministerial portfolios and by making concessions to the parties on national policy. The politics of confrontation gave way to the politics of compromise. Itō Hirobumi, the chief architect of the Meiji state, was so poignantly aware of the need for party support in the Diet that in 1900 he organized a party of his own, the Seiyūkai, which he hoped to mold into a "national party" drawing on a broad base of public support. His intention was not to promote the cause of party power or party government; rather, he hoped to smooth over potential conflict between his cabinet and the Diet and to assure that the Diet would serve the national interest rather than the partisan interests of the politicians. But it was testimony to the growing strength of the Diet that he felt constrained to organize a party at all.

The victories of the parties in the 1890's left most men in the Diet confident that the day of party rule would not be long in coming. But there was some disagreement on the means for bringing it about. The fires of protest, which had burned so strongly in the 1890's, still flickered in many breasts, and the tactics of frontal assault through Diet confrontations with the cabinet or public demonstrations against cabinet policy had much appeal. In 1905, for example, a group of disgruntled Diet members, allying with patriotic groups and chauvinist associations, organized popular rallies in Tokyo to protest the acceptance of the Portsmouth Peace Treaty by the Katsura cabinet. Some party leaders, like Inukai Tsuyoshi, a pugnacious wisp of a man later apotheosized as a "god of constitutional government," favored a union of all the parties in the Diet against the continuation of clique government and its policies. Opposed to these coalitionist tactics were party leaders who favored striking bargains with oligarchic protégés like Premier Katsura Tarō in order to expand the power of the parties. They felt that in the long run such tactical compromises would work to the advantage of the parties. By contrast, direct confrontation with clique government in the streets or in the Diet seemed futile. Such tactics might harden the attitude of the oligarchs toward the parties and postpone the advent of party rule.

The years following the Russo-Japanese War saw the slow triumph of the tactics of compromise over the tactics of coalition. The Seiyūkai, under the leadership of Hara Kei, an ambitious and astute ex-official with a genius for political maneuvering, established itself as a semipermanent government party through a gentleman's agreement with Katsura. In return for Seiyūkai support during the Russo-Japanese War, Katsura agreed to recommend as his successor the amiable and indolent Saionji Kimmochi, the nominal head of the party. During the five years that followed, control over the cabinet passed back and forth between the two men. The genro were by-passed in these transfers of power, but they gave their assent to them since both Katsura and Saionji were former protégés. Under both men, the Seiyūkai used its influence as progovernment party to build up an absolute majority in the Diet, to win ever increasing numbers of votes, and to attract financial and political support. As the most favored party in the Diet, it grew steadily in power.

The success of the Seiyūkai produced a sense of frustration among the minority parties in the Diet. Those who favored a grand union of the parties against clique government found the Seiyūkai, comfortable in its political position, less and less willing to embark on such a joint effort. The advocates of party coalition made their last effective effort when Katsura replaced Saionji once more in 1912. Brandishing the slogans "Overthrow clique government" and "Establish constitutional government," men like Inukai organized a "Movement for Constitutional Government." By giving vent to the long-accumulated public resentment of the oligarchs and their lieutenants, the movement stirred up much of the press and public. But it would not have succeeded in overthrowing Katsura's new government if the Seiyūkai had not decided to support it. When Katsura had come to power, he had announced his intention to form a party of his own rather than to rely on the Seiyūkai. Abandoned by their powerful ally, the Seiyūkai repaid him by defecting temporarily to the popular movement. Once Katsura was forced from power, however, Hara agreed to compromise with another oligarchic protégé, Yamamoto Gombei, who succeeded Katsura in 1913. The constitutional movement lost impetus, and the Seiyūkai managed to recover its position.

The organization of Katsura's new party, the Dōshikai, proved to have a significant long-run impact on the politics of compromise, however. Like Itō, Katsura felt that he needed a party of his own to manage the Diet. He was able to recruit a substantial following because many minority-party members who had rejected the tactics of coalition found themselves made impotent by the Seiyūkai's growing power. Sustained by a desire to compete with the Seiyūkai for votes and influence, they flocked to Katsura's banner. Even after Katsura's death in 1913, the party continued to grow under his successor, Katō Kōmei, a blunt and haughty ex-diplomat imbued with an admiration for English parliamentary politics. With the emergence of the new party, the tactics of coalition lost much of their appeal. The Diet was divided between two large parties more interested in competing for influence than in cooperating in attacks on the genro and their cliques. Diet politics became dominated by a pattern of two-party competition.

THE ESTABLISHMENT OF PARTY CABINETS

The genro, who had abdicated their role as cabinet makers between 1905 and 1912, nevertheless viewed the emergence of two strong parties in the Diet with some apprehension, for, although both parties were willing to compromise, neither forsook the long-run goal of party rule. Men like Yamagata were still convinced that the parties were "private cabals" and could not be trusted with control over the government. As a result, the genro renewed their efforts to stave off party rule by turning the parties against one another. In 1914, when the Seiyūkai-supported Yamamoto cabinet fell, the genro named an unlikely successor, Ōkuma Shigenobu, a veteran of the early party movement and a symbol of "true constitutional government." They urged him to rely on the support of the Dōshikai and other anti-Seiyūkai groups in hopes of breaking Seiyūkai power in the Diet. With the backing of the oligarchs and a large measure of official intervention, the anti-Seiyūkai parties won a resounding victory in the election of 1915, leaving the Seiyūkai a much diminished minority group. But the oligarchs did not intend to trade the tyranny of the Seiyūkai for the tyranny of the Dōshikai. When Katō showed an ill-concealed impatience with genro interference on matters of foreign policy, the oligarchs forced his resignation. In 1917, the cabinet of Ōkuma's successor, Terauchi Masatake, a protégé of Yamagata, provided electoral support to the Seiyūkai at the expense of the Kenseikai, a party newly organized out of the remnants of the Dōshikai.

The attempt to balance the Dōshikai off against the Seiyūkai and vice versa sustained the faltering grasp of the oligarchs only temporarily. Such divide-and-rule tactics did not solve the inherent dilemmas of clique government, nor did they cancel the effectiveness of the politics of compromise. No matter which party won at the polls, one of them was bound to hold the plurality necessary to force the premier to rely on its support. Moreover, the premiers continued to be impatient of oligarchic interference in policy and anxious to act independently. Even Terauchi, on coming to power, had told Yamagata that he was a grown man and could not run to the old man for counsel on every problem. As if this were not all, fewer and fewer members of the oligarchic cliques were willing to take on the vexatious task of the premiership. In the cabinet changes of 1912, 1913, and 1914, the genro had run through long lists of prospective candidates before finding one willing to serve. For all practical purposes the genro's circle of choice had been narrowed to the party leaders. In 1918, when Terauchi Masatake resigned on grounds of health, the genro found no willing protégé to replace him and chose instead the Seiyūkai president, Hara Kei. The politics of compromise, which had produced more than a decade of covert party rule, finally forced the collapse of clique government.

The end of clique government did not mean the firm establishment of party government, however. The genro regarded the appointment of Hara as a pragmatic experiment, not as a capitulation to the principle of party rule. They selected Hara because they thought he would make a cautious and pliable premier. Indeed, Yamagata frequently told his acquaintances that he and Hara agreed on most issues of policy, save the question of whether a majority party should dominate the Diet. But none of the genro ruled out the possibility of a return to nonparty cabinets if the Hara cabinet proved that party rule was not equal to the needs of the country.

The experimental character of the Hara cabinet became apparent in 1922, when, instead of nominating Katō Kōmei for the premiership, the genro returned to the practice of appointing nonparty cabinets. Their intention was not so much to perpetuate clique government as to appoint "national unity" cabinets headed by men of substantial public reputation who would command the support of the bureaucracy and the House of Peers as well as the political parties. In part this was prompted by the feeling that none of the party leaders—Katō, Inukai, or Hara's successor, Takahashi Korekiyo—were of suitable mettle to head a government.

The revival of nonparty rule proved only a partial success, however. The political parties, whose appetite for power had been whetted by the appointment of Hara, were reluctant to give wholehearted support to nonpartisan cabinets. The Seiyūkai did rally to Admiral Katō Tomosaburō in 1922 to prevent power from going to his rival, the Kenseikai. But both major parties withheld support from Admiral Yamamoto Gombei when he organized a "national unity" cabinet in 1923. And, when Kiyoura Keigo came to power in 1924, he attracted Diet support of only the Seiyū-hontō, a group of dissidents who had split from the Seiyūkai. The selection of three nonparty cabinets in a row proved too much for the leaders of the two major parties. In early 1924, adopting the coalitionist tactics advocated years before by Inukai Tsuyoshi, the Seiyūkai and the Kenseikai organized a second "Movement for Constitutional Government" to oppose the Kiyoura government. It attracted very little popular support, but it did force Kiyoura to dissolve the Diet and call an election. By cooperating in the election, the coalition parties managed to win a collective victory.

When Kiyoura resigned, Saionji, who was now "the last genro," had little choice but to nominate Katō Kōmei, whose party held a Diet plurality, as head of a coalition party cabinet. This event marked the establishment of party government in a way that the Hara cabinet had not. Katō's success was not based on a personal accommodation with the genro; it rested on Saionji's realization that there were no immediate alternatives to party government. Saionji did not rule out the possibility of appointing a "neutral," nonparty cabinet if circumstances dictated, but for the time being he was willing to follow what he thought was the natural drift toward "normal constitutional government." As a result, from 1925 until 1932 the premiership passed to the president of the majority party in the House of Representatives. The failure of clique government and the death of the oligarchs had cleared the way for overt party rule.

The emergence of party cabinets resulted from changing political practice, not from constitutional amendment or legal reform. It was a peaceful revolution in constitutional practice on the order of that which occurred in England during the 1830's and 1840's. The selection of party premiers was an attempt to recruit national leadership once clique government had been proved a failure. A few clique members, like Itō and Katsura, had been quick to realize during the first decade of the century that the parties represented the wave of the future, and by the 1920's most prominent public figures accepted this as a political fact. Even Tanaka Giichi, a former follower of Yamagata who had inherited leadership of the army, realized that the only path to the premiership lay through the parties, and in 1925 he accepted the presidency of the Seiyūkai.

But, in order for the selection of party premiers to become a binding precedent, as in England, the nurture of time was needed. "Normal constitutional government" could be maintained only if it rested on a broad consensus of those active in politics. Otherwise, in the absence of constitutional changes, it would face the same fate as clique government. The party leaders therefore felt strongly impelled to lay firm foundations for continued party rule.

The Challenge of Power, 1914–1930

In the long run, the political parties faced two main tasks in expanding their power and maintaining their ascendancy. One was to demonstrate their effectiveness in ruling the country and in satisfying the interests of the majority of the population. The other was to convince the public that party rule was the most appropriate form of government for Japan. In the parties' scale of priorities, the former task seemed more important than the latter. Party success in overcoming oligarchic opposition to party rule seemed already to have solved the constitutional problem. In any case, it was easier to appeal to men's interests than to change their values. The parties therefore devoted themselves primarily to the more immediate job of building a solid local base of power and extending their influence over the apparatus of government. In this they were rather successful. The constitutional structure hampered their efforts, but it did not check them completely. By the late 1920's the parties showed they could bend the political system to their own ends.

THE PARTIES AND THE EXTRAPARLIAMENTARY FORCES

One key problem for the parties during their era of hegemony was that of handling the complex decision-making apparatus that had been set up under the Meiji Constitution. Unlike the oligarchs, the party premiers of the 1920's could usually count on support in the Diet, but it was far more difficult for them to exercise influence over the civil bureaucracy, the House of Peers, or the Privy Council. These bodies could check the party cabinets in much the same way that the House of Representatives had once checked nonparty cabinets. Indeed, the oligarchs had intended that they restrain the rasher impulses of the popular elements in the political structure. The constitutional balance might have changed in favor of the parties, but there was still the need to maintain a balance. On the whole, the parties recognized this need for balance, working within the constitutional framework rather than attempting to alter it to strengthen their own legal powers.

Increased control over the civil service was a consistent aim of the parties. Since 1900 the bureaucracy had been sealed against outside influence by ordinances requiring that all posts in the civil service below the rank of cabinet minister be recruited through the higher-civil-service examination system. This precluded the possibility of patronage appointments by the parties in the event they came to power. Both major parties advocated some measure of civil-service reform, but each approached it from a slightly different direction. The Seiyūkai, under the influence of Hara Kei, was interested in opening most of the top echelons of the civil bureaucracy to free appointment in order to permit greater direct party control over the official hierarchy. In 1913, Hara succeeded in having the posts of the vice ministers, secretaries, and counselors of each civilian ministry made patronage posts, and in 1920 he also opened up certain key posts in colonial administration to free appointment. By contrast, the Dōshikai and the Kenseikai, under the influence of Katō, introduced a system of parliamentary vice ministers and counselors in 1914 and again in 1924. These officials were to be appointed from the Diet membership and given the power to oversee the operations of each ministry, but they had no power to intervene in the administrative process. Unlike Hara, whose constant aim was the expansion of direct party influence, Katō had a great respect for the English practice of keeping the professional civil service free of such influence.

In the long run, reform of the civil service proved of less importance to the parties than the creation of proparty elements among the professional bureaucrats—a far more effective way of making the civil service responsive to party pressure. The parties were particularly interested in partisanizing the prefectural bureaucracy, which played a key role in local politics. The prefectural governor controlled the passage of local ordinances, the disbursement of prefectural tax revenues, the appointment of some local officials, and the supervision of the local police. He was a powerful ally to local party activities if he lent them his support—and a powerful enemy if he did not. It was the Seiyūkai that took the first step in making prefectural governors into party supporters, but the Dōshikai-Kenseikai soon joined the game. By the early 1920's, many local governors were clearly aligned with one or the other of the two major parties. When the Seiyūkai came to power, "pro-Seiyūkai" prefectural governors were appointed to office, and when the opposition came to power, "anti-Seiyūkai" or "pro-Kenseikai" governors were appointed to replace them. In 1925 the Kenseikai home minister, Wakatsuki Reijirō, announced his intention of abandoning this practice, but in fact it continued through the late 1920's. Because the parties avoided appointing actual party men to bureaucratic posts, there never developed the kind of "spoils system" that characterized American politics in the early nineteenth century. But many Japanese observers, who were used to the idea of an impartial official class dedicated only to the interests of the state, found distasteful even this slight degree of party involvement in the bureaucracy.

The parties were also able to extend their influence in the House of Peers. As clique government declined, the leadership of the Peers began to break free of control by imperial appointees who owed their positions to oligarchic patronage. As late as 1914 the upper house was responsive enough to oligarchic pressure to bring down the Seiyūkai-supported Yamamoto cabinet by refusing to approve its budget. But, by the time Hara came to power in 1918, many of the younger peers, particularly the hereditary peers, had had their fill of playing puppet for the oligarchs. Capitalizing on this discontent, Hara established an alliance with the Kenkyūkai, the largest faction in the Peers, which agreed to support most of the Seiyūkai's legislative program between 1918 and 1922. This "vertical alliance" was supplemented by the formation of party-linked factions in the upper house made up of imperial appointees who had gotten their positions through party patronage. By the early 1920's the House of Peers was being partisanized by party influence.

The effects of this partisanization were not entirely beneficial to the parties. Many leaders in the Peers, particularly in the Kenkyūkai, began to harbor larger ambitions. They felt that if the political parties in the House of Representatives had come to play a larger role in politics with the decline of oligarchic influence, the factions in the House of Peers could too. With the reappearance of nonparty cabinets in 1922, the Kenkyūkai saw a chance to act. Members of the faction took ministerial positions in both the Katō Tomosaburō and Yamamoto Gombei cabinets. The most striking assertion of the peers' new political independence came in 1924, when Kiyoura formed his "cabinet of peers," recruited from the major factions in the House of Peers. This was such a radical departure from recent precedent that an immediate public outcry arose both in the press and in the Diet. When the coalition cabinet of Katō Kōmei came to power in 1924, it had an unspoken commitment to undertake some measure of peerage reform.

The difficulties of direct reform of the Peers were considerable, since such action required the consent of the peers themselves. Naturally they were not willing to countenance a major overhaul, and when the Katō government proposed certain modest changes, they reacted by holding up the budget and threatening to defeat the government's other legislation. As a result, the government was able to make slight alterations in the composition of the upper house but was forced to leave its powers nearly intact. Despite the failure of the reform effort, the Peers ceased to play a major active role in politics after 1925. Some of the younger activists in the Kenkyūkai had died off or lost influence, and there were many in the House of Peers who felt it should remain above partisan struggle, as the framers of the constitution had originally intended. By the late 1920's, custom seemed to be accomplishing what reform had not. The upper house retained its powers to check the actions of the cabinet and the lower house, but it no longer attempted to intervene in the formation of cabinets.

The Privy Council proved as resistant to structural reform as the House of Peers, but, like the civil bureaucracy, it was susceptible to political pressure. The premier could threaten to use his influence to dismiss councilors who opposed government proposals. Hara used these tactics in 1913 to force the council's approval of civil-service reform. Such confrontations were rare, and the party cabinets usually sought to persuade the council rather than to coerce it. For example, it was through negotiation and persuasion that Katō Kōmei succeeded in getting the council to accept the universal suffrage bill in 1925. The failure to carry out structural reform did leave the cabinets open to pressure by the council—in 1927 Privy Council objections to cabinet policy were important in forcing the resignation of the Wakatsuki government—but by the same token, cabinet pressure on the council in 1930 forced it to accept the ratification of the London Naval Treaty. The balance of power between the two depended less on the formal institutional structure than on the political skills and determination of the party leaders and the council members.

The reluctance of the parties to make major reforms in the constitutional structure reflected certain practical considerations. The procedure for constitutional amendment was cumbersome, but even if it had been easier the party leaders would probably not have used it. Manipulating the system was more convenient than reforming it. The professional bureaucrats, the House of Peers, and the Privy Council were willing to go along with the parties in most instances, and only infrequently did they attempt to check party actions. In effect, the party leaders tried to substitute themselves for the oligarchs in making the constitutional apparatus work smoothly. They lacked the prestige of the oligarchs, but they made up for this lack by their control over the Diet. Many have criticized the parties for failing to undertake the crucial task of structural change, since it left them vulnerable to extraparliamentary pressure by the other political elites. This vulnerability was not a fatal one, however, nor did it precipitate the decline of party rule. If anything, the parties proved vulnerable because they were able to make the national decision-making machinery run too well.

THE PARTIES AND VOTE-GETTING

The pursuit of Diet majorities was a perpetual concern of the parties. Unlike the power of the oligarchs and their protégés, party power depended less on personal influence and connections than on the ability to control the Diet. Often a party could strengthen itself by merging with other groups, as the Dōshikai did in 1916 to form the Kenseikai, or as the Kenseikai did in 1927 to form the Minseitō. But the primary means of building Diet strength was winning elections. A large part of party activity therefore centered on the cultivation of *jiban,* or local "electoral bases," throughout the country. This was a concern not simply of individual party members, whose personal political fortunes were decided by the ballot, but of the party leaders themselves, whose positions on the national scene depended on the collective strength of their parties in the Diet.

During the parties' rise to hegemony, the electorate remained quite limited in size. The electoral law of 1900, which was slightly revised in 1919, restricted suffrage rights to those who paid over ten yen in direct national taxes. In 1908, only about three percent of the total population thus had the right to vote. Moreover, most of these voters were rural, since the main national tax was the land tax and very few city dwellers, whatever the size of their income, owned enough landed property to qualify. The rural character of the electorate had enormous effects on the tactics of vote-getting. The small villages and provincial towns where most voters lived were still permeated with old habits of social deference, political conservatism, and localism that persisted from pre-Meiji days. Local politics tended to be dominated by local "men of influence." Often they were local landlords, but they might also be small bankers and businessmen, members of the prefectural assembly, the heads of town and village councils, or even school teachers and principals. They played the role of local opinion-makers and formed the main link between national politics and the local community. The rest of the voters, a mere generation removed from the days when the mass of the common people had no voice in politics, tended to follow their lead. In many ways, the situation was very much like that of big-city politics in the United States at the turn of the century, when local political bosses swayed the votes of the newly naturalized immigrants from Europe who came directly from a tradition of political passivity in their home countries.

In their election tactics the political parties aimed primarily at winning over the local "men of influence." As a result, the parties often showed less interest in clarifying their position on national issues than in cultivating personal ties with local political leaders and in catering to the economic interests of local communities. By the late 1890's men like Hoshi Tōru, a leader of the Kenseihontō, had already experimented with interest politics as a means of building political support in the city of Tokyo. But it was not until the end of the Russo-Japanese War that party politicians began to dip regularly into the pork barrel to build local support. After the end of the war, and particularly after the accommodation between the Seiyūkai and Katsura, it became common political practice for local Diet members, prefectural party officials, and even the highest party leadership to appeal to voters with promises of new schools, new roads and bridges, local harbor improvements and irrigation works, and new railroad branch lines. And, as the parties gained control over the cabinets, they were able to deliver on these promises. The central government's expenditure on such projects rose steadily. Much of the Seiyūkai's success between 1908 and 1915 can be attributed to its exploitation of local-interest politics. But politicians in other parties soon realized the usefulness of the technique, and by the early 1920's it was a well-established practice for local Diet members to act as lobbyists for the economic interests of their constituencies.

If the parties were careful to associate themselves with local economic interests to win votes, they established equally close ties with big-business interests to raise money. Although the electorate remained limited in size, election campaigns grew more and more costly after the Russo-Japanese War. In part this was due to the expansion of the electorate that resulted from the wartime boom. But the legitimate costs of electioneering rose considerably, and the practice of vote-buying also became more widespread. Candidates would often advance bribery money to voters through "election brokers," who made a profession of buying and selling votes. Many local candidates were able to finance themselves with their own funds, or with some local backing, but the parties still needed ever increasing amounts of money. For this they turned to the support of the banking and business interests in Tokyo and Osaka, who were as anxious to maintain cordial relations with the political parties as the big entrepreneurs of the Meiji period had been anxious to befriend the oligarchs. By the late 1910's big business was giving large contributions to both major parties.

Big business gave this financial support primarily to assure that the parties would follow policies favorable to the growth of large-scale modern industry and commerce, and the party leaders, who had inherited the Meiji urge to build up the country's economic strength, were generally willing to pursue such policies. Tax rates on business profits and personal incomes were kept low; subsidies and tax rebates were granted to key industries such as iron and steel; and tariff rates were kept high to protect infant industries, while import duties were kept low on raw materials and semimanufactures needed by Japanese industry. At the same time, some businessmen exploited their political connections with the parties for more immediate returns. A cordial relationship with the party in power gave individual businessmen advantages in competition for government contracts, provided opportunities to buy government-owned properties, and gave advance access to private information on government price supports, trade, and monetary policies. Having an inside track with the government was often very profitable. By contrast, however, the acceptance of bribery money by politicians in return for favors to businessmen seems to have been relatively rare, and usually it involved only rather small businessmen or minor members of the party's rank and file. But the borderline between overt corruption and informal influence-peddling seemed thin, and many critics looked with disgust on the growing "commercialization" of the parties.

The lavish use of election money, the exploitation of "pork barrel" legislation, and the pursuit of votes through conventional canvassing accounted for most of the successes of individual candidates at election time. But there was often a temptation for a progovernment party or a party in power to use its influence over the local bureaucracy to swing the tide of an election in its favor, particularly in hotly contested districts. Direct intervention of government officials in elections became common by the mid-1910's. Local police officials harassed the campaign workers of the opposition, while turning a blind eye to election irregularities committed by the government party. Sometimes local officials stuffed ballot boxes or falsified election returns. By the 1920's it became axiomatic that the party supporting the government in power was assured of electoral victory.

The vote-getting techniques of the parties were highly effective. Individual party members often faced difficulty in being reelected, and the turnover in Diet membership was high. But by the 1920's it was clear that election to the House of Representatives was not possible without the endorsement or financial backing of one of the two major parties. The result was a strengthening of the tendency toward two-party politics; the number of small parties in the Diet declined steadily, and the number of independent Diet members nearly reached zero. This increase in the strength of the two major parties did not mean that they were popular, however. Since voters were influenced by a variety of pragmatic appeals, from the promise of local economic benefits to the offer of bribery money, voting often meant political participation without political involvement. There was little interest in where the party leaders stood on national issues and very little concern with whether "true constitutional government" continued or not. And party politicians, as long as they continued to mobilize the vote, seemed little concerned about the level of political education within the country.

THE PARTIES AND THE LEFT WING

The means by which the parties built their electoral strength invited much public criticism. So did the tactics of compromise. By the time the parties secured preponderant control over the cabinet, there was a widespread feeling, shared by many party men themselves, that the character of the parties had declined since the first days of the Diet. By the beginning of World War I, the parties were usually referred to not as "popular parties," the commonest term in the early days of the Diet, but as "established parties" or "entrenched parties." There were also growing complaints of "party abuses," which meant the parties' use of state power for partisan ends. In the eyes of many, the parties appeared unrepresentative, their membership corrupt, and their actions self-serving. Such feelings gave rise to movements for the democratic reform of politics and eventually to the growth of an active left-wing movement.

The demand for democratization was strongest among a new generation of intellectuals, journalists, and younger party politicians who were frustrated by the gap between the promise of liberal political theory and the practice of parliamentary politics in Japan. These men drew psychological sustenance from the victory of the democratic powers in World War I, which toppled militaristic, bureaucratic regimes in Russia, Germany, and Austria-Hungary and brought a wave of democratic revolutions in its wake. They were also encouraged by signs of a "popular awakening" within Japan, particularly in the cities. The rising number of labor disputes, the growth of a new and militant labor-union movement, and the outbreak of widespread rioting over rice prices in 1918 convinced them that the people were no longer content to be docile subjects of the emperor but wished for a greater role in politics.

Reformist politicians and intellectuals, backed by the working-class movement and university-student activists, called for a broad program of change within the country. As Ōyama Ikuo put it, their ultimate goal was "politics which touch on the needs of the people." How this was to be achieved was not always clear, and the would-be reformers advocated everything from the legalization of trade-union activities to the abolition of the House of Peers. But the majority of them held that the most immediate task was the establishment of universal manhood suffrage. Many reformers held that the creation of a mass electorate was the key to the political transformation of the country. They hoped it would make politics more sensitive to popular demands, end the corruption and jobbery involved in vote-getting, and perhaps even open the doors of the Diet to representatives elected from among the common people. Unless universal suffrage were achieved, the people could not expect the government to heed their aspirations.

The political parties were not at first very responsive to these demands. Although Hara was touted as the first "commoner premier," he had little sympathy for the city workers, who he thought were better off than ever before, and he was contemptuous of reformist intellectuals, whom he regarded as showoffs and troublemakers. From the viewpoint of the discontented, his cabinet was a reactionary one. Hara put through a revision of the electoral law that created a large number of new rural voters by lowering the tax qualification to three yen, but he dissolved the Diet in 1920 when the opposition presented universal suffrage bills; he spoke of the need for the "cooperation of labor and capital," but he refused to pass laws legalizing trade-union activity; and he watched complacently as his home minister used the power of the police and the constabulary to arrest labor organizers and break major strikes.

The failure of universal suffrage, the unsympathetic attitude of the Hara ministry toward labor, and the onset of business recession in 1920 had the effect of radicalizing many of those who had joined in the call for democratic reforms at the war's end. They began to question the justice of the capitalistic economic order, which they felt kept profits for the few while the mass of the people faced unemployment, lacked decent working conditions, and suffered with minimal living standards. At the same time, since it was clear that the politics of the Diet were in the hands of the "have" class, many former advocates of parliamentary action now called for a "rejection of politics." If the ballot were denied to the people, they should resort to the tactics of "direct action" through greater working-class solidarity, through more militant labor tactics, such as the general strike, or through revolution. Although some liberals like Yoshino Sakuzō and Suzuki Bunji continued to advocate the tactics of moderate reform, others soon succumbed to the appeal of more radical political faiths, ranging from anarcho-syndicalism to revolutionary Marxism.

The radicalization of the left might well have continued unabated had the parties continued to hold the attitude of Hara. But such did not prove to be the case. The Kenseikai, together with several smaller groups in the Diet, began to press for a more positive response to reform demands. In part this was prompted by political opportunism. Since these parties remained in the opposition throughout the early 1920's, they had little to lose by advocating such policies, and, in fact, they had hopes of perhaps winning a popular following in the cities. But probably more important was their feeling that failure to meet popular demands for change would invite the spread of "dangerous thought." In the catch-phrase of the time, it was necessary to give "proper guidance" to the opinion of the masses by making timely concessions to popular demands. A "safety valve" for popular discontent was necessary. This feeling was shared by many reform-minded members of the civil bureaucracy, who likewise regarded social legislation as a more effective response to the unrest in the cities than repression or inaction.

The early 1920's saw a trickle of social legislation, drafted in the bureaucracy and passed by the party-controlled Diets. Many of these laws were modeled on similar legislation in the West. At the same time, the more reform-minded Kenseikai sponsored laws providing for the mediation of labor disputes in 1924 and repealing certain restrictions on the right of labor unions to strike or recruit members. It also attempted, in 1927 and again in 1929, to put through legislation regulating the organization of trade unions. But pressure from big-business organizations like the Japan Industrial Club, as well as resistance in the House of Peers, brought these efforts to nothing. Despite the failure of these laws, the party governments of the 1920's continued to let the labor-union movement grow. There were occasional crackdowns on Communist-led or Communist-influenced unions, but moderate unionism was tolerated if not encouraged.

Perhaps most important in defusing the potential discontent of the left was the passage of the universal suffrage bill in 1925. The Kenseikai, together with a number of small groups in the Diet, had proposed universal suffrage bills in 1921, 1922, and 1923. By 1923 there was general agreement that such a law was inevitable and necessary. Even the Yamamoto government announced its intention to support such a bill. But, appropriately enough, it was the coalition government of Katō Kōmei that brought it into being. By negotiation, maneuver, and persuasion, Katō managed to secure the approval of the House of Representatives, the House of Peers, and the Privy Council for a nearly fourfold expansion of the electorate from about 3 million voters to a little over 12.5 million. The effects of such a change were hard to foresee, and Katō called the passage of the bill "a leap in the dark."

The passage of universal suffrage brought the reformist elements on the left back to the tactics of parliamentary action. In late 1923 and early 1924, partly because "direct action" proved to have little practical effect, a number of liberal and left-wing intellectuals, labor leaders, and leftist activists banded together to organize a "proletarian party" movement. Its aim was to create a political party that would represent or defend the interests of the "new political forces" to be enfranchised by universal suffrage. The original intention was to organize one unified party, but a lack of ideological consensus, a split in the labor movement, and personal antagonisms led to the emergence of not one party but several. Roughly they fell into three main groups: the moderate liberal democrats, who advocated policies of social meliorism; the Marxist-oriented social democrats, who favored the use of parliamentary tactics but took as their ultimate goal the overthrow of "bourgeois" hegemony in Diet politics; and the communists and their sympathizers, who regarded the formation of political parties as merely an instrument for educating the masses in preparation for revolution.

Ironically, the main benefits of universal suffrage accrued not to the newly organized "proletarian parties" but to the older, established parties. Both the Seiyūkai and the Kenseikai (reorganized as the Minseitō in 1927) introduced new campaign techniques to lure the new mass of voters. They adopted in their platforms many of the reform demands made in the early 1920's, and they attempted to publicize themselves as parties "above class" that served all segments of the population. But the main strength of the established parties lay in the time-tested electoral techniques they had used in the past. Most of the new voters lived in the countryside, where they were easily absorbed into the local "electoral bases" of the two major parties. The "proletarian parties," by contrast, suffered from financial weakness, a lack of practical political experience, and a narrow base of urban support that rested mainly on the intellectual community, the white-collar class, and the miniscule labor movement. As a result, in the first election held under universal suffrage in 1928, the two major parties managed to capture 8.4 million votes out of the 9.8 million cast. Even after the onset of depression in the late 1920's, the established parties continued to win. At the height of hard times in 1930, the voters once more rejected the parties of the left, and the older parties were swept into power.

THE PARTIES AND FOREIGN POLICY

The era of party ascendancy was marked by some domestic discontent, but it coincided with a period of relative peace in foreign affairs. In part this peaceful lull was due to the stabilization of imperialist politics in East Asia following the Russo-Japanese War. But it also owed much to the attitude of the political parties. Like most other responsible elements in Japanese politics, the parties were committed to certain fundamental goals in foreign affairs: the protection of Japan's colonial possessions in Korea and Taiwan, the preservation of her "special rights and interests" in Manchuria and the Kwantung Peninsula, and the maintenance of her newly acquired status as a great power. In pursuing these goals, the parties favored using the tools of diplomacy and negotiation rather than the tactics of military threat and expansion advocated by some elements in the army. They were also committed to the principle of civilian domination in foreign policy. Not unnaturally, they regarded continued military interference in diplomacy a baneful residue of clique government.

Party independence in the making of foreign policy began in 1914 with the attempt of Katō Kōmei, Ōkuma's foreign minister, to break the hold of the oligarchs on foreign affairs. Largely on his initiative, Japan followed its ally England into World War I on the side of the Allied Powers. This angered Germanophiles like Yamagata, but entry into the war won Japan control over the former German concessions on the Shantung Peninsula in China. Katō's other essay in independent diplomacy, however, the Twenty-One Demands of 1915, proved to be a diplomatic disaster. Katō's intention was to reach an overall diplomatic settlement of outstanding problems with China in hopes of forestalling more militant moves by the army. Instead he succeeded only in arousing the anger of Chinese and exciting the suspicions of the Westerners. The oligarchs attempted to regain some of the influence lost under Katō by persuading Terauchi to organize the Extraordinary Council on Foreign Affairs, an official body that included representatives of two of the major political parties as well as members of the cabinet. But the council proved to be one more forum for the expression of party opinion, and far from bringing the parties into line it gave them a new voice in diplomatic affairs.

The Twenty-One Demands also illustrated the difficulties of following a unilateral policy in East Asia. With the end of World War I, international peace and amity seemed to be "the trend of the times," and the political parties, like the foreign ministry officials, were willing to ride with the trend. They began to stress the need for cooperation with the Western powers. The first sign of this new policy was their support of Japan's participation in the Siberian expedition of 1918, a joint American-British-Japanese venture aimed at putting pressure on the new revolutionary government in Russia. The parties also supported ratification of the Versailles peace treaty and entry into the League of Nations. But perhaps most important was their acceptance of the agreements reached at the Washington Conference of 1921–22, where the Western powers, prompted mainly by American initiative, attempted to substitute new collective-security arrangements in East Asia for the imperialist arrangements that had characterized prewar diplomacy there. At the Washington Conference the Japanese delegation, headed by Admiral Katō Tomosaburō, agreed to accept restrictions on naval construction that were to limit the strength of the Japanese navy in capital ships to a ratio of 6 to 10 with the English and American fleets. At the same time, the Japanese agreed to participate in an international guarantee of the Open Door policy in China. This moderate stance in Asian policy had the support of the professional diplomatic corps, the high echelons of the navy, and certain big-business elements. It became the keystone of the foreign policy of party cabinets in the mid-1920's.

The new trend in foreign policy was prompted by practicality rather than idealism. It was obvious that Japan would face diplomatic isolation in East Asia unless it followed the lead of the Americans and English, still the two dominant powers in the area. The Anglo-Japanese alliance, due to expire in 1921, was not likely to be renewed, and the bipartite agreements that Japan had signed with tsarist Russia to guarantee the Japanese position in Korea and Manchuria had been repudiated by the new Soviet government. Without these bilateral guarantees, cooperation in the new collective-security arrangements was the only diplomatic alternative left open to Japan to guarantee its position. At the same time, there was a strong feeling that unilateral demands backed by force or threat of force were less likely to be profitable in the long run than peaceful economic expansion. The presentation of the Twenty-One Demands in 1915 and the seizure of the former German concession in Shantung had provoked violent anti-Japanese sentiment in China but had gained Japan few concrete benefits. Trade, not territorial acquisitions, best served the national interest. It was also clear that a cooperative diplomatic stance in no sense weakened Japan's military defenses. Since the United States had agreed not to construct any new naval fortifications in the western Pacific, the ratio of naval strength agreed on at the Washington Conference permitted Japan to maintain naval hegemony in the area. Voluntary arms limitations permitted Japan to avoid a costly arms race with the United States yet still maintain a military and naval establishment strong enough to protect the home islands and the colonial possessions.

The new look in foreign policy was accompanied by attempts to reduce the influence of the army in Japanese politics. It encouraged civilian politicians to launch a drive against the special prerogatives of the army. There had already been signs of civilian discontent with the military before the Washington Conference. During the Siberian expedition, for example, Premier Hara revived the practice of limiting the authority of the general staff to the conduct of military operations, and, while Admiral Katō Tomosaburō was absent at the Washington Conference, Hara established a new precedent by serving temporarily as naval minister in his place. This was the first time a civilian politician had served in such a position. The emergence of "the spirit of the Washington Conference" emboldened other politicians to make more outspoken criticisms of the army in the Diet. Many reform-minded party politicians began to attack the special legal position of the army and its "right of Supreme Command." Some even introduced resolutions to abolish the requirement that the service ministers be military officers. Although the party leaders made no serious attempts to overhaul civilian-military relations in the early and mid-1920's, the public atmosphere was far less favorable to the military than it had been in some years.

The growing criticism of the military, coupled with the acceptance of a moderate approach to foreign policy, resulted in a demand for a reduction in arms spending. The onset of economic difficulty after the 1920 recession had left many business leaders, party politicians, and even the genro feeling that some retrenchment of government expenditure was necessary to get the economy back on an even keel. Since the new, cooperative foreign policy seemed to guarantee Japan's security without resort to a large military establishment, a cut in arms spending to an essential minimum seemed a good way to begin retrenchment. Such a policy was adopted by the Katō Tomosaburō cabinet in 1923 and was continued by the party cabinets that succeeded it after 1924. From 1919 to 1922, the percentage of central government expenditure devoted to military expenditure dropped from thirty-nine percent to twenty-two percent, and from 1923 to 1931 it leveled off at about sixteen percent.

Although the navy was generally agreeable to this policy, there were many in the army who were not. Doctrinal disagreements and factional rivalry among the army leadership, however, neutralized this discontent. General Ugaki Kazushige, war minister from 1924 to 1927, used the demand for army retrenchment as an opportunity to challenge those senior generals who believed in an outmoded, "infantry first" approach to tactics. Under pressure from the Katō Kōmei cabinet, Ugaki agreed to deactivate four army divisions, but he received in return permission to modernize and mechanize the army with the substitution of tanks, machine guns, and aircraft for manpower. At the same time, he managed to allay some of the hardships created by the reduction of army strength by introducing military training into the middle and higher schools in

1925. The policy of arms reduction, though it satisfied the demands of party and public opinion, in no sense weakened the military strength of the country any more than naval limitations did. On the contrary, it permitted the army to survive in a new and more efficient form.

The diplomatic and defense policies of the party cabinets in the mid-1920's were inspired by the diplomatic corps, but they also rested on compromise with the army and navy high commands. The upper echelons of the military services proved as amenable to cooperation with the parties as had the civil bureaucracy, the Privy Council, and the House of Peers. For instance, during the domestic debate over the London naval agreements in 1930, the Minseitō premier, Hamaguchi Yūkō, won the support of one faction of the navy for continued limitations on naval construction, even though the new settlement was far less advantageous to Japan than the one arranged at Washington in 1921. Since the parties were able to have their way with the military, they were reluctant to curb its formal powers, feeling that the costs of such tactics would far outweigh the advantages. Moreover, the party leadership, as well as most of those in top positions outside the parties, belonged to a generation accustomed to giving high priority to national security. For patriotic as well as political reasons they were reluctant to go too far in challenging the military services.

The Crisis of Party Rule, 1930–1932

Few observers would have denied the strength of the parties in the late 1920's. The steady succession of party premiers, the domination of the electorate by the parties, and the willingness of nonparty elites to compromise with party leaders left few doubts that they were firmly entrenched in power. Yet beneath this facade of political strength there was a decided element of instability. Limited but critical segments of the army and a burgeoning civilian right wing had come to feel that continued party rule would lead the country to disaster. More ominously, these discontented did not accept the rules of the parliamentary game. Unwilling or unable to dislodge the parties by votes or even by behind-the-scenes political maneuvering, they turned instead to the tactics of extraparliamentary violence. The parties, which had built their power within the framework of the constitution, were hard pressed to defend themselves against this new form of attack.

Discontent on the right had been growing since the mid-1920's. In part, it was stimulated by a feeling that the "weak diplomacy" of the party cabinets was bankrupt. The rise of barriers to Japanese immigration in the United States, Canada, Australia, and New Zealand kindled resentment against the Anglo-American powers, who seemed unwilling to accord the Japanese full equality despite their talk of cooperation. More important, the rapidly changing situation on the Asian mainland made many feel that a navy-oriented defense policy, coupled with a respect for China's territorial integrity, no longer served Japan's best interests. The reorganization of the Kuomintang in 1924, the growing anti-imperialist sentiment of the Chinese leadership, the outbreak of antiforeign demonstrations in Shanghai, and the launching of the Kuomintang's northern expedition in 1926 all caused alarm. So did the reemergence of the Soviet Union as a military power in the Far East. By the late 1920's many elements in the army, as well as a number of civilian politicians and officials, began to fear that areas like Manchuria and Mongolia might soon fall under either Chinese or Soviet domination. They were convinced that Japan had to move into these areas in order to maintain its status as a power in a world dominated by industrial and territorial giants such as Great Britain, the United States, and the Soviet Union.

To this discontent over foreign policy was added an upsurge of agrarian populist sentiment. Despite the parties' success in building up electoral bases in the countryside, many military officers and right-wing ideologues felt that the parties had neglected the interests of the rural proletariat. Although the parties were willing to cater to the needs of big business and local "men of influence," they had made few attempts to improve the lot of the poor peasantry. The problem of rural hardship became acute in the late 1920's. Agriculture had been hit by a decade-long slump after World War I, and with the onset of world depression after 1927 it was the farm villages rather than the industrialized cities that bore the brunt of economic distress. Semiskilled workers thrown out of work returned to the native villages; daughters of farm families employed in textile mills likewise lost their jobs; falling silk prices robbed many farm families of an important source of outside income; and a series of bumper crops resulted in a sharp drop in the price of rice. The plight of the countryside, though it did not produce a grass-roots movement against the parties at election time, did much to stimulate the spread of right-wing sentiments.

Right-wing discontent erupted into political action in 1931 and 1932. It did not take the form of an organized mass movement to overthrow party rule. Rather, it expressed itself in uncoordinated acts of political violence, military insubordination, and terrorism, which undermined public confidence in the ability of the parties to control the country effectively. This series of political shocks began with the seizure of Manchuria by the Kwantung Army in the fall of 1931. A group of middle-grade staff officers, working with some tacit support from the army general staff but independently of the civilian government, engineered the occupation of the area in hopes of creating an autonomous, pro-Japanese state that would supply Japanese industry with vital raw materials and give Japan a strategic foothold on the Asian mainland for protecting its colonies and special interests there against Russian and Chinese pressure. The Wakatsuki government proved unable to reverse this *fait accompli.* At the same time, parallel efforts were made to bring about a military *coup d'état* as well. Two major military insurrections were plotted in March and October of 1931, but both proved abortive. The top leaders of the army, who were more interested in reasserting military influence through legal and constitutional means, were apprehensive that the political activities of lower officials might disrupt army discipline. When the army high command failed to act, more radical elements in the army joined hands with civilian right-wing societies to purge the country of corrupt party rule through terrorism. In early 1932 a wave of bloody murders culminated in the assassination of Premier Inukai Tsuyoshi.

The Manchurian incident, the attempted military coups, and the rise of political terrorism created an atmosphere of national crisis that precipitated the final fall of the parties from power. The *jūshin,* or "senior statesmen," a group of former premiers and imperial court officials who had taken over the genro's function of nominating the premier, decided that the leaders of the political parties had lost control of both foreign policy and the domestic situation. They felt that the only way to surmount the crisis was to experiment once more with "national unity" cabinets. Their intention was not so much antiparty as antimilitary, and they hoped that the appointment of a neutral figure free of partisan ties could stop the country's slow drift toward a militaristic foreign policy and army insubordination. Since the parties had provided no institutional guarantees for the continuation of party rule, they were powerless to prevent the return to nonparty cabinets. Many party leaders protested the overthrow of "normal constitutional government." So too did a few moderate liberal intellectuals. But beyond this there was no very effective attempt to restore party rule, nor even a very spirited public defense of party rule in principle.

The ease with which party rule was brought to an end rested on certain long-run weaknesses of the parties. These weaknesses did not "cause" the fall of the parties but merely made it easy for much of the public to accept that fall with equanimity. First of all, there was the failure of the parties to achieve genuine popularity during their three decades of hegemony. Their electoral success rested on their appeals to pragmatic interests, not on their ability to generate emotional support. The mass of the voters cast their ballots with an eye to concrete economic benefits, whether in the form of park-barrel legislation, local subsidies, or bribery money. But their primary political loyalties were to the emperor or the nation rather than to the political parties. They had supported the parties for instrumental reasons more than for moral ones. Secondly, the growing sense of foreign crisis made many feel that the times were too unsettled to permit the parties to continue in power. The aggressive policies of the army were cloaked in the language of patriotism and national interest, which appealed to deeply rooted sentiments of nationalism. The highly patriotic content of primary education, the indoctrination of military conscripts, the establishment of reservist associations in the countryside, and the memory of Japan's heroic victories over China and Russia created a reservoir of popular chauvinism that reached even the remotest village. As long as the overseas adventures of the military succeeded, many Japanese felt the country was shaping a new national destiny for itself in Asia. They were not enthusiastic for a return to the more pacific foreign policies of the 1920's. Finally, the intellectual community, which had been alienated by the reluctance to move more rapidly toward social and political reform, remained indifferent to the plight of the political parties. On the contrary, many left-wing leaders saw the emergence of a national crisis as the beginning of the end for plutocratic rule and welcomed army radicalism as a motor for change. Moreover, many intellectuals were likewise caught up in the newly quickened sense of national purpose that began to envelop the country after 1932.

The end of party rule in 1932 did not mean an end of the parties, however. They did not die but merely faded in influence. There were no attempts to suppress the parties or to challenge their right to exist. Throughout the 1930's, the two major parties continued to dominate the Diet, voters continued to cast their ballots overwhelmingly in favor of the parties, party men debated the pros and cons of national policy in the Diet, and premiers continued to recruit party leaders to fill cabinet posts. Similarly, the whole structure of interest politics in local communities remained intact. Only in 1940 were the political parties finally dissolved, and a one-party system was organized to replace them. But even then the old bonds of party cohesion, the old local bases of support, and the old habits of political participation remained strong. As a result, when freed from the burden of military domination in 1946, the party system was quick to recover its strength, and a new era of party rule was under way.

Selected Readings

Duus, Peter. *Party Rivalry and Political Change in Taishō Japan.* Cambridge, Mass.: Harvard University Press, 1968. A study of the emergence of two-party politics, the establishment of party cabinets, and party attempts at social and political reform.

Goodman, Grant, ed. *Imperial Japan and Asia.* New York: East Asia Institute, Columbia University, 1967. A collection of essays on Japanese foreign policy from the late Meiji through the Shōwa period.

Iriye, Akira. *After Imperialism: The Search for a New Order in East Asia.* Cambridge, Mass.: Harvard University Press, 1965. A thorough study of international relations in East Asia in the 1920's that sheds much light on the motives behind Japanese foreign policy.

Marshall, Byron K. *Capitalism and Nationalism in Prewar Japan: The Ideology of the Business Elite, 1868–1941.* Stanford, Calif.: Stanford University Press, 1967. A brief but interesting account of Japanese businessmen's views on national politics and on the social role of business.

Maruyama, Masao. *Thought and Behavior in Japanese Politics.* London: Oxford University Press, 1965. A series of brilliant essays by one of Japan's foremost scholars and political critics on the popular intellectual milieu of prewar Japan. Extremely stimulating reading.

Morley, James W. *The Japanese Thrust into Siberia, 1918.* New York: Columbia University Press, 1957. A detailed study of one aspect of Japan's foreign policy that gives much insight into the workings of the Japanese political system.

Najita, Tetsuo. *Hara Kei in the Politics of Compromise, 1905–1915.* Cambridge, Mass.: Harvard University Press, 1967. An excellent study of the development of the Seiyūkai during the decade following the Russo-Japanese War.

Ogata, Sadako N. *Defiance in Manchuria: The Making of Japanese Foreign Policy, 1931–1932.* Berkeley, Calif.: University of California Press, 1964. An incisive account of the events that led to the end of party rule.

Scalapino, Robert A. *Democracy and the Party Movement in Prewar Japan.* Berkeley, Calif.: University of California Press, 1962. An influential interpretation of prewar party politics, reflecting postwar pessimism toward the viability of representative democracy in Japan.

Totten, George O., III. *The Social Democratic Movement in Prewar Japan.* New Haven, Conn.: Yale University Press, 1966. A meticulous examination of the proletarian party movement from its origins through the 1930's, at times overwhelming in detail.

Young, A. Morgan. *Japan in Recent Times, 1912–1926.* New York: William Morrow, 1929. A contemporary history based on English-language newspaper accounts that is filled with factual inaccuracies but conveys the atmosphere of the period.

Communism, Nationalism, and Democracy: The Chinese Intelligentsia and the Chinese Revolution in the 1920's and 1930's

JEROME B. GRIEDER

IT is tempting to think of the three decades that confront us here, the thirty years of political turmoil, militarism, and social disintegration from 1919 to 1949, either as an extended and increasingly dissonant coda to the great historical themes played out in the early years of the twentieth century or as an uncertain and sometimes cacophonous overture to the militant drama of the 1950's and the 1960's. The sudden disappearance of imperial institutions notwithstanding, much of "old" China survived the shock of the revolution of 1911, stubborn witness to the durability of that venerable traditional order. Habits of mind and conduct cultivated over the long centuries of Confucian imperialism did not succumb easily, even when the institutional structure they had supported no longer existed in any formal sense. "Republicanism," the cause for which a generation of revolutionaries had propagandized and plotted, meant nothing to the vast bulk of the Chinese people, bound still to the parochial prejudices of their forefathers, bred in ignorance of the modern world, condemned to a barren and hazardous livelihood. And to those few who, through education and experience, had become partisans of the new ideals, the new forms seemed no more than hollow mockeries, a "modern" veneer barely concealing the familiar contours of familial despotism, political ineptitude, and intellectual stagnation.

Thus did the inheritance of the past shroud the Chinese present in the wake of the 1911 revolution and the May Fourth movement. Yet in these years we may also discern, with the privilege of retrospection, other themes more suggestive of what was to come than of what had been. It was during this time, in so many respects a dismal and disheartening interlude, that the Chinese appropriated the revolutionary doctrine they would later transmute into the vengeful and hopeful creed of a resurgent nation; it was during this period, too, that the Chinese devised the political and organizational skills necessary to sustain such a resurgence and translated the republican myth of an earlier time into a genuinely populist strategy of political life. As we look back across those decades, then, it may sometimes seem that there were forces at work that led with quickening inevitability to the crescendo of 1949.

Such impressions possess something more than casual validity. But we would do well to try to think of these years not merely as a reprise, or only as a prelude. For the men whose thoughts and actions comprise the substance of this history, this was not time past but time present. They might look back upon what was their past with nostalgia or with revulsion; they might look to the future with confidence or with dread. But they lived in a time that had, for them, its own significance, a succession of singular days full of perplexities and of promise. In this spirit, then, let us try to rediscover what that significance may have been, and what the promise that gave them hope.

The May Fourth Movement and the May Fourth Era

On the morning of Sunday, May 4, 1919, some thousands of university and middle-school students swarmed into the streets of Peking to demonstrate —by their presence and by the placards they carried aloft and the slogans they shouted as they marched—their disapproval of the manner in which China had been treated at the Paris Peace Conference and, equally important, their sense of betrayal by their own government, the warlord regime of Tuan Ch'i-jui.

Nowhere more than in China had Wilsonian principles been taken to heart in the late teens, at least by the small and articulate minority of Chinese whose opinions constituted the "public" opinion of the day. The Chinese had persuaded themselves, moreover, that their token representation on the Allied side in the recently concluded war, and their participation in the peacemaking that followed, must signal the beginning of a new era in Sino-Western relations, an era that would bring to China the long-sought equality of status among nations. It was, of course, an idle hope. The European powers were too mired at Paris in the diplomacy of retribution to pay sufficient attention to the situation in the Pacific; nor was President Wilson prepared to make the Chinese case a test of those very principles that had roused such enthusiasm among Chinese students and intellectuals. The result of this indifference is well known: The Japanese, who had considerately taken over the administration of formerly German-leased territories in Shantung as their major contribution to the Allied victory, found themselves confirmed in this position at Paris. The Chinese were left with only shattered hopes, an overwhelming sense of betrayal, bitter disillusionment with the meaning of Western ideals, and a profound and smoldering anger.

Nonetheless, a new era was dawning for China, not in Paris but closer to home, in Peking and Shanghai and Tientsin and Hankow and the other centers of the disturbances that erupted in May and June of 1919. The students who inscribed, in their own blood on the whitewashed walls of university dining halls and dormitories, denunciations of the Japanese, their Western supporters, and their Chinese cohorts, the students who marched through the streets of the ancient capital or who carried the movement into the streets of other cities over the next days and weeks —these were the prototype of a new generation of intellectual and political leadership, the first representatives of a new force in China's revolutionary experience.

It was not the function of intellectual dissent that was new in China but rather its substance and the manner of its expression. Confucian society had always assigned to its intellectual elite—those versed in Confucian literature and sensitive to Confucian standards of right conduct—an important role as critics of the political order. Often this responsibility had been discharged only at the level of symbolic remonstrance, but on occasion criticism of imperial policy had been more forcefully expressed, by individuals or by groups, sometimes with dire consequences for the critics. The "student protest" organized by K'ang Yu-wei and Liang Ch'i-ch'ao among examination candidates gathered in Peking in 1895 had been somewhat in this tradition. But the student protests of 1919 were far different in scope and in intent. The temper of their challenge to authority is less reminiscent of the traditional style of criticism within the accepted limits of a reigning orthodoxy than it is suggestive of the kind of intellectual dissent that has become increasingly familiar the world over in the last half-century. The Chinese students of 1919 proclaimed their lack of confidence in the warlord government of the day. More than this, they denied the legitimacy of any government in which the Chinese people refused to place their confidence. It was this assertion—implied rather than articulated, at the time—that constituted the real impact of the May Fourth experience on later Chinese politics.

The students, of course, regarded themselves as spokesmen for the Chinese people, since the masses were as yet incapable of taking such an initiative themselves. In this sense the intellectual dissenters of the May Fourth period reflected a self-image much in the pattern of earlier Confucian history. To a significant degree, however, the May Fourth movement involved others besides the students. It received substantial support not only from the small urban professional class, largely Western trained —the teachers, journalists, lawyers, engineers, doctors, and technicians who serviced China's growing modern enterprises—but from the urban commercial class, from large manufacturers, and from small shopkeepers, who participated in the movement by supporting the anti-Japanese boycott. The May Fourth movement was the closest thing to a "mass" movement that the Chinese had experienced to that time. And it brought into prominence and temporary alliance social forces that would figure importantly in the tempestuous course of the next three decades: the dissident (if not yet entirely disaffected) younger intelligentsia, the more or less modernized (or Westernized) elements of the urban population, and the commercial bourgeoisie.

In these respects, 1919 appears an even more significant year than 1911. And it is not without cause that Chinese Communist historians are wont to trace the origins of the Communist movement to this period, partly because the May Fourth movement lent impetus to the popularization of Marxist-Leninist social and political analysis—theories that had barely begun to attract an intellectual audience on the eve of the events of 1919—and also because this informal collaboration between discontented intellectuals and nationalistic businessmen foreshadowed the revolutionary strategy later pursued with some success by the Chinese Communists.

So far, indeed, has a later generation gone in glorifying "the spirit of May Fourth" that we would do well to remind ourselves here of the limitations of the movement. First, and perhaps most significant, is the fact that it never spread beyond the cities. While the students marched through the streets of Peking and organized anti-Japanese boycotts among the shopkeepers of Shanghai, in the villages—even those on the very outskirts of such great centers of modern enterprise and political ferment—the peasants remained aloof, not disapproving, but mystified, and immune to the sense of injury that burned so deeply in the minds of the young intellectuals. May Fourth was an urban movement, involving only those upon whom the influence of the West, both as a source of inspiration and as an object of hatred, had been most pronounced. The May Fourth generation took scant cognizance of the afflictions of peasant life except in the most general terms; nor did it seek in any purposeful way the support of the peasantry. Years would pass before the brutal energy of the peasants' misery would be harnessed directly to the realization of revolutionary goals.

Nor, again, did the May Fourth movement touch in any very compelling fashion upon the lives and minds of the Chinese working class, even in the larger cities. In some places, it is true, dockworkers refused to unload Japanese ships, and there were instances in which rickshaw men refused to carry Japanese fares. "Workers" took part in some of the open-air demonstrations in North China. But for the most part the laborers in the textile mills, the match and tobacco and powdered-egg factories, the tiny, old-fashioned ateliers that crowded every thoroughfare—this con-glomerate class that would within a few years find itself addressed as the "proletariat" and thrust forward as the instrument and the beneficiary of revolutionary progress—played a subsidiary role at best in the unfolding events of 1919.

And, finally, we must take note of the limited political accomplish-ments of the movement, at least in the short run. The students succeeded in embarrassing the government of Tuan Ch'i-jui and in bringing it down in the summer of 1919; and, buried beneath an avalanche of outraged protests from home and from Chinese communities the world over, the Chinese delegation in Paris withheld its signature from the Versailles treaty. But Tuan Ch'i-jui was only one militarist, and warlordism re-mained the fashion in China. And the imperialist powers, Western and Japanese, were unmoved by the symbolism of the Chinese gesture at Versailles. The May Fourth movement did not purge Chinese politics of the corruption of militarism or bring China appreciably closer to the establishment of a more equitable relationship with the West.

But the May Fourth movement did have an enduring significance. It marked the reemergence of the intellectual elite as a self-conscious force in Chinese public life. The Confucian elite of an earlier time had van-ished, the ground cut out from under it by the erosion of Confucian standards of conduct and the destruction of the institutions that had been designed to cultivate and exploit the arts of Confucian culture. Now once again an enlightened and concerned minority stepped forward to exercise the time-honored responsibility of remonstrance on behalf of a dumb and passive people. Yet the past could not really repeat itself. The difference between the old elite and the new was that the old had served, for the most part unquestioningly, a system of public values that by the 1920's had been generally discredited and repudiated. The new elite, reclaiming a historical right to speak as the public conscience of the nation, did so at a time when public values were uncertain, when even the traditional assumption that the people must not speak for themselves was question-able. For the first time in the long history of Chinese political speculation, terms such as "individualism" and "human rights" challenged the right of the minority to assume that a sense of moral responsibility carried with it the privilege of political authority.

The vanguard of the May Fourth movement—the students and teach-ers, the opinionated and articulate urban professional groups, the writers and scholars, the bourgeoisie—represented a potentially useful revolution-ary force, a force that those who held political power or aspired to it would endeavor to exploit in the years that followed. But the movement itself was not the product of political calculation or ideological fanati-cism. It was, rather, a spontaneous outburst of genuine feeling. It is the intellectual liberality of the May Fourth period, the extraordinarily rich and free quality of the intellectual environment that engendered it, that make of that hopeful era a standard against which to measure the potential of the Chinese revolution. It was a time, rare in the history of any people and unprecedented in the experience of the Chinese, when the traditional image of the world had all but vanished. The forms that had given structure to the old society were held in disrepute even where they survived, as was largely still true with respect to the family system. Confucianism was reviled in substance and in form. The enormous body of classical literature, which had been for centuries the private preserve of the erudite Confucian scholar-bureaucrat, his bastion and his refuge, was now consigned—in the colorfully bitter phrase of one of the intellectual radicals of the day—to the privy. The classical written language itself, ornate, intricate, self-absorbed and supremely burdensome, was rejected in favor of a written language patterned on the colloquial. Perhaps nothing better symbolized the determination of China's young intellectuals to liberate themselves and their people from the weight of the past than this "literary revolution" and its implied challenge to the idea that education belongs to the few and bestows upon them a position of political and social preeminence. There was, in the ethos of the May Fourth generation, a profoundly democratic element, albeit tentative and unprogrammed. The May Fourth intellectuals were in some respects the lineal descendants of Confucian forebears, as I have suggested, but they had a different dream for their descendants.

In another significant respect the May Fourth era stands in sharp contrast to the tradition out of which it emerged. Never before had the Chinese been as willing to measure themselves against the standards of alien accomplishment, to set their own history against the perspective of a wider human history, or to aspire to membership in the world community, not only as a matter of political right, but with a sense of intellectual obligation. The venerable tradition of cultural self-containment and self-sufficiency that had been a natural consequence of China's historical experience had suffered fatal blows in the course of the nineteenth century. An invincible culture had revealed irreparable flaws. This realization had borne in fully upon turn-of-the-century reformers like Yen Fu and Liang Ch'i-ch'ao. But it was not until the May Fourth generation came into its own—the generation that had had its earliest image of the world shaped by Yen and Liang and had gone on to points they had never reached—that the harsh and unwelcome lesson was drawn with candor. The uniqueness of China's past and the sometimes imposing accomplishments of Confucian civilization could no longer excuse Chinese pretensions to uniqueness in the present or vouchsafe a comparable record of achievement in the future. In the May Fourth period a spirit of genuine cosmopolitanism flourished as never before.

The most obvious reason for this was the fact that among the leaders of this new generation, men older in experience than the students themselves though scarcely riper in years, there were many who had been exposed personally to the culture of the West, as students in European and American universities or in the universities of that remarkably Western (at least in Chinese eyes) Asian neighbor, Japan. These were men for whom, in many cases, the bare bones of "Western learning" had been clothed in the flesh of true appreciation for Western values. And when they returned to their professorships of law, or history, or literature, or philosophy, or to their bureaucratic posts, or to the practice of law or medicine in Shanghai or Tientsin, or to the pursuit of careers in journalism, engineering, banking and finance, communications, or transportation, these "returned students" brought with them, not only new ideas and aspirations, but a new capacity for critical comparison.

It was the May Fourth era, then, that marked the dividing line between tradition and modernity even more distinctly than the years that had culminated in the revolutionary dismemberment of the Manchu monarchy. As if to provide cosmic recognition of this transition, in the decade that followed the May Fourth movement the erstwhile advocates of intellectual and political reform passed physically from the scene: Yen Fu, disconsolate and misunderstood, in 1921; K'ang Yu-wei in 1927, clinging with anachronistic fervor to his monarchist loyalties right to the end; and Liang Ch'i-ch'ao, who had weathered the stormy crossing from monarchism to republicanism better than his old teacher, respected and mourned in 1929. Even Sun Yat-sen, the very personification of China's brief revolutionary tradition, passed from life into legend in 1925. (We will shortly turn our attention to the final years of that life and to the legend that grew out of it.)

This, then, was the May Fourth era, a time of bitter frustration and exuberant hope, of naive self-confidence and sophisticated self-criticism, of unparalled political cynicism and a remarkable resurgence of public conscience. It was a time when the glacial mass of traditional orthodoxy had begun visibly to crack and new ideas coursed like spring rivulets through the land, a time when, seemingly, the Chinese stood ready to assume the place they claimed for themselves as citizens of a modern world order and a modern civilization. Out of these years of intellectual ferment and social and political stagnation emerged the forces that would dominate the political life of China over the next decades, determining the destiny of its people and the fate of those ideals of democracy and cosmopolitanism that were the peculiar values of the May Fourth generation.

The Nationalist Revolution, 1924–1928

History has not treated the Nationalist movement kindly. Almost from the beginning it has had a bad press, though not always for the same reasons. And it has ended something short of victory, if not in total defeat. It is difficult now to disentangle the accomplishments of the movement from the hopes that once were held for it, the claims that were made in its name, and the burden of misfortune that was laid on it by circumstance. From today's perspective it is as hard to see in the artificial and ludicrously ponderous Nationalist regime that governs Taiwan any resemblance to the brash and radical revolutionary movement of forty years ago as it is to perceive in the sunken visage and vacantly benign smile of the aging Generalissimo the smooth cheek, the determined chin, and the imperious gaze of the young commander who led his anti-imperialist armies of liberation northward in the mid-1920's. Yet we must make the effort, for the Nationalists, in their time, were the masters of China and left upon it deep, if not indelible, evidence of their passing.

The Nationalist party of the 1920's was a hybrid organization. It traced its origins back to earlier revolutionary organizations, and in the person of Sun Yat-sen it had a leader with impeccable credentials as the spokesman for what had been most distinguished of that earlier revolutionary tradition. Yet it was also the product of a time closer at hand, the idealistic and iconoclastic May Fourth era. Its nationalism was rooted in the anti-imperialism of the late teens, the basic stuff of Chinese politics from that time forward. Yet it combined this with other, more exotic elements: a curious theory of the state that endeavored to reconcile republicanism with party elitism; intraparty organizational techniques that were fundamentally incompatible with the democratic principles the party nominally espoused; and an ambiguous economic program, based on a wide variety of sources, that failed withal to touch upon the pressing issues of social and economic reform in the countryside.

For much of this confusion Sun Yat-sen must be held responsible. It was, perhaps, no more than the confusion natural to one of such strangely mixed intellectual antecedents and uneven political experience: the peasant boy with a Western education, the physician turned revolutionary conspirator, the idealistic reformer, supremely confident of his own messianic importance, compelled to fight for his political life, matching wits with militarists to whom his visions were as dust.

Sun is certainly among the strangest figures to appear on the modern Chinese scene, in some respects the most complicated and enigmatic. As innumerable witnesses attest, he was a man of singular personal attractiveness despite the rather dour and ordinary impression conveyed by his photographs. He took with him to his grave in 1925 the extraordinary charisma that had enabled him to survive since the turn of the century as the leader of a fragmented revolutionary party. He left behind only a vague and ambiguous collection of speeches, manifestos, and political tracts to serve as the founding orthodoxy of the revolutionary government that fought its way to power in the years immediately after his death. Some of the frailties of the Nationalist regime that claimed him as its patron must certainly be laid to the peculiarities of the ideology that Sun bequeathed to his political heirs and to the reorganization of the party that Sun engineered in the last years of his life.

The reorganization of the Nationalist party (the Kuomintang, or KMT) was effected in the years 1923 and 1924 as a result of the convergence of several forces. An unbroken if not very straight line can be drawn between the Kuomintang of the 1920's and the various revolutionary factions that had coalesced into the prerevolutionary T'ung-meng hui, with Sun as one of its central personalities. The nature of that organization and the difficulties that beset it before and after the 1911 revolution are matters that lie outside the scope of this essay. Suffice it to say here that the failure of the revolutionary forces to realize their initial aims and the precarious conditions of Sun's life during the early years of the republic left him understandably scarred in spirit and mind. He sought relief from his profound sense of disillusionment in the belief that the revolution had foundered because his own leadership had been betrayed by the inability of his subordinates to understand his vision. By 1917 and 1918, years that saw Sun living virtually as an exile in Shanghai, a mystique of party leadership was already taking form in his mind, with ominous implications for the future development of his party.

It is impossible to speculate as to what Sun's fate, or that of his cause, might have been without the coincidental intrusion of two unrelated circumstances: the Bolshevik revolution in Russia and the May Fourth disturbances in China. Each of these contributed in its own way to the reshaping of the revolutionary movement in the early twenties. Of the latter I have already written at some length. Of the former more must be said when we examine the genesis of Marxist-Leninist ideas in China. Here we may confine ourselves to the observation that it was the May Fourth movement that provided a climate hospitable to the nationalistic revolutionary movement of the early twenties, aimed against the twin enemies of imperialism and militarism, and the Bolshevik revolution—or, more accurately, its representatives who came to China to assay the native revolutionary vein—that offered both inspiration and model for this experiment. From the outset, then, the reviving fortunes of the Nationalist party drew strength from sources that were, at certain levels, incompatible: the vigorously iconoclastic, self-critical, and cosmopolitan spirit of the May Fourth period, with its genuinely democratic inclination, and the rigid discipline of Leninist party organization and ideology, "democratic" only in a very limited sense and "internationalist" (where the Chinese were concerned) only in its rhetoric.

Sun found the Bolshevik—or Comintern—emissaries who sought him out in Shanghai congenial enough company, ready to applaud his revolutionary ideas and, more significantly, to offer, not only the kind of organizational advice that might help him mold the KMT into a more satisfactory revolutionary instrument, but substantial material assistance. For their part, the procession of Dutchmen, Indians, and Russians who made their way to China beginning in 1920, as representatives of the cause of world revolution under Comintern auspices, soon came to regard Sun and the Nationalists as useful allies, the most coherent revolutionary organization then on the scene and entirely amenable to the anti-imperialist policies espoused by the Comintern.

"Nationalism" (min-tsu chu-i), which had been first among Sun Yat-sen's celebrated "Three People's Principles" since shortly after the turn of the century, became in the final years of his life synonymous with anti-imperialism, and he became increasingly vituperative in his expression of it. The Bolsheviks, of course, cannot be given the full credit for this. The contemporary climate of opinion was laden with distrust of the Western powers, as we have noted. And Sun himself had reason to bear the West little good will, having been rebuffed repeatedly in his attempts since 1912 to secure Western support for his struggling cause. Yet, even while he denounced the West for having brought China to its present pass, Sun remained hopeful, almost to the moment of his death, of massive economic and technical assistance from the West and Japan. To this end he made, from time to time, remarkable proposals for foreign investment in China—proposals that, had they been implemented, would have compromised China's economic and political integrity to a far greater degree than even the most ambitious and avaricious imperialist of a former day would have dreamed possible. Partly for this reason, and also because of their long-standing preference for recognizing the Peking government whoever might control it for the moment, it was easy for the major powers to dismiss Sun's movement as devious, unrealistic and potentially dangerous to their own interests, even after Sun contrived to establish himself at the head of a "legitimate" republican government in Canton in 1920–21, as an alternative to the northern warlords, and reports began to circulate of the unusual popular support that his cause elicited from among the common people. The Soviets were more astute, perhaps, or more cynical. In any case, the conflict in Sun's mind between his genuine hatred for Western encroachment and his equally genuine admiration for Western economic and technical superiority proved irreconcilable also in the larger context of Nationalist party policy. From the beginning, the

Nationalist program was an unstable combination of anti-imperialism on the one hand and Western-oriented economic reform on the other.

The second principle in Sun's trinity was "livelihood," or the people's welfare (*min-sheng chu-i*). He insisted that the term went beyond the Western concept of "socialism" (Marxist or otherwise) to embrace principles of economic justice enshrined—at least in the rather romantic view of some of the more traditionally inclined of Sun's associates—in the most ancient Chinese visions of the good society. Sun's Comintern advisers laid upon him no obligation to recast his own economic theories in conformity with Marxist-Leninist principles or to accept the Marxist-Leninist analysis of Chinese social and economic classes. He was, in their eyes, a bourgeois nationalist and, for the time being, sufficiently useful as such. Sun's economic program remained vaguely defined, treating in grandiose terms such things as railway development and all but ignoring the urgent problems of economic and social reform at the village level and the responsibilities of the government in effecting such reform.

It was the last of Sun's three principles, however, the principle of "democracy" (*min-chu chu-i*), that suffered most in the reshaping of KMT ideology and organization. Before 1912 the assumption common to most of the republican revolutionaries seems to have been that popular sovereignty and the political forms associated with it, standing at the opposite pole from the autocratic despotism of the Manchu imperial structure, would spontaneously triumph once the autocracy had been toppled. The disasters that befell the republican cause during the ascendancy of Yuan Shih-k'ai quickly discredited such optimism, and the lesson was learned, perhaps, only too well. If republicanism had failed the first time for want of adequate preparation, the fate of democracy was sealed the second time by excessive planning. Sun wrote into his revised scheme a thorough and orderly revolutionary timetable, beginning with the seizure of power by military means and proceeding thereafter through a period of "political education," during which the people would be instructed in the use of their political rights and duties, to an ultimate condition of constitutional democracy. Sun did not live to see, nor perhaps could he have anticipated, the tendency of this progression to stop short of its final goal.

The agency charged with the responsibility for supervising the revolutionary process and the political education of the Chinese people was, of course, the Nationalist party itself. The party that emerged from the reorganization undertaken during Sun's last years has sometimes been described as a compromise between Leninist principles of party organization and the amorality of warlord politics. Such a description, however, is neither entirely accurate nor altogether just. Although patterned on the Leninist model, the reorganized KMT never attained the degree of inner discipline that Lenin imposed on the Bolshevik party. And, despite the fact that the KMT was compelled to absorb numerous warlord elements in the course of its rise to power, it maintained, for all its shortcomings, a broader and more compelling vision than had any of the warlord regimes that it replaced. Nonetheless, the Leninist-warlord image is a telling one. Sun's desire to establish the primacy of his own leadership within the party rendered it vulnerable to autocratic methods of control that were exploited by those who competed for the succession to party leadership after Sun's demise. And, almost from the outset, military priorities remained foremost in the drafting of party policy—partly, perhaps, as a result of the mentality of its leadership but also in consequence of the conditions it confronted.

Sun Yat-sen died in 1925, the leader of a reviving but still largely impotent revolutionary regime whose authority was confined to the southern province of Kwangtung and, by means of uneasy alliances with the local militarists, certain immediately adjacent areas. Sun died before even the first step toward the realization of his vision could be undertaken, the military reunification of the long-divided nation. But by the time of his death the forces that would make this possible were already coming into being. The revolution was arming itself with the assistance of its new Soviet allies, and at Whampoa, near Canton, an ideologically committed officer corps was in training under the military command of a young soldier named Chiang Kai-shek and the political guidance of an even younger recruit to the Chinese Communist party named Chou En-lai. Finally, a conscious attempt was being made to establish contact with the masses, to devise a revolutionary message that would be comprehensible to the workers and the peasants, and, by involving them in its realization, to provide a mass base for the revolutionary movement.

Ernest P. Young has remarked upon the propensity of China's revolutionary leaders in the pre–May Fourth era to speak of "social revolution" without committing themselves to the belief that the kind of social reforms so obviously imperative in the West would be similarly needful in China. Sun Yat-sen was as prone to this kind of thinking as were the political "moderates" like Liang Ch'i-ch'ao. Even under the influence of his Comintern advisers, Sun never acknowledged the relevance to China of the Marxist-Leninist concept of class antagonism, nor did he accept the idea that the victory of *his* revolution was contingent upon a fundamental revision of the class structure in China. By the early 1920's, however, there were others associated with the Nationalist movement who were of a different mind, most notably the Chinese Communists who had taken membership in the Kuomintang under the conditions of Sun's agreement with the Comintern. Like a magnet, the revolutionary government had attracted the disaffected and the idealistic to the south; Canton had become a haven and a rallying ground for men involved in the promotion of social revolution. Within the still limited jurisdiction of Sun's influence, the organization of workers and peasants made considerable headway.

From the outset, then, the Nationalist movement was divided against itself, though the extent of the rift remained concealed for some time. The burgeoning military establishment drew much of its support, and recruited a good share of its manpower, from the conservative "politicized" gentry that had risen to prominence in provincial politics over the first decades of the century, a class easily enough fired with nationalist and anti-imperialist sentiments but fundamentally hostile to the sweeping social reforms espoused by the Left, whether within or outside of the Kuomintang itself.

The revolutionary coalition that took form in South China in the early twenties was, then, inherently an unstable combination of forces. Yet for a few critical years it proved also an enormously potent combination. A little more than a year after Sun Yat-sen's death, the Northern Expedition was finally launched, the revolutionary armies being preceded by political cadres who prepared the way for its passing, igniting for the first time the tinder of social unrest in the countryside and readying the great centers of Western commercial enterprise along the Yangtze, from Hankow to Shanghai, for liberation from the imperialist yoke. Within a remarkably short time the warlords had been evicted from Central China and the wealthy Yangtze area claimed for the revolution. Then, after a few months' respite, the armies moved northward once more, extending their victory all the way to the ancient capital at Peking by the early summer of 1928. On October 10, 1928, the seventeenth anniversary of the 1911 revolution, the reunification of China was officially declared to have been accomplished, and the period of political education was inaugurated. Thus the revolution triumphed. But what was won had been won at great cost, not only to the enemies of the revolutionary cause, but to that cause itself.

The Origins and Development of the Chinese Communist Party, 1918–1928

Communism came to China, as we have noted, in the wake of the Bolshevik revolution in Russia, riding the wave of disillusionment with the West that followed naturally from the spectacle of European self-destruction and the diplomatic catastrophe at Paris. In that era of feverish intellectual experimentation and discovery, Marxism came to China as a hopeful idea, not as a seriously considered program of action or theory of organization. Its first adherents were intellectuals: Li Ta-chao, librarian at Peking National University, the intellectual center of the ferment of May Fourth; Ch'en Tu-hsiu, dean of the College of Arts at the same university and founder of *The New Youth,* the magazine that had been since 1915 the authentic voice of radical cultural reform; and a growing number of students, some returned from European and Japanese schooling (very few of the American-educated were early converts to the new faith), others raised in the native tradition of radicalism—like Mao Tse-tung (though no one would pay him much mind for several years to come).

For men such as these, Marxism kindled once more a hope that had been all but extinguished by the recent European debacle: the hope of harnessing the enormous power of Western technology to the task of raising China to membership in a new world order—a *moral* world order. And more, Marxism, as emended by Lenin, gave the Chinese a role to play in the unfolding drama and made of China something more than the passive victim or the passive beneficiary of a history it had no part in shaping. Lenin preached that European capitalism, having survived its first crises by casting its net to trap the resources and markets of the non-European world, would be destroyed when the strands of that net, the web of imperialist exploitation, were severed one by one. This, of course, simplifies what is in fact a complex theory of economic and political relationships. But the underlying message was simple enough, or seemed so to the Chinese: Drive the imperialists from China, and some part of the vitality of capitalism will be sapped; evict the Westerners from their privileged position in China, and all mankind will be brought some distance nearer to liberation from the bondage of capitalism itself. This, certainly, was a vision that fitted the mood of the moment in China. The difficult discipline of Leninist principles of party organization, like the rigid categories of Marxist class analysis, would take longer to learn.

It was the intellectualism, the somewhat academic bookishness of China's first converts to Marxism-Leninism, that encouraged the Comintern representatives to look elsewhere for an organized movement through which to pursue their own ends and finally to attach themselves to Sun Yat-sen and his Nationalists. At the same time, however, they set about educating the Chinese Marxists and transforming the Marxist study groups that had sprung up in Peking and Shanghai in 1918 and 1919 into the foundations upon which, in 1921, the Chinese Communist party was established. In the ensuing years substantial progress was made in turning the interests of the Chinese Communists in the direction of revolutionary organization. All the currents of political and social unrest that marked the rising tide of nationalism in the early 1920's bore the Communists along in increasing numbers: the student disturbances that erupted from time to time, most dramatically in the late spring of 1925, in the wake of bloody confrontations between demonstrators and foreign gendarmes in the concessions at Shanghai and Canton; the occasional attempts to organize the peasants against the scourge of rents and taxes and conscription; the boycotts that cut into British and Japanese trade; the strikes that sputtered and flared among dock workers, railway laborers, and workers in the textile industry.

Yet paradoxically the Communist party, the product of a nationalistic age and the instrument of nationalistic aspirations, remained throughout the first decade of its existence under the disastrous discipline of policies drafted far from the scene of conflict in China, by men whose understanding of Chinese conditions was scanty and prejudiced and who were concerned with the promotion of Chinese nationalism only as a means to the achievement of other purposes. The policies to which the Chinese Communist party was committed were determined, in substantial measure, in Moscow, in accordance with analyses of the revolutionary situation in China that reflected the established Comintern line of the moment. The Chinese Communists were accordingly instructed that the socialist revolution in China must remain for the time being subservient to the bourgeois-nationalist revolution aimed at the expulsion of imperialism. They were also urged to improve their urban base of operations in preparation for the ultimate triumph of the proletarian revolution.

Thus was the party compelled, even against the wishes of Ch'en Tu-hsiu, its first General Secretary, to ally itself with Sun's Nationalists in 1923. I have already described briefly the results of that alliance, fruitful for both partners for a time, yet distrustful from the first. Without doubt the Communists contributed significantly to the early successes of the Northern Expedition, providing much of the personnel needed for the political indoctrination of the areas through which the armies of liberation made their victorious progress. Yet neither the Communists nor the Nationalists—at least after Sun's death—regarded this kind of cooperation as permanently feasible. The Comintern policy, which after Lenin's death in 1924 became increasingly a matter of contention among his would-be successors, was clearly opportunistic: The Chinese Communists were to maintain a working relationship with the Kuomintang until such time as they were prepared to seize control of the revolution from within.

As it happened, however, it was the Kuomintang that took the initiative to sunder the alliance. As the wave of the Northern Expedition crested in April 1927, with the rich ports of the lower Yangtze open before it, Chiang Kai-shek moved swiftly and ruthlessly against his erstwhile allies. In Shanghai, workers who had risen in expectation of the impending arrival of the revolutionary forces were put down with savage determination. Throughout the ensuing spring and summer the "white terror" gripped the cities and countryside of Central China. Membership in the Communist party, which had grown from sixty or so at the time of the first party congress in 1921 to nearly sixty thousand by the early months of 1927, plunged precipitously. And the few thousand who survived were harried throughout the land as the urban organization so carefully nurtured was systematically laid waste—for Chiang's strength, too, was in the cities. For a few months the Communists maintained, still at the behest of Stalin and the Comintern, a tenuous relationship with the Kuomintang Left, which had, for personal as well as political reasons, established an opposition government in Hankow, upriver from Chiang's new capital at Nanking. But in midsummer, when the dissidents finally recognized their military vulnerability and came to uneasy terms with the Nanking regime, the last possibility for maintaining even the fiction of an alliance with bourgeois nationalism vanished. The Comintern, offering at this juncture what seem in retrospect counsels of desperation, urged the remnants of the party to launch urban insurrections in the hope of gaining a foothold from which to recoup the fortunes of their cause. Over the following months several such attempts were made in Central and South China, with uniformly unfortunate consequences for the Communists. By the end of 1927 the party's future seemed bleak indeed, with its membership decimated, its organizational structure shattered, its Central Committee living a precarious underground existence in Shanghai, and its leadership bitterly divided within itself in the attempt to assign responsibility for the recent debacle.

Yet a spark of life remained, far to the south, far from the urban centers that were the party's natural base and seemed not unlikely to become its grave as well. In the wake of the calamities of 1927, several small groups of Communists had come together in the mountains that marked the border between Hunan and Kiangsi. Their purpose, perhaps, was first and foremost self-preservation. But in that remote and formidable wilderness, protected by the terrain and by their own troops—the ravaged remnants of the same forces that had tried, a few months earlier, to invest the cities of Nanchang and Changsha and Swatow—they established not only a refuge but a government that would eventually claim jurisdiction over some tens of millions of Chinese. Isolated physically and ideologically from the representatives of party orthodoxy in Shanghai, the men who forgathered in Kiangsi in the spring of 1928 were preparing to take, knowingly or not, the first tentative steps toward the domestication of Marxism and the development of Chinese Communism. And, more than any other individual, the man responsible for this was Mao Tse-tung.

Mao's early history has been sketched elsewhere in this volume (see p. 177). He was, up to a point, the rather unexceptional product of an assuredly exceptional time: a boy born close to, but somewhat above, the poverty of peasant life; a boy whose rebellion against paternal despotism and parochialism had been clothed in the ideals of individualism and social justice that elicited such a response from young Chinese in the first two decades of the century; a young man who found himself, on the threshold of maturity, fully committed to the "new thought" and active in its promotion. What drove him, once across that threshold, in the direction he took is difficult to say. It is easy enough to record (following his own testimony) that by 1920, at the age of twenty-six, he had become a Marxist. By then he had read, in Chinese translation, a number of books by or about Marx; he had also struck up an acquaintance with Li Ta-chao in Peking and called upon Ch'en Tu-hsiu in Shanghai. We can only accept as a given, however, the temperament that kept Mao true to his new faith (or to his understanding of it) through the hazardous years that followed. Much of his own early work as an organizer and propagandist was carried on in his native Hunan, and it was as a representative of the Communist study groups of that traditionally radical province that Mao attended the founding congress of the Communist party in 1921—a happy coincidence from the point of view of later myth-makers, but hardly to be taken as evidence of Mao's importance in the party at this early date. During the period of Kuomintang-Communist collaboration, Mao worked in a number of capacities to promote the joint enterprise. Some of his time during these years was spent in Hunan, and after the collapse of the alliance in 1927 he repaired once more to his native province, first to organize an unsuccessful attempt to capture Changsha, the provincial capital—the so-called Autumn Harvest Uprising—and then, in defeat, to seek the refuge of the southern mountains.

This is not the place to reopen the debate over the doctrinal originality of the ideology that bears the Maoist imprint. Its most significant feature, at least in those early years, was the assertion that in China the revolution had to base itself on the peasantry. It is difficult to say with certainty what drew Mao to this conclusion. On the surface of it, it seems a sensible enough insight, in view of the vast preponderance of the peasantry in China and the relative insignificance of any class that could legitimately have been thought of in orthodox Marxist terms as a "proletarian" revolutionary vanguard. Lenin too, of course, had spoken of the revolutionary role of the "rural proletariat" in Russia. Other factors may also have entered into Mao's thinking: his own considerable experience with the Hunanese peasantry, among the most radical and best organized in China at the time of the Northern Expedition, and his acquaintance with Li Ta-chao, whose thought was marked by a pronounced populist strain. In any case, Mao went much further than Lenin had in accommodating the revolution to the interests of the peasantry: It was one thing to say, as Lenin had, that the peasantry (or at least its most impoverished elements) could participate in, and benefit from, the socialist revolution under the leadership of the proletariat; it was quite another thing to affirm, as Mao did in devising his own revolutionary strategy, that the socialist revolution could succeed on the strength of the peasantry alone—in other words, that the revolution could sweep out of the hinterland to engulf the cities and liberate the proletariat.

This, indeed, is what happened in the years 1947–49. But, although we may suppose that Mao, like all Marxists, drew reassurance from the conviction that history must move in the direction of eventual victory for the revolutionary cause, he can hardly have foreseen the precise manner in which his heresy would be vindicated. For the decade following his retreat to the Kiangsi-Hunan border area in the spring of 1928 belonged to the Nationalists.

The Nationalist Decade, 1928–1937

With the accession of the Nationalists to power in 1928, China was governed, for the first time since the demise of Yuan Shih-k'ai, by a government that could claim jurisdiction over all the country. The new regime presented an imposing facade. At Nanking, in the heart of the Yangtze Valley, which was the new government's real base of operations, a suitably majestic capital was laid out; and with proper ceremony the mortal remains of Sun Yat-sen were transported from their temporary resting place in the Western Hills outside Peking and interred in an ornate mausoleum outside Nanking, which became forthwith the central shrine of a new cult. Bolstered by the enormous resources of the Yangtze valley and the commercial and industrial wealth of Shanghai and the other treaty ports, the Nanking government attracted to its service many bright and active young men trained in the skills of modern enterprise: banking, communications, commerce, and transportation. It had at its disposal a modern army, tempered in the recent campaigns. And, unlike its warlord predecessors, it had a creed—a commitment to the reassertion of Chinese strength and dignity.

At the head of the new government, of its military as well as its civilian establishment, and of the party, was Chiang Kai-shek. Chiang had been born forty-one years earlier in Chekiang, the son of a salt merchant who had failed to make a success of that often lucrative business. The interest in military history and military science that became Chiang's primary concern originated when he was a very young man and led him to Japan, where he studied in a military school in Tokyo from 1908 to 1910 and thereafter briefly at the Japanese Military Academy. It was in Tokyo that he became acquainted with Sun Yat-sen and joined the T'ung-meng hui. In the autumn of 1911 Chiang returned to Shanghai and became active in the revolutionary movement in that city. Over the next ten years he served from time to time as a military adviser to Sun; he also went into business in Shanghai and developed—perhaps by necessity rather than choice—connections with the secret society that controlled the Shanghai underworld. By the early 1920's, when the Kuomintang began to gather strength in the South, Chiang was an established figure in the party, on cordial terms with Sun and, not illogically, Sun's choice as the commandant of the newly established Whampoa Academy. More than anything else it was the Whampoa experience that made Chiang's career in the party. Through it he came to exercise, in informal as well as formal ways, the control over the Nationalist military that gave him the necessary advantage in the succession dispute that followed Sun's death in 1925 and enabled him to dominate the political as well as the military operations of the party and of the new government.

Thus equipped and commanded, the Nanking regime set about to accomplish the principal aim of its foreign policy: the revision of the treaty system on which China's relations with the Western powers had rested for the preceding three-quarters of a century. In Nationalist thinking, the expulsion of imperialism remained the *sine qua non* of China's emergence as a modern nation. Although the new regime won recognition from the major powers, it soon discovered that it would not be permitted unilaterally to abrogate the treaties. It therefore directed much of its energy toward the kind of reforms that would serve to make the powers more responsive to Chinese aspirations, and in a number of crucial areas considerable progress was recorded. The banking system was thoroughly revised to make it—on paper, at least—a suitable agency through which to underwrite large-scale industrial investment and to handle the credit requirements of China's international trade. The legal system was restyled and modernized to bring it closer to Western standards. Ambitious programs were undertaken in railway and highway construction and in the development of communications. The educational system was revamped, with increased emphasis given to the development of facilities for advanced training and research. And, as we might expect, the military establishment was subjected to continuing retraining and reorganization, regardless of cost, with German advisers replacing the Russians of an earlier time.

In sum, the Nationalist government took it upon itself to see through to fruition the "self-strengthening" policies of a bygone day. The rhetoric was different, of course, largely shorn of its Confucian rationalizations, but the underlying impulse was strikingly similar: to effect change in those areas of Chinese life where the presence of the West impinged, where surfaces touched and the friction generated heat. Beyond this the Nationalists had little desire to go.

Or, if the desire was there in the minds of some at least, the opportunity was lacking. From the very beginning the Nationalist regime was compelled by the circumstances of its inheritance to maintain itself in the face of odds that seem in retrospect all but insurmountable. Although it claimed with some historical justice to be the heir of the revolutionary movement of the pre-1911 era, it was in hard fact the offspring of the age of warlordism. The victories of 1926–28 had been in many cases more apparent than real—political deals, rather than decisive military triumphs, that had brought under the Nationalist banner men whose loyalty to the cause was at best conditional. Any attempt Chiang might make to assert unequivocally his own authority or that of his government—as with the ticklish issue of troop disbandment—violated those conditions. Hence the Nanking regime was repeatedly beset by military challenges to its authority, sometimes aided and abetted by Chiang's political rivals within the party. It also faced challenges from without. In the South, the Chinese Communists gained sufficient strength by the early 1930's to present a measurable threat to the stability of the regime. And in the North, after 1931, the Japanese presence in Manchuria hung like a black cloud on the horizon, an ominous harbinger of impending disaster. In such circumstances it is hardly surprising—though it may be a matter for regret—that "national unity" remained the principal object of Chiang Kai-shek's domestic policy, in pursuit of which he was willing to sacrifice much of the program for social and political reform bequeathed to him by Sun Yat-sen. Nor is it surprising that military priorities remained uppermost in Chiang's thinking and that in consequence an uncontrolled and perhaps uncontrollable military budget sapped the economic vitality of the regime even at the best of times.

As I have suggested earlier, the social classes on which the Kuomintang relied most heavily for political and economic support—the large and small businessmen, the professional groups and the professional bureaucracy, and the landlords—were hardly likely to offer that support to any effort aimed at radical social change either in the countryside or in the cities. Nor did the Kuomintang possess the means of imposing policies directed toward such an end, even had it seen fit to do so. In accordance with Sun's wishes, and in some measure out of political necessity, the central government turned over to its provincial and subprovincial counterparts considerable economic authority, including a virtual monopoly on land revenue. The ability of the central government to modify economic conditions at the lowest level was correspondingly impaired, while at the same time Nanking was compelled to rely for its own revenues almost exclusively on the "treaty port sector" of the economy. It thus became, inevitably and with lamentable consequences, the political representative of the status quo.

OLD CHINA AND NEW. Recruits to the Nationalist armies, Peking, 1948. *Photo by Henri Cartier-Bresson. Magnum Photos, Inc.*

There were, finally, subjective reasons for the dissipation of the Nationalists' revolutionary zeal. Just as the reform program of the new regime reflected the mentality of the self-strengtheners of an earlier time, so too Kuomintang ideology sought its inspiration in the past. Confronted by the restless iconoclasm of the new intelligentsia, yet incapable of severing its own attachment to the image of a stable and durable system of values lodged in the past, the Kuomintang concocted an official ideology that was one part pious Sun Yat-senism and two parts romanticized Confucianism. The magnificence of China's traditional culture was recalled, and the antiquity and durability of China's civilization. Such Confucian virtues as frugality and sincerity were extolled. The Sage's birthday became once more a day of national celebration. Over and over again the Chinese people were reminded of the uniqueness of their place in mankind's history. Thus the Kuomintang sought to exploit the latent resentment that lingered in some quarters against the intellectual and social disruption consequent upon the coming of the West and Western values.

As we have noted, according to Sun's plan the Kuomintang was to serve during the period of "political tutelage" as the agency that would transform the Chinese people from a lethargic and politically inert mass into a responsible and enlightened citizenry, prepared to assume the burden and privilege of self-government. It was, to say the least, a naive expectation. Once in power, the party dutifully embarked on the task of political education. But it had neither the will nor the necessary administrative apparatus at its disposal to pursue this purpose in the manner Sun had envisioned. And it quickly became evident that in the thinking of the Kuomintang leadership "political education" was synonymous with loyalty to the party—or, as it was sometimes phrased in more grandiloquent language, loyalty to "the thought of Sun Yat-sen." Sun thus became in death the kind of tyrant that, for all his shortcomings, he had never aspired to be in life. And the doctrine of "tutelage,' on which he had placed his hope for the eventual democratization of Chinese political life, became no more than a justification for enhancing the control exercised by the party over every aspect of Chinese intellectual life. Thus the Nationalists subverted the promise of the May Fourth era, crushing its democratic aspirations beneath the shabby trappings of the party dictatorship, and, by invoking the dead hand of the past as a guide to the uncertain terrain that lay ahead, seeking to revive once more the ancient Chinese sense of spiritual isolation and supremacy.

In fulfilling the limited aims of their foreign policy the Nationalists were partially successful. A number of foreign concessions were returned to Chinese jurisdiction as a result of diplomatic pressure and a certain amount of economic harassment. By the end of the 1930's only Great Britain, France, Japan, and the United States retained the privileges of extraterritorial jurisdiction. More significantly, in a series of treaties signed in the latter half of 1928, the Nanking government recovered full tariff autonomy, a victory of especial importance in view of the regime's dependence on tariff revenues. Yet within a few years the underlying weakness of Nationalist strategy was becoming evident. From the outset the Nationalists had operated on the premise that the only prerequisite to China's attainment of "wealth and power" was the destruction of the imperialist edifice of political privilege and economic advantage. But, given the administrative and ideological deficiencies of the Nanking regime and its indifference to the need for far-reaching social reforms, there was more rhetoric than substance in its claim to speak as the voice of a resurgent nation.

The disparity between Nationalist claims and Nationalist accomplishments did not escape the notice of the new intelligentsia. The intellectuals were increasingly estranged from the government by the Kuomintang's attitude toward them, as reflected in its persistent efforts to regiment education, its distrust of even moderate criticism, its attempts to exploit the student movement for its own ends or to suppress it entirely, its resort to harsher and harsher methods in dealing with its opponents, and its sedulous promotion of its own sterile ideology.

Yet we must be careful not to exaggerate the extent of intellectual disaffection or its consequences. Many who recognized the political and intellectual debilities of the regime maintained allegiance to it nonetheless. For some, this was because the government patronized the kinds of specialized talent, the technical skills, that were the particular competence of the new intellectual elite. Others accepted the Kuomintang's unsteady progress toward the establishment of a more broadly based and genuinely representative political order—as exemplified in the drafting of a provisional constitution in 1931, coupled with a reaffirmation of the constitutional goals of the regime—as sufficient token to justify loyalty to it. Still others tolerated the Nanking government because the alternative to its policies, a thoroughgoing social transformation, appeared too drastic, too disruptive, and too unpredictable as to outcome. We would be wrong to think of the Nationalist regime as the private preserve of party hacks and ex-warlords. Such men were represented in its councils, to be sure, and in discouraging number. But throughout the 1930's it retained the services, and the loyalty, of highly educated, resourceful, and well-intentioned men who continued to believe that it could become what it was not, a force for progressive and enlightened change.

History has proved their confidence misplaced. But with their help the Nationalist government might have survived, and might even have evolved into a more hopeful regime, had it not been for the intrusion of circumstances that were, in varying degree, beyond Nanking's power to control. The first of these was the reassertion of Japanese interests on the continent; the second was the resurrection of the Chinese Communist movement.

The War and Its Aftermath

The Nationalist government was less than three years old when the Japanese occupation of Manchuria was launched in September 1931. Although six more years were to pass before the outbreak of full-scale hostilities in the summer of 1937, it is hardly an overstatement to say that the Nanking regime never recovered from that first fateful blow. For from that moment on Japan was an ever present menace. Not since the "concessions scramble" at the end of the 1890's and the allied occupation of Peking in the wake of the Boxer Rebellion had Chinese sovereignty been so ominously challenged. In such circumstances it was inevitable that the government's every move should be judged by its effect upon the Japanese; and Nanking, unable to resolve the crisis diplomatically, and unable or unwilling to meet it head on, felt the ground of its authority begin to shift beneath it.

From 1931 to the end of 1936, Chiang Kai-shek steadfastly refused to resist the Japanese threat by military means, to provoke the test of arms that seemed increasingly inescapable as Japanese pressure on North China mounted. Behind Chiang's policy there lay, perhaps, a level-headed assessment of Japanese strength and Chinese weakness and a realistic understanding of the eventual cost to China of the kind of militancy for which the Chinese clamored. But it was a politically hazardous policy, and it was implemented in the worst possible manner. China could do nothing about the Japanese threat, Chiang repeatedly insisted, until the country had been truly unified under the banner of the Kuomintang. To this end the Nationalists demanded total conformity to their principles and steadily increased the pressure against those—most notably the intelligentsia—who resisted such a demand. To this end also Nanking strove with increasing fury to eradicate the Chinese Communists from their southern stronghold by means of a series of "final extermination campaigns" that became the army's chief preoccupation in the early 1930's. To many Chinese this seemed an unjustifiable inversion of priorities, and the result was as inevitable as it was unfortunate for the Nationalists: It was the Communists who appeared as the true friends of liberty and the sincere nationalists, an advantage they were quick to exploit.

The Communist movement had gathered considerable strength since the early days of its confinement to the Kiangsi-Hunan border area. By

1931, when the Chinese Soviet Republic was officially born—with Mao Tse-tung as its chairman—the Communists had become adept enough as political administrators to govern a sizable territory and a substantial rural population. They had also become sufficiently skilled in the tactics of guerrilla warfare to withstand the repeated thrusts of Chiang's superior forces. And they had won unprecedented autonomy from the dictates of the Comintern, symbolized by the retreat of the party's Central Committee from Shanghai to Kiangsi in 1932. They remained, nevertheless, on the defensive militarily, and toward the end of 1934, in the face of mounting pressure, the Kiangsi base was abandoned. The exodus that followed, the legendary "Long March," brought the Communists in the course of a perilous year to safer ground in the Northwest. There they established a new Soviet Republic, with its capital finally settled at Yenan, in Shensi province. Thus began the "Yenan period," born out of retreat and to end, fifteen years later, in victory.

Much of the credit for this remarkable reversal in the fortunes of the Communist party must be attributed to the policies devised during the Yenan years and to the manner in which these policies were carried out. The policies of the Yenan period were generally moderate, designed to take advantage of the inherent appeal of a movement dedicated to genuine social and political reform and to exploit to full advantage the corresponding weaknesses of the Nationalist regime—but designed also to earn the sympathy and support of the majority of the people and to exclude as few as possible from participation in the revolutionary process. So, for example, while the Communists clearly dominated the political structure in areas under their control in the Northwest, they did not seek a monopoly on political representation. Similarly, the land-reform program was carried forward, both as a matter of principle and as a means of securing essential peasant support, but with a minimum of coercion and in such a fashion as to de-emphasize rather than exaggerate basic class antagonisms.

A like spirit of moderation pervades Mao's theoretical writings that date from the Yenan period, though occasionally, as in his celebrated lectures on literature and art delivered in the winter of 1942, the hard bedrock of doctrine thrusts above the surface. In other major theoretical pronouncements, however, the emphasis was inclusive rather than exclusive, promoting the idea of a coalition of classes as the basis for the transition toward socialism. (This was the message of Mao's "On the New Democracy," published at the beginning of 1940. It remained a guiding principle in "On the People's Democratic Dictatorship," published in mid-1949 on the eve of the Communist accession to power.)

In all of this there may have been an element of political calculation—more so, at least, than Western observers who witnessed the Communist experiment at first hand in the late thirties and during the war years were sometimes ready to acknowledge. But the Chinese Communists cannot be dismissed as political cynics. Especially in the development of the strategy of guerrilla warfare, directed against the Japanese and later against the Nationalists, they betrayed a keen and genuine awareness of the relationship between political loyalty and the preservation of a sense of human dignity. The peasants on whose support guerrilla forces necessarily depended were treated, as Chinese peasants had seldom been, like human beings. Thus, despite the obvious authoritarianism of the Communist party itself and all that it might imply in the event of an eventual Communist triumph, the Communist claim to the democratic inheritance of the May Fourth era was not entirely without justification.

A final factor that must be mentioned in accounting for the steady growth of support and sympathy for the Communist movement is again the issue of nationalism. Among the first acts of the Kiangsi Soviet Republic, in the early months of 1932, was a declaration of war against Japan. It was an inexpensive gesture at a time when the nearest Japanese troops were a thousand miles away, but it established a commitment that the Communists lived up to in later years. And during the Yenan period it was not Marxist-Leninism that rallied support for the Communist cause, nor even perhaps the social reforms to which they were pledged, so much as it was their purposeful exploitation of anti-Japanese sentiment at a time when, to more and more Chinese who lived far outside the limits of Communist jurisdiction, the Nationalists' preference for making war against their countrymen instead of throwing themselves upon the aggressor seemed an intolerable injustice.

In a number of ways the war that came in 1937 benefited the Communists. It distracted the attention of the Nationalists for a time, providing the Communists an opportunity to expand the range of their own military and political operations in North China, and in the end it destroyed their adversary. For the Nationalists the war was an unrelieved disaster. It drove them away from the sources of their wealth along the coast and compelled them to seek sanctuary in the wilderness, an environment they found far from congenial. Throughout the war they strove to maintain an enormous regular army and a burdensome governmental structure in an area that could not provide adequate support for either. By 1945 the symptoms of fatal decrepitude were already in evidence: a ravenous inflation, only momentarily checked by the postwar currency reforms; corruption that spread out of control through every level of the political hierarchy; and the loss of that sense of moral purpose without which no government can survive. For a few years, relying increasingly on repressive force, the Nationalists maintained their hold over a sullen people. Then, their mandate exhausted, they were engulfed by the revolution that swept out of the hinterland and were forced to seek a forlorn refuge a hundred miles off the coast of their former domains. The Nationalist era was at an end.

China's new rulers were—even as their predecessors had been—dedicated to the pursuit of national power. In 1949 it remained an open question whether they would prove willing or capable of realizing the vision of the age that had given life to their movement—whether they would seek to turn once and for all away from the isolation of the past and whether they would seek to transform the populist strategy that had brought them to victory into the enduring forms of a genuinely democratic state.

Selected Readings

Chiang Kai-shek. *China's Destiny. Annotated by Philip Jaffe.* London: Dennis Dobson, 1947. A fascinating distillation of Nationalist ideological positions.

Chow Tse-tsung. *The May Fourth Movement: Intellectual Revolution in Modern China.* Cambridge, Mass.: Harvard University Press, 1960. The standard work on this subject, covering not only the political movement itself, but the intellectual environment in the period 1915–23.

Grieder, Jerome B. *Hu Shih and the Chinese Renaissance: Liberalism in the Chinese Revolution, 1917–1937.* Cambridge, Mass.: Harvard University Press, 1970. A study of liberalism in prewar China, as reflected in the thought of its most persistent and consistent advocate.

Isaacs, Harold. *The Tragedy of the Chinese Revolution.* Rev. ed. Stanford, Calif.: Stanford University Press, 1951. An extensive account, based on numerous primary materials, of the growth of radicalism in Chinese politics in the 1920's.

Israel, John. *Student Nationalism in China, 1927–1937.* Stanford, Calif.: Stanford University Press, 1966. An authoritative study of the group that was sometimes the follower, sometimes the leader, in the political and intellectual history of the prewar decades.

Kwok, D. W. Y. *Scientism in Chinese Thought, 1900–1950.* New Haven, Conn.: Yale University Press, 1965. An examination of one of the major intellectual enthusiasms of modern Chinese thinkers, as represented in the ideas of Wu Chih-hui, Ch'en Tu-hsiu, Hu Shih, and a number of less well-known figures.

Levenson, Joseph R. *Confucian China and Its Modern Fate.* 3 vols. Berkeley, Calif.: University of California Press, 1958–65. The most provocative general treatment of modern China's intellectual transformation, from the Opium War through the establishment of the People's Republic.

Meisner, Maurice. *Li Ta-chao and the Origins of Chinese Communism.* Cambridge, Mass.: Harvard University Press, 1967. An intellectual biography of one of the first and most original Chinese converts to Marxism-Leninism.

Sharman, Lyon. *Sun Yat-sen: His Life and Its Meaning.* New York: John Day, 1934. A critical and often perceptive biography, based largely on Western-language sources but still the best general treatment of its subject.

Wang, Y. C. *Chinese Intellectuals and the West: 1872–1949.* Chapel Hill, N.C.: University of North Carolina Press, 1966. An extensive study of the great and (in Wang's view) in many respects unfortunate influence of Westernization of the modern Chinese intelligentsia as a factor in the erosion of the moral elitism of the traditional Confucian literati.

A New Deal for Japan
and Asia: One Road
to Pearl Harbor

JAMES B. CROWLEY

DECEMBER 7, 1941, was a somber day for Americans. Echoing the national mood before a joint session of Congress, President Roosevelt branded the Japanese onslaught on Hawaii "a date which will live in infamy." Instantly, Pearl Harbor became a national symbol infused with many meanings: the "duplicity" of the Japanese, the "end of isolationism," the "folly of unpreparedness," and the mission to "destroy" Japanese militarism once and for all. This instinctive reflex of a nation embarrassed and humiliated by the Japanese strike was later questioned by a small but turbulent stream in American historiography, best exemplified by the distinguished Charles A. Beard. Viewing the diplomacy of the Roosevelt administration as a concerted effort to join in the European conflict, these historians reasoned that the government had willfully pursued a rigid policy toward Japan, calculated to force the attack on Pearl Harbor and, thereby, to enable the United States to declare war on Nazi Germany. Variations on this "back door to war" thesis surfaced briefly but never gained academic respectability. Rather, the revisionist viewpoint was curtly dismissed. In Samuel Morison's terms, it was "history through a beard."[1]

---

[1] "Did Roosevelt Start the War? History Through a Beard," *Atlantic Monthly* (August 1948), pp. 91–97. For discussions of the "back door" thesis, see Charles A. Beard, *President Roosevelt and the Coming of the War, 1941: A Study in Appearances and Realities* (1948; reprinted, Hamden, Conn.: Shoe String Press, 1968); and Charles Tansill, *Back Door to War: The Roosevelt Foreign Policy, 1933–1941* (Chicago: Regnery, 1952).

With the onset of the Korean War, however, some historians perceived a new range of irony and paradox in American prewar diplomacy. Imperial Japan had indeed been destroyed in the war; and, as was equally evident, the prospects for peace in Asia, as well as American security, had not thereby been noticeably enhanced. On the contrary, the emergence of Communist China, allied to the Soviet Union, prompted some wistful regrets about certain aspects of American-Japanese relations along the road to Pearl Harbor.

> It is an ironic fact [observed George Kennan] that today our past objectives are ostensibly in large measure achieved. . . . Today we have fallen heir to the problems and responsibilities the Japanese had faced and borne in the Korean-Manchurian area for nearly half a century, and there is a certain perverse justice in the pain we are suffering from a burden which, when it was borne by others, we held in such low esteem. What is saddest of all is that the relationship between past and present seems to be visible to so few people.[2]

After this insight, some historians allowed that American policy might have been partially responsible for the Pacific War and for creating the historical tiger that Mao Tse-tung rode to power.[3] This concession, of course, remained distinct from the earlier revisionism that had charged the Roosevelt administration with willful deception. Blame or responsibility became less personal and more diffuse, being located in the cultural-national style of American approaches to the hard world of Realpolitik and balance of power.

The central thrust of Kennan's critique of the "legalistic-moralistic" syndrome of American diplomacy was blunted by the chilling atmosphere of the Cold War. The assertion that American diplomacy in the past had been too naive, too simple, served as no springboard for any sweeping reconsideration of prewar Japan or of the road to the Pacific War. Prewar Japan continued to be seen as a totalitarian-fascist nation that had brazenly sought to transform China and the rest of Asia into a Japanese colony. Criticism of American diplomacy understandably focused on its failure to form viable collective security pacts, which presumably could have contained—possibly attenuated—Japanese imperialism. Few historians were prepared to argue that the legalistic and moralistic dimensions of American diplomacy were really fundamental flaws. The inability to act in defense of these principles, on the other hand, drew many catcalls. In this sense, the Korean conflict and the Cold War reified the

[2] George Kennan, *American Diplomacy, 1900–1950* (Chicago: University of Chicago Press, 1951), pp. 48–49.

[3] For example, Paul W. Schroeder, *The Axis Alliance and Japanese-American Relations, 1941* (Ithaca, N.Y.: Cornell University Press, 1958).

initial clutter of meanings originally symbolized by Pearl Harbor—particularly the wisdom of preparedness and collective security. This truism reinforced the conviction that the world and the United States would have been better off if the American government had acted, in 1931, with the League of Nations to oppose the first manifestation of Japanese aggression in Manchuria. The symbolic meaning of Pearl Harbor was neatly capsulized in the axiom "It's better to fight a small war now than a larger one later." By not meeting force with force in Manchuria in 1931 the United States, it seemed, had condemned itself to Pearl Harbor and the Pacific War in 1941.

This historical axiom tended to preclude critical discussion of either the moral or the Realpolitik dimensions of American policy during and after the Korean War, and it tended, as well, to confirm the conviction that Japan's prewar diplomacy was atavistic aggression, pure and simple. This sentiment clearly furnished no incentive to reconsider the nature of prewar Japanese society. More recently, with the Topsy-like growth of the Vietnam conflict, consideration of some "new" concerns became viable for the American community—namely, the question of "Asian" nationalism, the heritage of "colonialism," the peculiar configuration of communist ideology and nationalist movements in an Asian setting, and the "relevance" of American power and ideals to contemporary Asian societies and politics. These concerns have not yet congealed into any fundamental reassessment of America's role in Asia, but they have raised, for the first time, serious doubts about American understanding of the dynamics of Asian racism and nationalism. To what extent these doubts will unleash a new, revisionist approach to the origins of the Pacific War remains uncertain. Nonetheless, one can already discern the glimmers of a "neo-isolationism" that talks about the "inevitability" of Chinese hegemony in Asia, about the United States as a "maritime-air power" whose security interests lie off the Asia mainland, about the United States as a Western nation with little, if any, racial or cultural ties with Asian countries, and about whether the United States is even an "Asian" power.[4] Whatever the implications of Vietnam for subsequent historiographical fads, one may reasonably conclude that fewer historians will henceforth deem Pearl Harbor a "day of infamy," the "end of isolationism," or the "beginning of a new era." More likely, Pearl Harbor will increasingly be seen as a by-product of Asian nationalism and as the conflict of an Asian

---

[4] Vietnam has obviously generated a new sense of inquiry about America's role in Asia. A few of the more thoughtful expressions of this mood are found in Arthur M. Schlesinger, *Bitter Heritage: Vietnam and American Democracy, 1941–1966* (Boston: Houghton Mifflin, 1966); Noam Chomsky, *American Power and the New Mandarins* (New York: Pantheon, 1969); and Hans J. Morgenthau, *A New Foreign Policy for the United States* (New York: Praeger, 1968).

country with Occidental nationalism and an Occidental nation. It was, lamentably, neither the first of these confrontations in the twentieth century nor, obviously, the last. This sad fact alone dictates a closer consideration of prewar Japan and the road to Pearl Harbor.

The Post-Versailles Decade:
The Dilemma of the Japanese Empire

Although the attack on Pearl Harbor occurred on December 7 by American reckoning, it was December 8 Tokyo time. On the calendar this was one day, but on the scale of historical consciousness it expressed a radically different time dimension. Pearl Harbor, from the Japanese standpoint, was no infamous deed. It was portrayed as a blow against the efforts of the Occidental powers to strangle Japan and to perpetuate their colonial and semicolonial rule in Asia. Commenting on the Imperial Declaration of War, Tokutomi Iichiro (elsewhere, Tokutomi Sohō) affirmed:

> We must show the races of East Asia that the order, tranquility, peace, happiness, and contentment of East Asia can be gained only by eradicating the evil precedent of the encroachment and extortion of the Anglo-Saxons in East Asia, by effecting the real aim of the co-prosperity of East Asia, and by making Nippon the leader of East Asia.[5]

To understand this standpoint, one must recognize that the syndrome of nationalism, colonialism, communism, and imperialism in an Asian setting was not a remote configuration that would become viable in the postwar era. For Japan it had been operative for many years, particularly since the Versailles peace settlement. At that conference, the Western powers had projected a new international norm based on the tenets of armament control, a League of Nations, the peaceful solution of disputes, and the principle of national self-determination. These worthy principles, however, were not applied throughout Asia. Among other distinctions, China was the one country outside Europe where the Western powers were willing to champion the principle of national self-determination and even here, initially, only as it applied to Japan's wartime acquisitions in Shantung. These alone were considered imperialistic and contrary to the new principles of international politics incorporated into the League of Nations.

From the Japanese standpoint, this criticism of Japan's China policy was both self-serving and suspect. The Western powers considered their treaty rights in China—rights that had been obtained earlier by "gunboat

[5] Cited in William Theodore de Bary *et al.*, eds., *Sources of the Japanese Tradition* (New York: Columbia University Press, 1958), p. 800.

diplomacy"—legally valid. And it seemed that the powers were less concerned with China's sovereignty than with safeguarding their own economic interests in China against Japanese incursions. As importantly, the Wilsonian rhetoric that World War I was "a war for democracy" appeared patently fraudulent. Japan may have been a great power by virtue of its military prowess; Japan may have been recognized as one of the Big Five nations and accorded membership on the Council of the League of Nations; but Japan was not recognized as an equal of the Anglo-Saxon nations. The principle of racial equality was not one of the guiding principles of the League of Nations or of the diplomacy of the Anglo-American nations. In addition, none of the Caucasian nations championed the Open Door principle in their colonial preserves. Discriminated against on racial and economic grounds elsewhere in the Pacific basin, Japan found itself confronted with the demands of the Western sea powers that it accept the Open Door in China and that it withdraw from Shantung. To many Japanese at Versailles, including Prince Konoe and Matsuoka Yōsuke, Wilsonianism became little more than a clever ideological ruse designed to check the growth of imperial Japan, to protect the semicolonial rights of the Western powers in China, and to promote Sino-Japanese hostilities. Without a willingness to accept Japan as an equal, or to propagate the Open Door elsewhere in Asia, the powers, in this perspective, were perpetuating Western imperialism in Asia and in China under the principles of disarmament and international justice.

If these sentiments were unfair, they were not completely wrong. Addressing himself to these issues in 1921, the prime minister of Australia reflected:

> For us the Pacific problem is for all practical purposes the problem of Japan. . . . America and Australia say to her millions, "Ye cannot enter in." Japan, then, is faced with the greatest problem which has bred wars since time began. . . . She feels that her geographical circumstances give her a special right to the exploration of the China markets. But other countries want the market, too, and so comes the demand for the "Open Door." . . . This is the problem of the Pacific—the modern riddle of the Sphinx, for which we must find an answer. . . . Talk about disarmament is idle unless the causes of naval armaments are removed.[6]

Prime Minister Hughes unquestionably pinpointed the central problem and the most grievous flaw of the post-Versailles approach to Japan and China. Unless Japan also had an "open door" throughout the globe, many social, economic, and political difficulties would fester. Hughes was prob-

---

[6] Cited in Lionel Wigmore, *The Japanese Thrust* (Adelaide, Australia: 1957), pp. 2–3.

ably correct, too, in preferring a recognition of Japanese primacy in China and Manchuria over a commitment to a struggle for the illusive China market. Although Hughes was, as well, willing to accept Sino-Japanese tensions as one consequence of his approach, he was wrong, one suspects, in believing that Japan could pursue an imperialistic policy in China without the dangers of war, first in China and later throughout Asia.

The problem of the Pacific, so keenly described by Hughes, was temporarily alleviated but not fundamentally resolved at the Washington Conference of 1921–22. In exchange for naval security against the Anglo-American powers, Japan pledged itself to respect Chinese sovereignty and the Open Door. Since the security interests of Japan and the commercial interests of the Western powers were well served by the Washington treaties, the conference was a diplomatic success. Still, these treaties created no viable sense of community among the sea powers and no sense of collective security. More decisively, the diplomatic accommodation discounted the dynamics of Chinese nationalism and the growing power of the Soviet Union. Throughout the 1920's, the Kuomintang gradually emerged as the dominant political force in China, and its program was rooted in a strong anti-imperialist, anti-Western platform. Although this anti-imperialism was directed initially against England and France, the demands inherent in the struggle with the Chinese Communists soon moderated this feature of Kuomintang policy. Parallel with this change, the Soviet Union supported the cause of the Kuomintang and solidified its position in Outer Mongolia and North Manchuria. This new dialectic—Soviet power and Chinese nationalism—confronted Japan with grave and complex issues affecting the vital economic and security interests of the empire. Alone of the Washington Treaty powers, it had continental possessions in Northeast Asia (Korea); alone of these powers, it had "semicolonial" rights in China (South Manchuria) that were the key to its overseas investments; of these powers, only Japan was non-Caucasian; and only Japan was singled out by the other sea powers as a potential threat to their economic interests in China. Furthermore, the maritime powers, especially the United States, championed the principles of "disarmament" and "peaceful resolution" of all international disputes as the hallmarks of responsible and civilized nations. Laudable as these principles were, none of the Western powers was apprehensive at this time over Soviet rearmament; and none of the European colonial powers faced a viable nationalistic movement that threatened its major colonial and semicolonial investments.

JAPAN's resolutions to ignore the "nonrecognition" posture of the Western powers toward Manchukuo and to withdraw from the League of Nations in 1933 were partly formed by these discontents with the Versailles and Washington Conference settlements. As importantly, the chemistry of domestic politics, especially of Taishō democracy, also contributed to the crystalization of an independent foreign policy toward Manchuria. Throughout the 1920's, Japan was plagued by a series of acute social and economic problems, compounded in several respects by rising public expectations and a dismal record in economic development. The agricultural sector, which embraced better than fifty percent of the population, literally stagnated, producing an absolute decline in rural living standards. Although Japan's GNP witnessed a modest five-percent per capita average consumption growth between 1922 and 1928, this performance was far inferior to that of the preceding two decades. Moreover, the gain accrued primarily to landlords, professionals, civil servants, and employees of the handful of large-scale industrial and commercial concerns. In essence, one saw, in tandem with an agrarian recession, an increasing inequality of living standards between rural and urban populations. These hard facts unleashed bitter indictments of the political parties as being handmaidens of Japanese landlords and capitalists. Along with these complaints and problems, the economy was plagued by three major crises—namely, the 1923 Tokyo-Yokohama earthquake, the 1927 bank crisis, and a continually adverse balance of payments, which dissipated the foreign-exchange reserves acquired during the 1916–19 wartime boom. Severe as these concerns were, they were aggravated by the 1929 Great Depression and by the government's decision in 1930 to go on the gold standard. This last step coincided with the collapse of the American silk market, one of Japan's major foreign-exchange earners, and a run on Japanese gold. By 1931 the nation was in the slough of a major depression, and responsibility for this plight naturally was projected onto those in political power—that is, onto the Minseitō cabinet and party politicians. Perhaps Herbert Hoover and the Republican party could have appreciated the political onus inherent in this context. In Japan, however, party cabinets and leadership by politicians were not traditional features of the political system as they were in the United States. They were, in fact, a recent innovation, operative for less than a decade.

By 1930, Japan was bedeviled by an ominous dialectic between foreign and domestic tensions. By its commitments to the League of Nations, the Washington treaties, and the Kellogg-Briand Pact, Japan had legally abjured the policy of overt aggression and imperialism in China, and it had embraced the tenet of armament limitation. Temporarily, this foreign policy brought tangible benefits, and its main advocates, the Minseitō party and big business, reaped the political benefits. By failing to articulate and implement a successful program of domestic economic and social reforms, however, the Minseitō was subjected to bitter criticism throughout the 1920's, especially among the intelligentsia, farm and labor organizations, and reform-minded bureaucrats. The services, naturally, resented the retrenchment policies of armament limitation. This cluster of internal dissatisfactions slowly became linked to the so-called spineless China policy of Baron Shidehara, the foreign minister in the Minseitō cabinets. Chinese efforts to compromise Japan's position in South Manchuria and the maturing power of the Soviet Union in the late 1920's raised significant and volatile doubts about the sagacity of Shidehara diplomacy, which played down the use of force in the protection of Japan's continental interests. As early as 1925, one of the two major parties, the Seiyūkai, questioned publicly this cautious China policy. Once in power, the president of the Seiyūkai, Baron (General) Tanaka, reaffirmed the traditional axiom of Japanese diplomacy since 1902: "If disturbances should spread to Manchuria and Mongolia, and threaten Japan's special position and interests in this region, the Imperial government must be prepared to combat this menace, regardless of where this menace may originate."[7] Implicit in this resolution was the conviction that the principles of armament reduction and the denial of force as an instrument of national policy were incompatible with the particular military, political, and economic ingredients brewing in the Manchurian cauldron.

Tanaka's forceful stance soon had tangible consequences. Japanese troops "intervened" in Tsinan, thereby blocking the "unification" campaign of the Kuomintang; and a few army officers in Manchuria arranged the assassination of Chang Hsüeh-liang, the major warlord of Manchuria. This last act precipitated a cabinet crisis that, combined with the Minseitō's opposition to the Tsinan intervention, toppled Tanaka's cabinet. Nonetheless, the Seiyūkai was firmly identified with a positive, or forceful, China policy, and this stance gave a new dimension to domestic politics. On assumption of office, the Minseitō, the party-bearer of Shidehara diplomacy, had to prove that it could cope with the Manchurian question by a policy of moderation and cooperation with the Anglo-American nations. This was a nettlesome assignment. The opposition party systematically argued that force alone would deter the Chinese from threatening Japan's position in Manchuria. Baron Shidehara and the Minseitō, however, adhered to a policy of increased armament limitation and a soft-line China policy. Ironically, Shidehara's diplomacy was severely compromised in 1930, not by a Sino-Japanese quarrel, but by the determination of the American government to extend the naval limitations of the Washington treaties.

In 1922 the powers had accepted a 10:6 ratio in capital warships between the Anglo-American nations and Japan. This ratio, however, was

[7] Cited in James B. Crowley, *Japan's Quest for Autonomy* (Princeton, N.J.: Princeton University Press, 1966), p. 32.

part of a package deal that included American nonfortification in the western Pacific, which in fact assured Japan an absolute superiority over the American fleet in the area. At the 1930 London Naval Conference, the Minseitō government indicated its willingness to accept additional limitations, so long as these would not compromise the principle of Japanese naval supremacy in the western Pacific. Both Japanese and American naval strategists believed this supremacy could be retained if Japan were given a 10:7 ratio in heavy cruisers, and the Japanese government understandably demanded such a ratio. Moreover, in actuality Japan had twelve heavy cruisers in 1930, while the United States possessed only one. Having an existing 12:1 ratio and realizing the undisputed centrality of the 10:7 ratio for the security interests of the empire, the Minseitō government publicly declared its commitment to this ratio as the *sine qua non* of its armament program. At London, however, the American government pressed for a 10:6 ratio and gained the support of Great Britain. Once again the Western powers confronted Japan with a united front, and again the Japanese government backed down. Under the Reed-Matsutaira Compromise, Japan accepted the "principle" of the 10:6 ratio, and the United States agreed it would not build its full allotment of cruisers under this principle before 1936. This guaranteed Japan a *de facto* ratio of 10:7 until 1936, when the sea powers would meet again to reconsider the treaties negotiated at the Washington and London conferences.

The domestic backlash of this treaty was severe. Under Article XI of the Meiji Constitution, the "right of supreme command" was entrusted to the general staffs; and this prerogative entailed responsibility for the security policies of the government. By compromising national security, the Hamaguchi cabinet opened itself to a barrage of discontent. The naval general staff, the opposition party, and a host of political lobbies and patriotic organizations passionately accused the government of "violating" the right of supreme command. Fortunately for Hamaguchi, the London treaty was not subject to the approval of the Diet. Only the oligarchic Privy Council could review the treaty, and then strictly on a procedural basis. The treaty gained the imperial sanction; and the Minseitō reaped the popular dissatisfaction. Indeed, Hamaguchi was shot by a young patriot who rationalized his deed on the grounds that the premier had flaunted the constitution and endangered the empire.

In the wake of this controversy, the Minseitō justified its quest for armament reduction on the premise that, in the midst of a depression, retrenchment was the orthodox prescription. By 1931 grumblings of discontent were discernible in the services, labor unions, the opposition parties, reservist organizations, the popular press, and the Minseitō itself. By mid-August, the Seiyūkai was mobilizing behind a powerful platform: The Chinese were threatening and insulting Japanese interests in Manchuria, but the government remained passive; the Western powers favored China, but the government had compromised the nation's security; and the country was wracked by a depression, but the government's fiscal policies were ineffectual. Most ominously, the war ministry decided that Shidehara's diplomacy was wrong and harmful and that it should "educate" the nation as to the "true situation" in Manchuria, including the "necessity" to use force in resolving the crisis there. Against this background, the Kwantung Army, with the connivance of the general staff, deliberately engineered an incident at Mukden on September 18, 1931. The public response was overwhelmingly in support of this deed, and the Minseitō cabinet faced a mortal threat to its authority and the foreign policy symbolized by Baron Shidehara.

Contrary to popular impressions, the Mukden incident was not followed immediately by a conquest of Manchuria. The Kwantung Army secured control of South Manchuria but was denied authority to move northward. Over the ensuing weeks, Premier Wakatsuki and Foreign Minister Shidehara desperately maneuvered to save their policies. Domestically they were subjected to a raging demand that Japan "settle" the Manchurian crisis by force, while internationally the Council of the League and the United States insisted that the clash over Manchuria be settled peacefully. Without the support of the sea powers, Japan could not compel the Nationalist government of China to negotiate a treaty that would confirm all of Japan's treaty rights in China. This situation reinforced public sentiment in Japan that the Chinese "understood only force" and that the Western powers were not prepared to act in defense of Japan's rights in Manchuria. Unable to harmonize these internal and external pressures, the Wakatsuki cabinet resigned on December 5 in favor of a Seiyūkai cabinet led by Inukai Tsuyoshi. The new government promptly sanctioned the move of the Kwantung Army into North Manchuria and to the Great Wall of China. Domestically the decision was applauded; but this move occasioned the enunciation of the famous nonrecognition principle. Approaching Japan's action in terms of the Kellogg-Briand Pact, the Western powers were relatively immunized against the plight and dilemma of the Japanese government. As crucially, they were unaware of the paradigmatic significance of Japan's thrust into Manchuria. What was peculiar to Japan in 1931 would later be common to all the European colonial powers. Just as these nations would try vainly to rely on force to safeguard their colonial rights against popular nationalistic forces, so, too, Japan resorted to force in 1931. At that time, however, the Imperial Army had sufficient power to crush Chinese resistance in Manchuria and to create the client or puppet state Manchukuo. Since this diplomacy flaunted the Kellogg-Briand Pact and the Nine-Power Treaty, the League and the United States refused to recognize its existence. Japan was now isolated, censured by the Western sea powers, hated by the Chinese, and opposed by the Soviet Union. Previously, whenever the powers had united against Japan's continental policy, Japan had always adjusted its diplomacy according to their dictates. This time, however, Japan was prepared to go it alone, to make its own destiny in Asia, independent of the wishes or guidance of the Occidental powers.

Manchukuo: The Solution of the Client State

Manchukuo, when combined with the nonrecognition response of the powers, forced a Copernican turn in Japan's foreign relations. This inevitably had pervasive domestic repercussions, the first of which were discernible by May 1932. Enthusiastic endorsements of the army's positive Manchurian policy reinforced demands that the government cope with the agrarian problem as decisively as the Kwantung Army had handled the Manchurian question. One extremist group decided to lash out at the political-economic-social establishment through a campaign of assassinations. The first two targets were Baron Dan Takuma, one of the nation's foremost industrialists, and Premier Inukai. Both were gunned down in May. The assassins were arrested, and they proved to be mainly a group of junior naval officers inspired by the agrarianist ideologue Gondō Seikyō. Unable to rationalize their violence with any coherent program or reform, these activists idealized Japanism (*Yamato damashii*) and the emperor, calling for a "renovation" of the national spirit and a "restoration" of the benevolence of imperial rule. As they interpreted contemporary Japan, the power structure—the parties, the zaibatsu, and the House of Peers—had all succumbed to Western values, especially to selfishness and individualism. Since they believed these leaders lacked a total commitment to the principle of social harmony (*chōwa*), they attributed the socioeconomic plight of the nation to a reliance on sectional and personal interest. In essence, these assassins assumed the "Western" values had anesthetized the nation's leadership against the peasant's plight. With this premise, they easily concluded that the murder of representative figures of the ruling establishment would shame these leaders into a return to the true Japanese social values and to a spontaneous readiness to institute the reforms essential to any resolution of the agrarian problem.

Inukai's death and the revelation that naval officers were the culprits stimulated apprehensions about the body politic. Normally the premiership would have gone to a leader of the Seiyūkai, the majority party; but times were not normal in the aftermath of the assassinations of May 1932. Japan was becoming diplomatically isolated, and criticism of politicians and plutocrats was boiling throughout the nation. Deeply concerned by the Seiyūkai's positive foreign policy, the last genro, Prince Saionji, feared these politicians would pursue an opportunistic and irresponsible foreign policy in order to cultivate the support of the services and the masses at home. Utilizing his authority as genro, Saionji opted for Admiral Saitō Makoto and a nonpartisan, whole-nation cabinet. If his motives were comprehensible, the consequences of Saionji's decision were momentous. Spurning the principle of parliamentary responsibility, Saionji had reconstituted an oligarchic cabinet that was not directly responsible to any legal institutions save the throne. Henceforth, political parties no longer wielded the premiership, and gradually leadership of the cabinet and, by definition, national policy would become virtually monopolized by the professional bureaucracy and the services.

The demise of party cabinets is commonly regarded as a retrogression in Japan's modernization process and as the beginning of fascism in Japan. Perhaps it was. Still, parties did not die in 1932; and the Meiji constitutional system was not legally flaunted after 1932. This return to the past—to whole-nation cabinets—was comprehensible and unsurprising. Japan, no less than the other industrial nations, was plagued by severe tensions during the Great Depression. Confidence in parliamentary government, in economic liberalism, and in individualism was shaken in even the most viable of Western republics and destroyed in many nations. In the United States, the Hudson patrician Franklin D. Roosevelt restored public faith in the democratic process with his promise of a New Deal. In central and eastern Europe, fascism flourished; and Hitler's New Order, concocted out of anti-Semitism and virulent racism, prevailed in Germany. Although the Soviet Union ostensibly had no unemployment problem in 1932, its solution of this problem was no less totalitarian than that of Mussolini or Hitler. Indeed, both Hitler and Stalin endorsed the premise that increased armament expenditure was both an effective economic stimulant and essential for national security. The increasing centralization of political power and the increasing role of the government in the economy, as well as the drift toward totalitarianism and militarism, were global traits of the 1930's. How much of Japanese politics of the 1930's may be judged as a "retrogression" or as "fascism" thus depends in large measure on how one evaluates the global dimensions of totalitarianism and militarism in that era and thereafter. Without handling this nettle further, one may reasonably say that the Saitō cabinet did not, at least by European standards, usher in an epoch of fascism. Throughout the 1930's, the Meiji constitutional system remained viable. There were no mass revolutionary movements; there was no single party claiming a political monopoly on the state's authority and denigrating traditional moral values; and there was no charismatic leader comparable to Hitler or Mussolini, nor was there an autocrat of Stalinesque dimensions. In short, Japan's increasing authoritarianism and militarism in the 1930's had a distinctive hue and configuration; and these are difficult to detect under the simplistic labels of "retrogression" or "fascism."

The Saitō cabinet inherited a political-diplomatic *fait accompli:* the commitment to build the state of Manchukuo. Within Japan, external criticism of Manchukuo acted primarily as a stimulant reinforcing the nativistic sentiments behind the new national mission. Initially, in 1932–33, the government's foreign policy expressed confidence and emulation—confidence in the propriety of Japan's actions in Manchuria and emulation of the Monroe Doctrine of the United States. "In a word," as one editorial phrased it, Japan must "advance with a policy of Asia for the Asiatics—an Asiatic Monroe Doctrine."[8] The nation sought, in Viscount Ishii's terms, "equality and security." Gratifying as these axioms were domestically, they provoked only censure and abuse abroad. The empire had to convince the powers of the credibility of a Japanese Monroe Doctrine, and, admittedly, this would take time and power. As the Saitō cabinet defined national policy in 1933, three objectives were paramount. First, Japan must enlarge the army in order to safeguard Manchukuo against the Soviet Union and Nationalist China. Second, the navy had to be strengthened so as to guarantee the security of the empire against the Anglo-American fleets. Third, China must be forced to recognize Manchukuo, sever its economic-diplomatic dependence on the Western powers, and cooperate with Japan for the mutual advantage of both nations.

Clarity of goals, however, did not affect certain realities. Resources were limited; the balance-of-payments problem was undeniable; and the Diet was unwilling to support any vast armament expansion or any comprehensive economic planning. This configuration of domestic and foreign facts had ominous implications. Not in 1932, or in any year thereafter, would Japan actually possess the twofold strategic capability essential for a viable Japanese Monroe Doctrine. The navy was not strong enough to repel the combined Anglo-American fleets; the army could not smash the Soviet Union; and the vastness of China was a Napoleonic nightmare. It was not surprising that by 1934 the optimistic language of "independence" and "Japan's Monroe Doctrine" had evolved into the more apprehensive slogan "The crisis of 1936." At this time, the Washington and London naval treaties would expire unless renewed, and the safeguards on fortifications and expansion would disintegrate. The prospect of a naval race with the industrial Anglo-Saxon nations, one might expect, should have transformed Japan into the most vociferous advocate of a renewal of the naval-limitations agreement. But, as Japan's naval authori-

[8] *Ibid.,* p. 188.

ties observed, the nation had made Manchukuo and a Japanese Monroe Doctrine the stated national goals. Unless Japan expanded its naval power, the powers would persist in their nonrecognition doctrine, and China would rely on the powers as the basic source of support for its anti-Japanese policy. Manchukuo, willy-nilly, meant the end of naval limitations, and the burdens of an armament race generated concern about the approaching "crisis" of 1936.

As the crisis mentality underlying Japan's foreign policies intensified, there was a striking increase in messianic Shintoist and Buddhist cults and in the number of patriotic societies. It was almost as if the nation's isolation had acted as a hothouse that nurtured and brought to bloom all the nativistic fauna in the sacred isles. If these groups were fragmented in terms of rhetoric and leadership, they all vented a common infatuation with the concepts of social harmony and the improvement of the people's livelihood under a benevolent Imperial Rule. None of these demands, laments, and complaints, moreover, were filtered through a belief in personal liberty, in the denial of hierarchy, or in faith in the parliamentary process. Reforms, not rights, were the stated political goals; and this reformist syndrome reverberated with the popular calls for "renovation" of the nation's spirit and "restoration" of the benevolence of Imperial Rule. Democracy and party cabinets became sordid ideals, soiled by their "Western" inspiration. As significantly, the emperor's advisers—the genro, the imperial household, and the ministers of state—were held responsible for the socio-economic ills plaguing the empire. Hence one heard increasingly strident accusations against the emperor's "evil advisers" and romantic appeals to the glorious tradition of the Meiji Restoration. Thus, although Japan did not experience any revolutionary movements, there was a raging nativism that envisioned a Shōwa restoration—that is, the emergence of a new group of leaders who, faithful to the nation's spirit (*kokutai*) and sensitive to "the demands of the times," would guide the country into a new era of security and propriety exactly as the Meiji oligarchy had done in the nineteenth century.

The whole-nation cabinets of Admiral Saitō and Admiral Okada Keisuke rode these treacherous political currents throughout 1932–36. Japan's isolation had enhanced domestic nativism, which in turn generated greater pressure for a return to Japan's political tradition—a restoration—and for a more strikingly apparent independent foreign policy. Admirals Saitō and Okada, however, displayed no interest in radical approaches to domestic or foreign problems. Unlike most of their critics, they were opposed to any direct confrontation with Nationalist China, insisting that Japan should first guarantee its security vis-à-vis the naval powers and the Soviet Union. Nor did they join those chanting contempt for the parties and the plutocrats. Entrusting the government's economic policy to

Takahashi Korekiyō, who served as finance minister in both their cabinets, premiers Saitō and Okada sanctioned a very successful reflationary program.[9] Between 1932 and 1936, governmental expenditures comprised twenty-two percent of the net domestic product. Three-fourths of this expenditure was deficit-financed, and approximately three-fifths of the governmental budget was for military expenditures. This pump-priming was linked with a decision to go off the gold standard and a devaluation of the yen by forty-three percent. The payoff was immediate: Japan's prices on the world market plunged dramatically, exports flourished, and by 1936 the nation again had a favorable balance of payments. Despite this performance, many of the younger bureaucrats and military officers preferred a far more radical program, including a graduated income tax, nationalization of basic industries, and the adoption of a five-year economic plan. None of these recommendations could be enacted, however, without the sanction of the Diet; and the political leadership in both houses voiced their opposition to these schemes. The ministers of state were subjected to two main strands of criticism. Within the government, their subordinates demanded dramatic and comprehensive reforms; outside the government, public opinion, as expressed in the proliferation of nationalistic societies, demanded even more nebulous reforms, a Shōwa restoration.

Despite the real accomplishments of Takahashi's reflationary policy, the Saitō and Okada cabinets had not visibly alleviated the agrarian problem, nor had they brought much benefit to small business concerns. This reinforced popular complaints that the whole-nation cabinets were not truly exercising authority in conformity with "the wishes of the Throne" and sustained the charge that these cabinets were merely "a clique of senior statesmen, financiers and noblemen." Acting on this popular conviction, a handful of army officers led their troops onto the path of direct action on the morning of February 26, 1936. Within three hours, Admiral Saitō and General Watanake were slain; the Grand Chamberlain, Admiral Suzuki, was seriously wounded; and Count Makino, Admiral Okada, and Prince Saionji barely eluded their self-appointed executioners. Seizing control of the war ministry and the heights overlooking the palace, these troops proclaimed their divine mission as the punishment of those leaders of the nation whose purpose in life was "the amassment of wealth, regardless of the general welfare and propriety of the people. . . . We believe it is our duty, as subjects of His Majesty, to remove

[9] On this program, see Hugh T. Patrick, "Some Aspects of the Interwar Economy," presented at the VI Seminar of the Conference on Modern Japan, San Juan, Puerto Rico, January 1968. This essay will appear in the forthcoming volume *Dilemmas of Growth in Prewar Japan* (Princeton, N.J.: Princeton University Press), edited by James W. Morley.

traitors and evil-doers surrounding the Throne and to destroy their head-quarters."[10] As they saw it, the evildoers were the nation's highest leaders, the emperor's personal advisers and the emperor's political servants, the cabinet.

This rebellion sent seismic shock waves throughout the nation. The army reacted firmly. The rebellious troops were directly ordered back to their barracks; and, when the officers refused to commit suicide for their behavior, court martials were held *in camera*, and the leaders were exe-cuted by firing squads. At the same time, however, the army called for a new government that would institute the type of reforms "appropriate" to Japan's domestic and foreign problems. Admiral Okada resigned, and the premiership was entrusted to a professional diplomat, Hirota Kōki. The new cabinet pledged itself to derive a unified national policy and to restore confidence in the nation's leaders. Throughout the spring, the Hirota cabinet appointed special investigating committees covering the whole gamut of domestic and foreign policies. One soon heard spokesmen for the government calling openly for major reforms. The Cabinet Inquiry Bureau, for example, recommended the creation of a central planning agency with the authority to introduce bills in the Diet, the nationalization of key industries, a reform of the House of Peers, and the formulation of a national ethic under which the parties would abandon "liberalism" and the government would cease "catering to" private interests.

> Now that capitalism has become a source of evil [this cabinet inquiry declared] we should not shrink from insisting on, determining and imple-menting a fundamental readjustment of the tax system so as to wipe out present evils and to create new circumstances which will lead to the rehabilitation of the national economy.[11]

The Hirota cabinet was unquestionably seeking greater centralization of power, and, as evidently, the parties were placed in greater jeopardy. Public sentiment was being cultivated by the government in the direction of a Shōwa restoration, a development that inherently compromised the prestige and the influence of the Diet in national politics.

After February 26, 1936, insistence on basic economic reforms and a unique national ethic became part of the official language of the minis-ters of state. Hitherto, save for War Minister Araki's speeches in 1932–33, this rhetoric had been the property of nativistic groups and organizations. After the February Twenty-sixth incident, the dream of a Shōwa restora-tion became the first axiom of the bureaucracy, the services, and the in-tellectuals, as well as of professional patriots. All these groups shared bonds of contempt for the symbols of "bourgeois democracy" and "Anglo-

---

[10] Cited in Crowley, *Japan's Quest for Autonomy*, p. 246.
[11] *Contemporary Opinion*, No. 121 (April 2, 1936), pp. 16–17.

Saxon liberalism"—that is, the parties and the zaibatsu. They believed, as well, that these sentiments were expressive of Japan's *kokutai.* This indictment threw the parties and big business further on the defensive. In this context, the parties also embraced the nativistic mystique of Imperial Rule and relied on the legal prerogatives entrusted to the Diet and the Privy Council—the personal gift of the throne—as their political fortress. No longer arguing the principle of parliamentary responsibility, the parties insisted that the imperial prerogatives given to the Diet were an intrinsic part of the *kokutai,* that these prerogatives were not to be challenged by assassination (as in 1932) or by rebellion (as in 1936). Hence, despite the momentous pressure exerted by the Hirota cabinet, they reasoned that the Diet alone could pass laws (reforms). Unless the government were willing to flaunt the Meiji Constitution, it had to work with the parties. Moreover, by virtue of its control over the budget, the Diet retained powerful political leverage on the cabinet.

Throughout the succeeding eighteen months, the Hirota and the (General) Hayashi cabinet proposed all sorts of economic and administrative reforms. The Diet steadfastly refused to enact any of these recommendations into law. Although it resisted the cabinet's demands for increased political power, the Diet did not oppose the armament dimensions of the government's program. On the contrary, it voted what both services demanded as essential to national security. Japan formally terminated the naval-limitations treaties and was saddled with the fateful prospect of an armament expansion race in which it would cope with the maturing might of the Soviet Union and with the combined Anglo-American fleets. The cost of isolation had become incalculable, but no one questioned directly the commitment to Manchukuo and to Japan's Monroe Doctrine. Still, adjustments were necessary. The constant pressure on the Chinese government had precipitated the Sian incident and the forging of a "united front" between the Kuomintang and the Chinese Communists. The buildup of the Soviet Maritime forces induced the signing of the Anti-Comintern Pact with Nazi Germany. In this context, the Japanese government decided to forgo further military pressure on China. The Hirota and Hayashi cabinets determined that the nation would concentrate on national defense, on a crash naval-army expansion program. Presumably, once this were attained the powers and China would resign themselves to the Japanese Monroe Doctrine.

This policy slighted the dynamics of Chinese nationalism. Although Japan was content with the status quo of 1936, which precluded the Kuomintang from the North China provinces, China, after the Sian incident, was determined to resist Japanese imperialism and to restore the authority of the Nanking government in North China. This policy also accentuated the need for greater planning and centralization. If the cabinet saw these latter imperatives clearly, the parties and big business adopted a different perspective and resolutely frustrated all attempts to impose some form of state socialism. Hoping to outflank the parties, the war ministry, in conjunction with the home ministry, patronized political parties favoring their ideas. But, in the spring election of 1937, the major parties prevailed. This political stalemate could be resolved in one of two ways. The government could attempt to by-pass the Diet and flaunt the constitution, or it could buy the parties back into the cabinet in an effort to gain greater parliamentary support. Preferring the latter alternative, the parties and the ministers of state turned to the scion of the Fujiwara class, Prince Konoe Fumimaro. Patron of the arts, protégé of Prince Saionji, and a leader of the House of Peers, Prince Konoe assumed the premiership openly articulating the call for reform and renovation.

> Evolutionary reforms and progress within the Constitution must be our watchdogs; but the country demands national reform, and the government, while neither Socialist nor Fascist, must listen to its call. The impetus of the great [Meiji] Restoration has carried us this far with honor and success; but now it is for the young men to take up the task and carry the country forward into a new age.[12]

Within a month, Konoe would discover his vision of a Shōwa restoration being first challenged and eventually destroyed by the outbreak of the China incident.

East Asia for the East Asians: The China War

When Prince Konoe became premier, his dominant concern was domestic politics, not foreign policy. The immutable national policy was an independent foreign policy pegged to Manchukuo and Japan's Monroe Doctrine. From the vantage point of Tokyo, the course of foreign policy had been charted. Japan would freeze the North China scene as it was, develop the resources of Manchuria and integrate them into the domestic industrial complex, and increase its strategic capability vis-à-vis the Western powers. The major ambiguity appeared to be the degree to which the government could impose economic planning and political reforms within the nation. There were, as well, two main currents of thought about China. Many, especially those in the services, regarded Chiang Kai-shek contemptuously as just "one more warlord." Since this perspective discounted Chinese nationalism and the military power of the Nanking government, it tended to rely on force as the arbitrator of

---

[12] Crowley, *Japan's Quest for Autonomy*, p. 398.

Sino-Japanese relations. Others, especially the foreign ministry and the general staff, preferred to stress Chiang's viability and the futility of a direct confrontation with the Nationalist government. Officially, cabinet policy reflected the latter opinion. But since 1931 Japan had followed an openly aggressive stance in Manchuria and North China. This policy naturally vindicated Chinese fears that Japan was plotting another Mukden incident in North China, and this policy, as noted, had been well received within Japan. On July 7, 1937, a minor incident broke out at the Marco Polo Bridge in North China, and it soon escalated into a major war.

The Konoe cabinet reacted with a call for a "local settlement" of the incident; Nanking, anticipating another Mukden, insisted that it would settle the crisis. Neither side would compromise; both mobilized troops to enhance their positions. The Konoe cabinet, on July 27, settled on a "fundamental resolution" of Sino-Japanese relations. As part of this resolution it demanded that Chiang Kai-shek create a "demilitarized zone" in the Peking-Tientsin region and sign a general treaty of friendship that would grant *de facto* recognition to Manchukuo. As the Konoe cabinet saw it, these stipulations were "worthy of winning the respect of the whole world" and "beyond the expectations of the Chinese." The Chinese evaluation came on August 14, when Nationalist bombers attacked the Japanese settlement in Shanghai. In retaliation, the Konoe government declared it would wage "a war of chastisement" until China lost "its will to fight" and reflected "on the errors of its ways." Despite this public stance, the army general staff thought the Konoe cabinet should reflect on its error—namely, that a war with China would be the wrong war, with the wrong enemy, at the wrong time. In contrast to popular sentiment and the confidence of the field armies, the general staff did not believe Chiang could be defeated strategically, nor did it relish the prospect of expending men and material in China while the Soviet Union continued its buildup in the Maritime Provinces. Throughout the fall, these strategists urged negotiations and concessions; but, after each tactical victory, the government sanctioned more operations. By December, Prince Konoe, believing that the nation was "winning one victory after another," concluded Japan could foster a new government in China that would cooperate with Japan's notion of its Monroe Doctrine. Overruling the advice of the general staff, the cabinet resolved, on January 16, 1938, that it, too, would play the dangerous nonrecognition game of diplomacy. Denying the legitimacy and viability of Chiang's government, the Konoe government pledged its determination to "annihilate" the Nationalist regime and to foster "new regimes" for a rejuvenated China.

Prince Konoe, throughout the unfolding tragedy, projected a leadership confident of its goals. Triumphs in the field reinforced this image. Mirroring the popular mood, the newspaper *Yomiuri* voiced its end-of-the-year assessment that "the cost of Japan's operations in China is incomparably smaller than her gains." Once confronted with a war of annihilation, however, the nation had to look forward to extended operations, a massive pacification program, and additional mobilization of men and material. The burdens this raised were inescapable, and the government soon requested an extraordinary budget of 4.85 billion yen. Inherently, this posed the danger of inflation and dictated strenuous efforts to control prices and wages. Confident that, in the midst of the conflict, the Diet would go along with all proposals, the Konoe cabinet linked this budget request with an omnibus Mobilization Bill and the proposed nationalization of electric power. The Mobilization Bill would have given the cabinet blanket authority to enact all sorts of ordinances, including the right to set wages, profits, and prices and to reorganize the great industrial concerns. To the parties and big business, this was anathema, as it would delegate the Diet's prerogatives to the cabinet and allow the government to control private business directly. By threatening opposition to the nationalization of electric power, the parties forced the government to yield on this point, and Prince Konoe affirmed that the Mobilization Bill "would not be applied during the present conflict in China." More significantly, the bill was amended to include the establishment of an Industrial Mobilization Committee, which would consider any proposed implementation of the mobilization legislation. Since this committee would include, as a majority, representatives of the parties, the Diet had, in fact, stymied the efforts of the cabinet to extend its legal authority over the economy. The government secured its supplemental budget and the nationalization of electric power, but it was not given a blank check to impose its dictates on the nation. Although this, of course, had no bearing on the escalation of the China war, at the least it moderated for a while the trend toward totalitarianism in Japan.

By the spring of 1938, Prince Konoe had thrust the nation forward in two complementary directions. He had committed the empire to the building of a new China, and he had sought to infuse the general Mobilization Bill with a reformist orientation. In actuality, neither goal had been realized. Chiang was not on the verge of capitulation, nor was the Diet abandoning its constitutional authority. Moreover, the dimensions of the China policy provoked a great deal of apprehension in the Diet, in the imperial-household ministry, and in big business. This uneasiness was heightened by an increasing awareness that the dynamics of the China incident were leading to greater campaigns and to a China policy that would threaten the treaty rights and interests of the sea powers. As one position paper phrased it for Prince Konoe, "Because of a lack of preparation, the conflict was ignited; because of a lack of preparation, this misfortune was enlarged; and, because of a lack of preparation, today we are burdened with a difficult task."[13] The nation would, these advisers observed, have to face facts, including the recognition that it had overlooked "the possibility of total Chinese resistance and miscalculating that the war would readily produce the internal political disintegration of China." Seeing it as it was, however, served as no prelude to an abandonment of the nonrecognition stance or to a search for an armistice.

Instead of trimming the sails of national policy, the Konoe cabinet linked the idea of a domestic Shōwa restoration with the resolution of the China conflict. Viewing the ultimate objective as a Japan-China-Manchukuo bloc, the government crystalized the notion of an East Asian confederation based upon Asian values, especially on the concepts of "cooperativism" and "the Kingly Way." As defined in Tokyo, this new league would not be "based on an imperialistic economic bloc relationship. Rather, from the standpoint of a new national economy which does not esteem national selfishness, this cooperative system will form an integrated unity which emphasizes the interests of each nation as the basis of cooperative relations."[14] The China incident had come full circle. Causes became effects, and limitations became stimulants. Chinese nationalism was no longer discounted, but Chiang Kai-shek became the symbol of the older generation of Chinese. The provisional government created by Japan no longer seemed a credible vehicle for China's regeneration, but these entities, infused with "the Kingly Way" and "cooperativism," would become midwives for a new central government. Chiang's forces were not to be destroyed on the field of battle, but the new war of attrition would become the basis for reforms at home. Japan would no longer stumble into the China hinterlands lacking the compass of a clear national purpose; it would plunge deeper into China as part of the blueprint for the construction of a new China and a new Japan. On November 11 Prince Konoe displayed the new mission in a public address, averring that Japan harbored "no territorial ambitions" in China and that it wished to bring about "eternal peace" in East Asia.[15] China, Konoe sighed, had been "the victim of the imperialistic ambitions and rivalries of the Occidental Powers." He hoped the Chinese people henceforth would cooperate with Japan in ending this age of Western imperialism. "Japan is eager to see a new order in East Asia—a new structure based on true justice." Presumably, in the midst of conflict, China and Japan

[13] James B. Crowley, "Prince Konoe and His Brain Trust, the Shōwa Kenkyūkai," presented at the VI Seminar of the Conference on Modern Japan and to be published in the forthcoming volume *Dilemmas of Growth in Prewar Japan*, edited by James W. Morley.

[14] *Ibid.*

[15] Cited in Royal Institute of International Affairs, *Documents, 1938* (London: 1940), pp. 348–49.

would create a New Asian Order and usher in an age of eternal peace in Asia.

Having guided the nation into the holy war of a New Asian Order, Prince Konoe resigned the premiership in favor of Baron Hiranuma. The Hiranuma cabinet, of course, championed the new immutable mission and, as the China conflict dragged on, applied greater pressure on British interests in North China. It also sought to achieve some type of military alliance with Nazi Germany. Seventy-five times the cabinet discussed an Axis pact, and seventy-five times the naval minister, Admiral Yonai, balked at the proposal. This acrimonious internal dispute terminated abruptly on August 23, when Germany and Russia signed a "nonaggression" pact.

The Nazi-Soviet alliance humiliated the Hiranuma cabinet and heightened concern with the Soviet Union. The outbreak of the European war, on the other hand, automatically weakened Britain's position in China. Hiranuma resigned, succeeded by another whole-nation cabinet headed by General Abe. Apropos Europe, the new government adopted a policy of "strict neutrality." Reiterating the New Asian Order as the "immutable China policy," Abe stoically proclaimed that Japan would "inflexibly oppose all who obstruct her mission." In view of the new European development, Wang Ching-wei, second in prestige only to Chiang Kai-shek, chose to cooperate with Japan's China policy. The powers, the Soviet Union, and Chiang Kai-shek, however, remained inflexibly opposed to Japan's mission. While the Abe government organized the Wang regime in Nanking, it also prepared the budget for the coming year. The estimate was almost breathtaking, totaling some 10.3 billion yen, with 4.4 billion charged directly to the China incident. To cope with this burden, the government proposed a series of new taxes, including a general income tax, a classified income tax, and a corporation tax. Since representatives of the political parties held no major cabinet portfolio, the budget and the tax proposals provoked bitter complaints and set the stage for another battle with the Diet.

To defuse this crisis, Abe resigned in favor of Admiral Yonai, who promptly nominated four party leaders to his cabinet, including Sakurauchi Yukio as finance minister. Except for Ikeda Seihin's brief tenure in 1938, every finance minister after the February Twenty-sixth incident had been a bureaucrat. Yonai's appointment of Sakurauchi was a conciliatory gesture to the Diet, one designed to head off any major debate over national policy. It almost succeeded. On February 2, however, the venerable Saitō Takao amazed his Diet peers and infuriated the cabinet with a scathing parliamentary indictment of the nation's China policy. "The government," Saitō began, "should abandon its so-called notion of keeping eternal peace in East Asia. . . . The Konoe declaration [of November 1938] which stated this national purpose may, in fact, be detrimental to the future of our nation."[16] From Saitō's perspective, all wars were struggles in which "the strong subjugate the weak." To depict war as a holy mission for justice and morality was hypocrisy. Japan, he feared, lacked the resources to subjugate China, and he questioned the ability of Wang Ching-wei's regime to rule China. Overlooking the limitation of national strength, concluded Saitō, "the government was using the beautiful sounding notion of a sacred war in vain; and, disregarding the national sacrifices involved, it is constantly harping on the notion of international justice, moral diplomacy, and co-existence and co-prosperity."

For the first time, the course of Japan's China policy had been censured publicly in the Diet. The cabinet, particularly the service ministers, were livid with anger. The war minister insisted the China incident was not "a war of survival" and that the New Asian Order was "an ideal possible to realize. . . . A million Japanese troops in China are inspired by this conviction and one hundred thousand have died for it."[17] From the administration's perspective, Saitō's speech was treasonous: Saitō had denied the moral purpose of the incident; he had cast doubt among the people and demoralized the soldiers in the field; and he was lending aid and comfort to Chiang Kai-shek's regime. As the naval ministry phrased it, "He views the China incident as a conflict which is substantively the same as wars waged by Caucasians. . . . He defiles the meaning of this sacred war and of the special racial character of the Japanese people."[18] Confronted by this passionate reaction to Saitō's speech, the parties drummed Saitō out of the Diet. Saitō's banishment marked the last expression of direct criticism of the holy war in the Diet; his fate also illustrated, better than any single political event, the degree to which the government had, by its conduct of the China war, circumscribed the limits of dissent. The China incident had become a sacred crusade. The Diet, at this point, could not act as a viable restraint on the direction or dimension of the mission to build a New Asian Order. It could and did battle the government's maneuvers to acquire direct control over big business and to smash the major parties' control of the Diet.

With the startling Nazi blitzkreig in Western Europe, the Saitō episode receded rapidly from public consciousness. The fall of Holland and France, Dunkirk, and the Battle of Britain had two crucial consequences

---

[16] "Saitō daigishi ensetsu ni tai suru shoken" [Assessment of Representative Saitō's speech], Archives, Self Defense Agency, War History Division, *Kihon Kokusaku Kankei* [Concerning basic national policy], Vol. 3. The document includes, as an appendix, the complete text of Saitō's speech.

[17] Newspaper clipping, Hugh Byas Collection, Sterling Memorial Library, Box 36, Yale University, New Haven, Conn.

[18] Self Defense Agency, "Saitō daigishi ensetsu ni tai suru shoken."

in Japan: The parties and the Diet itself were threatened by a political New Order movement organized by Prince Konoe; and Premier Yonai, a staunch opponent of any alliance with Germany and of war with the Anglo-American nations, was maneuvered out of office in favor of Prince Konoe.

Resigning from the Privy Council, Prince Konoe joined the euphoric mood occasioned by the Nazi blitzkreig. Advancing the slogans "Strengthen the national defense state," "Renovate foreign policy," and "Establish a new political system," Konoe conspired against the Yonai cabinet, confident that he could institute major political and economic reforms and move the nation forward toward the realization of a Greater Asian New Order. Both objectives were to be pursued by means of an Axis alliance. In contrast to Admiral Yonai, Prince Konoe was not inclined to pause and wait until the outcome of the European conflict was decided. He believed that reforms at home and expansion into Southeast Asia were the order of the day and that the latter could be attained without war with the United States. Within four months, the Konoe government forged the Axis alliance, launched the "Imperial Rule Assistance Movement," granted *de jure* recognition to the regime of Wang Ching-wei, and proclaimed the establishment of a Greater East Asian Co-Prosperity Sphere as the new divine mission.

In essence, the "resolution of the China incident" no longer served as the first principle of national policy. Instead, access to the resources of Southeast Asia, hopefully by diplomatic means, had become the cardinal goal. Accordingly, the dream of a New Asian Order was supplanted by the vision of a Greater Asian Co-Prosperity Sphere.

Asia for the Asians:
The Pacific War

Throughout the fall and winter of 1940, Foreign Minister Matsuoka waged what he liked to call "my blitzkreig diplomacy." By strident rhetoric and brandishment of the Axis pact, the Konoe government sought to cajole the United States into some type of accommodation. The hopes and gestures prompting Matsuoka's diplomacy proved futile. The United States kept its fleet at Pearl Harbor and transparently supported the Dutch East Indies in its diplomatic travails with Japan. The sale of vital raw materials to Japan dwindled ever so slowly, and the American fleet grew month by month. By the spring of 1941, the Konoe government had to abandon the euphoria of the preceding year. The Western powers were responding effectively and collectively to Japan's southern policy. In this context, the government became wary of the "encirclement" by the powers, and, more decisively, it labeled control of the resources of Indochina and the Indies as requisites "for the self-existence and defense" of the empire. No longer, in short, were these resources deemed important for a New Asian Order; they had become part of the security requirements of the empire.

When Japan launched its southern policy in the summer of 1940, the quest for a Greater Asian Co-Prosperity Sphere by diplomatic means was not completely bizarre. By nineteenth-century standards, the Konoe government held many trumps. England was absorbed in a life-and-death struggle; France and Holland were occupied by Japan's ally; the United States' first concerns were Europe and the defeat of Germany; and Japan's existing military capabilities in Asia exceeded those of the European powers and the United States. Consequently, many Japanese judged the behavior of the Roosevelt administration to be "inscrutable." Others attributed it to "fanatical crusaders like the thorough-going Christian Secretary of State, Cordell Hull, who divides the world between Christians and Heathens" and to "an obstreperous State Department which holds firmly-opinionated ideals about international diplomacy. It has now come to the point whereby presumably no diplomatic moves should be made by any foreign state without the blessing of the American State Department."[19] This bitterness toward the United States strengthened the conviction that the objectives of American policy were, first, to block Japan's access to the resources of Southeast Asia; second, to gain naval superiority in the Pacific; and third, to force Japan out of China and Manchuria. This bitterness reinforced other sentiments as well. "Success of this American policy would forever compel Japan, as in the past, to kowtow to the United States. With the sentinel of the Far East in economic chains, the Orient would once again become the playground of Western economic imperialists."[20] Rather than endure this fate, it seemed time to "call any American bluff" and to move forcefully into Southeast Asia. Once Japan obtained control over these resources, it would for the first time be able to translate this economic might "into political and social power, as has been done in the past by Western countries. Consequently, racial equality would become an established fact."[21]

These sentiments no doubt afforded many psychological gratifications in an international context warranting increased apprehension. Still,

---

[19] "Beikoku sansen o chūshin to suru gaikō tembō" [Diplomatic prognosis centering on the participation of the United States in the war], February 22, 1941, pp. 1–2, in *Kaigunshō, chōsaka, kaichō kenkyū shiryō (toku) A dai yongō* [Research Department, Naval Ministry: Research Document (Special) Series A, No. 4], Commander Ogi Collection, Daitō Bunka Library, Tokyo.

[20] *Ibid.*, p. 10.

[21] *Ibid.*, p. 27.

Japan had no success in its diplomacy with the East Indies officials, and American power continued to expand. In early June, Germany invaded Russia, providing the world and Japan with another display of Nazi recklessness and ambition. This war automatically relieved Japan of its concern with the Soviet forces. The empire could, therefore, concentrate its forces on the southern area. Although Foreign Minister Matsuoka and some army personnel wanted Japan to join its ally in the dismemberment of Russia, the cabinet and the Supreme Command resolved to push southward, even at the risk of war with England and the United States. Despite this decision, the government decided to launch a concerted effort to obtain the resources of the East Indies by diplomacy. At the same time, however, the government decided to move into South Indochina, as this would be an essential staging area for any southern operations. This move, in turn, prompted the United States to impose a total embargo on Japan. Japan now confronted an ominous timetable. Without oil imports, the fleet could not function for longer than two years. The Supreme Command calculated that Japan could not take offensive operations after January 1941, and it recommended that Japan make the decision for war before October 1941.

On September 6, in an imperial conference, the Konoe government decided on war with the United States unless there were viable prospects of any diplomatic settlement of the oil embargo and of Japan's access to the East Indies. In addition, Japan's terms included the cessation of aid to Chiang Kai-shek and the pledges that the United States would not acquire any military bases in Southeast Asia or the Soviet Union and would not strengthen its military bases in the Philippines. Desperately seeking some way out of the course he had previously charted for Japan, Premier Konoe proposed a summit conference with President Roosevelt. The request was denied. Since no reasonable prospect for diplomacy was discernible, Konoe chose to resign rather than lead the nation into war with the United States. This action also vexed the senior statesmen, for they could not reach a clear-cut decision on a new premier. The Lord Keeper of the Privy Seal, Marquis Kido, finally ended the stalemate by ruling that the statesmen had voiced "a feeling of negative support" for War Minister Tōjō. By default, therefore, the premiership went to General Tōjō. At the same time, the Lord Keeper informed the new premier that he was not bound by the September 6 imperial conference. Tōjō, in Kido's words, was given "a blank slate."

In actuality, however, General Tōjō had no blank slate. He could neither disregard nor negate the consequences of Japan's past policies. Most ominously, the Supreme Command promised no victory in case of war with the United States, only the prospect of a protracted war and the vague hope of a negotiated settlement. Nonetheless, it preferred war to peace. Without access to the resources of Southeast Asia, Japan, after March 1942, would confront the superior naval power of the United States for the foreseeable future. In essence, Japan's primacy in Asia and its China policy since 1931 were at stake. Admiral Nagano responded to this situation with the resignation of a warrior:

> Even if there is a war, the country may be ruined. Nevertheless, a nation which does not fight in this plight has lost its spirit and is already a doomed country. Only if we fight to the last soldier will it be possible to find a way out of this fatal situation.[22]

The foreign ministry promised no diplomatic resolution with the United States. Still, the Tōjō cabinet made one last effort to avoid war. It agreed to withdraw from South Indochina and to refrain from aggression in Southeast Asia if the United States would end the embargo, assist Japan in obtaining necessary material from the Dutch East Indies, and cooperate with Japan in its settlement of the China incident.

The American response of November 26 was a categorical refutation of Japan's foreign policy since 1931. Some historians regard this famous Hull memorandum as "an ultimatum" because it demanded the withdrawal of Japanese troops from Indochina, China, and Manchuria; the recognition and support of Chiang Kai-shek's government; and the abandonment of all extraterritorial rights in China. Technically, Hull's note was not an ultimatum, since it contained no explicit threat of force. Operationally, however, it meant war. The Tōjō government was talking about an accommodation that would confirm Japan's current China policy and would provide access to the resources of Southeast Asia. The American government, however, proposed the abandonment of a national mission that had guided the Japanese empire for almost a decade. The wisdom of this Hull note of November 26 will be debated by diplomatic historians for years to come. Presently, one may note that the American Secretary of State believed that an acceptance of the Japanese proposals would have made the United States "a condoner of Japanese crimes, a silent partner in Japanese imperialism, a traitor to China and Russia, and an active accessory in building up a threat to America itself."[23] In contrast, the Tōjō government was convinced that the Hull proposals signified an American determination to crush Japan and maintain the political-economic supremacy of the Occidental powers over Japan and the rest of Asia.

---

[22] Cited in Nakayama Masai, *Ichi gunkoku shugisha no chokugen* [Candid statements of one militarist] (Tokyo: 1956), p. 180.

[23] Schroeder, *The Axis Alliance and Japanese-American Relations, 1941*, p. 77. See also Cordell Hull, *The Memoirs of Cordell Hull* (New York: Macmillan, 1948), Vol. 2, p. 170.

The divergent standpoints underlying Japanese and American policies were clearly revealed on the afternoon of December 7, 1941, shortly after the attack on Pearl Harbor. In the memorandum presented to the American government, Ambassador Nomura reviewed the diplomatic negotiations during the preceding eight months. As the Japanese saw it, the American government was "always holding fast to theories in disregard of realities," and the United States "may be said to be scheming for the extension of the war." The Japanese memorandum observed in addition:

> It is a fact of history that the countries of East Asia for the past hundred years or more have been compelled to observe the *status quo* under the Anglo-American policy of imperialistic exploration and to sacrifice themselves to the prosperity of the two nations. The Japanese Government cannot tolerate the perpetuation of such a condition since it directly runs counter to Japan's fundamental policy to enable all nations to enjoy each its proper place in the world.[24]

Cordell Hull, on the other hand, dismissed this briefly.

> In all my fifty years of public service I have never seen a document that was more crowded with infamous falsehoods and distortions—infamous falsehoods and distortions on a scale so huge that I never imagined until today that any Government on this planet was capable of uttering them.[25]

Given these dissimilar views of history, Pearl Harbor was inevitable. For one nation, the beginning of the war was "an act of infamy"; for the other, it was "a blow for the liberation of Asia under Japanese leadership." If neither of these convictions presently seems fully persuasive, incontestably they were persuasive in 1941.

Hiroshima: The End of an Aspiration?

Tokutomi Iichiro, as noted earlier in this essay, praised the declaration of war on the United States as a divine mission to bring peace and happiness to Asia. Several years later, with the sacred islands violated by an occupying army and the country in ruins, Tokutomi reassessed the conflict.[26] Paraphrasing the Chinese sage Sun Tsu, he confessed that the Japanese people knew neither themselves nor others. By this he meant

[24] U.S. Department of State, *Papers Relating to the Foreign Relations of the United States: Japan, 1931–1941* (Washington, D.C.: U.S. Government Printing Office, 1943), Vol. 2, p. 786.

[25] *Memoirs*, p. 1096.

[26] International Military Tribunal for the Far East, *Defense Document 632*, deposition of Tokutomi Iichiro, February 20, 1947.

they had not been faithful to their own traditions—that is, they had both succumbed to the bad examples of Western imperialists and badly miscalculated the strategic power of the United States. "The folly of the Japanese," Tokutomi allowed, "is indeed unsurpassed." Nonetheless, he would not concede the validity of the historical perspectives of Japan's conquerors, nor would he acknowledge the moral condemnation of Japan by the victors. Japan, Tokutomi maintained, had gone to war for three reasons—namely, self-existence, self-defense, and self-respect. The war was a protest, an "explosion of dissatisfaction and malcontent with [the] unfair treatment the World Powers accorded to Japan as an independent state." While he recognized the propriety of Western "laughs and jeers" at Japan's inept diplomacy and leadership, Tokutomi felt that any "censure or condemnation of Japan for it on their part will never be considered an act of fairness in the eyes of God." Western historians may, and have, adopted a contrary judgment. The crucial point is not the "validity" of Tokutomi's conviction but the comprehension of the historical perspective sustaining this conviction. In prewar days, few Japanese regarded the developments of the 1930's—expansion, the end of party cabinets, increased governmental power—as aberrations or retrogressions in the course of modern Japanese history. In postwar Japan, despite caustic indictments of prewar leadership and policies, few Japanese have questioned the sentiments articulated by Tokutomi vis-à-vis Western moral condemnation of Japan. One should therefore recognize that, from a Japanese standpoint, the rhetoric of a Shōwa restoration and a New Asian Order was comparable to the demand for independence and autonomy heard in the Meiji era. One may assume, too, that this drive for independence and equality—for a sense of national identity and national purpose separate from that of the dominant Occidental powers—was not interred in the mushroom cloud over Hiroshima.

Clio is a fickle muse. Japan's prewar leaders envisioned an age of basic domestic political and economic reforms and the end of Western colonialism. Both aspirations were, in large measure, realized in defeat and occupation. The dream of an Asian community of nations, free from Occidental political and economic domination and guided by Japanese leadership, remains unfulfilled. As Japan gains greater independence and economic power in the postwar era, one may wonder whether this aspiration may not also rise phoenix-like out of the destruction of imperial Japan. Will Pearl Harbor become, as Hayashi Fusao recently intoned,[27] less a symbol of the evils of prewar Japan than a historical milestone in a Hundred Years' War of the Asian races in their struggle against Western imperialism?

[27] *Daitōa sensō kōteirou* [Affirmation of the Greater East Asian War], 2 vols. (Tokyo: 1964–65).

Selected Readings

Beard, Charles. *President Roosevelt and the Coming of the War, 1941: A Study in Appearances and Realities.* 1948; reprinted, Hamden, Conn.: Shoe String Press, 1968. Despite its polemical style, a provocative analysis of American policy.

Borg, Dorothy. *The United States and the Far Eastern Crisis of 1933–1938.* Cambridge, Mass.: Harvard University Press, 1964. The most authoritative study on the subject.

Butow, Robert. *Tojo and the Coming of the War.* Princeton, N.J.: Princeton University Press, 1961. An excellent critical study of Japanese foreign policies.

Byas, Hugh. *Government by Assassination.* New York: Knopf, 1942. A brilliant re-creation of Japanese popular opinion during the early 1930's.

Crowley, James B. *Japan's Quest for Autonomy: National Security and Foreign Policy, 1930–1938.* Princeton, N.J.: Princeton University Press, 1966. A recent reassessment based on Japanese sources.

Feis, Herbert. *The Road to Pearl Harbor: The Coming of the War Between the United States and Japan.* Princeton, N.J.: Princeton University Press, 1953. A solid diplomatic narrative by a distinguished historian.

Maxon, Yale. *Control of Japanese Foreign Policy: A Study of Civil Military Rivalry, 1930–1945.* Berkeley, Calif.: University of California Press, 1957. A suggestive analysis of civil-military relations, based on the records of the Tokyo Military Tribunal.

Ogata, Sadako. *Defiance in Manchuria: The Making of Japanese Foreign Policy, 1931–1932.* Berkeley, Calif.: University of California Press, 1964. An incisive study of the Mukden incident.

Rōyama, Masamichi. *Foreign Policy of Japan, 1914–1939.* Tokyo: Japanese Council, Institute of Pacific Relations, 1941. An informative apologetic for Japan's role in East Asia.

Schroeder, Paul W. *The Axis Alliance and Japanese-American Relations, 1941.* Ithaca, N.Y.: Cornell University Press, 1958. A perceptive reappraisal of American diplomacy.

Storry, Richard. *The Double Patriots.* London: Chatto & Windus, 1957. A popular but sometimes unreliable account of ultranationalism in prewar Japan.

Wohlstetter, Roberta. *Pearl Harbor: Warning and Decisions.* Stanford, Calif.: Stanford University Press, 1962. An excellent critique of intelligence analysis and the Japanese strike on Pearl Harbor.

Yenan Communism

and the Rise of the

Chinese People's Republic

MAURICE MEISNER

COMMUNIST China, it is often said, is a nation imprisoned by the traditions of its historic past. "The more [Mao Tse-tung] seeks to make China new," a distinguished historian has written, "the more he seems to fall back on old Chinese ways of doing it."[1] One need not accept the view that Chinese Communism is the carrier (albeit an unconscious one) of the millennial Chinese cultural tradition to recognize that the legacies of the Chinese past weigh heavily on the Chinese revolutionary present. Institutional forms, social habits, and patterns of thought and behavior that evolved over some three thousand years cannot be so easily disposed of—not even by the most iconoclastic revolutionaries operating in the most favorable of historical environments. And, while there can be little doubt that the leaders of Communist China are revolutionary iconoclasts, they find themselves in something less than the most favorable of environments, and not for cultural reasons alone. For the survivals of the cultural past have been accompanied and supported by a terrible heritage of economic and social backwardness and massive poverty. Mao Tse-tung's famous statement that China is "poor and blank"—an expression of his great faith in the future emergence of a "new China"—is only half true. China is indeed poor, but it is hardly blank, for archaic elements of the past remain and impose cruel burdens on the present. And "cultural revolutions," however fervently pursued, are not likely to achieve a viable new culture or a "new China" unless accompanied by massive economic and social transformations.

Yet, if Chinese Communists bear the burden of "traditional China," they are also the bearers of other and more recent traditions. They carry,

[1] John K. Fairbank, *China: The People's Middle Kingdom and the U.S.A.* (Cambridge, Mass.: Harvard University Press, 1967), p. 3.

in their own particular fashion, the "Western" Marxist tradition—the tradition that was adopted rather than the one that was reluctantly inherited. And there is a third tradition, neither inherited nor adopted by Chinese Communists but of their own making—the Chinese Communist revolutionary tradition forged in the bitter wars and civil wars of the two decades that culminated in the establishment of the Chinese People's Republic in 1949. These two new "Chinese" traditions also bind and shackle in various ways, but they convey new values and proclaim a future different from that which the Confucian tradition of the more distant past would dictate.

It is the purpose of this essay to explore certain themes in these two new traditions to which Communist China is heir. In such an exploration, the much celebrated Yenan period of Chinese Communism (1935–47) assumes a place of very special importance. The Yenan era not only proved decisive for the rise of Communist power in China; it also came to be seen as the heroic phase of the Chinese revolution—it is the experiences of those years that Chinese Communists today celebrate as the most pristine and noble expression of their revolutionary heritage. The Yenan period was also the time when Mao Tse-tung first seriously attempted to come to grips with Marxist theory, to understand and evaluate the Marxist-Leninist doctrine he had adopted, and to rationalize Chinese Communist political practice in terms of Marxist-Leninist theory. In the process, that theory was both explicitly and implicitly revised, and "Maoism" emerged as a dinstict and distinctive variant of Marxism, and one with enormous consequences for the future. The now famous "thoughts of Mao Tse-tung" are in large measure (though by no means entirely) the thoughts and writings of Mao in Yenan. And, finally, it was in the highly nationalistic milieu of the Yenan era that Chinese Communist theorists and historians felt the need to tie themselves to the Chinese historical and cultural tradition, to establish a meaningful relationship with the historic past by interpreting it through the prism of Marxist historical theory and in the light of contemporary Chinese revolutionary experience.

Much of what is distinctive about Communism and Marxism in China, therefore, was crystalized in the Yenan period. And, although the heroic Yenan years are now long past, the concepts, phrases, and slogans that emerged from that time are still heard—in recent years, as crescendos announcing new revolutionary dramas.

For Chinese Communists, it is "the Yenan spirit" that is celebrated—celebrated not only in history books but as a living model to be emulated in the present for revolutionary tasks yet to be completed. And for contemporary "China watchers," it is "the Yenan syndrome" that is pondered. Why is it, they wonder, that this allegedly pathological element in the

Chinese body politic has not yet been safely buried in history books?

Whether "spirit" or "syndrome," Yenan still lives in the present, in the minds of men both inside and outside China. To understand why this is so, it is necessary to turn to the history of the Yenan years, to see what "Yenan Communism" was and how it came to be.

The Political and Psychological Significance of the Long March

The conclusion of the epic Long March marked the beginning of the epic of Yenan. It was in October 1935 that Mao Tse-tung led what remained of the Communist First Front Army through the last lines of enemy soldiers guarding Mount Liu-p'an in Kansu province and entered the northern portion of Shensi province. And there, in that remote and relatively primitive area of China's vast and sparsely populated Northwest, Chinese Communist revolutionaries from many provinces found refuge in the months and years to come. It was a precarious haven, to be sure, but one that provided sufficient time and opportunity to establish a new base area from which the revolution was to begin once again, grow and develop in new ways, and eventually emerge victorious.

Mao marked his arrival in Shensi with a poem that expresses something of his feelings at the time the Long March neared its end:

> Lofty the sky
>   and pale the clouds—
> We watch the wild geese
>   fly south till they vanish.
> We count the thousand
>   leagues already travelled.
> If we do not reach
>   the Great Wall we are not true men.
>
> High on the crest
>   of Liup'an Mountain
> Our banners billow
>   in the west wind.
> Today we hold
>   the rope in our hands.
> When shall we put bonds
>   upon the grey dragon?[2]

2 "Mount Liup'an," translated from the Chinese by Michael Bullock and Jerome Ch'en in Jerome Ch'en, *Mao and the Chinese Revolution* (London: Oxford University Press, 1965), p. 337.

Although Mao wrote his poem in a style borrowed from the past, in the classical Chinese *tzu* form, and employed traditional phrases and allusions, the content pointed prophetically to the future. However much else was uncertain in the autumn of 1935, Mao was certain that the new battles to be fought were to be with "the grey dragon," the Japanese invaders who had occupied Manchuria and parts of North China and who threatened a full-scale war to conquer all of China. The struggle to "put bonds upon the grey dragon" was soon to begin—perhaps sooner than Mao then anticipated—and was to dominate the next decade of Chinese history. As we shall have occasion to observe, this struggle was to prove of crucial importance in molding the nature of Yenan Communism and was to have critical implications for the fate of the Chinese Communist revolution.

But, while Mao anticipated something of the future in his poem, he also reflected on the year past, looking back to "count the thousand leagues already travelled"—and no doubt to count the dead and missing as well. For few of those who began that incredible, six-thousand-mile journey survived to reach "the Great Wall"—or, more precisely, the new revolutionary stronghold the Communists were to establish just to the south of that ancient northern fortress. Of the approximately 100,000 men and 35 women (80,000 soldiers and 20,000 administrative party cadres) who began with Mao from Kiangsi on the night of October 15, 1934, only about 8,000 survived the torturous trek to the north to arrive in Shensi a year later. Among the many dead—left along that circuitous and now legendary route through the treacherous mountains, rivers, and marshes of western China—were many of Mao's closest friends and comrades and one of his two younger brothers, Mao Tse-t'an, killed in one of the many bloody battles fought with pursuing Kuomintang troops and warlord armies along the way. Among the missing—and never to be found—were two of Mao's children, who remained behind with sympathetic peasant families in Kiangsi, along with many other children too young to undertake the march.

The Communists call the migration from Kiangsi to the Northwest the "Twenty-five-thousand-*li* March" (a distance of approximately eight thousand miles) and celebrate it as a great victory for the Red Army and a defeat for the Kuomintang. Actually, it was only about eighteen thousand *li*, but it was long enough and sufficiently heroic. This is not the place to relate the history of the epic or to celebrate it. The Long March will stand on its own as one of the most extraordinary chapters in the annals of military history and as a truly remarkable saga of human courage and endurance. Measuring it by any standards of human accomplishment, and quite apart from one's political persuasions, few would disagree with

Edgar Snow's assessment that it was "an Odyssey unequaled in modern times."[3]

But the heroic adventures and the great human drama of the Long March should not be allowed to obscure the fact that it was born out of political failure and the prospect of military catastrophe and nearly ended in complete disaster. The Communists did not choose to leave Kiangsi but were forced to do so. Having successfully withstood Chiang K'ai-shek's first four "encirclement and annihilation" campaigns (1930–33), they had neither the economic nor the military resources to resist the new "blockhouse strategy" that Chiang's imported German military advisers had devised for the fifth campaign. Surrounded by almost one million Kuomintang troops and increasingly hard pressed by the effects of an ever tightening economic blockade, the Communists found their position had become untenable by early 1934, and in the summer of that year they undertook preparations to retreat from the Soviet areas in the Southeast.

The abandonment of the Chinese Soviet Republic, which the Communists had built with such painstaking efforts for over half a decade, and the abandonment of the peasants who had supported them to the terrible reprisals the Kuomingtang was to inflict, marked a political defeat of very considerable magnitude. And the fact that the largest part of the Red Army was destroyed during the ordeals of the next year can hardly be seen as a Communist victory, much less a defeat for the Kuomintang. The exhausted and ill-equipped survivors of the Long March who reached Shensi in the fall of 1935 celebrated not a military and political triumph but rather the fantastic fact that they had managed to survive at all. They were indeed heroic, but they were not victorious. Their victory was still to come, and it was to come in the context of new and very different political and historical circumstances.

Yet the Long March was the prelude to what proved to be the victorious period of the Chinese Communist revolution, and in that sense it was an event with momentous political and psychological consequences. Politically, the Long March is important because it was the time when Mao Tse-tung achieved effective control of the Chinese Communist party, a position of influence and authority that had eluded him during the Kiangsi period. The internal political history of the Chinese Communist party in the early and mid-1930's is much too complex a subject to deal with here, and much of the story remains obscure.[4] It is clear, however,

[3] *Red Star Over China* (New York: Random House, 1938), p. 177. Snow's original account (pp. 177–96) remains the best description of the Long March to appear in English.

[4] Much that had hitherto been obscure or unknown is detailed in John E. Rue's revealing account *Mao Tse-tung in Opposition, 1927–1935* (Stanford, Calif.: Stanford

that throughout most of the Kiangsi period Mao was engaged in an almost continuous political struggle with other Communist leaders and factions, most notably with the Comintern-supported "Twenty-eight Bolsheviks," a group of young Chinese Communists trained at Sun Yat-sen University in Moscow to do Stalin's bidding in China. Although Mao officially was chairman of the Soviet government in Kiangsi, his influence over both party and army affairs was never complete and was steadily eroded by the growing power of the Twenty-eight Bolsheviks, led by Wang Ming and Po Ku. Not only were the policies he advocated often overruled, but he sometimes found himself in the most precarious of political positions, and at no time more so than in the waning months of the Kiangsi era. In July 1934 Mao was deprived of all authority in both party and government and, according to some sources, was placed under house arrest for a time prior to the beginning of the Long March in October. Indeed, the military operations of the Long March itself were originally directed largely by a Comintern military adviser, Otto Braun, a German known by the pseudonym Li T'e. As a military strategist, the Communists' German adviser had proved a good deal inferior to the Kuomintang's German generals, von Seeckt and Falkenhausen.

It was not until the troops on the main line of the Long March stopped at the town of Tsunyi in Kweichow province in early January 1935 that the power of Li T'e and the Twenty-eight Bolsheviks was effectively broken. There Mao called an enlarged meeting of the party's Politburo, and from that fateful conference he emerged as the chairman of the Politburo and the head of the reorganized Revolutionary Military Council. His leadership was not to go unchallenged, but he was now sufficiently in control of the party (and of enough of the army) to pursue his own policies and his own strategy of revolution. The incubus of the Comintern finally had been thrown off, and Mao had achieved party supremacy in defiance of Stalin. It was an event unprecedented in the history of communist parties in the Stalinist era and one having the greatest significance for the future course of the Chinese Communist revolution.

The Tsunyi conference also defined the destination and purpose of the Long March, hitherto unsettled matters that had provoked heated controversies among Communist leaders. "Go north and fight the Japanese" was the official battlecry that now emerged. Some dissented, most notably Chang Kuo-t'ao (and perhaps Mao's long-time comrade in arms Chu Teh). While Mao moved north, Chang led the Fourth Front Army west-

---

University Press, 1966) and in Stuart R. Schram's excellent biography *Mao Tse-tung* (New York: Simon & Schuster, 1967).

ward to Sinkiang and Tibet,[5] although Chang and Chu eventually were to rejoin Mao in Shensi in 1936.

It is impossible to know whether Mao's determination to march to the north was motivated primarily by nationalist impulses to defend the nation against the Japanese threat or was part of a grand revolutionary design to capitalize on the growing forces of popular nationalist feelings and harness them to Communist ends. No doubt both considerations were involved, but, as events were soon to demonstrate, it was in any case a situation in which Chinese nationalist and Communist revolutionary considerations coincided. One can credit Mao with either great foresight or great luck. However that may be, the Long March had brought him to a position of supreme leadership in the Chinese Communist party and had brought the revolutionaries he now led to a geographical position from which they could both stimulate Chinese nationalist feelings and mobilize them for revolutionary purposes.

The psychological effects of the Long March are perhaps as important for the history of the Chinese Communist revolution as its political implications, although here one encounters a more intangible realm of affairs that it is difficult to assess with any degree of assurance. There can be little doubt, at least, that the experience of the Long March served to reinforce Mao's already deeply ingrained voluntaristic faith that men with the proper will, spirit, and revolutionary consciousness could conquer all material obstacles and mold historical reality in accordance with their ideas and ideals. If the Long March demonstrated anything, it was the ability of men to defy the most overwhelming odds, to triumph over the most formidable and fearsome barriers that nature could present and that other men might erect. For those who survived the ordeal—and for those who were inspired by the story of their survival—the experience, however bitter it was at the time, gave rise to a renewed sense of hope and a deepened sense of mission. These are necessary (even if not necessarily sufficient) ingredients for any successful revolutionary effort. Men must be able to hope before they can act; they must possess not only ideals and a sense of mission but hope and confidence that they will be able to realize their ideals and their mission through their own actions. More than any other event in the history of Chinese Communism, it was the Long March—and the legendary tales to which it gave rise—that provided the essential hope and confidence, the faith that determined men could prevail under even the most desperate conditions. And, more than

[5] Much of this whole episode remains mysterious. According to Chu Teh's later account, he was imprisoned by Chang and forced, under threat of death, to accompany him to Sinkiang (see Agnes Smedley, *The Great Road* [New York: Monthly Review Press, 1956], pp. 328–32). Chang Kuo-t'ao was expelled from the party in 1938.

any other individual, it was Mao Tse-tung who radiated and inspired this confidence, as is well reflected in a statement that appears in the "autobiography" he related to Edgar Snow not long after the conclusion of the Long March:

> The victorious march of the Red Army, and its triumphant arrival in Kansu and Shensi with its living forces still intact, was due first to the correct leadership of the Communist Party, and secondly to the great skill, courage, determination and almost super-human endurance and revolutionary ardour of the basic cadres of our Soviet people. The Communist Party of China was, is, and will be, faithful to Marxism-Leninism. . . . In this determination lies one explanation of its invincibility and the certainty of its final victory.[6]

What is expressed and conveyed here (even though in Marxist-Leninist idiom) is not only confidence in the future, and in those deemed capable of molding the future in accordance with Communist hopes, but also the kinds of values that were regarded as essential to the eventual realization of those hopes. The now familiar Maoist virtues of unending struggle, heroic sacrifice, self-denial, diligence, courage, and unselfishness were values not espoused by Mao alone but carried and conveyed by all (or at least most) of "the veterans of the Long March," for they had come to regard these values as essential to their own survival and to that of the revolution to which they had devoted their lives. These values lay at the core of what later came to be celebrated as "the Yenan spirit"; they were held by the makers of the Chinese Communist revolutionary tradition, and they are still conveyed by those who have inherited that tradition.

Many more died during the Long March than survived it, and this fact alone made its peculiar contribution to "the Yenan spirit." The survivors' consciousness that they had lived while so many more had died lent an almost sacred character to their revolutionary mission and gave rise to a religious sense of dedication.

This overwhelming sense of mission and dedication may be attributed partly to what Robert Jay Lifton has referred to as "the survivor's characteristically guilt-laden need to contrast his own continuing life with others' deaths."[7] One way to attempt to transcend this feeling of guilt, or of grief, is to make an extraordinary personal commitment to a collective revolutionary effort, to create a future that will vindicate and justify the sacrifices that have been made. This "survivor formulation," as Lifton has termed it, is particularly useful for understanding something of Mao Tse-tung's mentality in the Yenan period and after. Although it is doubtful

---

[6] Cited in Snow, *Red Star Over China,* p. 167.

[7] *Revolutionary Immortality: Mao Tse-tung and the Chinese Cultural Revolution* (New York: Random House, 1968), p. 14.

that Mao has been tormented with an overriding sense of guilt, he has exhibited an acute awareness of his own defiance of death while so many of those who surrounded him were killed in the course of revolutionary struggles. Among the dead were not only untold numbers of close friends and revolutionary comrades but many members of his own family.[8] In an interview with Edgar Snow in 1965, Mao recounted his personal losses and described some of the many instances when he himself faced seemingly certain death but miraculously managed to escape. Mao found it "odd" that he had survived and commented that "death just did not seem to want him."[9]

This sense of having defied death undoubtedly contributed enormously to Mao's perception of himself as a man of destiny who would lead his followers to the completion of their sacred revolutionary mission. And if others did not necessarily share Mao's special sense of destiny and infallibility, they had had similar experiences, suffered equally heavy personal losses, and acquired a similar sense of being "survivors." This psychological legacy of the Long March became one of the components of Yenan Communism, and it manifested itself in a very special commitment to carry on the revolutionary struggle.

Thus, for "the veterans of the Long March," and for those who inherited their values and sense of mission, the sheer fact of survival became a matter of enormous psychological significance. It was also a matter of great political consequence, for it was testimony not only to the validity of the mission but to the wisdom of the leader and his policies. Indeed, the cult of Mao Tse-tung was doubtless born out of the Long March, for Mao was the prophet who had led the survivors through the wilderness. And if Shensi was not the promised land, later revolutionary successes were to seem to fulfill his prophecies. Although one does not find in the Yenan period anything resembling the more extreme forms of the worship of Mao and his "thought" witnessed in recent years, a certain mystique and sense of awe had already begun to develop around his name and person. As early as 1937, Edgar Snow reported that Mao had acquired the reputation of leading "a charmed life."[10] The "faith in Mao" that emerged from the experiences (and the legends) of the Long March, and

[8] During the Long March, as we have noted, Mao lost two of his children and a younger brother. Earlier, in 1930, his younger sister and his wife, Yang K'ai-hui, the "brave Yang" Mao mourned in one of his most moving poems ("Reply to Madame Li Shu-yi," in *Poems of Mao Tse-tung,* translated and edited by Wong Man [Hong Kong: Eastern Horizon Press, 1966], p. 54), were captured and executed by Kuomintang authorities in Changsha. A second brother was killed during the Yenan period, and a son later died in battle in the Korean War.

[9] Edgar Snow, "Interview with Mao," *New Republic,* Vol. 52 (February 27, 1965), pp. 17–23.

[10] Snow, *Red Star Over China,* p. 67.

that grew and deepened in the Yenan years, is the foundation upon which the more recent cult of Mao has been erected.

In Communist China today, no event in the history of the revolution is more celebrated than the Long March. The story is told and retold in an endless flood of memoirs, novels, films, poems, and history books. To be able to claim one was "with Chairman Mao on the Long March" is the highest of revolutionary honors. An entire floor of the Revolutionary Museum in Peking is devoted to the celebration of the epic, complete with a huge, electronically controlled map that traces the journey in minute detail. But, although the story is told in museums, the Long March has not yet been "museumified." It is not yet merely an event of historical significance to be commemorated on appropriate occasions; it remains a heroic model from the revolutionary past to be emulated on all occasions. The stories and legends of the Long March (much embellished and glorified in the retelling) convey to new generations of Chinese the past revolutionary examples of "arduous struggle," dedication, and self-sacrifice, values still deemed relevant for the revolutionary present. Its continuing symbolic significance has been manifested in various forms, but never more strikingly than in 1966 and 1967, when various Red Guard groups undertook their own exhausting "long marches" to testify to their claims to be the rightful heirs to the revolutionary tradition and to demonstrate their devotion to continuing the revolution.

In celebrating the heroism of the Long March, contemporary Chinese Communist accounts present the event as a great victory that in turn guaranteed the inevitable victory of the revolution. Victory did not seem so inevitable at the time, however. When Mao reached Shensi in October 1935, only about eight thousand haggard and half-starved men remained of the First Front Army. While they celebrated their survival, they had little else to celebrate. In assessing the situation, Mao was a good deal more candid than later Communist writers. In a report prepared in December 1936, he wrote:

> Except for the Shensi-Kansu border area, all revolutionary bases were lost, the Red Army was reduced from 300,000 to a few tens of thousands, the membership of the Chinese Communist Party was reduced from 300,000 to a few tens of thousands, and the Party organizations in Kuomintang areas were almost entirely wiped out. In short, we received an extremely great historical punishment.[11]

To be sure, Mao attributed the disaster to the ideological and political errors of his recently vanquished party opponents and duly expressed confidence in ultimate victory and in the new strategy he proposed to

[11] "Strategic Problems of China's Revolutionary War," in *Selected Works of Mao Tse-tung*, Vol. 1 (London: Lawrence & Wishart, 1954), p. 193.

achieve that victory. But his appraisal of Communist fortunes at the conclusion of the Long March was bleak and accurate.

The military forces under Mao's control in Shensi were augmented in
late 1935 by several thousand Communist partisans who had been engaged in guerrilla warfare in the Northwest since 1931 under the leadership of Liu Chih-tan, a Whampoa graduate and former Kuomintang army
officer whose heroic exploits had given him something of a Robin Hood
reputation among the peasants of his native Shensi. In addition, several
thousand other Communist troops, who had abandoned a small and precarious base area in Hunan province, reached Shensi in September 1935,
several weeks prior to Mao's arrival. In 1936 these forces were joined by
the remnants of two other armies, which had taken different, but equally
difficult, routes to the North: the army under the command of Ho Lung,
which had been operating in Hunan, and the troops led by Chang Kuo-t'ao
and Chu Teh, which arrived from Kiangsi by way of Sinkiang. Yet by
late 1936 the Red Army in Shensi numbered no more than thirty thousand
men, a pitifully small and poorly equipped force compared to the pursuing Kuomintang army and various hostile warlord armies allied with
Chiang K'ai-shek.

The Yenan Era and Peasant Revolution

If the Communist military position in 1936 was precarious at best, the
social and economic environment in which they now found themselves
was hardly any more promising. Northern Shensi was one of the poorest
and most backward areas of modern China. Centuries of erosion of its
loess topsoil had made its lands barren and infertile, capable of supporting only a relatively small and extremely impoverished population—"a
very poor, backward, underdeveloped, and mountainous part of the country," as Mao Tse-tung once remarked to a foreign visitor who had toured
the province.[12] And, to Chou En-lai in 1936, it seemed a most inauspicious
place to revive the revolution. He complained:

> Peasants in Shensi are extremely poor, their land very unproductive . . . .
> The population of the Kiangsi Soviet numbered 3,000,000 whereas here
> it is at most 600,000 . . . . In Kiangsi and Fukien people brought bundles
> with them when they joined the Red Army; here they do not even bring
> chopsticks; they are utterly destitute.[13]

[12] Cited in Jan Myrdal, *Report from a Chinese Village* (New York: Pantheon,
1965), p. xxvii.
[13] Cited in Edgar Snow, *Random Notes on Red China, 1936–1945* (Cambridge,
Mass.: Harvard University Press, 1957), pp. 60–61.

And what of Yenan itself, the most sacred city to which pilgrimages are made to view the historic revolutionary places, especially the austere wooden houses and cave dwellings where Mao and others lived and worked during that legendary decade? Although an ancient city, founded some three thousand years ago, it cannot claim a particularly distinguished history. As Chinese civilization moved southward over the centuries, Yenan became a remote and unknown frontier town, used mostly as an advanced military outpost to defend the northern borders against nomadic invaders from central Asia. It was little more than a dreary and impoverished market town of perhaps ten thousand people when it was occupied by Communist troops at the end of 1936 and established as the administrative capital of what was to be called the Shensi-Kansu-Ningsia Border Region. The wretched poverty of the entire area in which the Communists now operated was reflected in the bleakness of Yenan. The town's famous museums and shrines exhibit no ancient, historic glories but are products of modern revolutionary history—and, in a sense, are the result of an accident of history. ("We didn't pick it" was Mao's terse reply to a sympathetic American writer who once politely praised Yenan's harsh climate.)[14]

But it is Yenan the time, not Yenan the place, that Chinese Communists celebrate. Yet how did the time become one to celebrate when the place was so unfavorable? How did a force of thirty thousand revolutionaries, isolated in an area so remote and so lacking in economic and material resources, grow within a decade into a powerful army of more than a million men and acquire the massive peasant support upon which its momentous and overwhelming victory was to be based?

Little light is shed on these questions by pondering that most quoted of Maoist maxims: "Political power grows out of the barrel of a gun." To be sure, an important modern Chinese political reality is reflected in this slogan: The disintegration of traditional Chinese forms of political authority and sources of legitimacy had produced a twentieth-century historical situation in which the effective exercise of political power was in fact largely dependent on the control of effective military force. But Mao Tse-tung was not the first to discover this particular secret of modern Chinese political life. Chiang K'ai-shek, for one, had learned the lesson earlier, and it was, in fact, Chiang's control of an effective army in 1927 that was mainly responsible for the Communist disasters of that year. Moreover, "political power grows out of the barrel of a gun" is hardly a formula for political victory, even if it is a more or less accurate description of the character of modern Chinese politics. Still less is it an ex-

[14] Anna Louise Strong, *Tomorrow's China* (New York: Committee for a Democratic Far Eastern Policy, 1948), p. 18.

planation for the victory prepared during the Yenan decade. For the fact remains that in 1936 the Communists in Shensi had few guns (even fewer guns than men to hold them), and they possessed what guns they had in an environment where the economic and human resources necessary for the development of military power were severely limited. It is, in short, necessary to explain how they acquired guns—and the men willing to use them—in order to understand how Communist political power did in fact grow in China.

We shall turn shortly to the many internal prerequisites for the Communist military and political success. But first it is necessary to take note of a crucial external factor—the Japanese invasion and its effects—that transformed the Chinese political scene and redefined the internal prerequisites for revolutionary victory.

For those inclined to ponder the role of "accidents" in history, the Japanese invasion of China is undoubtedly a most intriguing case. Were it not for the Japanese attempt to conquer China in 1937, it can plausibly be argued, the conditions essential to the Communist victory would not have been present. Yenan would have remained an obscure and unheralded market town in a remote Chinese province, unknown to Chinese and foreigners alike. No one in Peking today would be celebrating "the Yenan spirit," and no "China watchers" would be deliberating the implications of "the Yenan syndrome." The whole course of recent Chinese history—and indeed of world history—would probably have been profoundly different.

Those who are inclined to seek universal patterns of historical development can find in the Japanese invasion of China a classic case of one of the oldest and most persistent of historical patterns: the intimate relationship between war and revolution. For students of communism, it is of special interest to note that all *indigenous* communist revolutions (with one dubious exception[15]) grew out of conditions created by major wars; more precisely, they grew as war and foreign invasion undermined the power and authority of existing socio-political orders. The Russian October Revolution of 1917 was in large measure the product of conditions created in Russian society by World War I. And it was the foreign invasions of World War II that produced the conditions for successful communist revolutions in Yugoslavia and Vietnam as well as in China.

However intriguing it might be to pursue the question of the relationship between war and revolution (and this is a matter that deserves the most serious consideration), there is little to be gained from viewing the

---

[15] The exception, of course, is the revolution led by Castro in Cuba. The case is dubious because a good argument can be made that the Cuban revolution did not become communist until well after Castro had achieved state power.

Communist revolution in China solely in terms of some inevitable and universally valid model of this relationship. For the Communist success, as we shall have occasion to observe, was by no means the inevitable historical result of the Japanese invasion.

Nor can we interpret the Japanese invasion itself—and its results—as simply an "accident" of history. There were compelling political, economic, and ideological forces—as well as a variety of factors operating in the realm of international diplomacy—that led to the Japanese decision to attempt to conquer China. And that decision was not uninfluenced by the Chinese historical situation—or, more precisely, by Japanese perceptions of the weakness of China. Yet, if the invasion was not a historical accident, it was to China an external event, in the sense that it was determined by forces over which Chinese had little or no control. Neither the Nationalists (who lost a good deal of their credentials as Chinese nationalists by their feeble responses to the Japanese threat) nor the Communists (who gained considerable political capital by their consistent advocacy of national resistance to the foreign invaders) could decisively influence the course of Japanese policy in China.

It is not likely to prove fruitful to speculate about what might or might not have happened had circumstances been different; but it is important to understand just what did happen in the existing circumstances. As we have just suggested, these circumstances—the Japanese occupation and its effects on Chinese society—proved highly favorable to the realization of Communist ends. For one thing, the Japanese undermined the foundations of the Kuomintang regime, for the Nationalists were driven from the major cities, which were their primary sources of financial and political support. For the Kuomintang, the ravages of war resulted in incredible economic chaos and bureaucratic corruption—and, eventually, in almost total demoralization. More importantly, such administrative authority as the Kuomintang had managed to exercise in the countryside was largely destroyed, and members of the gentry-landlord class, upon which that fragile authority had rested, either fled the rural areas or were left militarily and politically defenseless. At the same time, the Communists, already experienced in working in the villages among the peasantry and adept at guerrilla warfare, were given access to vast areas of the countryside. For, while the Japanese invaders were able to occupy the cities, where the Kuomintang had been based, they did not have the manpower to effectively control the countryside, where Communist guerrilla bases multiplied rapidly during the war years. The retreat of Kuomintang military forces to the west in the face of invading Japanese armies, and the concurrent collapse of Nationalist governmental authority in much of China, allowed the Communists to break out of their remote sanctuary in Shensi and expand their military and political influence through vast areas of the countryside in northern and central China. Although the increasingly powerful Yenan base area remained the political and ideological center of the Communist revolution, Communist cadres operated in many parts of rural China, gaining the political support of tens of millions of peasants and organizing many for guerrilla warfare behind Japanese lines. Some Communist organizers filtered southward from Shensi, others were survivors from earlier guerrilla bases in central China, and many more were new adherents to the Communist cause. The gradual growth of peasant-supported Communist political and military nuclei in many parts of China during the war years was to prove decisive when the revolutionary struggle with the Kuomintang was resumed with full fury in 1946 in a massive civil war.

Much of the enormous popular support the Communists gained during the war years was based on patriotic appeals for national resistance to the foreign invaders. The new banner of modern Chinese nationalism had replaced the old "Mandate of Heaven" as the symbol of political legitimacy in twentieth-century China. As that banner began to slip from old Kuomintang hands in the 1930's—at first because of their seeming unwillingness to defend the nation against the Japanese threat and then because of their obvious inability to do so—it was quickly picked up and eagerly hoisted by new Communist hands. During the war years, Yenan was not only the revolutionary center but also (for increasing numbers of Chinese) the symbol of Chinese nationalist resistance to the Japanese. From the cities many thousands of students and intellectuals migrated to Yenan to join the Communist (and now also the nationalist) cause—and there, at the Northwest Anti-Japanese Red Army University, many were trained (and also "ideologically remolded") to become important political, administrative, and military cadres for the rapidly expanding Communist base and guerrilla areas. Of far greater political importance was the Communists' ability to organize the peasantry on the basis of patriotic as well as socio-economic appeals. The Japanese occupation not only intensified the economic crisis in the countryside but gave rise to the most bitter antiforeign sentiments among the peasants. These the Communists were able to transform into a modern mass nationalist movement and utilize for revolutionary political ends. This new Communist political opportunity was greatly facilitated by the ruthless policies pursued by the Japanese invaders—the brutal and indiscriminate military forays into the villages of northern and central China, which Japanese soldiers could plunder and punish but could not hold and occupy. Indeed, in the areas to which the Communists were able to gain access, the mobilization of the peasant masses on the basis of an anti-Japanese nationalist program contributed enormously to the military and political successes of the Yenan period.

In view of the strong tendency to interpret Chinese Communism as a species of Chinese nationalism or to view the Communist revolution as a case of a new elite riding to power on a fortuitous wave of mass nationalism, it is important to keep the whole phenomenon of "peasant nationalism" in proper historical perspective. For one thing, the Chinese peasants' sense of identification with China as a political entity and resistance to foreign intruders and invaders are not phenomena that suddenly appeared on the Chinese scene in 1937; both are age-old features of Chinese history. Even armed peasant resistance to modern imperialist incursions has a rich, almost century-old history prior to the Japanese invasion, beginning with the Opium War of 1839–42. Second, it would be highly misleading either to overestimate the spontaneous origins of the peasantry's precisely modern sense of "national consciousness" or to underestimate the role of Communist cadres in instilling that modern sense of nationalism in the strategy of "people's war." The Communists did not suddenly become nationalists during the war because they had become immersed in a nationalistic rural environment; they were ardent nationalists long before 1937, and they played a crucial role (through both propaganda and organization) in transforming the elemental antiforeign response of the peasantry into a truly modern nationalist response. By forging bonds of solidarity among peasants from various localities and regions, the Communists created a nationwide movement of resistance and imbued it with a sense of national mission that otherwise would have been absent. The Chinese Communists, in large measure, brought Chinese nationalism to the countryside; they did not simply reflect it.

Furthermore, however important Communist nationalist appeals were in gaining mass peasant support, socio-economic issues were at least equally important. The war intensified the already horrendous economic burdens of the peasantry and thus increased the attractiveness of the Communist program for land reform. To be sure, the official land policy of the Yenan period was a relatively moderate one by Kiangsi standards. Instead of the outright expropriation and division of landlord holdings, the Communists adopted a program for reductions in rents and interest rates, partly to conform to the terms of the tenuous wartime alliance with the Kuomintang but more importantly as an attempt to enlist the support of landlords and "rich peasants," as well as the masses of poor peasants, in the struggle against the Japanese occupation. But the reduction of rent to no more than one-third of the crop and the elimination of the many extralegal means through which landlords and bureaucrats traditionally exploited peasants in China were hardly unappealing measures to those who had been subjected to the most merciless forms of economic, as well as social and political, oppression.

Moreover, the officially "moderate" agrarian policies were by no means universally followed. In many cases large landholdings were in fact expropriated and distributed among land-hungry peasants, especially in areas where landlords fled with retreating Kuomintang armies. Where the gentry-landlord elite remained, collaboration between Chinese landlords and Japanese occupiers was not uncommon; in exchange for political services performed—which is to say, the traditional gentry function of "social control"—the Japanese allowed the gentry their traditional economic privilege of exploiting the peasantry. In such cases, the traditional hatred of the landlord for socio-economic reasons was intensified by new, nationalist resentments, and the Communists appealed to both feelings simultaneously, promoting class as well as national struggle. The fact of the matter, then, is that expropriation and division of gentry landholdings was a highly popular policy in much of the countryside; and where it occurred, the Communist party—if it had sufficient military predominance to guarantee the security of the peasants and their newly acquired land—won over masses of loyal peasant followers.

The view that the Communists acquired their massive peasant support in the Yenan period by a combination of nationalist appeals and moderate land policies that did not radically change existing social relationships is simply not tenable. Conditions and policies of course varied greatly from area to area. In some areas, social revolutionary actions were sacrificed to obtain the support of all rural classes in the interests of national unity; in others, radical land policies proved more effective in gaining peasant support than purely nationalist appeals; and, in still other areas, neither nationalist nor socio-economic appeals were effective. But, even where the officially moderate land policies were pusued, traditional agrarian relationships were profoundly transformed: The local political power of the gentry elite was broken, its social authority and prestige were gravely undermined, and such reduced economic power as it still held was dependent on the grace of the new holders of political and military power in the local areas—the cadres of the Chinese Communist party. In the areas under Communist control in the Yenan era, the undermining and sometimes the destruction of the power of the gentry-landlord class—the ruling elite of Chinese society for two thousand years—marked the beginning of a social revolution that was to culminate in the late 1940's and early 1950's in the elimination of the gentry as a social class throughout China. It was to be the first genuine social revolution in Chinese history since the establishment of the imperial order in 221 B.C.

Thus the Japanese invasion, by removing the Kuomintang armies and bureaucracies from vast areas of China and by undermining the power and prestige of traditional power-holders and elite groups (warlords and gentry), created conditions highly favorable to the Communists—and perhaps ones that were crucial to the eventual Communist victory. The invasion did not in itself create a revolutionary situation (for that already existed), but it did much to intensify and aggravate conditions conducive to revolution and to provide new opportunities for revolutionary action. But "revolutionary situations," however mature, do not in themselves create revolutions. Only men make revolutions—and only on the basis of their consciousness, their perception of the situation in which they find themselves, and their will and ability to transform that situation in accordance with their revolutionary goals. The war, in short, by no means guaranteed the inevitability of a Communist victory. And the successes and specific characteristics of Yenan Communism did not spring spontaneously from any "objective" imperatives of the wartime situation. Rather, they owed much to the way in which the Chinese Communists perceived the Chinese historical situation and to the way in which they were disposed to go about changing it. Thus, to understand the Yenan era and its distinctive revolutionary and ideological legacy, it is necessary to take into account subjective as well as objective factors, particularly the intellectual and ideological predispositions of Mao Tse-tung.

The Origins of Maoism

Although "Maoism" did not crystalize into an official ideological orthodoxy until the Yenan period, its historical existence as a distinct (and distinctively Chinese) interpretation of Marxism began with the introduction of Marxism in China in 1918–19. To view Maoism as simply the ideological product or reflection of the "objective" conditions of Yenan Communism is to ignore the historical truism that men are the producers as well as the products of history, and that the way in which they make history depends, at least in part, on the way they perceive objective reality. Neither Yenan Communism nor Mao Tse-tung are exceptions to this proposition; much of what went into the making of the former was molded by the now famous "thoughts" of the latter. And Mao did not arrive in Shensi in 1935 with an empty head.

In fact, when Mao became a convert to Marxism and communism in 1919, the basic intellectual predispositions that were to mold his understanding and interpretation of Marxism and his concept of revolution were already present, and they were to be reinforced by his revolutionary experiences in the 1920's and early 1930's. While it is well beyond the scope of this essay to trace the intellectual development of Mao Tse-tung, it is possible to identify certain abiding traits of the Maoist mentality that provided the essential intellectual and ideological prerequisites for the successful Yenan strategy of revolution.

By no means the least important of Mao's early (and persisting) intellectual orientations was a profoundly voluntarist belief that the decisive factor in history is human consciousness—the ideas, the wills, and the actions of men. This faith in the ability of self-conscious men to mold objective social reality in accordance with their ideas and ideals survived the influence of the more deterministic tenets of Marxist theory, as Mao began to assimilate that theory in the 1920's and 1930's.

The survival of this fundamental voluntarist impulse, it might be noted, was greatly facilitated by the manner in which Marxism had come to China in the wake of World War I. Unlike Russia and the Western countries, China lacked a Marxist social-democratic tradition. The early Chinese converts to communism were drawn to Marxism and Leninism by the chiliastic message of the Russian Bolshevik revolution (which promised both national liberation and worldwide revolution) and were committed to a Leninist-style revolution long before they became familiar with Marxist-Leninist theory. These early communists (such as Li Ta-chao, China's first Marxist, and his disciple, Mao Tse-tung) tended to interpret Marxist theory in the light of their revolutionary expectations rather than to redefine those expectations on the basis of their new Marxist creed.

To be sure, Mao derived from the objective laws of historical development proclaimed by Marx some degree of assurance in the historical inevitability of a socialist future (and he soon learned to repeat the relevant Marxist formulas). But, in the final analysis, his faith in the achievement of that future was not based upon any real Marxist confidence in the determining, objective forces of socio-historical development; it stemmed rather from a profound confidence in the revolutionary consciousness and activism of men determined to bring about that future. For Mao, in other words, the essential factor in determining the course of history was conscious human activity, and the most important ingredients for revolution were the attitudes of men and their willingness to engage in revolutionary action.

This implied, among other things, that revolution in China need not be dependent on any predetermined levels of social and economic development and that immediate opportunities for revolutionary action need not be restricted by orthodox Marxist-Leninist formulas. It also implied a special concern for developing and maintaining "correct" ideological consciousness, the ultimately decisive factor in determining revolutionary success or failure. Correct thought, in the Maoist view, is the first and essential prerequisite for correct revolutionary action, and it is this assumption that lies behind the emphasis on the peculiarly Chinese Communist techniques of "thought reform" and "ideological remolding" developed and refined in the Yenan period. The Cheng Feng campaign of 1942–44 for the rectification of "undesirable" ideas and ideological tendencies was the most intensive application of a general Chinese Communist policy.

This whole emphasis on ideological solidarity was of central importance to the successful conduct of guerrilla warfare in the Yenan period. In a "guerrilla" situation, where centralized forms of organizational control are by definition precluded, the forging of the strongest possible commitments to a common ideology and a common manner of thinking (and thus of acting) becomes a matter of supreme importance. The fact that Maoism was already disposed to stress the importance of "subjective factors" goes a long way toward explaining why the Communists adopted the strategy of guerrilla warfare and why they were able to employ this strategy so successfully.

If Mao's voluntarism mitigated the more deterministic implications of Marxist theory, his particularly powerful nationalistic proclivities were equally important in making Marxism a more flexible ideological instrument for revolution in China. As was generally true for Chinese intellectuals who were attracted to communism and Marxism in the May Fourth period, nationalist resentments against Western imperialism and nationalist aspirations for a future "new China" were very much involved in Mao's original conversion to Marxism. Quite apart from the nationalist appeals of the Leninist theory of imperialism and specific Soviet appeals to Chinese nationalist sentiments (both of which promised China an important place in the world revolutionary process), Marxist theory itself satisfied profoundly important nationalist needs. For Mao, as for others, Marxism appeared to be the most advanced product of modern Western thought; but, unlike other Western ideologies and models, it rejected the West in its present capitalist and imperialist form (and thus also rejected the present Western imperialist impingement on China). At the same time, Marxism served to reaffirm the rejection of the already discarded "prenationalist" values of traditional China, which now could be conveniently dismissed as "feudal." In other words, Marxism had the great nationalist appeal of assigning both "precapitalist" China and the capitalist West to the same "dustbin of history" while simultaneously looking toward a "postcapitalist" future in which China would take its rightful place in a new international socialist order.

It goes without saying that Mao has always had a certain feeling of national pride in the Chinese past and that he has been at least as much concerned with the future power and glory of the Chinese nation as with the fate of the international proletarian revolution. But it might also be said that from the beginning Mao's especially deep-rooted nationalist impulses gave rise to the belief that the Chinese revolution was more or less synonymous with the world revolution—or at least that China had a very special, indeed almost messianic, role to play in the world revolutionary process. As early as 1930 Mao felt sufficiently confident to proclaim publicly that China was more revolutionary than other countries and to predict that "the revolution will certainly move towards an upsurge more quickly in China than in Western Europe."[16] In the Maoist conception of China's special place in the world revolution, genuinely internationalist aspirations and goals were no doubt inextricably intertwined with Chinese nationalist impulses. But it was in this treacherous area of "messianic revolutionary nationalism" (as Trotsky once called it) that Mao departed from other Chinese Marxists whose nationalist passions were restrained by more orthodox Western Marxist considerations.

The nationalist element in Mao's Marxist world view was reflected not only in his long-standing hostility to the Russian-dominated Comintern (and, in the late 1950's, in his open hostility toward the Soviet Union) but also, and more importantly, in his conception of revolution within China. Central to this conception was the conviction that the real enemies were not so much within Chinese society as without. The real enemy was foreign imperialism, and in the face of that continuing threat China stood as a potentially proletarian nation in a hostile capitalist-imperialist world order. Although internal class divisions were important and class struggle necessary, in confronting the external foe, it was assumed that Chinese of all social classes could gather under the revolutionary nationalist umbrella held up by the Chinese Communist party—and those who could not, or would not, were excluded from membership in the nation, or at least from "the people," excommunicated as representatives of foreign imperialism. Political circumstances permitting, class struggle thus could be subordinated to national struggle—and, indeed, the two could be regarded as more or less synonymous. In fact, if the main enemy was external, then a "united front" of all Chinese opposed to foreign imperialism was not only necessary for national survival but also conducive to the eventual realization of international communist goals. In Mao's eyes, nationalist struggle was not necessarily incompatible with the pursuit of Marxist internationalist goals.

A third intellectual orientation that decisively influenced the Maoist

[16] "A Single Spark Can Start a Prairie Fire," in *Selected Works of Mao Tse-tung,* Vol. 1, p. 118.

adaptation of Marxism-Leninism to the Chinese environment may be described as essentially populist. The populist-inspired notion of a "great union of the popular masses"[17] that Mao advocated at the beginning of his revolutionary career in 1919 survived the influence of Marxism and modified the influence of Leninism. Populist impulses reinforced Mao's nationalist-inspired faith in the basic unity of the Chinese people in the face of intrusion by alien forces and led him to attribute to "the people" an almost inherent revolutionary socialist consciousness. "In the masses is embodied great socialist activism" is a recent Maoist slogan that derives from an early Maoist-populist faith, expressed in 1919 in the affirmation that "our Chinese people possesses great intrinsic energy."[18]

Moreover, Mao's populist impulse, with its essentially rural orientation and its romantic celebration of the rural ideal of "the unity of living and working," served to define "the people" as the peasant masses (for the peasantry, after all, constituted the overwhelming majority of the Chinese population) and led him to prize the spontaneously revolutionary energies he believed they possessed. Thus, Mao's populism drew him to the countryside at a time when the Communist revolution was still centered in the cities. In his famous (and heretical) "Hunan Report" of March 1927, he found in the Chinese peasantry an elemental revolutionary force so great that it would sweep away everything before it—including, he predicted, those revolutionary intellectuals who proved unwilling or unable to unite with the peasant masses. Then, as later, he expressed profound distrust of the "knowledge" brought by urban intellectuals and profound admiration for the innate "wisdom" of the peasantry.

Many other characteristic features of the Maoist mentality are typically populist. One might mention, for example, Mao's hostility toward occupational specialization, his acute distrust of intellectuals and specialists, his profoundly antibureaucratic orientations (and indeed his general enmity toward all forms of large-scale, centralized organization), his anti-urban bias, and his romantic mood of heroic revolutionary self-sacrifice. These, as well as many other aspects of the thought of Mao, bear striking similarities to what is generally understood by the term "populism." To be sure, Mao is not simply a populist in Marxist guise (any more than he is simply a Chinese nationalist in communist dress), but it is important to note that populist ideas and impulses have significantly influenced the manner in which Mao has understood and employed Marxism.

To understand the reasons for the Communist success in the Yenan

[17] This was the title of an article by Mao published in the summer of 1919. For a translation of extracts from the article, see *The Political Thought of Mao Tse-tung*, edited by Stuart R. Schram, rev. ed. (New York: Praeger, 1963), pp. 105–06.

[18] *Ibid.*, p. 106.

period, it is of special importance to take into account Mao's genuinely populist faith in the peasant masses as potential bearers of socialist revolutionary consciousness. For it is this faith that permitted—and indeed dictated—the much celebrated Maoist notion of "the mass line," the various principles and rules by which Communist cadres became intimately involved and identified with the peasant masses. The Maoist maxim that intellectuals and party cadres must become the pupils of the masses before they can become their teachers was in fact widely practiced in the Yenan days. Had it been otherwise, the Communists could never have acquired the mass support and cooperation among the peasantry that was so essential to the successful employment of the strategy of "people's war."

In attributing a latent socialist consciousness to the peasantry, Mao, it should be noted, departed not only from Marx but from Lenin. For Marx, the bearers of socialist consciousness were the urban proletariat, and he rarely missed an opportunity to express his contempt for "the idiocy of rural life." And for Lenin, socialist consciousness was to be imposed on the "spontaneous" proletarian mass movement by an elite of revolutionary intellectuals organized into a highly centralized and disciplined communist party, with the peasantry playing an ambiguous auxiliary role in the revolutionary process. Mao departed from Leninism not only in his virtually total lack of interest in the urban working class but also in his conception of the nature and role of the party. The party was sacrosanct to Lenin because it was the incarnation of "proletarian consciousness." In his mind, there was no question about who should be the teachers and who the pupils. For Mao, on the other hand, this was precisely the question, and it has remained unanswered; he has never really defined the relationship between the organized "proletarian consciousness" of the party and the spontaneous "proletarian consciousness" of the masses in a purely Leninist fashion. His faith in the party as the bearer of revolutionary consciousness was never complete, for it was accompanied by the populist belief that true revolutionary knowledge and creativity ultimately emanate from the people themselves.

There were, to be sure, objective factors that influenced Mao's rather ambiguous view of the role of the party. Military power, after all, was the crucial factor in determining the outcome of the Chinese revolution, and the influence of the party as such tended to be subsumed by the Red Army. Moreover, unlike the Russian Revolution, the Chinese Communist revolution did not involve the sudden seizure of state power. It was based, rather, on the relatively gradual growth of popular support and, eventually, on the revolutionary activities of millions, often largely spontaneous, that were to take place in many local areas where communication was slow and difficult. This created a revolutionary situation that was hardly conducive to control and direction by a highly centralized party apparatus.

The voluntarist, nationalist, and populist impulses that governed Mao's understanding and interpretation of Marxism in the years after 1919 formed the essential intellectual and ideological prerequisites for the development of the Maoist strategy of peasant revolution and the successful employment of this strategy in the Yenan period. Although the Japanese invasion intensified China's socio-economic crisis and created political conditions favorable to the growth of a revolutionary movement, it was not inevitable that a revolutionary movement would in fact grow and emerge victorious. It is most unlikely that orthodox Marxist-Leninists could have appreciated fully the revolutionary opportunities offered, much less have taken advantage of them to build a communist movement on a purely peasant base. It was precisely Mao's ideological unorthodoxies that allowed the Communists to seize upon these opportunities. It was his voluntarist faith in the power of the human will and consciousness to shape historical reality that permitted him to ignore (or redefine) those Marxist socio-economic prerequisites and Marxist social-class considerations that might otherwise have restricted the possibilities for revolutionary action. It was his nationalist-populist impulses that made him look to the broadest possible sources of national revolutionary support and directed him from the cities to the countryside. And it was his populist trust in the spontaneous revolutionary energies of the peasant masses that allowed him to develop and pursue the unorthodox strategy of "people's war." Such were some of the essential ingredients in the emergence of a distinctively Chinese Marxist revolutionary mentality that proved instrumental in transforming a "revolutionary situation" into a genuine social revolution with the most momentous historical consequences.

Yenan Marxism

The Yenan era was Mao's most productive period, both as a Marxist theoretician and as a revolutionary strategist. The bulk of the writings that were later to be canonized as "the thoughts of Mao Tse-tung"—and eventually presented as universally valid revolutionary theory on as lofty a doctrinal level as the works of Marx, Engels, and Lenin—were composed during the Yenan period, especially in the years 1937–40.

A textual analysis of these writings, however, throws very little light on the much debated question "What is Maoism?" or on the problem of the relationship of "the thoughts of Mao Tse-tung" to the Marxist and Leninist traditions. The majority of Mao's Yenan writings deal with matters of military strategy—and, it is argued by some, Mao's real innovations as a "Marxist-Leninist" lie in this rather nontheoretical realm of affairs, in his long treatises on the tactics and techniques of guerrilla warfare and in his detailed discussions of the practical and specifically Chinese political and economic factors involved in the conduct of revolutionary war. Moreover, in his more theoretical writings, which are concerned with problems of Marxist theory and politics, most of the distinctive features of the Maoist version of Marxism are only implicit, and what is distinctive is often concealed and obscured by the restatement of standard Marxist-Leninist formulas. In fact, a good case can be made for the proposition that Mao's real contributions and innovations as a Marxist did not appear until the postrevolutionary period (particularly after 1955), when he directed his attention to the problems of building a socialist society in an economically backward country—especially to the problem of how to prevent the bureaucratic degeneration of a socialist revolution in the postrevolutionary era.

However that may be, Mao's Yenan writings are important for a number of reasons. First, they established Mao's reputation as an independent Marxist theoretician. Having achieved *de facto* political independence from Moscow, the Chinese Communists could now claim to have established ideological independence as well—in the form of a body of doctrine that was hailed as having applied the "universal truths" of Marxism-Leninism to the specific conditions of the Chinese historical situation. Second, Mao's treatises on "dialectics" and "contradictions" provided a rudimentary philosophical basis for the distinctive features of Maoism. Finally, the Marxist theoretical writings of the Yenan era (by Mao and others) were designed to reaffirm the Marxist-Leninist orthodoxy of the Chinese Communist party, to convey some rudimentary knowledge of that doctrine to many newly recruited members of the party, and, most importantly, to rationalize Chinese Communist political practice in terms of Marxist-Leninist theory.

Although this last task was accomplished to the satisfaction of Mao and other Chinese Communist leaders, it was done without dealing with the most crucial ideological problem raised by the Chinese Communist revolution in general and the strategy of the Yenan period in particular. The Maoist theoretical writings say virtually nothing about how a communist party almost totally separated from the cities and the urban proletariat and based entirely on peasant support could carry out a socialist revolution. This posed not only a grave Marxist theoretical dilemma but also a very practical revolutionary problem. While the peasants were very much interested in socio-economic reform and the redistribution of land, not even Mao, with all his faith in the inherent "socialist activism" of the peasant masses, really believed that the peasants as a class were inclined (spontaneously or otherwise) to socialism in the abstract, much less to the collectivization of land, which the building of a socialist order presupposed. At their radical best, the peasants were interested in the equal distribution of land on the basis of individual peasant proprietorship—an agrarian revolution, to be sure, but one that precluded a true socialist reorganization of society, by either Marxist or non-Marxist definitions. The class composition of the Chinese Communist movement and the social aspirations of the Chinese peasantry both implied that the revolution could not pass logically or practically beyond what in Marxist terms is called the "bourgeois-democratic stage." There is nothing in either Maoist ideology or Chinese social reality to suggest that the peasantry as such is the bearer of the socialist future.

Who, then, were to be the agents of socialist revolution? There are Maoist answers to this question, but they are not easily found in Maoist theoretical literature. Here we find only repetitions of the stale Marxist orthodoxy that the socialist revolution is to be led by the proletariat and the equally withered Leninist orthodoxy that the Communist party is the representative of the proletariat and the incarnation of "proletarian consciousness." This is supplemented only by the concept of "the people's democratic dictatorship," a notion that was born in the united-front strategy of the Yenan era (in Mao's essays on "new democracy" and "coalition government") and formally proclaimed in 1949, on the eve of the official establishment of the Chinese People's Republic. The formula provides for a government representing a coalition of four classes (proletariat, peasantry, petty bourgeoisie, and national bourgeoisie) but also for a coalition under "proletarian hegemony"—which is to say that political power ultimately resides in the "proletarian" Communist party.

For the purposes of the present essay, there is little to be gained by embarking upon a discussion of the political and ideological implications of these particular formulas. The fact of the matter is that during the crucial Yenan years of the revolution the Chinese Communist party lacked the active support of the Chinese urban proletariat and made very little effort to acquire it. Indeed, such an effort was largely precluded by Maoist revolutionary strategy, which, in both theory and practice, assumed that the crucial forces of revolution resided in the countryside and in the peasantry, and that the mobilization of these forces would lead to a situation in which the revolutionary rural areas would encircle and eventually occupy the nonrevolutionary cities.

What turned out to be crucial in determining that the revolution would move beyond the bourgeois-democratic stage to socialism were the "subjective factors" in history (upon which Maoism itself places such great emphasis), most particularly the conscious determination of Mao and the Chinese Communist leadership to pursue socialist goals. However unorthodox they have been in their strategy of revolution, Maoists have remained firmly committed to orthodox Marxist goals. If they have not identified themselves with the actual proletarian class, they have identified themselves with the political and social goals and the messianic, historic mission that Marx attributed to that class. And this "subjective factor" proved of enormous historical significance in determining the character and direction of the Chinese revolution.

What is thus implicit in Maoist theory, and demonstrated in Maoist practice, is the notion that the bearers of socialism are those who possess true "proletarian consciousness" and that the latter can exist quite independently of any specific social class. This consciousness is not dependent on the actual presence of the proletariat, nor, on the other hand, is it attributed to the peasantry upon whose revolutionary energies and actions the Communist success was based. Thus "proletarian consciousness" can be attributed to a revolutionary elite (the party and its leaders), which holds the socialist goal firmly in mind and directs the mass movement toward the realization of that goal. In a broader sense, "proletarian consciousness" is seen as a potential, inherent in "the people" as a whole, for all men are potentially capable of achieving (through revolutionary action) the spiritual and ideological transformation necessary to acquire a true proletarian spirit and a socialist world view.

This emphasis on the role of consciousness in the making of history and revolution reflects, of course, long-standing Maoist voluntarist and populist predispositions and also the uniquely Maoist treatment of the Marxist theory of class struggle. Mao, to be sure, has always been intensely concerned with objective class conditions in Chinese society and has been an ardent promoter of class struggle, both in theory and in practice. But he also has tended to define "class position" less on the basis of objective social class than by moral and ideological criteria. While for Marx the existence of a potentially revolutionary proletarian class was the prerequisite for the rise of revolutionary proletarian ideas, for Mao the existence of men with appropriate revolutionary ideas is sufficient to prove the existence of a revolutionary proletarian class. Perhaps the most radical ideological expression of this entire voluntarist trend is to be found in the Maoist treatises that conclude with the proposition that under certain conditions "the subjective can create the objective."

Another radical Maoist precept that dictated that the revolution would not and could not stop at the bourgeois-democratic stage, China's economic backwardness and the social composition of the Chinese Communist party notwithstanding, is the doctrine of "uninterrupted" (or "permanent") revolution. This doctrine proclaimed the necessity for a continuous process of ideological transformation and revolutionary social and political struggle, proceeding through increasingly radical phases of social development directly into the communist utopia of the future. Although the theory of permanent revolution was not formally put forward until later, it was implicit in the Maoist ideology of the Yenan era and had its philosophical roots in Mao's writings on dialectics, particularly his essays "On Practice" and "On Contradiction," which were originally speeches delivered in the summer of 1937. Here the world was seen as being in a state of eternal flux, and social and historical reality as a process of constant and inevitable change and development because of the internal contradictions inherent in all phenomena. Quite apart from the controversial question of their philosophical merits or deficiencies, the essays reflected a highly activist mentality and prophetically proclaimed the message that change, in increasingly radical directions, was permanent and necessary.

It might also be noted (and this was another prophetic pointer to the future) that Mao's emergence as an independent Marxist theoretician in the Yenan years posed a grave challenge to Moscow's authority in the world communist movement in general, and to Stalin's claim to universal Marxist-Leninist ideological and political infallibility in particular. For Mao had embarked upon "the Sinification of Marxism" (to use his own words of 1938), and the celebration of his "creative adaptation" of Marxism-Leninism to Chinese conditions and of his claims to theoretical innovation was to become increasingly explicit—and for Stalin, increasingly defiant—over the years. The celebration was to grow into claims of universal validity for "the thoughts of Mao Tse-tung"—valid, at least, for the vast non-Western areas of the world, where communist revolutions are possible and, according to the Maoist view of the world, inevitable.

The Yenan Revolutionary Tradition and Its Legacy

The Yenan period not only proved decisive for the Chinese Communist victory of 1949 but bequeathed to the victors a heroic tradition of revolutionary struggle that has since been canonized as "the Yenan spirit" and "the Yenan style." Since those who fashioned the Communist victory in the Yenan era were the ones who became the leaders of the People's Republic, it is hardly surprising that the policies they pursued and their responses to the problems of the post-1949 period have been significantly influenced by their experiences in those earlier and more heroic days. "The Yenan spirit" is not simply praised in Communist China to commemorate the heroism of days past; it has also become a model to be applied to achieve new revolutionary goals in the "postrevolutionary era." As recent political events have demonstrated dramatically, not all Chinese Communists have perceived the Yenan model in the same manner; at least, not all are convinced that it is completely relevant to contemporary Chinese needs. But many Chinese Communists, and most notably Mao Tse-tung, remain fundamentally committed to the Yenan spirit of revolutionary struggle.

In the broader sense, the Yenan revolutionary tradition includes the whole historical experience of Chinese Communism in this decisive phase of the revolution. Everything from the distinctively Chinese Communist methods of organization and tactics associated with the strategy of guerrilla warfare to Maoist philosophy and the Maoist version of Marxism-Leninism is part of this tradition.

The Yenan revolutionary tradition can be more narrowly defined as the distillation of this entire experience (as it was perceived then and reinterpreted later) into a system of social and ethical values and the concept of an ideal (and idealized) Yenan revolutionary cadre that exemplified these values. While the unique methods of organization developed in the Yenan period were enormously important in determining the manner in which political power was organized and social control exercised in China after 1949, the system of values that emerged from the Yenan era has perhaps proved to be of equally great historical significance. What Chinese Communists today celebrate as "the Yenan spirit" is in fact largely concerned with spiritual and ideological matters and, more specifically, with the kinds of social and ethical values deemed appropriately revolutionary for the present, even though they are attributed to a heroic revolutionary past.

Many of the values conveyed by "the Yenan spirit" have been mentioned earlier. Here it need only be noted that they are essentially ascetic values, which demand a highly disciplined and completely selfless life orientation. The highest and most prized virtue is struggle (and self-sacrifice) in behalf of the people. Such struggle is not necessarily seen as an end in itself; it receives its ultimate ethical sanction in the promise that it will eventually lead to the realization of the communist utopia of the future. But unselfish revolutionary struggle is in itself ethically valued and typically described in Chinese Communist writings as "saintly and divine" and the source of true happiness. In the Maoist theory of dialectics, struggle is seen as inevitable and infinite; and in Maoist moral theory, the spirit of revolutionary struggle is presented as the most sacred of revolutionary virtues.

Other Maoist moral maxims are more commonplace—hard work, diligence, self-denial, frugality, altruism, and self-discipline. Such values are attributed to "the Yenan spirit" and have been imparted to the Chinese people in various ways in recent decades. In the Yenan decade these values were in fact practiced by Chinese Communists, for they were imposed by the harsh imperatives of revolutionary struggle and the spartan and egalitarian style of life that such struggle demanded. In the Maoist view, however, men imbued with such values not only were responsible for revolutionary success in the past but remain essential for the building of a communist society in the future. The ideal, self-reliant Yenan guerrilla leader who "became one" with the people, who "combined ability with virtue" and was always ready to sacrifice his life for the revolution, became the prototype for the later model of the "new communist man" who exemplifies these ascetic values and revolutionary commitments.

The generalization and idealization of the Yenan model reflects Mao's voluntarist faith that the truly decisive factor in history is man—or, more precisely, ideologically self-conscious men motivated by the proper revolutionary will and the proper moral values. It also reflects his populist faith that all men are inherently capable of the spiritual and ideological transformation needed to make them "new communist men" and that such a transformation is the prerequisite for both the economic and political actions that will lead to the achievement of genuine Marxist goals. Such men are more important than machines and technology, in the Maoist view, and ideological-moral solidarity is more important than any artificial unity that formal bureaucratic organization can provide or impose.

This whole galaxy of Maoist beliefs owes much to the Yenan experience (although the success of the Yenan period owes much to these beliefs as well), for the Yenan experience seemed to confirm the view that determined men inspired by the correct ideology and spirit can triumph over the most formidable material obstacles. The Yenan era began with thirty thousand poorly armed revolutionary soldiers, isolated in an area that offered only the most meager material resources. A decade later, that small force had grown into a regular army of a million men, supported by several million more peasants organized in local partisan groups. More importantly, it had grown on the basis of a massive popular social revolution that involved the active and meaningful cooperation and participation of tens of millions of peasants.

At the end of World War II, when the uneasy Kuomintang-Communist truce inevitably collapsed and led to open civil war, Kuomintang armies enjoyed a four-to-one superiority in manpower over regular Communist military forces and an even greater superiority in modern military technology, largely supplied by the United States. Yet the Communist victory in the massive battles that marked the civil war of 1946–49, however bloody and difficult, was surprisingly swift. It was, as Stuart Schram has so well put it, "one of the most striking examples in history of the victory of a smaller but dedicated and well-organized force enjoying popular support over a larger but unpopular force with poor morale and incompetent leadership."[19] On October 1, 1949, Mao stood high on the Gate of Heavenly Peace in Peking to officially establish the Chinese People's Republic, while Chiang K'ai-shek and those who remained in his army and bureaucracy had already fled to the island of Taiwan, there to impose their rule on a hostile population and to find a haven granted by the grace of the American Seventh Fleet.

When the peasant soldiers of the Red Army occupied Peking and the other major cities of China in 1949, it was an almost anticlimactic climax of the Chinese revolution. Though the people of the cities generally welcomed the Communists as liberators (or at least as the lesser of two evils), the urban classes had made only the most minimal contribution to the victory of that revolution. The decisive battles had been fought (and the real dramas had taken place) earlier—and in the countryside.

The dramatic Communist success in the civil war, and the whole Yenan experience on which that success was based, undoubtedly served to reinforce the Maoist belief in the primacy of moral over material forces, of men over machines, and to bolster the faith that the truly creative revolutionary forces of society resided more in the countryside than in the cities. What is more, the Chinese revolutionary experience gave rise to powerful antibureaucratic orientations and to what some writers call "an antitechnocratic bias"—the Maoist preference for the ideologically pure generalist (modeled on the ideal Yenan guerrilla leader) over the technologically proficient (but ideologically deficient) expert. This is not a bias against technology as such, it should be noted, but rather a profound concern for the social uses of modern technology and its bureaucratic and elitist implications.

These intellectual and ideological orientations, accompanied by the ascetic values associated with "the Yenan spirit" of heroic revolutionary struggle, are some of the major components of the Chinese Communist revolutionary tradition. The implications of this legacy were largely muted during the early years of the People's Republic, years that saw the final steps in the destruction of the more than two-thousand-year-old

[19] *Mao Tse-tung,* p. 225.

gentry ruling class and a period when the consolidation of Communist political power and economic development where the main revolutionary orders of the day. But new bureaucratic and technological elites were to emerge from the new Communist forms of political organization and economic development. And it was in response to this that the Yenan legacy was to reemerge in the years after 1955 as a harbinger of new policies and strategies of social and economic development that seemed to defy the "laws" of "the modernization process." These historically un-precedented Maoist strategies were designed to pursue economic de-velopment in a manner consistent with the realization of Marxist goals, and they have kept China in a state of virtually continuous revolutionary ferment for more than a decade. It is much too early to pass historical judgments on either the validity or the viability of this Maoist search for a uniquely Chinese route to communism.

Selected Readings

Chassin, Lionel M. *The Communist Conquest of China: A History of the Civil War, 1945–1949*. Cambridge, Mass.: Harvard University Press, 1965. A detailed narrative history of the massive battles that marked the final stage of the civil war between the Communists and the Kuomintang.

Ch'en, Jerome. *Mao and the Chinese Revolution*. London: Oxford Uni-versity Press, 1966. A perceptive account of the life and times of Mao Tse-tung, including thirty-seven of Mao's poems in English transla-tion.

Johnson, Chalmers A. *Peasant Nationalism and Communist Power: The Emergence of Revolutionary China, 1937–1945*. Stanford, Calif.: Stanford University Press, 1962. A study of the Communist-led peas-ant resistance movement against the Japanese invaders in the Yenan period. The author presents a thought-provoking (and controversial) interpretation of the nature of Chinese Communism in terms of the concept of "mass nationalism."

Mao Tse-tung. *The Political Thought of Mao Tse-tung*. Edited by Stuart R. Schram. Rev. ed. New York: Praeger, 1963. An excellent and care-fully edited collection of selections from the writings of Mao, pre-ceded by a stimulating analytic essay on Mao and Maoism.

Meisner, Maurice. *Li Ta-chao and the Origins of Chinese Marxism*. Cambridge, Mass.: Harvard University Press, 1967. A study of the reception and interpretation of Marxist theory in China and an analy-sis of the early intellectual origins of "Maoism."

Rue, John E. *Mao Tse-tung in Opposition, 1927–1935*. Stanford, Calif.: Stanford University Press, 1966. A very important and highly informative account of the Kiangsi era that throws new light on the most obscure period of the Chinese Communist revolution and the career of Mao Tse-tung.

Schram, Stuart R. *Mao Tse-tung.* New York: Simon & Schuster, 1967. The most extensive—and the best—biography of Mao Tse-tung to date. The author also presents a brilliant and comprehensive history of Chinese Communism from its beginnings through the early phases of the "Cultural Revolution."

Schurmann, Franz. *Ideology and Organization in Communist China.* 2nd ed. Berkeley, Calif.: University of California Press, 1968. A monumental study that provides, among other things, an extraordinarily perceptive analysis of the Chinese Communist "manner of thinking."

Schwartz, Benjamin I. *Chinese Communism and the Rise of Mao.* Rev. ed. Cambridge, Mass.: Harvard University Press, 1958. A brilliant pioneering study of the history of the Chinese Communist movement from 1918 through the Kiangsi period.

Snow, Edgar. *Red Star Over China.* Rev. ed. New York: Grove Press, 1968. The classic, first-hand account of the Chinese Communist movement in the early Yenan days by the famous American scholar-journalist. Includes Mao's only (and invaluable) "autobiography," related to the author in a series of interviews in Shensi, and a fascinating description of the Long March.

Van Slyke, Lyman P. *Enemies and Friends: The United Front in Chinese Communist History.* Stanford, Calif.: Stanford University Press, 1967. An important study of one aspect of Chinese Communist revolutionary strategy, placed in fruitful historical perspective.

The Phoenix Risen

from the Ashes:

Postwar Japan

HUGH T. PATRICK

IN September 1945, and indeed for close to a decade thereafter, no one could conceive that by the late 1960's Japan would be not only the strongest nation in Asia but the third largest industrial power in the world, a major ally of the United States, and its second largest trading partner, after Canada. The purpose of this essay is to describe Japan's resurgence to the forefront of the world's nations.

Japan was utterly defeated in World War II, crushed militarily and economically, its ideological foundations of romantic traditionalism, expansionism, and nationalism fully discredited. Major cities were in rubble and their populations dispersed throughout the countryside. Japan lost in World War II almost three million people; its empire of Taiwan, Korea, Manchuria, and various mandated territories; and one-quarter of its capital stock of machines, equipment, buildings, and houses. This included virtually all its merchant shipping and textile equipment, the major prewar industry. Not all was due to the direct destruction of war. In the last desperate days, for instance, textile spindles were taken out of factories and melted down as scrap to make munitions, and much equipment had deteriorated due to lack of maintenance. Probably more important, soil fertility had declined sharply because of the virtual cessation of chemical and other fertilizer inputs. Acute shortages of goods and bottlenecks, combined with deficit financing and immense bank-note issues at war's end, were to provide the basis for a rampant inflation that was to plague Japan throughout the immediate postwar years.

Moreover, Japan was subject to military occupation by the victorious Allies, a prospect which the populace naturally regarded with great initial trepidation. As it turned out, however, the Occupation was not essentially punitive but was instead perhaps the greatest social experiment ever attempted. Highly idealistic and ambitious, its fundamental objective was to re-create Japan as a democratic society—not simply in political and economic institutions and in the sources and balances of power, but even in values and ideology. For all the inefficiencies and even mistakes during the Occupation, and for all the alterations the Japanese have made since it ended, any overall assessment must conclude that the Occupation was highly successful. This success was possible, however, only because the Japanese wanted it so. It was not simply that the Japanese cooperated with the Occupation—though that was essential—for the changes that came about have been far too great and lasting. It was that most of the seeds of change fell on fertile ground; those that did not have ultimately fared far less well.

Nonetheless, from the Japanese point of view the goal of "democratization" was not the most important one: For most people in the early postwar years the most immediate problem was simply how to survive, how to meet the pressing material needs for food, clothing, shelter. As conditions gradually improved, such economic objectives still continued to loom large for both individual family and nation. Indeed, the pursuit of rapid economic growth and rising living standards has remained predominant in Japan's postwar national objectives. And success in the economic sphere has been a requisite of Japan's continued democratization and of its resurgence as a world power. Accordingly, this essay focuses mainly on Japan's economic performance in arising, like the legendary phoenix, from the ashes of World War II.

From Occupation to Restoration of Sovereignty

The occupation of Japan was essentially an American operation, even though policy was nominally determined by the eleven-power Far Eastern Commission in Washington. General Douglas MacArthur, Supreme Commander of the Allied Powers (or SCAP, which referred both to MacArthur and to the administrative bureaucracy of the Occupation), by dint of personal authority and personality wielded considerable decision-making power in addition to overseeing the implementation of policy. SCAP worked through the Japanese government, utilizing rather than replacing it, by means of formal directives and informal, continuous guidance. Most members of the SCAP staff were American. Ranging from fervent New Dealers to conservative businessmen, they encompassed a wide spectrum of attitudes and values, as well as a wide variety of military and civilian skills.

Quite naturally the immediate objective of the Occupation was to demilitarize Japan, first by destroying all armaments and halting all military production, then by physically taking control of the entire country, purging military, political, and business leaders, and punishing those found guilty as war criminals. This was meant, over the long run, to destroy the economic and political bases of military strength and to curtail Japan's willingness to use war as an instrument of national policy. A considerable amount of punitive feeling colored Occupation policy at the beginning: Japan deserved its plight, which was the outcome of its unpardonable aggression against others, and it should be expected to pay for the damage it had done. Nonetheless, mere retribution never dominated policy and was soon submerged in the zeal for reform.

The shifting policy regarding reparations payments for damage done to Allied nations is indicative of the changing attitude. The sum of the claims of the Allied nations was huge. It was soon decided that Japan could not afford payments drawn from current production, but that much of her industrial capacity—especially in iron and steel, machinery, and chemicals—was war-related and hence "surplus," so it could be dismantled and shipped to damaged neighbors. It was difficult to decide exactly what was surplus, since in fact any reduction in capacity slowed Japan's ability to support itself economically. At first, "surplus" capacities were defined as any plants and equipment beyond those needed to maintain a standard of living equal to that of the countries Japan had occupied, but this was soon amended to Japan's prewar (1934–36) standard. Quickly realizing that it would ultimately have to foot the reparations bill, sending aid goods in as Japan sent reparations out, the United States renounced its claim to reparations and put pressure, not entirely successfully, on others to do so as well. The wrangling delayed the first reparations shipments of industrial equipment until 1947, by which time a series of U.S. special missions was drastically scaling down the program. The cumulative value of the shipments, which continued until the end of the reparations payments under Occupation auspices in 1950, was less than $50 million, one-fifteenth of the sum programmed in 1947.

A fundamental premise of SCAP was that only if Japan were democratized could it become a peaceful, useful member of the world community of nations. As a democracy Japan would not want to be aggressive, to wage war; moreover, democracy was a desirable end in itself. *Demokurashii* soon became a byword in Japan, with a bewildering variety of connotations to the enthusiastic but often perplexed Japanese man in the street. (Was it more democratic for a man sitting on a crowded streetcar to offer his seat to a woman, because of the raised status of the female, or not to offer his seat on the grounds that men and women were equally entitled to the seat?)

Nevertheless, the political institutions and behaviors appropriate to a democratic society were obvious enough, and the institutions, at least,

were soon established—though corresponding behavior has not always
followed, and certainly not always the kind of behavior Americans would
expect. Restrictions on political, civil, and religious liberties were removed, and rights were guaranteed. The state was separated from the
Shinto religion. Universal suffrage was extended to include women. The
system of nobility was eliminated and aristocratic titles abolished. The
emperor was replaced by parliament as the core of the political system;
he renounced any claims to divinity and was reduced to a (continuingly
popular) symbol of state.

The establishment of parliamentary democracy was an essential feature of the entire process. The country was governed by a prime minister and his cabinet, both elected by parliament (the Diet). Members of
the Diet, in both the House of Representatives and the House of Coun-
cillors, were elected; most power resided in the former (the lower house).
Political parties were quickly reestablished and covered a spectrum extending all the way to the Japan Communist party.

Many of these changes were embodied in the 1947 constitution, the
basic law of the nation. This is one of the most idealistic constitutions in
the world in the political, social, and economic rights it guarantees its
citizens. This idealism is further manifested in Article Nine, which re-
nounces the use of war and the maintenance of armed forces. The sweeping changes embodied in the 1947 constitution were very much of American instigation. When the rather conservative Japanese cabinet came up
with proposals for constitutional revision in 1946, the plan did not involve
significant changes. MacArthur then had his staff draw up a model document, which became the basis for the new constitution. Despite the general public's awareness of the American origins of their constitution, it
has been widely accepted by Japanese. In recent years conservative elements have urged constitutional amendment, without success, mainly
hoping to eliminate Article Nine and to raise somewhat the position (if
not the power) of the emperor.

The constitution is the political and legal manifestation of the changes
in values and social relations at which SCAP aimed: the replacement
of authoritarianism and paternalism with equality and individualism.
Changes in the educational system were also designed to promote new
values. The mythology of imperial divinity, coupled with the romantic
nationalistic views of the special world role of the chosen Japanese people, was denigrated, as was the military. While there is now less pressure
to conform than earlier, and some increase in individualism, nonetheless
this theme is rather alien to as group-oriented a society as Japan's, and
the society remains collectivistic. The people continue to have a highly
developed awareness of self and nation as uniquely Japanese. When children the world over were asked "What are you?" the most common

response was "a human being," "a child," or "a boy" or "a girl." In Japan the overwhelming response was "a Japanese." Yet the traditional ideals of loyalty to and self-sacrifice for the nation have receded in primacy, while the improvement of material well-being and the enjoyment of life have assumed much higher standing among the goals of most Japanese.

The efforts toward democratization involved major economic reforms. It was deemed essential for democracy in Japan to establish a competitive economy with a more equal distribution of power and a wide, relatively egalitarian distribution of income, wealth, and ownership of the means of production and trade. Gradually, it also came to be realized that these institutional and redistributive changes were not enough. Only economic reconstruction and satisfactory economic growth, resulting in prosperity and rising levels of living, would provide the economic environment in which incipient democracy could be nurtured. The way to build a competitive economy was to break up concentrations of economic power in the hands of businessmen and landlords and to develop new, countervailing power bases among industrial workers and tenant and other small farmers.

Perhaps the most thorough reform was that of farmland ownership. Japan had long been, and still is, a country of intensively cultivated family farms of miniature (2½ acres, on the average) size, broken down into even smaller, noncontiguous plots. Prior to reform, less than 10 percent of Japanese farmland was in holdings of 125 acres or more. Tenantry was widespread; in fact, about 45 percent of the land was farmed by tenants. Approximately two-fifths of the farm families cultivated land that they partially owned and partially rented, one-third owned nearly all their own land, while one-fourth were essentially tenants, cultivating almost exclusively land rented from others. Landlords, mainly local residents, were relatively wealthy, powerful, paternalistic, and traditional. Landlord-tenant problems had become exacerbated during the interwar period, and land-reform programs had been planned, but never implemented, by the Japanese bureaucracy. SCAP thus served as a catalytic agent, rather than originater of a new idea, and prompted a stronger reform than might otherwise have occurred.

The basic aim was simple: to end tenantry by transfer of land ownership from landlords to their farming tenants. The method was land purchase and sale under government auspices, not confiscation. In principle, landlords were to be fairly compensated; land values were determined on the basis of official 1945 prices, and payment was made partly in cash, partly in low-interest, thirty-year bonds. Tenant purchasers were extended easy-payment terms. However, by the time the actual transactions took place, in the years 1947–49, inflation had reduced the real value of the transaction price to only 1 percent of prewar land prices.

The land reform virtually eliminated farm tenantry and landlordism. Farm size was restricted to a maximum of 7.5 acres (30 acres in Hokkaido), which was well above the actual average. Change in ownership did not mean much change in the organization of production, which was still based on family farms. The new owners did have greater incentive to invest in land improvements, and in this they were much encouraged by the relatively high demand, and thereby prices, for foodstuffs. The agricultural sector was the first to reattain prewar living standards, and has continued to prosper. Consequently, the goal of sturdy farm families, independent of landlord control, has been achieved. Old patterns and values do not change quickly, however: Farmers remain the most conservative political force in Japan.

A second mass base for power to compete against the established powers of business and government bureaucracy (it being clear that the military was to be elminated as a power group) was comprised of industrial workers. <u>A major objective of SCAP policy was to develop a strong, independent trade-union movement.</u> The pertinent SCAP section was staffed by many American union leaders of very liberal persuasion. Even so, it is unlikely that they anticipated the rapidity and enthusiasm with which unionization was to sweep Japan or the highly political course unionism was to take at the national level. Unions were formed in most enterprises of any size. By 1950, 56 percent of industrial employees were unionized, a high-water mark that has now receded to about 35 percent, though absolute membership continues to rise. Initially, membership included both top and middle management (after all, that seemed most democratic), but this soon ended as unions settled into bargaining with management for employee benefits. Most bargaining on economic issues took place, and has continued to do so, at the individual firm level, so Japan has been characterized as having enterprise unionism. Industrywide bargaining remains the exception, though national federations of unions have increasingly attempted, in annual "spring offensives," to use leading industries to establish patterns of wage increases that can serve as the bases for negotiations by other industries and individual enterprise unions.

Many unions at the individual firm level joined industrywide organizations; most of these in turn joined one of several national federations. Unions at the national level have been highly political: They have tended to stress political more than economic objectives, have been very active politically, and have provided the main support for the moderate to extreme-left political parties. This emphasis on politics was in large part a response to the depth and rapidity of economic, political, and social changes in postwar Japan. It also reflects the nature of the original (and continuing) union leadership at the national level. Most union leaders were leftists who had been active in the prewar labor movement, had been imprisoned in the late 1930's and early 1940's for refusing to recant, and, following Japan's defeat, had emerged from prison as (in both Japanese and American eyes) about the only heroic figures around. These men quickly took charge of the nascent union movement and imparted to its national organizations the political focus that has since been dominant.

While building a strong union movement and an egalitarian agricultural system and disbanding the military, SCAP aimed at both reducing the concentration of business power and establishing a competitive business environment. The legal and institutional arrangements were reasonably simple. What was much more difficult—and never successfully achieved—was to obtain widespread acceptance from the Japanese business and government bureaucracy of the belief that free competition was of inherent social benefit. Most Japanese have never accepted the view that the Adam Smithian "invisible hand" would automatically guide the selfish, profit-maximizing behavior of firms and optimizing behavior of individuals to create the maximum output and lowest prices for the benefit of consumers. Rather, they have historically accepted the "visible hands" of government guidance and business cooperation (in cartels and otherwise) as means to attain satisfactory economic results. The Japanese place more emphasis on the costs of a competitive system, the possible overcapacity and misallocations in specific industries and attendant cyclical fluctuations in business activity. They frequently term as "excess competitions" situations that would be regarded in the United States as simply intense, but not undesirable, degrees of competition. Because the ideology of free competition has not become ingrained in Japan (leaving aside the question of how extensively it is really practiced in Western nations), the Occupation reforms were eroded more in the business sector than elsewhere in the economy. But this moves us ahead of our story; first, the reforms themselves.

A variety of interrelated reforms was undertaken: dissolution of the zaibatsu conglomerates; elimination of cartels and monopolies; breakup of extremely large firms; and enactment of rules for fair play in business. This last included antitrust and antimonopoly legislation; prohibition of unreasonable restraints on trade, production, sales, and pricing; and establishment of the Fair Trade Commission to monitor and enforce these rules.

Zaibatsu dissolution was the most thoroughly implemented and lasting of the reforms. The zaibatsu—of which the four largest were Mitsui, Mitsubishi, Yasuda, and Sumitomo—were family-owned conglomerates, usually controlled through a holding company, of firms operating in mining, manufacturing, commerce, banking, and insurance. They functioned on a highly interrelated basis—buying from, selling to, financing, and insuring one another and handling one another's sales. They had amassed great wealth and economic and political power, and inevitably they were completely involved in the wartime economy.

There were two strands in the reform: removal of the zaibatsu families from ownership, control, and position, and dissolution of the conglomerates. The holding companies were ended, and all shares in the underlying companies owned by zaibatsu family members were confiscated and sold, both to employees of the constituent firms (who obtained about one-quarter of the shares) and gradually, on the open market, to large numbers of middle-income Japanese. In compensation the zaibatsu families received bonds that bore no interest and could not be sold or redeemed for ten years, and zaibatsu family members were not even permitted to work for the firms they formerly had owned. All this was so effective that the families have never been able to return to power; by and large they have slipped into comfortable obscurity, at least in terms of economic and political power if not in terms of social status.

The breakup of the zaibatsu conglomerates was less easy. All interlocking directorships and stockholdings came to an end. Subsidiaries and affiliates were spun off into separate, independent companies. A few very large zaibatsu firms, particularly the trading companies, were broken down into separate companies; for example, Mitsubishi Trading Company was divided into about a hundred small trading companies. However, the established buying-selling-financing-trading patterns remained, so that ex-zaibatsu firms have continued to do business extensively with one another.

Originally, being zealous to establish a competitive environment (and perhaps having some punitive motives), SCAP considered some 1,200 operating companies for breakup into smaller units. Personnel in the SCAP sections for industry and finance had come primarily from American business and banking; they were somewhat less inclined toward "New Deal" measures than were their labor counterparts. Probably more important, it was felt that too much splitting up of Japanese companies would retard economic recovery, and recovery came to be an increasingly important objective after the first two years of occupation. By 1948 the list of companies designated for "reorganization" had shrunk to 325. In fact, only 28 companies were ultimately broken up, and 10 of these were electric power companies.

The reforms did much to redistribute income, wealth, and ownership of the means of production as well as to provide countervailing bases of power in a relatively more competitive economy. The wealthy owners of large corporations were hurt further by the great corporate losses from bombing, deterioration, reparations, and government repudiation (at SCAP insistence) of its guarantees on loans made to firms for war production. The tax system was also used to restructure the distribution of income and wealth. In 1946 sharply progressive special taxes were levied on war profits and on wealth, and in 1949 SCAP pushed through reforms of the tax system. Much greater emphasis was placed on direct, progressive taxes on personal and corporate incomes, and less on sales and other indirect taxes that tended to be regressive. Local governments were given greater autonomy, including a larger tax base and an automatic share in certain taxes collected at the national level. While many of the specific reforms were later weakened, and even the roles of direct taxes and local autonomy were eroded, in general the new tax system remained even after the Occupation had ended.

By far the most important, if somewhat erratic and untended, force for redistributing income and wealth was inflation. Strong inflationary pressures had built up during the war. They were exacerbated by the government's heavy deficit financing and extensive money creation via the Reconstruction Finance Bank, which readily made loans to industries essential for reconstruction—coal, fertilizer, electric power, transport, iron and steel—using funds obtained by selling its bonds to the Bank of Japan, the central bank. Thus the price level, computed on the basis of 1934–36 prices, was 9 times higher at the end of 1945, 145 times higher at the end of 1947, and about 300 times higher in 1949, when the inflation was finally halted as part of the Dodge Plan reforms. Some inflation was inevitable, given the exigencies of postwar shortages and bottlenecks. However, a combination of wage, price, budget, and bank-credit controls could have halted the inflation sooner had SCAP not been at first unwilling to take responsibility for economic policy and then slow in developing effective anti-inflationary measures.

The Japanese government itself adopted a rather noncooperative and even deceptive attitude toward attempts to halt the inflation—although it is probably too extreme to say that the Japanese government was deliberately attempting to undermine the Occupation reforms and to shift the burden of support of the economy to the United States by making aid imports essential since exports were uncompetitively priced. In large part the Japanese government's attitude reflected the high priority it attached to economic recovery even at the expense of inflation; it wanted to be sure resources were attracted to essential industries, and loans seemed the easiest way to accomplish this. Moreover, anti-inflationary measures were bound to hurt, and the party in power would lose popular support. Big business had immense wartime loans to repay to banks, with the government no longer guaranteeing the loans; business therefore benefited from being able to raise the prices of its goods and from repaying the loans with money of sharply reduced purchasing power. Business did suffer from sharply reduced depreciation charges, in real terms, for its plant and equipment, but this was eventually remedied when firms were allowed to increase the book value of assets in line with the post-inflation price level.

Inflation hurt holders of bonds, deposits, and other fixed-interest financial claims; rent recipients; pensioners; and to some extent wage earners, because wages lagged in adjusting to the upward-spiraling prices. Particularly hard hit were agrarian ex-landlords and zaibatsu families, since they were stuck with nonsaleable bonds whose value in terms of purchasing power had declined to only about 5 percent of what it had been initially. In contrast, ex-tenants and other landowners, owners of corporate shares, and owners of other real assets did not suffer, and in some cases even benefited, from inflation, since the prices their assets could command increased at least as rapidly as the general price level.

Why did the Japanese accept, or at least tolerate, these striking changes in income distribution, ownership of assets, and political power? By and large the adjustments represented transfers from a small minority to a large majority of the Japanese, who quite naturally responded favorably. The previous holders of power and wealth were under attack politically, economically, and socially, so they were not able to sustain their vested interests. Finally, because Japan was utterly defeated and close to chaos, tremendous sacrifices could be demanded of everyone simply to get the country back on its feet.

The assumption underlying the initial economic policy of the Occupation was that Japan had brought the devastation upon itself, so it would have to suffer the consequences and had no right to expect outside assistance in economic recovery. In practice, however, from the beginning SCAP could not remain completely aloof from economic reconstruction problems and issues. The difficulties were simply too great. Japan was one of the most devastated of all the countries that had fought in World War II. Industrial production in 1946 was only one-fifth of the wartime peak and one-third of the 1934–36 level. Agricultural production had fallen off some two-fifths from prewar levels—a less extensive but more serious decline, for by early 1946 Japan was on the verge of starvation.

To "prevent disease and unrest," General MacArthur prevailed upon Washington to begin large-scale aid shipments of food and medical supplies. Moreover, it was soon apparent that a requisite for successful political democratization was an adequate economic base, brought about by reconstruction and satisfactory economic progress. To achieve this, U.S. aid was essential. The form of aid changed gradually from foodstuffs to fertilizer, petroleum, and industrial materials like cotton. By 1949, when the aid program was drawing to a close, the United States had provided Japan with a total of almost $2 billion in aid. Aid paid for 38 percent of Japan's imports during the Occupation—a period when Japan's export earnings were negligible because of the loss of prewar markets and lack of productive capacity. In per capita terms, U.S. aid to Japan was relatively modest: $27 for Japan, as compared with $77 for West Germany, $51 for Italy, $122 for the United Kingdom, and $103 for France. Legally this aid was a loan rather than a gift, to the eventual surprise of most Japanese and Americans. In the late 1950's Japan made an agreement, based on the formula worked out in similar negotiations between the United States and West Germany, to repay the aid at a rate of about 25 cents on the dollar.

SCAP and U.S. concern for economic reconstruction deepened as the world environment changed and perceptions altered as to how Japan might best fit into it. By 1948 the Cold War had divided the world, and China could no longer be relied upon to become the stabilizing influence in Asia, as had earlier been hoped. Japan appeared increasingly to be the most likely among major Asian nations to become a stable democracy, a strong economy, and a close ally of the West. This caused a shift in American attitudes from a policy of punishing Japan and keeping Japan weak in competition with its neighbors to one of regarding Japan as the "workshop of Asia" and good friend of the United States.

The effect of this shift in attitude was that Occupation economic policy placed increasing emphasis upon recovery and decreasing emphasis upon reform. The land and labor reforms had already been completed, but the breakup of large industrial and financial enterprises other than zaibatsu holding companies, and the breakup of the latter's buying and selling interrelationships, had really only begun. As already noted, the quite ambitious SCAP industrial-reform program was allowed to wither away at the implementation stage, since SCAP realized that most companies could correctly point to retardation of their recovery if they were to be split up or otherwise disrupted. In a sense, the more long-range reform goals gave way to the immediate tasks of recovery.

In growth-rate terms recovery was rapid, but this recovery began from such a low 1945–46 base (when output was probably at a level not above that prior to World War I!) that even rapid rates of improvement were insufficient to reconstruct the economy quickly. Not until 1954 or 1955 was Japan able to reattain prewar per capita levels of productivity, national income, and personal consumption. In crude economic terms, Japan lost eighteen years of economic growth in embarking on its disastrous World War II adventure; it took that long to come back up to the prewar level.

Thus, Japan was still a very weak country when the Allied nations agreed in 1951 to end the Occupation and to restore sovereignty to Japan by signing a peace treaty. Actually, General MacArthur had suggested this course as early as 1947. In addition to continuing problems of reform and recovery within Japan, the increasing intensity of the Cold War, the hardening anticommunist position of the United States, and Russia's unwillingness to agree to a peace treaty all slowed the ending of the Occupation. The outbreak of the Korean War in June 1950 marked its *de facto* end, for American attention was now focused on Korea, and SCAP turned over responsibility for domestic affairs to the Japanese government. The war also intensified the American resolve to have a peace treaty signed, and the United States pressured its Western and Asian allies to agree.

The peace treaty was signed on September 8, 1951, and went into effect on April 28, 1952, when Japan was once again (legally, at least) an independent nation. Russia and Communist China refused to participate. Russia and Japan resumed diplomatic ties in 1956, restoring correct, if cool, relations that have been marred by Japan's tie with the West and disputes over continuing Russian control of two small islands just north of Hokkaido and over fishing rights in adjacent waters. China and Japan have not yet (as of mid-1969) normalized relations. Other Asian nations signed the peace treaty, but several—notably Burma, Indonesia, and the Philippines—refused to accepted a clause in which they would have given up rights to reparations. An important aspect of Japan's foreign policy in Asia in the 1950's was negotiations with these nations on reparations; settlements were concluded in all cases. Under the peace treaty the United States retained the right to occupy and administer Okinawa and the other Ryukyu Islands and Iwo Jima and the other Bonin Islands; only later, under the Eisenhower administration, was Japan's "residual sovereignty" recognized. The desire of the Japanese to resume full sovereignty, particularly over Okinawa, has been an increasingly important issue during the 1960's, which the return of the Bonins in 1968 did little to resolve.

The peace treaty did not mean that Japan was immediately or automatically accepted back into the community of nations. In 1952 Japan was still weak: Its standard of living was low (gross national product per capita was about $250[1]), still below the prewar level; its foreign trade was far below prewar levels, yet the need for imports was and would continue to be acute; it had virtually no means of defense from external aggression; it still had relatively little self-confidence; and it faced a world beset with its own postwar adjustment problems, hostile or at best indifferent to Japan. To Japanese leaders, it was clear that the country needed a sponsor in its political, economic, and security relations with

---

[1] Calculated on the basis of 1960 Japanese prices and converted at the official exchange rate. As is the case with other low-income countries, conversion of local currency into dollars in terms of real purchasing power would yield a considerably (perhaps 50 percent) higher figure.

other nations. A neutralist policy of going-it-alone would have been very difficult and probably not very fruitful.

Naturally, perhaps inevitably under the circumstances, Japan turned to the United States for this support. The United States was anxious to establish an alliance with Japan and willing to support it in the international arena. In addition, the United States was clearly the strongest nation in the world and was by far Japan's largest trading partner (almost one-third of exports and imports, eight times greater than Japan's next trading partner). Moreover, because the American presence in Japan remained strong despite the ending of the Occupation, Japan may not really have had any other viable alternatives, even though Prime Minister Yoshida and the other leaders may not have felt the need for such alternatives. It is perhaps in the context of a partnership between an omnipotent nation and a weak but willing nation that the U.S.-Japanese security treaty, signed at the same time as the peace treaty, should be appraised. Under this arrangement the United States guaranteed Japan's security from external attack and was allowed to maintain bases and military forces, but not nuclear weapons, in Japan. Japan's commitment has been limited to maintenance of its internal security and, eventually, to limited defense against possible external threat; it undertook no security responsibilities for areas beyond its own territorial limits.

In terms of Japan's self-interest, its alliance with the United States has paid off handsomely. The United States sponsored Japan's entry in 1956 into the United Nations and into such U.N. affiliates as the International Monetary Fund and World Bank, into GATT (the world trade organization), and in the early 1960's into OECD (Organization for Economic Cooperation and Development). This sponsorship, together with Japan's own strenuous efforts, enabled Japan to dissipate, or at least substantially mitigate, the hostilities and discriminatory measures of other nations. By the early 1960's, if not sooner, Japan was recognized and accepted as a major nation.

The economic payoff was perhaps even greater. Japan benefited from U.S. special-procurement dollar expenditures for the Korean War, as well as from continuing access to America's rapidly growing import market (despite the recurrent irritation of U.S. restrictions on textile and other commodity imports) and to the U.S. short-term and long-term private capital markets. The U.S. security umbrella meant that Japan did not have to devote much of its resources to defense and could utilize them instead for growth-producing investment and the raising of living standards.

Of course, the alliance with the United States has not been without its costs. Japan was committed generally to follow the U.S. line in international affairs. Until the late 1950's its trade with China was severely restricted, more so than that of European nations though less so than that of America, with its total boycott. Even today, Japan has not followed the subsequent lead of European nations in making long-term export credits available to China, no doubt in large part due to American pressure (the American position is that it does not see why Japan should have easy, even preferential, access to American funds if Japan is going to, in effect, relend them to China).

Most important, as Japan's remarkable economic performance of the 1950's continued into the 1960's, Japan no longer remained a weak client needing paternalistic U.S. sponsorship. The evolution in the relative power positions of Japan and the United States has brought new strains as well as opportunities to the alliance. Japan quite naturally has wanted greater independence and more equal partnership. The nature of Japan's economic performance since the end of the Occupation is hence the next matter for consideration.

The Economic Miracle: From Reconstruction to Super-Fast Growth

The 10.8 percent real growth rate of Japan's national income between 1946 and 1954 was rapid, but this rate was derived from the extremely low base of the early postwar years. It represented little more than the result of eliminating bottlenecks, restoring to operation the existing capacities that had been partially damaged, and returning the country to prewar levels of productivity and per capita income. Similar patterns of reconstruction and rapid growth occurred during the same period in Europe, notably in West Germany. Once recovery was completed, there seemed to be no reason to expect continued rapid growth. Indeed, in a 1956 governmental five-year projection, 6.5 percent was regarded as the maximum sustainable growth rate.

In fact, the Japanese economy has continued its rapid surge of growth right up to the present, at a rate far greater than that of virtually any other country in the world, whether communist, democratic, or autocratic. Between 1954 and 1967, Japanese gross national product (GNP), measured in constant prices to adjust for the mild inflationary trend, grew at an average rate of 10.1 percent, almost three times as fast as the growth of the American economy for the same period. The power of compound interest is such that in 1967 Japan's GNP was 3½ times larger than it was in 1954. This performance is unparalleled in history. It brought Japan from a populous but relatively weak nation in the mid-1950's to the forefront of world powers by the late 1960's. I will consider some of the implications of this performance in the next section, but it is desirable to examine first the changing structure of the economy, the role of cyclical fluctuation, and the causes of the exceptional growth performance.

The most important change in the structure of production is the rise in the relative share of manufacturing and construction, which has grown from about 28 percent in the early 1950's to 36 percent in the late 1960's, and a concomitant decline in agriculture, forestry, and fishing from 22 percent to less than 12 percent. Yet agricultural performance generally has been very good, certainly better than in prewar years. In the growth of rice, which remains the single most important crop, better seeds, more fertilizers, and insecticides have raised output, particularly in the 1950's. Agriculture is becoming more diversified in response to rising consumer demands for vegetables, fruits, dairy products, and meat. However, the growth of labor productivity in agriculture, while outstanding when compared with that of most countries, has lagged behind the rapid increases in industrial productivity.

The principle increases in output and productivity have occurred in industrial activity—manufacturing, construction, electric and other forms of power, and transportation. With this growth have also come substantial changes in the form of manufacturing output, in response to domestic and foreign demand and in accord with Japan's ability to produce. These changes might be summed up by the terms diversification, sophistication, and efficiency.

Historically, Japan's manufacturing was dominated by cotton and silk textiles, though machinery and armaments were of increasing importance in the 1930's. By the 1960's Japan had developed an extremely diversified manufacturing sector capable of producing (though not always efficiently) almost every product existing in the world. These ranged from the world's largest ocean tankers to cameras, computers, and color television sets, as well as the traditional textiles and various souvenir trinkets. Areas of particularly rapid growth include iron and steel, chemicals, petrochemicals, machinery, and consumer durables such as television sets, transistorized items, washing machines, refrigerators, and, more recently automobiles. With diversification has come increasing sophistication of product, as is obvious from this random sample of the items produced.

Japan is not simply a diversified producer of manufactured goods but, on the whole, a highly efficient producer. It has been able to enhance the quality of products while reducing their costs. Its technological level is now highly advanced in many sectors, and in pig iron, shipbuilding, radio receivers, and a few other areas its technology is preeminent. In the case of most highly sophisticated items, however, such as integrated circuits, military and large commercial aircraft, and certain kinds of precision tools, Japan still remains somewhat behind the most advanced technology of the United States and Europe. Most Japanese industries are making rapid technological strides and combining labor and capital efficiently, so their competitive power at home and abroad continues to grow.

Japanese growth, while rapid, certainly has not been smooth. The postwar economy has moved ahead in great spurts. Booms have developed that have generated real growth rates as high as 12, 13, and 15 percent. These rates simply cannot be sustained: Bottlenecks develop, actual and potential export products are diverted to domestic uses, imports of needed industrial materials and other goods increase rapidly. The result has inevitably been periodic balance-of-payments crises, which are then attacked by temporarily slowing down what the Japanese term the "overheated economy" by means of restrictive monetary (and sometimes fiscal) measures. As soon as the balance-of-payments difficulties are resolved, the restraints are removed and the resumption of rapid growth encouraged, and achieved, once again.

This cycle has usually had a course of three to four years. While the amplitude of fluctuation has been great, this is primarily because in boom periods the growth rate substantially exceeds the average rather than because the recession phases are severe. Indeed, not only are the recessions brief—generally about twelve months—but they are very mild: There is only a slowdown in growth, not an absolute decline in output. The slowest growth rate in any postwar year was 2.8 percent (in 1954); and the simple annual average of growth rates for the *recession* years of 1954, 1958, 1962, and 1965 is 3.9 percent—better than the average growth rate of the United States *for the entire period.*

So far it has been impossible to arrive at a comprehensive explanation of Japan's postwar growth performance that defines adequately the relative importance of the major causal factors. Three interrelated factors have clearly been of great importance: a large supply of highly motivated, relatively skilled (or at least trainable) labor for industrial uses; a very rapid rate of technological innovation and transformation; and an impressively high rate of capital formation and saving.

Prior to World War II Japanese industrialization had not proceeded far enough in its absorption of labor to reduce the absolute number of workers in agriculture to substantially below early Meiji levels. Wartime bombing and postwar repatriation further swelled the numbers in agriculture. When we add to this the labor in other areas of low productivity, such as small-scale manufacturing, fishing, retailing, and other services, we find, in the early postwar years, an immense stock of labor in relatively low productivity uses. Moreover, population growth was rapid in this period. The legalization of abortion (for reasons of economic as well as physical or psychological health) sharply reduced the birth rate beginning in the early 1950's, but the lagged effect on new entrants into the labor force was only beginning to be felt in the mid-1960's. Japan has, in other words, been a country of relatively ample labor supply.

Japan's labor force, moreover, is highly motivated—making it industrious and hard-working. It is also well educated. Nine years of education are mandatory, most children go on to senior high school, and a higher proportion of each age group continues to college than in any other country except the United States. An important reform policy of the Occupation was to increase the number of colleges and universities and generally to stress enlarged educational opportunities. Educational attainment is the most important means for achieving social and economic upward mobility in Japan, and most Japanese parents are highly education-conscious, encouraging their children to become better educated than their parents and saving assiduously to meet the rising costs of higher education. All this has resulted in a labor force that is better trained in both general and specific vocational skills and, perhaps equally important, is receptive to further learning on the job. The improvement in the quality of labor has thus been substantial, but probably not strikingly more so than in other industrial countries. The supply of labor and its improvements in quality have been supportive and even essential factors for rapid growth, but they have not been the initiating cause. Roughly estimated, approximately one-quarter of Japan's growth in output can be attributed to the combination of increase in the labor force and its re-allocation from lower to higher productivity uses.

The transfer of labor from agriculture and other low productivity uses has been accomplished primarily by the movement of young people when they first enter the labor force as school graduates. Only one-tenth of farm children remain in agriculture; the others migrate to factory and related jobs in nearby towns and larger cities. By the mid-1960's large firms, which typically hire only new entrants into the labor force and retain them for their entire work life, were complaining of shortages of labor, but this was really only in terms of new entrants. There has also been movement among the economically active into more productive, higher-paying jobs. Thus, more than half of farm-family income is derived from nonfarm activities; often the father works in a nearby factory, while much of the farming work is done by his parents and his wife.

One of the most impressive facets of the Japanese economic performance has been the improvement in productivity due to technological innovation. Japanese business has been highly oriented toward innovation in physical production processes, primarily in adopting and adapting techniques that had quick commercial application. So far there has been much less emphasis on basic research. This has been especially true in regard to foreign technology, which has been inducted into Japan on a larger and more diverse scale than has ever occurred elsewhere.

Several points stand out about this immense foreign technological inflow. First, Japan's increasing isolation from the West after 1937 meant that by 1955, when the technological inflow began to assume substantial proportions, the gap between Japan's level of technology and the best technology available in the West had widened substantially. Moreover, prewar Japan had not reached the frontiers of advanced technology in most fields.

Second, and probably as important as the technological gap itself, has been Japan's enhanced capacity to absorb foreign technology on a large scale. By the 1950's Japan had a sufficient quantity and variety of managers, engineers, and skilled technicians to learn foreign technology without excessive difficulty and to adapt as well as adopt. This general ability is the cumulation of the long process of development. It probably was enhanced by the production requirements of war and again by certain of the postwar reforms.

Third, access to foreign technology has been obtained almost entirely by licensing arrangements, purchase of patents, and technical tie-ins of Japanese private firms with their counterparts abroad. Very little has come in by the route of direct investment in Japan by foreign business; where that has occurred it usually has been in the form of a joint venture between Japanese and foreign firms, with management often in Japanese hands. Until the late 1950's few foreign firms regarded the Japanese market as particularly good, in view of the difficulties of doing business there. The Japanese government has had a consistent policy of opposition to foreign direct investment for a variety of reasons: fear of foreign control of strategic sectors; concern that Japanese firms in specific industries would be outdone by competitors; concern that foreign firms would not fit into, and indeed might possibly disrupt, the government's informal (but close) relations with and controls over business; an evaluation that royalty and license payments, while expensive, would be less than the profits that would be made by foreign firms; and plain xenophobia. The policy has gradually become less restrictive as the United States and other countries have put pressure on Japan to "act like other advanced nations." In addition, as Japan approaches the technological frontier of knowledge in specific areas, it has only one foreign company with which to bargain, rather than the several or more firms that control the areas of slightly less advanced technology. This foreign firm frequently utilizes its superior bargaining position by requiring a share of profits—usually through a joint venture—rather than settling solely for a licensing arrangement.

Technological innovation has by no means been limited to adoption of foreign technology but has included considerable improvement and commercial application of Japan's own research and development efforts.

Shipbuilding is just one example. Japanese shipbuilding firms have become preeminent in the world, notable especially for their immense petroleum and other bulk carriers. Optics—including cameras, binoculars, and electron microscopes—is another field relying heavily on domestically developed technology. Adaptation of a given technology to obtain superior performance has been an important factor in enhancing productivity. Typically, large firms surround a new machine or process with many engineers, whose job is not simply to learn but to make numerous small adjustments and improvements. This is expensive, but it pays off. One Japanese steelmaker was able to produce 3,500 tons from a unit of 2,500-ton rated capacity. Other examples abound. No overall evaluation exists, but this approach has probably led to increases in productivity of from 10 to 20 percent above rated capacity.

Two final points should be made about the high rate of technological innovation. First, innovation has been concentrated mainly on the physical production process. Japanese firms have done much less to reduce overhead costs—to improve administration, finance, sales, and so on. It may well be that production processes, precisely because they are essentially "physical" and "technical," somehow justified any needed adjustments in human responses and interpersonal relationships. This is much less true of administrative activities, where changes may seem to impinge much more upon certain established patterns of human relationships and behavior, while the changes in themselves may seem not worth the disruption. Why minimize the amount of cash balances, when a firm thinks in the context of its total relationship to its lending bank? Won't an otherwise desirable change in distribution strategy undermine and perhaps even bankrupt the entire inefficient network of wholesalers, subwholesalers, and retailers that has been connected to the firm for so long? It is not surprising that innovation has come about less rapidly in management than in production.

Second, innovation has meant not just that a few large firms are utilizing the latest techniques but that modern technology has been dispersed throughout the economy. About 40 percent of Japan's total labor force now works with high productivity in modern plants using recent equipment and technology. It is this widespread improvement in production methods that has brought about the rapid growth rate of aggregate productivity and output in the economy as a whole.

Both labor force and technological innovation have been closely interrelated with the third major cause of Japan's rapid growth—the high rate of investment. The increasing production of labor in all uses, the growth of the labor force, and the shift of labor to relatively higher productivity uses have all required additional amounts of invested capital. Not all, but many, technological improvements have been embodied in the new machines and other equipment, domestically produced or imported, that constitute an important share of investment. Only with a rapid rate of new investment could innovation have been so substantial and pervasive and output per worker increased so much.

A high proportion of investment has been in business plant and equipment and in government fixed investment in transportation and other forms of social overhead necessary for growth. The final column of Table 1 indicates just how rapid the increase in investment has been. The inevitable consequence has been a continual rise in the proportion of the economy's output being plowed back into facilities for further growth, as shown in the other columns of Table 1. The share of gross (private plus public) domestic investment in GNP went from 25–30 percent in the mid-1950's to 35–40 percent in the 1960's. This is the highest rate ever achieved for any length of time in peace in a private-market-oriented economy—that is, on a voluntary, noncoercive basis. Similarly, fixed investment in facilities, excluding housing, rose from about 18 percent of GNP to 27–30 percent. The most rapid growth occurred during the investment boom of 1959–61. Since then the rate of growth of investment has leveled off somewhat, but at a significantly higher proportion of GNP.

The overall strategy of growth has been to plow investible funds into the expansion of private production facilities in order to increase output as rapidly as possible. This strategy provided the basis of policy under the Occupation and has continued to be used since. At the beginning government initiative was important in the reconstruction of basic industries. Thereafter investment has been made increasingly by private business on its own initiative. Thus it is misleading to use the term "strategy" if it is interpreted to imply a highly centralized decision-making authority with full control over the allocation of resources. Although the relationship between government and business is close—with there being considerably more government influence than there is in the United States on private business decisions regarding production, pricing, new investment in expansion of capacities, and so on—nonetheless the government has not been able to predict well or judge in detail, much less control, the amount of private investment that will be undertaken. Policy-makers have been surprised to see higher-than-anticipated surges of private investment in productive capacity following each recession. Although they have a favorable impact on growth, the rapid increases in investment have caused the unsustainable booms already discussed. Government policy has not succeeded in holding back private investment by direct controls or "administrative guidance" (informal pressure and consultations, backed with veiled threats of more serious action), so the government has generally waited until the last moment and then applied general restraints through fiscal and monetary policy. In large part this slowness to act has been a problem of lack of will rather than lack of means: The government in power has always had a pro-growth bias and never wants to appear to be choking off the boom prematurely.

TABLE 1

Gross National Product and Its Uses
(based on 1960 constant prices)

	1952	1957	1962	1967	Average Annual Rate of Growth†
Gross national product (in billions)*	$21.4	$32.2	$52.7	$84.8	9.6%
USED FOR (IN PERCENTAGE OF GNP)					
Private consumption	59.8%	57.8%	54.3%	51.2%	8.5
Food, beverages, and tobacco	31.0	27.9	21.8	18.4	5.9
Clothing	7.5	7.7	7.5	6.4	8.4
Housing services	7.3	7.0	8.7	8.4	10.6
Other	14.0	15.2	16.3	18.0	10.8
Gross private investment	17.5	26.2	27.5	32.0	14.1
Plant and equipment	11.7	16.2	21.2	20.7	13.9
Housing	3.1	3.5	4.0	5.3	13.6
Inventories	2.7	6.5	2.3	6.0	15.5
Government purchases	19.6	16.1	17.8	16.3	8.3
Consumption	13.2	9.6	8.1	6.8	4.8
Investment	6.4	6.5	9.7	9.5	12.6
Fixed	6.0	6.2	9.2	8.5	12.2
Housing	0.3	0.4	0.4	0.4	12.7
Inventories	0.1	−0.2	0.1	0.6	24.9
Net sales abroad	3.1	0.0	0.4	0.5	−4.4
Exports	10.2	11.1	11.9	14.9	12.4
Imports	7.0	11.1	11.5	14.3	14.9

* Converted at the offical exchange-rate parity of 360 yen = $1.
† Estimated from beginning- and end-year data.

NOTE: Because of rounding, subcomponents may not add precisely to the next level of aggregation.

SOURCE: Government of Japan, Economic Planning Agency, *Annual Report on National Income Statistics, 1968* and *1969*, pp. 78–81.

All this suggests an economy in which private enterprise has been terribly eager—much more so than in other countries—to invest in order to expand productive capacity and output. This is essentially correct, and it does not have to be explained by reference to some exotic form of business behavior peculiar to Japan. Investment has paid off—in both higher profits and larger-sized firms. Businessmen have had very optimistic expectations that have, on the whole, been fulfilled. In a sense they have been self-fulfilling; as many firms in all types of industries have tried to grow rapidly, they have generated greater demand for each others' (and thereby their own) products. Technological innovation, which has been so greatly oriented toward quick commercial application, has indeed paid off in profits. Profit rates on new investment rose substantially in the late 1950's and early 1960's, and although they apparently have receded somewhat since, new investment still remains profitable in most sectors.

A further important motivation in large business enterprises has been each firm's concern about its ranking relative to other firms, measured in terms of output or sales. Because stock ownership has become so widely distributed, most large business enterprises are in fact controlled by management. It cannot be completely impervious to the stockholders, but so long as profits appear adequate management has great independence of action. Management apparently does not conceive of its role as one solely of maximizing profits; it also attempts to enhance, or at least maintain, its status in the industry, commonly measured by its relative sales ranking. Thus, aggressive firms, not quite at the top of the heap, attempt to increase their share of the market. This shows up particularly during booms, when some firms race ahead to expand capacity regardless of pressures from the government and from other firms in the industry. This competitive spirit is an important reason for the high rate of business investment.

The high rates of investment flow have naturally resulted in a tremendous increase in Japan's capital stock. The private sector's fixed capital stock more than tripled between 1950 and 1964, while that of the government doubled. Of the increase in private fixed capital, 45 percent was in manufacturing, followed by 14 percent in agriculture; 11 percent in electricity, gas, and water; 9 percent in commerce; and 7 percent in transportation and communications. With the growth rate of the population being much slower, the amount of capital per worker in the economy has more than doubled.

Investment has to be financed out of saving, either domestic saving or the borrowed savings of foreigners. In Japan the extraordinarily high rate of investment has been matched by an extraordinarily high rate of domestic saving. Corporate business retains a high proportion of its profits for investment in expansion. The large amounts of government savings (defined as tax and other revenues minus current expenditures for government services) are invested in facilities for transportation, communications, education, and public services. One-third of gross saving consists of depreciation funds, generated by the rapid investment itself and by favorable depreciation rates.

Most impressive of all is the fact that private individuals—wage and salary earners, dividend and rent recipients, farmers, and owners of unincorporated nonfarm enterprises—provide one-third of gross saving. Even though income levels are below those in the West, all groups save a higher proportion of income than that saved in other advanced countries. For example, during the 1960's urban wage earners in Japan have been saving about 15 to 20 percent of their disposable income—more than twice the savings rate of workers in the United States. Farmers have a somewhat lower but still significant rate of about 10 percent. Owners of unincorporated enterprises have even higher savings rates—on the order of 25 to 35 percent, though the data are poor.

The relative importance of the various factors causing these high savings rates has not yet been well sorted out. Probably the inadequate retirement programs of government and business are an important influence; people save for their old age. With credit expensive and not readily available, there is considerable target saving for housing, purchase of consumer durables, and children's education. Small-business owners have similar difficulties in borrowing and have even greater incentive to plow back earnings than do large firms. The wage system of large and increasing semiannual bonuses probably has had an important impact on wage-earner saving. Lurking in the background of the explanations is the vaguely articulated feeling that the Japanese are frugal; in one sense a tautology, the use of the term implies something about the Japanese preference for future versus present consumption, their desire to protect against possible future adversities, their desire to pass on wealth to their children, and so forth.

In Japan, even more than in most other advanced economies, different individuals and groups have been doing the saving and the investing. Despite the very high rate of savings out of profits, corporate business investment has grown so rapidly as to require external financing—through stock and bond issues and through borrowings, mainly from financial institutions. Large firms are heavily in debt; net worth is only 20 percent of total liabilities. Stock issues have constituted only about 5 percent of industrial funds, and bonds even less. From management's viewpoint issuing stock is expensive, since new shares are issued at par (which is usually considerably less than the market price) and dividends, unlike interest, come from profits after taxes. Bond issues are limited because, with interest rates on bonds pegged by government pressure below those on long-term loans and other competing interest rates, there are few buyers. Commercial banks and other financial institutions have filled the gap by extensive lending, both long and short term. In turn, individuals tend to hold their savings in time deposits and other financial forms. Thus the financial system has been an efficient and effective intermediary between savers and investors, its allocation of credit enabling the growth of business investment to occur.

There has been a wide variety of other, perhaps lesser, causes of postwar Japan's outstandingly successful economic performance. The government, as already indicated, has placed domestic economic growth at the top of its list of policy objectives. It has relied on private enterprise to produce the goods, restricting its own role mainly to refraining, wherever possible, from competing with business for resources (allowing business first claim on investible funds for expansion); aiding and encouraging business with special tax concessions, loans to "important" industries, and provision of the social overhead facilities essential for maintaining private production; and producing optimistic but realistic five-year plans (really projections) that business has taken sufficiently seriously to regard as minimum targets (and indeed they have always been exceeded). Because of the no-war clause in Article Nine of the constitution and the security umbrella provided by the arrangements with the United States, government expenditures on defense have been negligible, less than 1 percent of GNP in contrast to 6 percent in the prewar years 1934–36. Resources have thus been freed for more productive uses and have so been used.

Of major importance has been Japan's ability to obtain and pay for the imports essential for this growth process. Because Japan is densely populated and has a relatively small land space, of which only about 15 percent is arable, a high and increasing level of GNP per capita can be achieved only by main reliance on industrial output. Yet Japan lacks sufficient supplies of the basic mineral and plant materials used in industrial production. It has to import all, or virtually all, of its petroleum, iron ore, bauxite, mineral phosphate, cotton, wool, natural rubber, and soybeans; 60 to 80 percent of its coking coal, hides, salt, sugar and wheat; and more than 20 percent (on a caloric basis) of all its foodstuffs. Japan, like all nations, imports substantial amounts of sophisticated machinery in which other countries have a comparative advantage; examples include large commercial jet aircraft, certain kinds of ship engines, and special steel manufacturing equipment. Virtually all of Japan's imports can be regarded as necessities, since the importation of manufactured consumer goods is a negligible proportion of the total.

Access to, and the ability to pay for, imports has thus been an extremely important objective, not just in terms of domestic economic policy, but as the cornerstone of foreign policy. Japan has achieved this objective remarkably well, due both to its own efforts and to favorable changes in the world trading environment. World trade has grown more rapidly than ever before in history as world GNP has increased and as trade restrictions have been successively reduced. Japan also benefited from the decline in world prices of raw materials during the 1950's, a decline that saw the price index of Japanese imports drop by 20 percent, more than offsetting the 10 percent drop in Japan's export prices. And, perhaps most essential, while importing at a rate considerably more rapid than that of the world as a whole, Japan has succeeded in expanding its exports equally rapidly (see Table 1), at more than double the world rate. This was essential for Japan to be able to pay for its import requirements.

Japan's superior export performance is attributable to a number of factors. Japan is a highly export-conscious nation. The government bureaucracy, businessmen, and even the general public—indoctrinated with such national slogans as "Prosperity through exports and stability through saving"—are so aware of the importance of exports that the latter have become virtually an end in themselves rather than a means of paying for imports. Considerable effort goes into analysis, projections, and achievement of export performance. Exports receive special consideration in the financing of their productive capacity, production itself, and sales; in inspections and other controls over quality; in the legalized formation of production and distribution cartels; and in various other, more subtle ways. Exports have done so well basically because of increased supply capacity resulting from the industrial investment boom, the competitive production of entirely new products, enhanced price competitiveness relative to other advanced countries resulting from the reduced labor cost per unit of output (wage increases have been rapid but productivity gains even more rapid), and changes in the composition of Japanese exports from commodities for which world demand in trade was growing slowly to those with rapid growth. Typical is the relative shift to transistor radios, color television sets, cameras, and automobiles and away from cotton and silk textiles, the prewar mainstays. In other cases world demand for a commodity may be growing less rapidly, but Japan has sharply increased its market share by cost-cutting and capacity-expanding investment along with technical change; shipbuilding and iron and steel are the most important examples.

In the final analysis, much of Japan's economic success must be attributed to the human factor. Japanese are a highly achieving, energetic, pragmatic, and restless people always on the lookout for new opportunities. The basic attitude toward many economic problems is that they can be solved through growth. The size of the slice of the pie becomes less important when the pie is rapidly becoming larger. Japanese are willing to work hard, to learn new methods, to save for the future, and to undertake the entrepreneurial risks inherent in any new production and investment.

The Political Economy and Welfare of Growth

Super-fast economic growth since the end of the Occupation and reconstruction has wrought great changes in Japan, changes that continue rapidly and whose implications are only beginning to be understood. In this section, I will briefly consider living standards, the evolution of Occupation reforms, the emergence of a new "establishment," and the political system and government-business relationship.

Rapid economic growth has brought a major improvement in family incomes and standards of living. The benefits of growth have been widely distributed, so virtually everyone is substantially better off. This has been accomplished mainly through higher wages and better employment opportunities rather than through social expenditures, which have remained a small proportion of governmental budgets. Thus, those who have benefited least from growth are the aged, the widowed, the older unskilled day laborer, and other deprived groups who are unable to provide fully for themselves. Discrimination has probably reduced the benefits accruing to Korean residents in Japan and to the outcast group of Japanese (the *burakumin*, or *eta*). Nonetheless, the improvements have been sufficiently widespread that there are no major groups who feel they have been completely left out of Japan's economic progress.

For the economy as a whole, disposable income per person[2] (adjusted for price rises and taxes) almost tripled between 1952 and 1967, growing at an average annual rate of 8.2 percent. It is very difficult to make direct comparisons with disposable-income levels in other countries, since Japanese typically consume somewhat different commodities and in different proportions and since the relative prices of commodities (say, fish and refrigerators) vary according to country. The official exchange rate, which is derived from the relationship between goods imported and exported (a relatively small proportion of total goods and services in most economies), clearly understates the real purchasing power of money in almost all countries. For example, Japan's disposable income per capita in 1967, measured at the official exchange rate, was $770. Measured in purchasing

---

[2] This is about one-third less than GNP per capita and one-sixth less than national income per capita. The main differences are corporate-retained income, government revenues less transfers to individuals, and (for GNP) depreciation allowances. Disposable income can be either spent for consumption or saved.

power, in terms of United States relative prices in 1965 dollars, the disposable income per capita was approximately $1,200. This was about four-ninths of the U.S. level and somewhat lower than that of major European countries aside from Italy.

Personal consumption per capita also has risen rapidly, at an average annual rate of 7.3 percent between 1952 and 1967. As Table 1 indicates, the share of food and clothing in total consumption has declined; with higher incomes people have been able to devote more to recreation, consumer durables, and other discretionary uses. Most household durables are more widely diffused than in Europe. For example, 96 percent of Japanese homes have television sets, 78 percent refrigerators, 85 percent electric washing machines, and 54 percent vacuum cleaners, though only 13 percent have automobiles and 4 percent room air conditioners.

The consumption pattern has been somewhat lopsided, in that housing and public amenities (such as urban water-supply and sewage systems, better roads, prevention of air and water pollution, and solution to problems of urban congestion) have lagged. Thus in some ways urban living has worsened rather than improved for the middle class. This is an inevitable result of the priority that government and the financial system gave to business investment and of government investments in transportation and other facilities that directly supported private production. Metropolitan-area housing is expensive, chiefly because land costs are high, yet mortgage credit is available for only a small proportion of total cost. Hence, while the gap between demand for and supply of private consumption goods has narrowed since the late 1950's, for public goods it has widened. While a reallocation of investment toward relatively more housing and public services would probably slow down the measured growth rate, it would probably also do a great deal to enhance the general welfare. Indeed, it is not readily apparent why these lags have been tolerated. Perhaps the postwar reconstruction syndrome, with its justification of personal sacrifices for the sake of growth of output, has continued to be important. Perhaps, too, here as in other democratic political systems, the demand for public services is not always well articulated. As a consequence of organized interest-group pressures, in Japan even more so than in other democracies, government policy has focused on producers rather than consumers. Perhaps foreign observers overestimate the extent of demand for public goods; individuals in what has been a relatively low-income country by Western standards may simply prefer private consumption. And no doubt the very nature of rapid growth produces such imbalances, since it is not possible to synchronize completely all sectors of the economy.

While all family incomes have risen substantially, the equality of income distribution has decreased somewhat from that of the early postwar years. This has been a result more of growth-oriented policies and of changes emanating from growth itself than of any attempt to undermine the Occupation reform objectives. And certainly income distribution appears to be about as equal as it is in the United States. A variety of forces have tended to reduce equality. In order to raise the saving rate, the government provided incentives to save by giving favorable tax treatment to dividends and interest; this favored the relatively wealthy. Capital gains, other than those on land, generally are not taxed; and business expense accounts, especially for top management, have become increasingly large. The government has also tolerated systematic understatement of income and profits by small business. In its *de facto* strategy of allowing private business first claim on resources, it has held down its social welfare expenditures (which typically benefit the poorest in a society), in sharp contrast to postwar Europe and the United States.

In the early 1950's older workers, those with longer service, those with more education, and those working in larger firms received much higher wages than young, low-seniority, less educated workers in smaller firms. Since then, all these differentials have substantially narrowed, thus raising the relative position of lower-income workers. While some of the general rise in wage rates (78 percent in real terms between 1953 and 1967) may have been attributable to labor union activity (though this is not at all clear), the general increase and the narrowing differential have been due primarily to the rapidly growing business demand for labor combined with the practice of large firms of hiring only young people.

Despite the substitution of small tractors and other capital equipment for the labor that has been pulled away from agriculture, labor productivity has almost inevitably grown less rapidly in agriculture than in manufacturing. This would suggest a worsening of the relative income position of farmers, but two things have occurred to prevent that. First, the government has allowed the prices of agricultural products to rise relative to those of manufactured goods. This was done in two ways. The government, which purchases most of the rice crop every year for resale to consumers, has responded to political pressure from farmers by raising its purchase price every year; the purchase price in 1967 was 94 percent above that a decade earlier and was more than double the world trade price. This suggests the second mechanism for the increase in prices of agricultural products: To protect domestic agriculture and to transfer income from consumers to farmers, the government has severely restricted the competitive importation of foodstuffs. As demand for agricultural products—especially fruits, vegetables, dairy products and meat—has gone up along with higher incomes and standards of living, supply has increased in response, but less rapidly, so prices have risen.

The second factor greatly to affect farm wealth, if not income itself, has been the rapid increase in land values, particularly near urban areas. Postwar growth has accelerated the rate of urbanization; more than two-thirds of the population now live in cities. Metropolitan housing has expanded into agricultural land; so too have factories. In the process, the price of urban land increased 925 percent between 1955 and 1967, in contrast to a 10 percent rise in the wholesale price index and a 60 percent rise in the consumer price index. Both urban landowners and farmers near cities have become wealthy. The value of farmland has also risen because agricultural output (and its price) per unit of land has increased. Only farmers in the hinterlands—located far from markets and owning hilly, marginal land—have had their land value decline as young potential farmers move instead into urban jobs. One of the unexpected side effects of the Occupation land reform was that ex-tenants became increasingly wealthy as land values rose. Former landlords have fumed and organized to demand additional government compensation, but the extra amounts they have received have not been large.

Growth has not been without its problems. I have already mentioned the lagging growth of housing and public services, particularly in urban areas. These have been an important component of the stresses and strains of urbanization. Another problem has been a persistent rise in consumer prices of about 5 percent annually since 1959. Even though money wages and incomes have increased more rapidly, housewives have protested vociferously. The five-year economic plans in the 1960's stipulated a maximum increase in consumer prices of about 2 to 3 percent per year; but, as the economy has grown more rapidly than projected in the plans, so too have prices.

The rise in consumer prices has been mainly in services, agricultural commodities, and goods produced by small manufacturers, where wages have risen more than productivity. Prices of goods produced by large firms, where productivity increases are greatest, have risen only slightly or in some cases actually fallen. Accordingly, wholesale prices and, of particular significance, export prices have not tended to go up much. The situation is epitomized by the case of prices of services. For example, it is difficult to increase substantially a barber's productivity: The only ways he can increase his income are to raise prices and to reduce quality (no free hair wash and shave). In the process of economic development it is natural to have changes in the relative prices of goods and services as demand and productivity changes occur. In a buoyant, growing economy with high aggregate demand it is not surprising to find the consumer price index rising.

On the whole, the increase in consumer prices has not been especially harmful. In fact, real incomes have risen. The consumer-price rise is due primarily to the absolutely and relatively increasing wage rates for young, unskilled, low-income labor, which have tended somewhat to equalize income distribution, at least among the lower 60 percent of the population. Deflationary policies to prevent consumer-price rises not only would have slowed the real rate of economic growth but would have hit particularly the low-income wage earners, whose wages would have increased much less rapidly.

While both agriculture and small business in general have prospered —though not without their difficulties—big business, finance, and commerce have prospered most of all. Their rate of new investment and technological innovation has been more rapid, their share in output has been rising, and their power in society increasing. Japan is as much a big-business society today as it has ever been.

Big business has close and extremely complex relationships with the central government bureaucracy and with the Liberal-Democratic party (LDP), the conservative political party in power. Government is much more involved in business decision-making in Japan than in most other private-enterprise, market economies. Ministry of International Trade and Industry (MITI) officials keep in virtually daily contact with large firms. MITI tries to assist large firms in a variety of ways; in exchange it applies informal pressures (termed "administrative guidance") to reduce "excessive" or "wasteful" competition among firms, to synchronize new capacity-expansion programs among firms and industries in line with stable growth and other objectives, to arrange cartels to prevent "excessive" price declines in recessions, and the like. Ministry of Finance (MoF) and Bank of Japan (BoJ) officials are in daily contact with the major commercial banks. Politicians serve, in one of their functions, as brokers between business and the government bureaucracy. There has been a high degree of consensus at the general level among businessmen, government bureaucrats, and the LDP politicians. The slogan "What is good for the country is good for Mitsubishi, and vice versa" is substantially, if not completely, operative.

At times, of course, conflicts do arise: The government bureaucrats want businessmen to toe the line more than they are willing to do, or certain industries want favors that bureaucrats feel are not in the national interest. The process by which conflicts are resolved is not well understood, nor is it clear whether government dominates business or business dominates government. The LDP and its party leaders rely heavily on financing from big business; the elected leaders in a sense control the government bureaucracy but also need its expertise for advice and implementation. The bureaucracy has strong legal and extralegal ("guidance") powers over business. However, bureaucrats retire early (typically at age fifty-five); many move into prestigious and well-paid positions in large firms with which they formally dealt as bureaucrats. The three-way interplay is subtle and not well understood; which group comes out ahead depends very much on the specific issue and its context at the time.

The interrelationships among big businesses and among business, government bureaucracy, and LDP politicians are rather close, personal, and informal. In the Japanese meritocracy—where social mobility is achieved in large part through education and where the more prestigious the university (and the more difficult to pass the entrance examination) the greater the chance of being hired by big business or government ministry and eventually succeeding in politics—most of the senior government and business officials, and many politicians, are bound by school ties that are close and important. Graduates of the same university have a special call on each other, which is intensified where they were classmates or studied under the same professor. And these school ties are reinforced by intermarriage among families.

All this has led observers to speak of a Japanese "establishment"—five hundred or two thousand or some other number of important individuals who, on the basis of their business, government, and/or political affiliations and common education and acquaintanceship, make the important decisions for Japan. There is some truth to this appraisal, but it is difficult to know how much. The groupings are in fact somewhat diffuse and pluralistic, a situation that shows up particularly in the case of specific issues. Despite the general homogeneity of the leadership group, there does not seem to be a fully cohesive, unified elite that can and does determine all major decisions.

What has prevented any such overwhelming, monolithic establishment from emerging? Three interrelated factors are important. First, the specific interests of various groups differ, and at times are in conflict, when concrete issues arise. I have noted already that this occurs among the three major groups: big business, LDP politicians, and central-government bureaucrats. It also occurs within each group. Second, some of the pressures that help influence and shape policy decisions emanate from outside—from opposition political parties, unions, small business, farmers, intellectuals. Third, while Japan is a group-oriented society, placing emphasis on harmony, consensus, and cooperation, the Japanese people are at the same time highly competitive.

Business, government bureaucracy, and society in general have all tried in various ways to reconcile the inconsistent elements between competition and cooperation. Young college graduates entering a large firm or government ministry compete intensively, yet on a friendly basis, with other new entrants—but do not compete with slightly older persons who entered earlier. Over ten to fifteen years, all will advance to at least a middle level on a straight seniority basis; a younger person will virtually never be promoted over the head of someone older. But within his group (referred to as his "entering class") an individual strives to be best. His rewards, rather than being faster promotion and higher salaries, are increasingly interesting and influential jobs and the opportunity to be promoted eventually into the ranks of top management. The individual working in a large firm seldom quits to move to a new firm (unless it is an affiliate); his sense of identity with his original employer is strong and pervasive, and he views the organization as both competing and cooperating with the world.

The firm acts in the same way. It is highly competitive with other firms in the same industry. As already noted, it places great value on enhancing, or at least maintaining, its market share and its size ranking in the industry. At the same time, rival firms in the same industry are willing to cooperate when it seems mutually beneficial to their dealings with other industries, with the government, or with foreign competition at home or abroad. Firms are most likely to cooperate in cartel arrangements during the stress of recession periods. They agree to restrict production in order to keep prices from declining too much and perhaps also agree to restrict new investment. Yet even here cooperation does not always win over competition. Of all the anti-recession cartels established (typically with MITI's encouragement and blessing), only about one-third have effectively restricted production and maintained prices; for another third the results are ambiguous; and the remaining third of the firms did not in fact adhere to the agreements restricting output, so prices fell and these cartels were a failure. During boom periods firms are less likely to cooperate so much with each other. Aggressive firms, not quite at the top of the heap, hope to increase their market shares. They are unwilling to participate in industrywide agreements to coordinate and limit the overall expansion of capacity to anticipated future total market size (by keeping their new investment down to some fixed rate based on historical relative size of the firm) on the grounds that they would thereby be locked into their present relative position.

Another reason for lack of overall business unity is that on many issues various industries have interests that conflict fundamentally with those of other industries. For example, certain industries want to import cheap machinery or intermediate goods, while Japanese producers of these goods quite naturally dislike such foreign competition. Similar conflicts exist within purely domestic markets. And there are conflicts between big businesses and small and between business (which would like large imports of cheap food to hold down prices and union demands for wage increases) and agriculture.

A further source of conflict within the big-business sector is the re-emergence and strengthening of competing business "groups" encompassing affiliated firms in mining, manufacturing, commerce, and finance. Superficially these appear suspiciously like the prewar zaibatsu, and indeed some of the groups have familiar names: Mitsui, Mitsubishi, Sumitomo—but Fuji instead of its Yasuda predecessor. Group member firms buy from, sell to, and finance one another; members participate jointly in establishing new enterprises in newly developing fields. The groups compete vigorously with one another across a wide range of industrial sectors.

A "group" differs significantly from a prewar zaibatsu in that a single family no longer owns or otherwise controls it, no centralized holding company exists, stock ownership is widely diffused, and control is typically in the hands of management. Consequently, each firm is immeasurably more independent than it was in prewar times. Decisions are not made by a single, higher authority. Although the presidents of the main firms in the group meet regularly to solve problems of mutual concern, and similar arrangements exist for lower staff levels, conflicts among firms are not easily resolved. Often an arbitration committee is established, usually chaired by the head of the bank in the group. The committee tries to reach a reasonable compromise, for otherwise a discontented firm might consider pulling out of the group—although this is, of course, truer of those firms at the periphery of the group than of those at the core.

Similar pluralistic features are also characteristic of the government bureaucracy and the political parties. Government ministries have a tradition of considerable autonomy and independence of views and are jealous in guarding their powers. Different ministries frequently view specific policies in quite different ways, deriving from a complex of different goals, ways of thinking, and perceptions of what their respective constituencies are and what they need. For example, the Bank of Japan appears to place considerable emphasis on price stability, the Ministry of Finance on the restraint of budgetary expenditures to the level of revenues, MITI on expansion of industrial production and improvement in productivity, the Ministry of Agriculture and Forestry on improvement of agricultural incomes (by expansion of production, restriction of imports, and higher prices for farm products), and the Economic Planning Agency on stable growth and efficient resource allocation. Not surprisingly, ministries are often at loggerheads. Even within ministries there are different groups—often based on personalities and internal politics as well as on alternative views on policy. For example, MITI is frequently regarded as monolithically protectionist and favoring *dirigisme,* cartels, and industrial concentration and planning; yet one group within MITI holds that the virtues of relatively free, market-oriented competition—its advantages of increasing output and quality, improving productive efficiency, and holding down prices—more than compensate for the problem of possible excess capacity and other alleged costs of "excess competition."

The pluralism of the Liberal-Democratic party derives in large part from its division into a series of competing factions, which combine and recombine in efforts to achieve and maintain power through the holding of the party presidency (and hence prime ministership) and of important party offices and cabinet posts. The factions share a common overall ideological and policy framework (alignment with the United States, emphasis on economic growth in domestic and foreign policy), while differing somewhat on certain specific issues. Factions formed around leaders have been based on personality, long-time personal ties, and the ability of a leader to obtain funds to finance the election campaigns and other activities of his faction. In addition to their heavy contributions to the LDP and its central fund-raising organization, many big enterprises make contributions to selected specific factions or individuals. Thus, competition among industries or business groups tends to spill over and reinforce competition among LDP factions.

Yet the LDP is not simply the captive of big business—it cannot afford to be. While much of its financing comes from large business contributions, it must seek elsewhere for the votes needed to keep it in power. Thus, it has to shape policies so as at least to ameliorate conditions for farmers, small businessmen, white-collar workers, professionals, and workers (particularly those who are not militantly organized by unions). Moreover, even though it retains control of the parliament, the LDP has to provide reasonable alternatives to the policy positions of the opposition parties.

While business is tied to the LDP, unions and their members in larger enterprises have consistently supported the parties to the left. SOHYO (General Council of Trade Unions), the largest labor confederation, has been the mainstay of the largest opposition party, the Japan Socialist party. (The JSP too is split into factions, based on both personalities and ideology.) Unions inclined more toward middle-of-the-road policies support the moderate Democratic Socialist party, while a few unions that are more extreme support the small Japan Communist party. Komeito (Clean Government party) is the political organ of Soka Gakkai, a fundamentalist Buddhist sect that has grown considerably in the past fifteen years. Its supporters do not belong to any clearly identifiable, organized economic group; generally they are urban, somewhat alienated, relatively lower income, and either workers in small establishments or housewives.

Thus the Japanese economic and business environment has evolved in ways considerably variant from those envisaged by the SCAP reformers. The main differences lie in Japan's only partial acceptance of competition and in its relatively greater acceptance of direct government influence on business decisions. Antimonopoly legal provisions were substantially weakened soon after the end of the Occupation and have eroded further since then, though LDP attempts at additional legislative easing in the late 1950's and early 1960's were blocked by widespread opposition. Nonetheless, interlocking directorships and stock ownership are once more permitted. More important, anti-recession production and other cartels have been made legal, subject to MITI and the Fair Trade Commission. The latter has been relatively weak, unable really to restrain the trends toward restriction of competition.

Concomitantly, there has been a gradual trend in many industries toward the increasing concentration of production in a relatively small number of large firms. Following the SCAP deconcentration efforts, Japanese industry was certainly less concentrated in the 1950's than before the war and no more concentrated than industry in the United States. Concentration was even somewhat lessened by the rapid growth of new firms. Since the late 1950's, however, the trend has reversed: The top three, five, or ten firms are gaining an increasing share of total output. Since the mid-1960's the tendency has accelerated due to the increasing number of mergers among large firms in major industries. This trend, together with the growth of groups of affiliated firms, suggests an increasing concentration of economic power—though far less than that of the 1930's.

Two factors mitigate the adverse effects of increasing concentration of the industrial structure. First, intense competition persists among firms in a given industry and among groups. This is reflected by the rather substantial changes that occur in the relative ranking of the top ten firms in any industry. Second, where the government has tolerated or encouraged restrictions of competition, it has put pressure on firms to improve productivity, cut costs, and reduce—or at least not increase—prices. This has been possible because increasing concentration has been a consequence in part of economies of very large-scale production.

The Future

The Japanese phoenix, revitalized and stronger than ever, has soared. Can it continue to fly so well? Which way will it fly? Phrased more prosaically, will Japan's economic growth continue unabated? Will the primacy of economic growth in domestic and foreign policy objectives persist, or will new goals become more important?

It is beyond the cope of this essay to analyze these questions in detail.

The odds are high (perhaps 70 percent) that over the coming decade the economy will grow at an average annual rate of at least 7 to 8 percent, somewhat slower than the super-performance of the past decade. Investment and saving rates will remain a high proportion of GNP, though not an increasing one as in the past. Foreign technological inflow will continue, even though much of the cream has been skimmed. Domestic innovation, and particularly the diffusion of advanced technology among a larger number of firms and a larger proportion of the labor force, will become relatively more important. Labor supply, while tightening, will remain more ample than in Europe, particularly since the institutional practices of large firms of hiring only new graduates and retiring their employees at fifty-five are eroding. Agriculture will constitute a major problem area, but its relative importance—now less than 20 percent of labor force and 12 percent of GNP—will continue to diminish.

While the predominant share of this growth in output and incomes will be used to increase private consumption and to provide the investment fuel for further sustained growth, a rising margin will be available for other uses. These resources are likely to be allocated to the improvement of housing, roads, water and sewage systems, and other public services.

Japan's resurgence to the forefront of world industrial nations—Japan is third now in total GNP behind the United States and Russia, though considerably lower in per capita ranking—has given the people a renewed self-confidence and national pride. Yet Japan's international political influence, its ranking as a world power, lags behind. Moreover, to many Japanese it appears that the country does not have sufficient independence. In part this impression derives from the earlier realities of the bipolar Cold War, when Japan as a weak nation quite naturally aligned itself with the United States and relied upon the American nuclear umbrella to provide security from external aggression. Thus, there are now some doubts being raised about the single-minded emphasis on economic growth, and new questions are now being asked. What should be Japan's future world role? How can greater independence be achieved and, at the same time, national security guaranteed?

No consensus is yet discernible in the emerging debate on these and related issues. In rather cautious ways the government has tried to develop a somewhat more positive foreign policy, particularly in the economic sphere. It has substantially increased its economic aid to less developed countries, particularly those in Asia. It has also attempted to mediate in various disputes, particularly among Asian nations, so far without notable success.

The issue of national security most starkly delineates these new developments within Japan. The issue is in flux still, with neither goals nor means for achieving them fully articulated. The extremely strong pacifist feeling, a continuing consequence of World War II, remains an important factor, though apparently affecting the young postwar generation less than the generation that directly experienced the war. Several alternative approaches are under debate. One, the policy of the LDP, is to maintain the present military alliance with the United States while obtaining greater independence from U.S. controls on smaller matters and redefining the Japan-U.S. partnership in more equal terms. This would allow Japan to use its resources for domestic growth and foreign aid and investment. But will it be independent enough? How independent can a nation be in today's world? And how about the U.S. commitment—how will American post-Vietnam security policy evolve?

The Japan Socialist party has taken a completely different position: neutralism without military power. Japan should align itself with no bloc but should be friendly with all nations. No one will want to attack Japan, so it is not necessary to have a defensive military force. Security can be guaranteed by an international pact signed by the United States, Russia, and China. Yet there seems no evidence that such a pact is feasible. More important, is Japan willing to lie defenseless, depending solely on the good will of other nations? Isn't the risk too high for Japan's own national interests?

A third alternative—neutralism with security guaranteed by Japan's own military forces—has a strong (though by no means overwhelming) logical basis. It has not yet really entered the debate, however, because a major premise is that Japan would have its own nuclear armaments. This at present remains anathema to most Japanese. Nonetheless, if Japanese nationalism takes the path of complete independence (and semi-isolationism), and if some external threat to Japan's security is clearly and strongly perceived, it is quite possible that this alternative could evolve from either the position of the left or that of the right. As it happens, atomic weapons and delivery systems are well within Japan's technical and economic capacity. Policy-makers have kept the choices open, pushing the development of atomic energy for peaceful uses and the development of missiles and guidance systems for basic space research. An allocation of perhaps 5 percent of GNP per year for five years should provide Japan a moderately sophisticated nuclear weapons system. This could be where the extra margin of resources from growth will go.

Japan's single-minded and highly successful pursuit, since the end of World War II, of economic reconstruction and growth of production and improvement in living standards is clear and noteworthy. It seems unlikely that Japan's future actions will be so overwhelmingly dominated by the goal of economic growth. But to what extent will economic objectives—growth, greater social welfare, improvement of public services—

continue to be predominant? Or will the nation increasingly seek other goals? If so, how will it try to achieve them? These issues make Japan an exciting and important country to watch in the crucial coming decade.

Selected Readings

Allen, George C. *Japan's Economic Expansion*. London: Oxford University Press, 1965. A standard introduction to Japan's postwar economy; more descriptive than analytical.

Cohen, Jerome B. *Japan's Economy in War and Reconstruction*. Minneapolis: University of Minnesota Press, 1949. A detailed, rather technical description and analysis of Japan's economy during World War II and the first part of the Occupation.

Correspondents of *The Economist*. *Consider Japan*. London: Gerald Duckworth, 1963. A superior piece of journalism that explores the question of why Japan has grown rapidly and England slowly. Follow-up articles appear in the November 28, 1964, May 27, 1967, and June 3, 1967, issues of *The Economist*.

Dore, Ronald P. *Land Reform in Japan*. London: Oxford University Press, 1959. An integrated, broad-gauged appraisal of Japan's agrarian economy, society, and polity as affected by the land reform.

Hunsberger, Warren S. *Japan and the United States in World Trade*. New York: Harper & Row, 1964. A policy-oriented study of Japan's foreign economic relations, particularly trade with the United States; with an extensive bibliography.

Japan, Economic Planning Agency. *Economic Survey of Japan*. Tokyo: The Japan Times, annual. The annual white paper on the economy. An invaluable source of contemporary data, description, and analysis, together with interesting evaluations of contemporary and future problems. Translation is mediocre but generally understandable.

Klein, Lawrence, and Ohkawa, Kazushi, eds. *Economic Growth: The Japanese Experience Since the Meiji Era*. Yale Economic Growth Series. Homewood, Ill.: Irwin, 1968. Rather sophisticated papers on Japan's long-run growth, including the postwar period. Several papers treat only postwar topics.

Komiya, Ryutaro, ed. *Postwar Economic Growth in Japan*. Translated by Robert S. Ozaki. Berkeley, Calif.: University of California Press, 1966. Papers of a Japanese conference held in 1963; particularly good essays on fiscal and monetary policy by Tachi, balance of payments by Kanamori, personal savings by Komiya, and postwar executives by Noda, together with useful, pungent commentaries.

Langdon, Frank C. *Politics in Japan*. Boston: Little, Brown & Co., 1967. A behaviorally oriented explanation that provides a good introduction to Japanese politics.

Levine, Solomon B. *Industrial Relations in Postwar Japan*. Urbana, Ill.: University of Illinois Press, 1958. A dated but standard work on the development of trade unionism and the respective roles of management, labor, and government in industrial relations.

Lockwood, William W., ed. *The State and Economic Enterprise in Japan*. Studies in the Modernization of Japan. Princeton, N.J.: Princeton University Press, 1965. Five papers on the postwar economy, from a 1963 conference on Japan's economic modernization, that include Lockwood on "new capitalism," Patrick on cyclical instability and fiscal-monetary policy, and Scalapino on labor and politics.

Martin, Edward M. *The Allied Occupation of Japan*. New York: American Institute of Pacific Relations, 1948. A description by a State Department offical of the objectives of the Occupation, the methods of implementation, and conditions within Japan during the first two years.

Patrick, Hugh T. *Monetary Policy and Central Banking in Contemporary Japan*. Bombay: University of Bombay Press, 1964. An examination of Japan's financial system during the 1950's and early 1960's, with particular emphasis on the instruments of central-bank monetary control.

Scalapino, Robert A., and Masumi, Junnosuke. *Parties and Politics in Contemporary Japan*. Berkeley, Calif.: University of California Press, 1962. An analysis of trends in postwar Japanese politics and the Japanese political process, culminating in a case study of the crisis related to the 1960 revision of the U.S.–Japanese security treaty.

Vogel, Ezra F. *Japan's New Middle Class: The Salary Man and His Family in a Tokyo Suburb*. Berkeley, Calif.: University of California Press, 1967. A sociological study of the new middle class of salaried, white-collar employees of large business corporations and the government and their families, based on field work in a Tokyo suburb in 1958–60.

Yamamura, Kozo. *Economic Policy in Postwar Japan: Growth Versus Economic Democracy*. Berkeley, Calif.: University of California Press, 1967. The author argues that there has been an erosion, under the impact of subsequent rapid-growth policies, of Occupation democratization policies in the areas of concentration of economic power, industrial (market) structure, and income distribution; interesting analysis and data.

Yanaga, Chitoshi. *Big Business in Japanese Politics*. Studies in Political Science, No. 2. New Haven, Conn.: Yale University Press, 1968. A discussion of the relationship of big business and its organizations to the government bureaucracy and political parties; includes several case studies.

Yoshino, M. Y. *Japan's Managerial System: Tradition and Innovation*. Cambridge, Mass.: M.I.T. Press, 1968. An interesting explanation and appraisal of the evolution of Japan's business ideology, organizational structure, personnel practices, and decision-making processes, with emphasis on recent changes in traditional attitudes and practices.

Communist China:

Moderation and Radicalism

in the Chinese Revolution

SHINKICHI ETŌ

T HE Communist revolution in China, especially in the past few years, has fascinated a worldwide audience. Unquestionably a historic tide of tremendous change is surging through China, and the entire world is aware that China is in the middle of what its leaders call the Great Proletarian Cultural Revolution. Although it is impossible to chart the full range and intensity of this revolutionary tide, various theories—some critical, others adulatory—have been advanced to interpret its scope and meaning. These divergent interpretations call to mind the tale of a group of blind men, each feeling and probing a small part of a large elephant, each conjuring up a distorted image of the beast, each confident that his was the reliable description. If observers of China have much in common with these blind men, nevertheless, there is no denying that the term "Cultural Revolution" has become a sort of universal shorthand for the Chinese Communist revolution and that the small, red handbook of the thoughts of Mao Tse-tung has become a bible for China's youth and for radical student movements throughout the world. Contemporary China, as symbolized by Mao's little red book and the concept of the Great Cultural Revolution, has captured the imagination of students and intellectuals in a way comparable to the memorable impact of the Bolshevik revolution. Thus, regardless of the mystery and ambiguities surrounding the Great Cultural Revolution, there is no reason as yet to question Chou En-lai's original judgment that it is "the gravest matter that may affect the fate and the future of our Party and the State."[1]

The Great Cultural Revolution began inauspiciously, in the spring of 1966, when an apparently small group of prominent officials and intellec-

[1] *People's Daily*, May 1, 1966.

tuals in the Chinese Communist party were criticized publicly and censured by official party organs.[2] Among those particularly singled out for vitriolic criticism were Chou Yang, the chief of the party's Central Propaganda Department; Ch'ien Po-tsan, a distinguished historian; Meng Chao, the vice president of Peking University; and T'ien Han, a famous playwright; along with Wu Han, Teng To, and Liao Mo-sha. In conjunction with this indictment of hitherto respected and reputable Communist intellectuals, Chou En-lai proclaimed that the prime problem confronting the party was "the fierce long-term struggle between the proletariat and the bourgeoisie in the ideological field to see who will fight and which will win."[3] By seemingly confining the issue to ideology and his criticism to intellectuals, Chou conveyed the impression that the problem of the class struggle in China was to be found primarily in the ideological and cultural fields. At this time, outside observers were completely unaware that this Great Cultural campaign coincided with the purge of P'eng Chen, the mayor of Peking, or that it was the opening move in a major campaign designed to disgrace and eventually to oust Liu Shao-ch'i, who was then heir apparent to Chairman Mao Tse-tung. Ignorant of these political overtones, observers felt the issue of the Cultural Revolution to be much like earlier party discussions of the problem of ideology and culture. In 1958, for example, during the Great Leap Forward, Liu Shao-ch'i had himself defined and interpreted the Cultural Revolution as a matter of spreading education among the masses and of reforming bourgeois intellectuals.[4] In the spring of 1966, it seemed that the party and Chou En-lai were addressing their remarks to the same problem in essentially the same terms.

This impression was soon corrected. In June, the party organs started to invest the concept of the Cultural Revolution with explicit political overtones bearing on the leadership of the party and the state. "The basic problem of the revolution," declared the *People's Daily*, "is that of power. . . . Possessing power means possessing everything, and not possessing power means losing everything. . . . The class struggle between the proletariat and the bourgeoisie in the ideological realm is basically a struggle for seizing leadership."[5] This shift in focus was clarified further in August 1966, at the Eleventh Plenum of the Central Committee of the Chinese Communist party. Here, the party formally ruled:

> The Great Proletarian Cultural Revolution now under way is a great revolution touching people to their very souls and is a new stage of our

[2] *Liberation Army's Daily*, April 18, 1966.

[3] *People's Daily*, May 1, 1966.

[4] *Collection of the Documents of the Second Meeting of the Chinese Communist Party's Eighth National Congress*, Japanese ed. (Peking: Foreign Languages Press, 1958), pp. 52–53.

[5] *People's Daily*, June 1, 1966.

country's socialist revolution for deeper and wider development. . . . Our immediate purposes are to crush those in power who are treading the capitalist road, to criticize bourgeois and reactionary academic "authorities," to criticize ideologies of the bourgeoisie and all exploiting classes, to reform education, literature and fine arts, and to reform all upper structures not suitable to the economic foundation of socialism, thus to help strengthen and develop socialist institutions.[6]

With this pronouncement, the Central Committee was, in effect, declaring war on "those in power" who presumably had not been sufficiently revolutionized—that is, had not truly transformed their class character into that of the proletariat. The injunction implicitly advanced the contention that only by "crushing" these bourgeois elements could the socialist system be strengthened and developed. If the logic of this reasoning was comprehensible within the framework of Marxism-Leninism, one vital question remained: Who within the state were "treading the capitalist road"?

Before probing this question, we must consider briefly some traits common to all revolutionary movements. In the drive for political power, the leaders of any revolutionary movement necessarily espouse comprehensive revolutionary goals. Once political power has been realized, however, the question of the tempo of the march toward the original goals inevitably becomes a vital and divisive issue among the new wielders of power. The result is usually a terrible power struggle, one that often compels a change in the revolutionary goals themselves. In the Russian Revolution, for example, Lenin's shift to the New Economic Policy marked a change in the revolutionary tempo, and Stalin's famous fight with Trotsky and Bukharin was a power struggle among revolutionary leaders. The question of the tempo of revolutionary change was also intrinsic to the Great Proletarian Cultural Revolution launched in 1966. So too, the question of who within the party were "treading the capitalist road" signified the onset of an ill-defined but undeniable power struggle among the leadership of the Chinese Communist party.

Discussions of the tempo of the revolution were not, of course, a new concern in the Chinese Communist movement. Liu Shao-ch'i had previously addressed himself to this very question. Speaking at the second meeting of the Chinese Communist party's Eighth National Congress in 1958, Liu had declared, "The question of the speed of construction is the most important question placed before us amidst the victory of the Socialist revolution. In a word, our revolution is intended to develop social productivity most quickly."[7] In Liu's judgment, the best way to promote

[6] Hong Kong *Wen Hui Pao*, August 9, 1966.
[7] *Collection of the Documents of the Second Meeting of the Chinese Communist Party's Eighth National Congress*, p. 53.

social productivity was to predicate all plans on an objective assessment of existing social conditions. At the same time, he acknowledged that, if the party were meticulously cautious with its programs, it would tend to wipe away the "revolutionary character" of the revolution. At that time, however, Liu's call for cautious programs and adherence to long-term revolutionary goals carried no stigma of being bourgeois or antisocialist. No less a revolutionary than Liu, Mao Tse-tung, in his younger days, had also ridiculed the proponents of radical policies within the party. "Developing the economy," he had said, "is the correct line, but development does not mean reckless or ill-founded expansion. Some comrades who disregard the specific conditions here and now are setting up an empty clamour for development; for example, they are demanding the establishment of heavy industry and putting forward plans for huge salt and armament industries, all of which are unrealistic and unacceptable."[8] One may reasonably conclude, therefore, that prior to 1956 disagreements over the tempo of the revolution were characteristic of the leadership of the Chinese Communist party and that the call for moderate and cautious programs in pursuit of long-term revolutionary objectives was characteristic of many leaders, including Mao Tse-tung as well as Liu Shao-ch'i.

The question then becomes one of why, in 1966, Liu Shao-ch'i, P'eng Chen, Chou Yang, and other leaders were suddenly subjected to the wild accusation that they were not real Marxist-Leninists but bourgeois and antisocialist. The answer, in my opinion, should be sought in a historical perspective that regards the Great Cultural Revolution as part of a ten-year dispute within the party over the speed of the socialization of China. Throughout the decade 1956–66, the party experienced a series of major crises—for example, the episode of the "great freedom of speech," the Sino-Soviet dispute, and the Vietnam war. These crises stimulated continuous debates about the tempo of the revolution, debates that eventually provoked serious factional struggles within the party. The onset of the Cultural Revolution in 1966 was the consequence of this factionalism. It would be incorrect, therefore, to regard the Cultural Revolution simply as a narrow power struggle in the sense of a factional competition to become Mao Tse-tung's heir, although this element is surely present. Since, however, the nature of factionalism in the Communist party is not yet clearly delineated, the best one can say at this time is that the Cultural Revolution is unquestionably a fierce struggle for power in the broadest sense of the term—that is, a power struggle, at all party levels, that includes disagreements about the vital issues of the tempo of the Communist revolution in China. To comprehend this power struggle, we

[8] "Economic and Financial Problems in the Anti-Japanese War," in *Selected Works of Mao Tse-tung*, English ed. (Peking: Foreign Languages Press, 1965), Vol. 3, p. 113.

must understand the historical currents in China's recent past, especially those evident since 1957. It is the intent of this essay to interpret the Great Cultural Revolution in the context of these historical currents.

The Revolution: Times of Moderation

In the course of a revolution, policy changes are often accompanied by a change in leadership. In the October Revolution in Russia and in China's Communist revolution, however, changes in basic policies have been accomplished without changing leaders. Under the continuous leadership of Mao Tse-tung, the People's Republic of China has repeatedly, since its inception in 1949, tried and altered radical and moderate policies almost in a trial-and-error manner. It is consequently impossible to categorize the history of Communist China neatly into clear-cut periods of moderate and radical policies. Radical policies have contained moderate elements, and moderate policies have had radical components; shifts in policies have sometimes been wide, at other times narrow. Still, in general terms, it is possible to discern two definite periods of moderate policies. The first was 1949–50, the initial stage of the founding of the People's Republic of China, and the second was 1953–57, following the negotiation of the Korean armistice. The intervening years, 1950–53, were distinguished by a move toward radical policies, including a campaign to suppress "counterrevolutionaries," implementation of a major land-reform program, and involvement in the Korean War.

The second period of moderate policies, 1953–57, was characterized by adoption of the first Five-Year Plan of economic growth, followed by the policy of "long-term coexistence and mutual surveillance" toward those who were not official members of the party. Domestically, this was the time of the mild, "let a hundred flowers bloom" approach to intellectuals, and foreign policy was keynoted by the so-called Five Peaceful Principles, respecting the spirit of the Bandung conference. Temporarily, these policies seemed to have been remarkably effective, especially in the economic realm. Even Western observers invariably praised highly the economic rehabilitation realized under the Five-Year Plan. Against this background, the party gained considerable self-confidence in its policies and programs. Addressing the Eighth National Congress of the Chinese Communist party in September 1956, Mao Tse-tung euphorically affirmed the "decisive triumph" of the socialist revolution in China.[9] "We have," Mao added, "conducted correct activities; but we also have committed a num-

[9] *Collection of the Documents of the Eighth National Congress of the Chinese Communist Party,* Japanese ed. (Peking: Foreign Languages Press, 1956), Vol. 1, pp. 9–15.

ber of mistakes." Modesty, not pride or arrogance, Mao reasoned, was therefore the most appropriate path to revolutionary progress. "We have no reason to be self-conceited and high-hatted," he cautioned. The immediate imperatives, Mao judged, were unity and solidarity—unity within the party; party solidarity with the various races, or nationalities, in China, as well as with all democratic classes and parties in the nation; and, of course, unity and solidarity with the Soviet Union.

In reference to economic matters, Mao spoke of a "step by step" building program; and, in another setting, he reiterated the centrality of rationalism in economic planning. "People's thinking must adapt to the changed conditions. Of course, no one should go off into wild flights of fancy, or make plans unwarranted by the objective situation, or insist on attempting the impossible."[10] Mao's call for prudent leaders and moderate programs, as well as his categorical affirmation of the "decisive triumph" of the socialist revolution in China, were comprehensible in the context of the apparently dazzling successes of the Five-Year economic program.

Mao's opening remarks to the congress also marked the opening move in the party's affirmation of the principle of collective leadership. The party's rejection of Maoism and the cult of individualism in 1956 was partly influenced by the de-Stalinization movement then under way in the Soviet Union. It coincided, too, with the heady optimism inspired by the achievements of the Five-Year program. The denial of Maoism by the party was best exemplified by the famous "Report on the Revision of the Party Constitution," submitted at the Eighth Congress by Teng Hsiao-p'ing, the secretary general of the party's Central Committee.[11] Here, Teng caustically berated party leaders for the evil trait of "commandism" and sarcastically ridiculed the practice of praising the role of party leaders in the realms of art and literature. Apart from these general indictments, Teng criticized the reluctance of the leadership to convene formal conferences to discuss programs and policies, as well as the fact that, when conferences had been held, they had always degenerated into mere formalism. Teng complemented these savage observations with words of praise for the principle of collective leadership. On this subject, Teng's report endorsed the ban on public birthday celebrations for party leaders and the prohibition against using their names for place and street names. Collective leadership, not individualism, Teng stressed, had been the guiding axiom of the party since 1949, and, he concluded, no one in the party had been free from mistakes and faults in all his activities.

[10] "Opening Speech of the Eighth National Congress of the Chinese Communist Party," in *Collection of the Documents of the Eighth National Congress of the Chinese Communist Party*, p. 5.

[11] *Collection of the Documents of the Eighth National Congress of the Chinese Communist Party*, pp. 243–50.

The thrust of this report was unmistakably directed at any personification of the party's leadership and progress. Adhering to this approach, the Eighth Congress officially revised the party's constitution, pointedly eradicating, in the process, any reference to "Mao Tse-tung's thought."[12] Maoism was no longer sanctioned in principle. Indeed, the party, with Mao's public approval, affirmed the principle of collective leadership, credited this principle with the realization of the "decisive triumpn" of the revolution in China, and sanctioned the course of modesty and moderation as the proper path for the party and the state.

The presentation of Teng's report and the favorable response it evoked have led some experts on Communist China to view the achievements of the Eighth Congress in terms of personal alignments and factionalism. In particular, the congress has been depicted as a contest between Mao Tse-tung and Liu Shao-ch'i for party control, with the Liu faction emerging as the victor.[13] This judgment, in my opinion, is exaggerated. Various sources indicate that Mao remained the firm leader in the Chinese Communist party, and I tend to believe that any conflict that existed between Mao and Liu was either obscure or insignificant. Obviously Mao agreed, or pretended to agree, with Teng's report and officially admitted that the party had made many mistakes and party members should be modest enough to accept any criticism.[14] In brief, there is reason to believe that in the context of 1956 both Mao and Liu espoused the moderate course and the principle of collective leadership. No one, in 1956, imagined that within a decade the "decisive triumph" of the revolution would be denied and China's crisis would be depicted as a "life or death struggle" against bourgeois and antisocialist elements. No one, in 1956, anticipated that Mao's call for personal modesty and "step by step" program would be displaced by the canonization of the thoughts of Mao Tse-tung, that Mao would be proclaimed "the greatest contemporary living Marxist-Leninist,"[15] or that the government would declare that "the attitude toward the thought of Mao Tse-tung is the yardstick to measure who is a real revolutionary, who is a sham revolutionary, who is a Marxist-Leninist and who is a revisionist. All opponents to the thought of Mao Tse-tung are the staunch enemies of the revolution and of the people."[16] Similarly, in

[12] *Ibid.*, pp. 240, 250.

[13] For example, Ho Yü-wen (Ying-chih), "Why Did Mao Tse-tung Bow Out?" mimeographed by the Public Security Investigation Agency, Japanese Government, March 17, 1959, p. 26.

[14] "Speech at a Chinese Communist Party's National Meeting on Propaganda Activities," in *Selective Reading of Mao Tse-tung's Works, Chia* ed. (Peking: People's Publishing Office, 1965), Vol. 2, pp. 500–20.

[15] "Official statement of the Eleventh Plenary Session of the Eighth Central Committee of the Chinese Communist Party," *People's Daily,* August 14, 1966.

[16] *People's Daily,* July 1, 1966.

1956, few foretold that the program of "solidarity" with all democratic parties would become a prelude to a tough "antirightist" campaign; and few believed that "friendship and solidarity" with the Soviet Union would yield to a passionate Sino-Soviet ideological dispute which seemed to confirm the saying that, to believers, heretics are more hateful than pagans. The prevailing mood in 1956 was optimism about the future and confidence that existing policies and programs would confirm the "triumph" of the Communist revolution in China.

Turning Point: 1957

Speaking in February 1957 before an audience of some 1,800 party members, Mao delivered a discourse "On the Correct Handling of Contradictions Among the People."[17] Here, Mao again reaffirmed the *ta-ming ta-fang*, the "great freedom of speech" principle. Although this address was not officially published, it is commonly believed that Mao wholeheartedly championed the free-speech movement, allegedly reasoning that listening to the people was equal to being advised by the people and that the people should tell everything they know and everything they want to tell. A month later, before some 380 party propaganda operations men, Mao cast the *ta-ming ta-fang* principle in a different mold.[18] Mao insisted, as usual, that while the Chinese Communist party was a great party, it also had shortcomings. It was essential, therefore, that the party should become a Marxist party, which would not fear criticism. By listening to the people, Mao maintained, the party could conduct a rectification campaign against the harmful traits of subjectivism, bureaucratism, and sectarianism. Thus, in this second speech, the context of the *ta-ming ta-fang* principle intimated that it had the ulterior purpose of marshalling and organizing criticism against revisionism within the party. In conjunction with this speech, party literature invariably urged nonparty democratic groups to follow the path of "the great freedom of speech," and in early May bold criticisms directed against the party by nonparty members began to be officially published. The party was castigated as a dictatorship under which only party members exercised power and nonparty men were entrusted with sinecure positions, and the demands for a *p'ing-fan*, a retrial of those who had been falsely accused of crimes and errors by the party, surged to the forefront. The invitation to honor "the great freedom of speech" had been accepted with gusto, thereby causing a major crisis within the party.

[17] *Ibid.*, March 3, 1957.

[18] Mao Tse-tung, "Speeches at a Chinese Communist Party's National Meeting on Propaganda Activities," pp. 510–12.

The party reacted promptly. On June 8, in a dramatic *volte-face*, it called for a program of "correct rectification."[19] At the same time, a large-scale antirightist campaign was launched. Thus, for example, when an anti-Communist demonstration began at the Hanyang First Middle School, the death penalty was promptly meted out to the three ring-leaders of the demonstration.[20] And on June 18 a significantly revised version of Mao's February rally speech on the "great freedom of speech" principle was published. In this published text, "On the Correct Handling of Contradictions Among the People," six criteria for judging the propriety of behavior and ideas were appended to the *ta-ming ta-fang*. Armed with this text, the party then utilized "the great freedom of speech" as a means to identify and attack "rightist" groups and individuals. In brief, those who had embraced the "great freedom of speech" movement and had castigated the party soon found themselves the targets of a raging antirightist campaign organized by the party as part of that very movement.

The party used the crisis fomented by "the great freedom of speech" in two decisive ways: to enforce discipline within the party and to locate, criticize, and purge those who were critical of the party line. The repression thus raised the question of whether the *ta-ming ta-fang* movement had been a carefully planned feint designed to flush out rightist elements, or whether the party leaders had launched this movement confident that China would not follow the example of either the Hungarian incident or the Poznan riots. The prevailing opinion is that Mao had sincerely championed the *ta-ming ta-fang* but that Liu Shao-ch'i and others had been apprehensive about the movement since its inception.[21] How accurate this opinion is remains an open-ended question. One should note, however, that there were some similarities between the opening phase of "the great freedom of speech" in 1958 and the "great democratic debates" that were to become part of the Great Cultural Revolution. In both instances, mass activities and speaking out in public were positively encouraged by the party, but, when public pronouncements and actions deviated from the framework and direction of the party, they quickly came to be criticized and punished by the party organizations.

Shortly after the crackdown on critics of the party, the government, on October 15, 1957, negotiated the Sino-Soviet Agreement on New Technical Aid for Defense.[22] By this agreement, the Soviet Union promised to provide China with sample nuclear arms and the technical data essential

[19] *People's Daily*, June 8, 1957.

[20] *Ibid.*, September 7, 1957.

[21] For example, the remarks of Vukmanovic, former vice president of Yugoslavia, in *Mainichi*, January 18, 1967.

[22] *People's Daily*, August 15, 1963.

for their production. A month later, during his visit to Moscow, Mao Tse-tung delivered his famous speech, "The East Wind Prevails Over the West Wind."[23] As is well known, Mao expressed the judgment that the strength of the socialist forces now surpassed that of the capitalist nations. With this axiom, Mao reasoned as follows: (1) In the event of a war between the socialist and capitalist camps, one-third to one-half of China's population would be destroyed; (2) the socialist forces would be triumphant and would socialize the world, and, in a few decades, China's population would be restored to its original size; (3) Communist China had yet to complete its reconstruction and desired peace with the capitalist nations; and (4) if recourse to war were intended by the capitalist nations, then China was prepared for war. Several months after presenting this doctrine of "The East Wind Prevails," the Chinese Communist party proclaimed the "Three Red Flags" program—that is, the people's communes, the Great Leap Forward, and the socialist construction movement. Under the Five-Year Plan adopted in 1956, the government had set as its targets for 1962 an increase in annual food production to 250 million tons and an annual steel production of 12 million tons. As part of the Three Red Flags program, however, this schedule was drastically increased to a target of 290 million tons for food production and 10.7 million tons for steel production, both to be realized by the end of 1958.[24] This shift heralded a dramatic change from the moderate "step by step" pace to the quick march of the Great Leap Forward. It marked the beginning of the second radical period of the Chinese People's Republic.

What Made Them Radical?

From 1953 to 1957, Communist China had pursued a course of moderate change. In 1958, the party accelerated the tempo of the revolution. Why? Again theories vary, but, tentatively, six considerations seem relevant to the onset of the second period of radical policies in the history of Communist China. First, as a consequence of the antirightist campaign launched in reaction to the "great freedom of speech" movement, it seems that the more radical, or left-wing, element of the party gained ascendancy. By 1958 this shift was reflected in the highest levels of the party. Second, the launching of Sputnik and the Soviet ICBM tests in 1957 were interpreted by Mao and his followers as "a new turning point," signifying the strategic superiority of the socialist bloc over the capitalist nations.[25]

[23] *Ibid.*, October 31, 1958.
[24] *Ibid.*, August 1, 1958.
[25] *Ibid.*, October 27, 1958.

Third, given this "new turning point," they believed China no longer needed to fear the threat of nuclear attack. This new and favorable international environment reinforced the opinion that an "objective" appraisal of the new conditions warranted a more rapid socialization of China and a hard-line foreign policy toward the capitalist nations. Fourth, as Marxist-Leninists, all the Chinese Communist leaders believed in the basic assumption that increased socialization of the state would increase productivity. There was no disagreement about the eventual benefits of state socialism. Of course, those who had devised and directed the first Five-Year Plan (for example, Ch'en Yün and Teng Tzu-hui) and those who, like Li Wei-han, were in charge of the united-front operations and were responsible for the coalitions with the so-called right-wing elements preferred a moderate cause. In 1958, they argued that moderation was still the most appropriate tack, the most effective approach given the actual domestic situation in China.[26] Still, they too subscribed to the goal of socialism, and by 1958 they were the minority within the party. Fifth, agricultural productivity had stagnated in 1957, enhancing the view that an intensive promotion of collectivization (a program already under way) would surely increase agricultural productivity and achieve the socialization of the villages.[27] This viewpoint was buttressed by a "new equilibrium theory" that denied the advantage of a balanced development of the total economy, reasoning in favor of a breakthrough in one sector of the economy on the premise that this would then automatically bring about a rapid development of the whole economy.[28] Sixth, the party leadership shared the belief that China would have to compensate for its deficiency in capital resources by an effective mobilization of manpower and by a program of ideological education that would improve the quality of the manpower base.[29] In brief, then, the shift to a radical tempo in 1958 was a consequence of the convergence of several factors: The more radical, or leftist, leaders had become dominant in the party; new appraisals of the international balance of power enhanced a general mood of radicalism; and the apparent stagnation of the existing agricultural policy seemed to vindicate the proponents of a greater intensification of the commune program.

The promulgation of the Three Red Flags program in 1958 symbolized

---

[26] *Collection of the Documents of the Eighth National Congress of the Chinese Communist Party*, Vol. 2, pp. 194–244, 431–54.

[27] T'an Chen-lin, "Report to the Second Plenary Session of the Eighth Central Committee of the Chinese Communist Party," *Collection of the Documents of the Second Plenary Session of the Eighth National Congress of the Chinese Communist Party*, Japanese ed. (Peking: Foreign Languages Press, 1958), p. 103.

[28] *People's Daily*, February 28, 1958.

[29] Vukmanovic, *Mainichi*, January 18, 1967.

the ascendancy of the more radical elements within the party. But the long-term struggle for party leadership did not disappear, and there were strong currents beneath the surface that flowed counter to the official radicalism.[30] Some party elements questioned part of Mao's "East Wind Prevails" theory and respected the Soviet judgment that the capitalist nations still retained the capability of total destruction. These elements, moreover, were anxious to capitalize on Soviet aid, especially in the field of nuclear weaponry, and they were sharply critical of those who minimized the danger of nuclear war and abused the Soviet preference for "peaceful coexistence" with the capitalist nations. Other elements, especially those convinced of the need for technical expertise and pragmatic programming, were repelled by the party's insistence on applying the "new equilibrium theory" at all levels of planning. Still other elements were distressed by the passionate, in fact compulsive, demand for ideological purity that unleashed a virulent antirightist campaign entailing the purge of more than 2,000 party members. Nevertheless, those who championed the so-called Maoist viewpoint had gained the upper hand within the party by 1958 and had thrust the state publicly into the Great Leap Forward movement under the banner of the Three Red Flags program.

Many China experts presume that Liu Shao-ch'i and Teng Hsiao-p'ing were, from the beginning, wholly antagonistic to the Great Leap Forward program. This contention, however, should be qualified. The Three Red Flags program—the people's communes, the Great Leap Forward, and the socialist construction movement—was officially adopted at the Second Plenary Session of the Eighth Central Committee, held between May 5 and 23, 1958. During the important preparatory stage of this session, Mao was in Canton, suffering from ill health. The agenda was prepared under the direction of Liu Shao-ch'i, the vice chairman, and Teng Hsiao-p'ing, the secretary general of the party.[31] It is unlikely, therefore, that Liu and Teng were, at that time, adamantly opposed to the principles symbolized by the Three Red Flags. Inasmuch as they were proponents of economic rationalism and pragmatic programming, they were, no doubt, chary about radical innovations. Still, there is little reason to assume, for example, that they were opposed to the basic idea of the people's commune movement. Under their leadership, the party had already endorsed the communal principle in theory, and in fact the government had already organized pilot communal projects. In the spring of 1958, these projects appeared to be remarkably successful and to offer the possibility of appreciably augmenting agricultural productivity. More-

[30] Donald S. Zagoria, *The Sino-Soviet Conflict, 1956–1961* (Princeton, N.J.: Princeton University Press, 1962), pp. 157–59.

[31] Ho Yü-wen, "Why Did Mao Tse-tung Bow Out?" p. 14.

over, as noted earlier, Liu had publicly affirmed in 1958 that "our revo-lution is intended to develop social productivity most quickly." In brief, Mao and Liu were both at this time proponents of a faster revolutionary tempo, with Liu preferring to step up the pace slowly and Mao anxious for more rapid acceleration.

The dominant sentiment within the party favored the Maoist view-point. In this mood, the party ruled in favor of a crash program in agri-culture and in industry, a program that stressed communes and the mobilization of workers and intellectuals by a zealous ideological cam-paign. By the end of August, according to official figures, 30 percent of all farm households in the nation had been communized.[32] And, judging by the press, those in charge of the communal movement were unani-mously reporting fantastic increases in productivity and total popular approval of the communal style of life. On the basis of these reports, the government even declared jubilantly that the communes had resulted in a striking increase in the yield of rice, in some instances to more than five hundred *tan* per *mu*.[33] Comparable statistics were marshalled on behalf of the production of steel by the "backyard furnaces" that had been programmed into the Great Leap Forward. These statistics and prognoses probably disarmed the initial reservations voiced by Liu and Teng against any radical implementation of the Three Red Flags pro-gram and instilled greater confidence and enthusiasm among those in the more radical party circles, including Chairman Mao.

Beginning in July, however, the successes of the "backyard furnaces" and of the people's communes, which had received such fulsome praise, were subjected to closer scrutiny and questioning. At a party conference held at Peitaiho in August, these critical voices became quite audible. Few details are known about this Peitaiho conference. There is reason to believe, however, that the Great Leap Forward policy was subjected openly to severe internal criticism but that, mainly because of Mao's strong adherence to the policies in effect, the party, after weeks of debate, announced on September 10 that the existing Three Red Flags program would continue.[34] With the dismal fall harvest and the inventory of the products produced by the backyard furnaces on hand, however, no one could deny any longer that the Great Leap Forward and the communes had been an unmitigated economic disaster. The Sixth Plenary Session of the Eighth Central Committee, held at Wuchang from November 18 to December 10, 1958, was a somber affair. After listening to the newly re-

[32] Statistics Bureau of the People's Republic of China, *Glorious Ten Years* (Peking: People's Publishing Office, 1959), p. 36.

[33] Compare Masatane Sugi, tr. and comp., *Four Hundred* Tan *Yield per Ten* Mu: *The Experiment of the Century* (Tokyo: Riron-sha, 1960).

[34] *People's Daily*, September 10, 1958.

vised reports on productivity, party officials conceded that the communes had, in fact, sharply reduced production. The "miraculous" rice yields cited in earlier reports had proven, on inspection, to have been rice planted just for show; and the vaunted backyard steel production was branded as no better than dregs, completely unusable for anything except simple farm tools.[35] The economy was in deep trouble, and the nation faced an acute food shortage and even the possibility of mass starvation. The pressing problem was no longer how far the nation could leap forward; the government had to cope with serious shortages in all sectors of the economy.

In this bleak context, Mao advised the party congress that he would not again assume the post of chairman of the party,[36] and five months afterwards Liu Shao-ch'i was elected chairman. Eight years later, speaking of this startling proposal, Mao confessed, "I was dissatisfied, but I was unable to do anything."[37] Two theories have been advanced by China experts to explain Mao's withdrawal at this Wuchang conference. One holds that Mao was forced to resign by the Liu faction, which had opposed the Great Leap Forward program from the beginning; the other maintains that Mao, assuming personal responsibility for the failure of the Great Leap Forward, voluntarily resigned his chairmanship before any explicit anti-Maoist mood could congeal in the party. If, as was suggested earlier, Mao and Liu had not already been seriously at odds during the formulation of the Three Red Flags program, disagreement between the two set in during the summer of 1958, when Liu responded quickly to the negative evidence but Mao preferred to discount it and to forge ahead with the communes. This disagreement, however, was not a personal power struggle between the two men. It was, as had happened in the past, a divergence of opinion over the tempo of the revolution. Thus, it would be a mistake to assume that Mao was personally attacked or deprived of power by the Liu faction at the Wuchang conference. In subsequent years, Mao enjoyed extremely high prestige in the party and was permitted to conduct his activities freely. It is reasonable, therefore, to conclude that Mao had retreated voluntarily from office in order to escape personal onus for the failures of the Great Leap Forward policy and that he was willing to entrust Liu and Teng with formal leadership during the inevitable reaction to the adverse consequences of that policy.[38] It would be a mistake, moreover, to assume that, with the Wuchang conference, Mao had become deeply antagonistic toward Liu's policies or

---

[35] Shigeo Oketani, "Steel Manufacturing by the Indigenous Method," *Chūō Kōron*, Vol. 79, No. 8 (August 1964), pp. 142–43.

[36] *People's Daily*, December 18, 1958.

[37] *Mainichi*, January 5, 1967.

[38] *Asahi*, January 7, 1967.

the Liu-Teng faction. Mao's later contention that he was "dissatisfied" with the outcome of the Wuchang conference should be read as a retrospective exaggeration. His sharp antagonism toward the Liu-Teng group and the genesis of the Great Cultural Revolution were most likely the consequences of events subsequent to 1959.

"Our Operations Had Not a Few Defects"

Little by little, following the Wuchang conference of December 1958, the Three Red Flags program was amended. Almost unnoticed, the third moderate stage of the revolution set in. By 1961, Liu Shao-ch'i could boldly admit that "our operation had not a few defects," and the party again publicly encouraged another free-speech movement.[39] This time, however, it took pains to constrict "free speech" by the sixfold criterion postulated by Mao's "On the Correct Handling of Contradictions Among the People," which had been published in June 1957. In addition, "free speech" was technically restricted to academic and cultural fields.[40] Nonetheless, a mood of liberalism soon spread throughout Chinese literary circles, and fine satires by Teng To, Wu Han, T'ien Han, and others appeared, one after another. This third moderate period has been termed the *Hsiao ming-fang*, or "small freedom of speech," and throughout it the party meticulously avoided any dramatic statements such as characterized the "great freedom of speech" campaign of 1957. Officially, party rhetoric praised the Three Red Flags and reasoned that the new moderation was part of this program—that, in fact, it was based upon the achievements of the Three Red Flags movement.

In other words, the radical tempo symbolized by the Three Red Flags was never denied in theory. In this sense, the genius of Mao's thought lies in its skillful combination of radicalism and flexibility. Thus, for example, when the party stressed "expertise" over "redness" in this third phase, it wrapped this change of policy in such terms as "flying high Mao Tse-tung's banner, thoroughly implementing the Three Red Flags and displaying the revolutionary spirit of Yenan, we will build our country into a powerful Communist State."[41] In short, the party, under the leadership of Liu and Teng, never denigrated Mao or Maoism. While conceding mistakes and defects in party organization, Liu was always careful to avoid any public criticism of the people's communes or any

[39] *People's Daily*, June 30, 1961.

[40] Dennis Doolin, "The Revival of the One Hundred Flowers Campaign: 1961," *China Quarterly*, No. 8 (October–December 1961), pp. 34–38.

[41] Kan Tzu-ts'ai, "Seventy-Article Educational Charter," *Tsu-kuo*, Vol. 40, No. 13 (December 24, 1962), pp. 16–19.

concrete censuring of the Great Leap Forward policy. Rather, under Liu's chairmanship, the party attributed the economic disasters caused by the communal movement to "natural calamities." At the same time, it adopted specific steps to cope with these so-called calamities of nature. The "backyard furnaces," for example, were legally abandoned under the "Seventy Article Industrial Charter," and the "Sixty Article Agricultural Charter" of 1960 was clandestinely labeled an "anticommunistic movement" by the people.[42] While manifestly praising Mao, Maoism, and the Three Red Flags, the party had, in fact, returned to the more flexible policies of the second moderate period.

There were, beyond doubt, great controversies within the party over the procedural question of how to combine the radicalism of the Three Red Flags with the specific task of recovering the productivity lost by the implementation of this program. Adherence to the principles of the Three Red Flags would have been an acceptance of the radical, or left-wing, approach to public policy, while any effort to promote agriculture by an outright appeal to the egoism of the peasant would have been subjected to the accusation of right-wing deviationism. Debates and controversies surely raged, generating passionate feelings about the course and tempo of the revolution. Unfortunately for historians, these arguments were not waged publicly. The Chinese Communists prefer understatement, calling these years "an adjustment period." Indeed they were, as the party supported the Maoist stand verbally while denying it in practice. Thus, for example, such "rightist" policies as the *san-tzu i-pao* and *tan-kan-feng* were sharply denied in the official statements of the party, but these policies were adopted nonetheless in order to cope with the economic crisis. The *san-tzu i-pao* was the program of expanding the amount of farmland the peasant could cultivate freely for himself while, at the same time, linking the produce of this land with a "free market" and a "free accounting system" in which each household was responsible for the producing, selling, and reporting of its production and income. The *tan-kan-feng* policy was a program for small-scale industry that entrusted it to private management and a free market comparable to that given to the peasant under the *san-tzu i-pao*. The party, under the direction of Liu and Teng, steadily castigated these policies in theory, but it also implemented them by endorsing specific exemptions and regulations.

A similar pattern prevailed in the educational realm. Under the Three Red Flags program, as mentioned earlier, the party had stressed the quality of "redness" over "expertness." In 1960, the government promulgated the "Seventy Article Educational Charter," which began with a ringing reaffirmation of the principles of the Three Red Flags and a theoretical

[42] "The 'Anti-Communistic Movement' and the 'Sixty-Article Agricultural Charter,' " *Tsu-kuo*, Vol. 36, No. 12 (December 18, 1961), pp. 5–8.

emphasis on redness over expertise. But then the charter proceeded, in substance, to contradict this theory. Intellectuals, for example, were notified that they should not spend more than three hours a week in physical labor, and workers were advised that they should not devote more than three hours a week to political studies.[43] In April 1961, once the acute food shortage had been alleviated somewhat by a good spring harvest, the government started to broadcast daily appeals to the students, urging them to "read hard" and to recognize that "to study is the essential duty of students." By April, the party's lip service to the rhetoric of "redness over expertness" had, in fact, been converted into a program directing Chinese "to be red and expert at the same time," and Ch'en Yi stressed repeatedly the necessity for expertise in the party.[44] As part of this switch in tone, some twenty-six thousand party members who had been purged as "rightists" during the heyday of the Great Leap Forward were officially restored to party respectability. This pattern—a rhetorical affirmation of the ideology of the Three Red Flags joined with a practical negation of the specific programs adopted as part of the Great Leap Forward—also duplicated itself, albeit to a lesser degree, in the realm of foreign policy. Here, too, the tough ideology of the "East Wind Prevails" doctrine was praised in theory, while in fact, following the 1958 Wuchang conference, specific policies and behavior became more prudent and flexible.

On foreign-policy matters, the leaders of Communist China have not been inclined to compromise or make concessions on issues involving what they call "fundamental principles."[45] Moreover, once they have transformed a question or issue into a matter of basic principles, they set in motion what can be called "the law of accumulation of involvements,"[46] which brings about a series of reactions and deeds that make it virtually impossible to return to the state of affairs existing before the "principles" were invoked. The most obvious illustration of the "accumulation of involvements" is the Sino-Soviet dispute. Beginning in 1950, with the Sino-Soviet security and trade pacts, the Soviet Union was idolized as the exclusive model for China's economic and technological development. Once Mao's doctrine of "the East Wind Prevails" became a cardinal principle of China's policy, however, the dispute with the Soviet Union over how to cope with the capitalist nations became a question of strategy, not tactics. China's distrust of the Soviets came to the forefront after 1959

[43] Kan Tzu-ts'ai, "Seventy Article Educational Charter," pp. 16–19.

[44] "A Lecture to Graduating Students of the Peking Municipal High School," March 19, 1962, in *Chung-kuo Ch'ing-nien* [Chinese youth], No. 17 (1961).

[45] Shinkichi Etō and Tatsumi Okabe, "Principles of Action of Chinese Foreign Policy," *Jiyū* (March 1965).

[46] Shinkichi Etō, "Doctrine of Non-Intervention," *Chūō Kōron*, Vol. 80, No. 8 (August 1965).

and fostered the accusation that Russian leaders were "revisionist traitors" who were compromising with the imperialists. This charge bred another principle—namely, that the confrontation with Soviet revisionism was as important as the fight against imperialism. In response, of course, the Soviet Union withdrew its advisers, ceased its aid program, and challenged the "chauvinism" of the Chinese. In turn, the Chinese pursued a course of "self-reliance."

This Sino-Soviet pattern of dispute accumulating on dispute became linked to another issue that the Chinese Communists have considered to be a matter of fundamental principle—the insistence that Taiwan is an inherent part of the People's Republic. During the civil war, and especially in the early years (1949–53) of the Peking government, the Communists branded Chiang Kai-shek a traitor and named American imperialism as the most important single force sustaining Chiang's regime on Taiwan. Yet, in the second moderate phase of the revolution (1953–57), even Mao expounded as a possibility the doctrine of a peaceful liberation of the island by Nationalist-Communist cooperation. But in the second radical period, along with the Three Red Flags, the Chinese Communist party adopted, as a matter of principle, a policy of confrontation with Taiwan and American imperialism. This policy began when the Chinese initiated the bombardment of Quemoy and Matsu and has, in theory, remained unchanged. Indeed, it became deeply interwoven with Chinese policy vis-à-vis the Soviet Union when, during his visit to Peking in 1959, Khrushchev urged a policy of coexistence toward the United States and Taiwan. Even though Mao had articulated the same line several years before, the party promptly condemned Soviet "revisionism" as being synonymous with the imperialist's "two China" policy.[47] The Chinese Communists would not let the Soviet Union pressure them into compromising the "principle" of liberating Taiwan, and, instead, they responded with the accusation that the Soviet Union was a traitor to the socialist bloc.

The Chinese Communists have not been able to deny the ideological principles enumerated as part of the Three Red Flags. In terms of internal affairs, as noted, this fact did not prevent the practical modification of radical principles during the third moderate period (1959–66). In terms of foreign affairs, however, the theoretical adherence to radical principles automatically intensified the rift with the Soviet Union, without causing any amelioration in China's anti-imperialist posture. Even so, in reference to Asian countries, as opposed to the Soviet Union and the United States, the Chinese Communists have been flexible. Toward India, China adopted a hard-line approach, precipitating the 1962 clash. But

[47] *People's Daily*, September 1, 1963.

the advantages won on the battlefield were not pursued; and, more important, between 1962 and 1964 the Chinese government concluded border demarcation treaties and nonaggression pacts with Pakistan, Burma, Mongolia, Afghanistan, Nepal, and Cambodia. In these cases, China articulated no general or fundamental principles that would have precluded a search for accommodation. More strikingly, the Chinese Communists have attenuated their passionate abuse of their former enemy, Japan. When the Soviet Union started to pull out of China, the Chinese sought to open trade with Japan, but in 1958 the tough diplomacy of the Kishi cabinet provoked a suspension of all trade. Yet, despite Japan's role as a past invader of China, despite Japan's existing alliance with the United States, and despite Japan's recognition of Taiwan, the Chinese Communists did not invoke any "principle" against Japanese trade. On the contrary, once the Ikeda cabinet was organized in 1960, the Peking regime softened its verbal abuse of Japan and called for a resumption of trade under the slogan "Friendship trade." This led, in 1962, to the so-called L-T (Liao Ch'eng-chih and Takahashi Tatsunosuke) accord, by which an informal trade system was established. And in 1964 the Chinese Communists went so far as to discuss the possibility of organizing a conference between Japanese and Chinese government officials.[48]

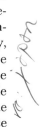

In effect, beginning in 1959 and continuing for several years thereafter, Communist China maintained a theoretically hard-line approach toward the Soviet Union and the United States. In domestic affairs, it reaffirmed, in theory, the basic principles of the Three Red Flags movement. At the same time, however, it pursued a cautious and softer diplomacy vis-à-vis the Asian nations on its borders, and it sharply slowed down the pace of socialization in order to recover the agricultural and industrial productivity that had been disrupted by the Great Leap Forward.

The Class Struggle

As has been outlined, the policies of the Chinese Communist party have made pendulum-like swings between moderate and radical programs. Each of these swings has represented a shift in political power within the party. In the first Five-Year Plan of the second moderate period, for example, those who stressed economic rationalism came to the forefront; but they were overshadowed in the second radical period by those who championed the communal movement. Throughout these swings, the party skillfully combined both right- and left-wing elements, granting each a large measure of flexibility. Perhaps the most outstanding example

[48] Shun'ichi Matsumoto, "My Visit to Communist China," *Kasumigaseki-kai Bulletin,* July 1964.

of this practice has been the career of Ch'en Yun.[49] A strong proponent of economic rationalism, Ch'en abruptly disappeared from public view at the onset of the Great Leap Forward program, only to resurface during the acute financial crisis of 1962, when he was again entrusted with important positions. The tension between the right and left factions of the party became very acute by 1963, when it seemed, from the viewpoint of the more radical Maoist elements, that the party was moving toward capitalism in the economic recovery program directed by Liu Shao-ch'i and Tseng Hsiao-p'ing. In view of the dismal record of the communes, however, the Maoists could hardly criticize the economic rationalism symbolized by a Ch'en Yun. Instead, they directed their fire against the "cultural" aspects of the programs adopted after the 1958 Wuchang conference.

Under the "small freedom of speech" movement, a number of fine satires appeared. The most outstanding satirist, Wu Han, even subjected Chairman Mao to some sharp criticism; and, in addition, the writings of Teng To, T'ien Han, and Hsia Yen reflected a caustic approach to the party's programs under Mao's leadership. Responding to this development at the Tenth Plenary Session of the Central Committee in 1962, Mao demanded and received a party resolution stressing the absolute need of all party members "not to forget the class struggle."[50] In December, Mao blasted the tendency of the party to entrust the fine arts to men who were inclined to ignore the class struggle and to advocate feudalistic and capitalistic art. Six months later, in June 1963, Mao, claiming that almost all works in the fields of art and literature had failed to adhere to the directives of the party, preached the need for a basic reform of the cultural aspects of the revolution. Another indicator of this sense of unrest among the left-wing elements of the party was the accusation by Chiang Ch'ing, Mao's wife, that the Peking opera should be revamped because it was being staged in ways that perpetuated traditional values.[51]

These salvos by Madam and Chairman Mao symbolized a keen dissatisfaction with the moderate programs of Liu Shao-ch'i and Teng Hsiao-p'ing. In view of the economic successes realized under these men, this unrest could not pass beyond an indirect indictment of the writers and artists for their failure to depict the class struggle in the cultural fields. In February 1965, however, the American involvement in Vietnam provided the more radical elements of the party with a new issue. From September to October, during a series of party conferences, Mao made

[49] *Mainichi*, January 28, 1967.

[50] *Liberation Army's Daily*, June 6, 1966.

[51] Later, some would declare that Chiang Ch'ing's critique of the Peking opera was the start of the Cultural Revolution. (*Liberation Army's Daily*, January 7, 1967.)

many appeals to the sense of crisis confronting the nation, linking the failures in the cultural fields to the threat raised by the United States. Finally, on November 10, under Mao's instructions, a hitherto obscure member of the editorial staff of the Shanghai *Liberation Daily,* Yao Wen-yuan, savagely abused the distinguished Wu Han, deputy mayor of Peking, a prominent member of the Philosophy and Social Science Department of the Chinese Academy of Sciences, and one of China's most respected writers.[52]

In 1959 Wu Han had written a drama, *The Dismissal of Hai Jui from Office,* patterned after an upright mandarin of the Ming dynasty. Most of Yao's criticism of this play voiced sentiments common to the left-wing partisans of proletarian literature; that is, he stressed that while Hai Jui may have been a respectable individual, he was, nonetheless, a representative of the landlord class. Unlike earlier abuses of Wu Han's play, Yao's literary criticism concluded with a polemic on national policy. "Everyone knows," Yao remarked, "that, in 1961, when our country faced economic difficulties for a while because of the natural calamities in three consecutive years and when imperialism, reactionaries of various countries, and modern revisionism aggravated anti-Chinese moves, goblins started a gust of *tan-kan-feng* and *fan-an-feng.*"[53] (Reference to these "goblins," especially the *fan-an-feng,* meant the demand for a retrial of those who had been expelled from the party for being "rightists" during the apex of the Great Leap Forward program.) In his drama, Wu Han had praised Hai Jui's recovery of lands for peasants from crafty landowners and bureaucrats and his retrial of those who had been convicted under false charges. In allusion to this, Yao said,

> What superiority of private management do they advocate, why do they demand the return to private economy, and why do they demand recovery of lands? This means nothing but destroying the people's commune system and restoring evil rule by landlords and rich farmers. It is imperialists, landlords, rich farmers, reactionaries, villains and right-wingers who convicted countless working people under false charges in old society. Having lost the right to make up false charges, they claim that their being overthrown is illegal. What kind of acquittal are they crying for wilfully?[54]

In brief, Yao branded all that Wu Han had said, whether intentional or not, as opposing the Great Leap Forward and the people's communes.

Prior to the essay, literary and academic disputes had been restricted to the areas of arts and learning. Yao Wen-yuan's polemic, however, was

[52] *People's Daily,* November 30, 1965; also, *Mainichi,* April 27, 1967.
[53] *People's Daily,* November 30, 1965.
[54] *Ibid.*

a frontal attack on Wu Han's political positions, and it has been popularly regarded by the Maoist elements as the starting signal of the Cultural Revolution. Thus, the Red Guard journal *Tung-fang Hung,* in an editorial against the Liu-Teng policies, declared:

> The Great Cultural Revolution began with *The Dismissal of Hai Jui from Office.* Chairman Mao pointed out that the critical point of *The Dismissal of Hai Jui from Office* was the question of political struggle and that this drama should be completely criticized on this issue. Liu Shao-ch'i, in conspiracy with the P'eng Chen Group, however, made frantic efforts to drag the political struggle of *The Dismissal of Hai Jui from Office* into the alley of academic debates. . . .[55]

The Maoists, as represented by the party hack Yao Wen-yuan, argued, in effect, that the class struggle should never be forgotten, that Wu Han had ignored this point, that Wu's drama about Hai Jui was a satire on the Great Leap Forward policy, and that the writings of Wu Han were the prelude to a revival of capitalism.

The Class Struggle Reflected in the Party

The blistering polemic against Wu Han was followed by comparable indictments of P'eng Chen, Chou Yang, Ch'ien Po-tsan, Teng To, Teng Hsiao-p'ing, and Liu Shao-ch'i. Sometimes the radical critics voiced far-fetched accusations; at other times they invoked such nebulous criteria as "anti-Maoist" or "antisocialist." Essentially, however, the logic of the Maoist elements was based on four points.[56] First, they charged that Liu Shao-ch'i and company were pursuing bourgeois policies, especially in their enforcement of moderate aims in opposition to the Great Leap Forward. Second, they claimed that these men had forgotten the fundamental principle of the class struggle, with the result that they not only had placed cultural and academic disputes into a bourgeois framework but also had protected bourgeois thought after it had appeared. Third, they charged that Liu's group advocated the increase of productivity by appeals to the egoism, individual initiative, and equality of all human beings, a cluster of traits that completely ignored the issue of class struggle.

[55] *Tung-fang Hung,* December 31, 1966.

[56] The criticisms of Liu Shao-ch'i that appeared in early 1967 are especially concrete and interesting. See, for example, Ch'i Pen-yü, "Patriotism or Traitor-ism," *Red Flag,* No. 5 (1967). A bulk of other criticisms of Liu appeared in the Red Guard journals *Chan-pao* [War report], *Tung-fang Hung* [East is Red], *Shou-tu Hung-wei-ping* [Capital city Red Guards], and *Chingkangshan* [Mount Chingkang]. These are reprinted in Japanese translation in the mimeographed "Collection of Materials Concerning the Great Cultural Revolution of Communist China Obtained from Red Guard Papers, Continued," *Mainichi,* April 6, 1967.

Fourth, they insisted that Liu's group had distorted Mao's personal instructions on the centrality of the class struggle in all fields.

These criticisms obviously represented a powerful reaction to the moderate policies pursued after 1958. As important, the critics stressed the principle of the class struggle as their decisive ideological axiom. With it, they branded the moderate policies of Liu Shao-ch'i as revisionist, as policies that were reviving capitalism. This indictment constituted the main thrust of the Maoist position, and it meant that the targets of the Great Cultural Revolution were not confined to a limited segment of the nation, to a few die-hards of the old capitalistic system or their fellow travelers. The proponents of the Cultural Revolution were attacking the leaders of the party itself—specifically, those who had been responsible for the moderate economic, cultural, and diplomatic policies of the post-1958 period.

Of the four main types of criticism articulated by the Maoists, the accusation that the party leaders had distorted Mao's instructions was the most delicate issue. In May 1963, the party adopted ten articles for farm-village operations, the so-called Anterior Ten Articles.[57] These articles were allegedly drafted by Mao himself, and they placed extreme emphasis on the principle of class struggle. In September 1963, however, the party drafted a set of concrete instructions for the implementation of the Anterior Ten Articles.[58] These instructions, popularly known as the Posterior Ten Articles, substituted the process of "unity-criticism-unity" for class struggle and instructed the cadre to treat those elements who had followed mistaken policies as "contradictions among the people" that could be reformed by a process of education. The ultimate goal, according to the Posterior Articles, was the increase of production for "mutual enrichment."

These articles, as well as the earlier, moderate "Sixty Article Agricultural Charter," which had censured the communal movement, were prepared under the direction of Teng Hsiao-p'ing, P'eng Chen, and Liu Shao-ch'i.[59] In view of the generally moderate policies pursued by these men after 1958, as well as the specifics contained in the Posterior Articles, the Maoists believed that these men were waving the Three Red Flags theoretically in order to subvert their principles in practice. And, in fact, their accusations were partly correct. A content analysis of the *People's*

---

[57] Chinese Communist Party, "A Decision on Some Problems of Immediate Farm Village Operations" (draft), reprinted by the National Security Bureau of the People's Republic of China (Taipei: 1965).

[58] Chinese Communist Party, "Regulations Concerning Some Concrete Policies of the Socialist Education Movement in Farm Villages" (draft), reprinted by the National Security Bureau of the People's Republic of China (Taipei: 1965).

[59] "The Many Crimes of Teng Hsiao-p'ing," in *Chan-pao*, No. 3 (January 19, 1967).

Party editorials after 1958 reveals a marked decrease in references to Mao Tse-tung. Unquestionably, at all levels, Mao's personal leadership and prestige were weakened in the 1958–65 period. This fact, plus the successful agricultural policies of the so-called revisionists, undeniably intensified a feeling of crisis among the radical Maoist elements. This feeling, combined with developments in the army and American involvement in the Vietnam war, unleashed the Great Cultural Revolution.

The dismal consequences of the Great Leap Forward had produced a shift to moderation after 1960, including a gradual but undeniable downplaying of Chairman Mao. The agricultural crisis, which led to moderation in governmental policies, also posed grave problems to the People's Liberation Army.[60] The soldiers, deeply disturbed by the threat of starvation to their families, became demoralized. Discipline collapsed in many units, orders were disobeyed, and riots even broke out. This problem could not be resolved by appeals to personal incentives, as it could in the civilian sector. In contrast to the party, which turned to economic rationalism and the downplaying of Mao's thought, the army, under the leadership of Defense Minister Lin Piao and Chief of the General Staff Lo Jui-ch'ing, launched a vigorous ideological campaign in order to restore discipline and morale. In short, the military directed a campaign to study the thoughts of Chairman Mao—a program that, of course, canonized Mao within the army. Later, one unanticipated consequence of this campaign would be the army's crucial support of the Maoist elements during the Cultural Revolution.[61]

American Aggression: Will It Attack China?

Although the initial impetus behind the army's stress on Mao's thoughts had been the problem of morale, the program was reinforced by American involvement in the Vietnam war. When American troops were directly committed in February 1965, the People's Liberation Army faced the old but always new question of whether it should counter the external threat with a modern military-industrial response or a conventional

---

[60] A rich source of this kind of information is *Kungtso T'unghsün* [Work bulletin], a classified periodical for Liberation Army officers released by the Department of State in 1964. Problematical points are concisely presented in Akira Kawaguchi, "The Undercurrent of the Great Cultural Revolution: A Clash of Two Stands over the Process of Modernization," *Monthly Report of Research*, Japanese Ministry of Foreign Affairs, Vol. 8, No. 4 (April 1967).

[61] Yūji Muramatsu, "This Is China," *Yomiuri*, April 18, 1967; Masanori Kikuchi, "The Undercurrent of the Great Cultural Revolution," *Asahi*, May 13, 1967; Reporter Hori, "The Background of P'eng Chen's Deposition," *Tokyo Shimbun*, May 23, 1967; Reporter Yoshida, "The Course of China," Part II, *Asahi*, September 8, 1966.

people's guerrilla war. In addition, the struggle against Western imperialists was now entangled with the problem of Sino-Soviet relations.[62] When the United States started to bomb North Vietnam, it had made certain calculations designed to control the extent and stages of escalation. From the Chinese perspective, however, there was a great deal of uncertainty about the ultimate intent and scope of the American action. If the United States were to bomb Chinese positions, China would have to cooperate with the Soviet Union. This, of course, would entail a radical shift in tone, if not an outright abandonment of Mao's abuse of the Soviet Union. And, in fact, during the opening months of the bombing of North Vietnam, the Chinese ceased all criticism of the Soviet Union, resuming their diatribes only after it became manifest that the United States was determined to avoid a major war against North Vietnam.

The uncertainty about American policy, when coupled with the acrimonious Sino-Soviet dispute, posed grave strategic issues for the Chinese. In 1959, Defense Minister P'eng Te-huai had been purged, first, for arguing that China could not confront the American imperialists without a close military alliance with the Soviet Union and, second, for insisting that industrial strength was the key to a modern army, thus putting himself at odds with the radical Great Leap Forward movement. As a consequence of his approach, P'eng was replaced by Lin Piao, who was an advocate of the radical movement.

At first, Lin had the firm support of General Lo, the chief of staff. When confronted with the American intervention in the Vietnam war, however, General Lo began to disagree with his superior. On May 11, 1965, General Lo presented the outlines of his "aggressive defense" strategy in the *People's Daily*.[63] He argued that it would not suffice to possess one or two (presumably nuclear) weapons. A modern army, he insisted, must have a firm economic foundation, which would require a great deal of time to construct. Until China developed an industrial complex, Lo reasoned, it would have to bide its time by allying itself with the Soviet Union and by supporting revolutionary movements throughout the world. Lo's "aggressive defense" was a restatement of Marshall P'eng's doctrine, and it contradicted the basic strategy of Mao Tse-tung. On September 3, 1965, Marshall Lin Piao set aside Lo's strategy with a ringing affirmation of Mao's reliance on a people's war.[64] Here, Lin faithfully praised the strategies employed by Mao against the Japanese invaders in 1937–45. In

[62] Compare Tatsumi Okabe, "Communist China's Strategic Thought," in *Chōsa Geppō* [Monthly report of research], Ministry of Foreign Affairs, Vol. 8, No. 3 (March 1967).

[63] Lo Jui-ch'ing, "An Article Written to Commemorate the Victory over German Fascism and to Carry Through the Struggle Against American Imperialism," *People's Daily*, May 11, 1965.

[64] "Long Live the Victory of the People's War," *People's Daily*, September 3, 1965.

particular, he argued that the imperialists were mounting a major war and that Chinese territory, not the United States, would be the field for a confrontation with American imperialism. With this premise, Lin reasoned that China should lie in wait for the American invaders and then drown them in a sea of seven hundred million Chinese. As part of this strategy, Lin called for arming the people with the thoughts of Mao Tse-tung as the first priority.

From some points of view, Lin's strategy appeared outdated, a reliance on bygone campaigns. Still, if one assumes, as Lin and Mao apparently did, that the United States would attack China before it could build a modern military-industrial complex and that the Soviet Union would betray China and encourage the American imperialists, then the strategies of Lin and Mao become much less irrational. Assuming a Soviet-American conspiracy against China, Lo's strategy would be a disaster. Underlying these two strategic doctrines is a considerable difference in assessments of international politics. On the basis of available evidence, one must surmise—though it is by no means certain—that Mao and Lin believe that the United States will attack China and that the Soviet Union will not be a reliable ally. In any case, it is clear that the American involvement in Vietnam has contributed to the popularity and effectiveness of Lin's concept. In this sense, the Vietnam war contributed directly to the Cultural Revolution, to the sense of crisis confronting China, and to the stress on Mao's thoughts as the basis for resolving domestic and foreign problems.

Six Principles of Communist China

During the past twenty years, the policies of Communist China have oscillated between moderation and radicalism. Against this background, the inception of the Great Cultural Revolution can be seen as a sharp reaction to the third moderate period. Despite this oscillation between the moderate and radical poles, however, one can discern some basic principles or patterns that could be called characteristic of contemporary China. In general terms, the policies of Communist China are governed by six basic principles: (1) an affirmation of the infallibility of Mao Tse-tung, (2) a nationalistic Chinese Marxism-Leninism, (3) a principle-oriented flexibility, (4) Mao's four principles of guerrilla warfare, (5) the centrality of a military orientation, and (6) an emphasis on spiritual elements. Although all six traits are important, the most significant principle has been the infallibility of Mao.

1. As mentioned, Marshall Lin relied on the potency of political indoctrination based on the thought of Mao. The Liberation Army's campaign to study Mao's thoughts and ideas was later emulated on a nationwide scale in the Cultural Revolution. Particular emphasis was placed on the

indoctrination of the younger generation, which had not personally experienced the difficult and bloody days of the pre-1949 Chinese Communist movement. Consequently, Chinese leaders invariably decorated their speeches and writings with the stereotyped expression, "under the accurate leadership of Comrade Mao Tse-tung." Even the successful nuclear tests were proclaimed to be an accomplishment of "hoisting the great red flag of Mao's thought." So, too, a victory by Chinese ping-pong teams in a contest with Japanese teams was attributed to the "stubborn-minded military gymnastic battalion" of the team that had "armed themselves with the spirit of Mao Tse-tung."[65]

This adulation of Mao's thoughts has also affected the party's official interpretation of its own history. It has claimed, for example, that several serious mistakes were made by the leadership of left-wing adventurers during the Kiangsi Soviet era in the 1930's, and that not until Mao assumed party leadership at the Tsun-i conference in 1935 did the party start, for the first time, to march along the "correct" line of the revolution. Actually, however, a study based on original Chinese Communist sources from the Ch'en Ch'eng collection clarifies the powerful and vital role Mao played in the Kiangsi Soviet.[66] Accordingly, Mao should share the responsibility for some of the early decisions that have since been credited to left-wing adventurers.

From some points of view, it may seem absurd that victory in ping-pong games and success in nuclear weapons are equally attributed to the inspiration of Chairman Mao. What it signifies, however, is that, whether or not the old revolutionary actually participates in decision-making activities of the party, all contending elements, moderates and radicals, advance and defend their proposals by means of references to the thoughts of Mao. The writings of Mao Tse-tung are utilized as precedents and guideposts in all policy discussions and decisions. If only for this reason, therefore, it is imperative that anyone interested in studying Communist China digest thoroughly the works of Mao. This is an indispensible requisite for an understanding of contemporary policies and attitudes of the Peking government.

2. Closely related to the adulation of Mao is the fact that Chinese Communist leaders are and have been primarily nationalists. China suffered many humiliations from Westerners in the past century, and Chinese intellectuals, particularly the younger ones, resented deeply the political disintegration and the turmoil of their homeland. They turned to Marxism-Leninism merely as a means by which to achieve their nationalistic desires—to recover China's national integrity and dignity. Moreover, the historical context of the Chinese revolution differed radically from

---

[65] *People's Daily*, April 20, 1965.

[66] Ryoko Ishida, "The Political Leadership of Mao Tse-tung in the Kiangsi Soviet" (M.A. thesis, Department of International Relations, University of Tokyo, 1965).

that of the Russian Revolution. On the eve of the October Revolution, the major target of the Russian revolutionists was the annihilation of the bourgeoisie in Russia. Since the domestic class struggle was the crucial issue, Lenin, in order to protect the domestic revolution, advocated peace with Imperial Germany, no matter how harsh the German demands might be. In contrast, on the eve of the Chinese revolution, the major target of the Chinese revolutionists was Japan. In this context, the Chinese Communists, in order to protect their revolution, advocated a national united front and a war against the foreign invader. While the Russian revolutionaries in 1917 and 1918 shouted, "Peace in order to protect the revolution!" the Chinese Communists firmly believed that "a righteous war against foreign imperialism" was indispensable in achieving the ends of their revolution.

This past history is not unrelated to contemporary differences of opinion between Soviet and Chinese leaders. As the Sino-Soviet dispute became increasingly tense, there emerged an image of China shared by the Soviet Union and the Western world—namely, that Communist China is inherently expansionistic and is distinguished by atavistic ideas of Sino-centrism. Thus, for example, R. V. Vyatkin and S. L. Tikhvinskii, two leading Sinologists in the Soviet Union, bitterly indicted recent Chinese historical studies as being jingoistic and contrary to Marxism-Leninism.[67] Unquestionably, many outsiders fear that Communist China will eventually claim territorial rights over peripheral areas formerly under the hegemony of the Ch'ing dynasty. In fact, Mao once wrote that the imperialist states had stolen many of the Chinese tributaries and a part of China's territory—that Japan had occupied Korea, Taiwan, the Ryukyus, the Pescadores, and Port Arthur; that England had occupied Burma, Bhutan, Nepal, and Hong Kong; that France had taken Vietnam; and that even tiny Portugal had occupied Macao.[68]

This proclamation has often been cited as tangible evidence that China, under Mao, is seeking a restoration of these areas, but this seems highly unlikely. First of all, any such territorial claims would threaten the people in those areas and drive them to an anti-Chinese position, which would run counter to the great importance the leaders of the Chinese Communist party have in the past placed on the subjective feelings of native people. Second, China's short-term strategy is to isolate American imperialism and to create as broad a united front as possible against the United States. The ultimate long-term strategy is to bolshevize the world. In order to achieve both aims, China needs to foster friendly relationships

---

[67] Compare R. V. Vyatkin and S. L. Tikhvinskii, "O Nekotorik Voprosak Istoricheskoi Nauki v KNR," *Voprosy Historii*, No. 10 (1963).

[68] "The Chinese Revolution and the Chinese Communist Party" (pamphlet), Hong Kong, 1940, p. 10.

with its neighbors. Third, the border agreements that China concluded with its neighbors in 1960–63 make it obvious that China's second short-term strategy is to stabilize its borders. In every border agreement, China was quite flexible, often yielding ground. Fourth, the Chinese Communists have a long experience of national humiliation and of nationalist struggle, and they understand the fierce nationalism of their neighbors. With the exception of the Sino-Indian border dispute, China has maintained an attitude of self-restraint toward its Asian neighbors. The Chinese leaders have been careful and calculating, and it is unlikely that they will resort to any aggressive action unless they feel certain that China can draw some profit from it. One could interpret various events as indicative of China's territorial ambitions—for example, the Sino-Indian border dispute, Mao's claim to Outer Mongolia,[69] and the Taiwan issue. However, there are other explanations for these events, and, although one cannot deny the possible existence of a Sino-centric mentality in the psychology of the Chinese Communists, China's nationalistic fervor seems unlikely to be transformed into unlimited expansionism or the atavism of the old Sino-centrism as long as its neighbors do not seem to threaten China's major principles and interests.

3. The doctrinal praise of Mao's thought and the nationalistic basis of Chinese Communism have not produced excessive rigidity or dogmatism in specific foreign or domestic policies. On the contrary, a principle-oriented flexibility has distinguished the thought and behavior of Communist China. "We should," Mao affirmed, "be firm in principle; we should also have all the flexibility permissible and necessary for carrying out our principles."[70] In restating one of Lenin's maxims, Mao insisted that the "soul" of Marxism is the careful analysis of specific conditions.[71] And, in his famous essay "On Contradiction," Mao defined "investigation" as the process of ascertaining what principle ought to be applied in any given concrete situation and then how flexible the specific acts should be in order to achieve the correct principles.[72] In practice, Mao and the party have constantly adhered to "principles," while at the same time displaying surprising flexibility in practice. In 1936, for example, the party defined the formation of an anti-Japanese national front as the basic principle involved in the concrete situation of Chinese politics. With this prin-

---

[69] In his conversation with the delegates of the Japanese Socialist Party on July 10, 1964, Mao told them that in 1954 he had asked Khrushchev and Bulganin to return Outer Mongolia to China.

[70] Mao Tse-tung, "Report to the Second Plenum of the Central Committee of the Seventh National Congress, March 5, 1949," in *Selected Works of Mao Tse-tung*, Vol. 5, p. 372.

[71] "On Contradictions," in *Selected Works of Mao Tse-tung*, Vol. 2, p. 26.

[72] *Ibid.*, pp. 41–42.

ciple, the party decided that the "main contradiction" in this context was the conflict between Japanese aggression and the resistance of the Chinese people. Acting on this "investigation," the party abandoned its hitherto basic principle, land reform, in order to reach an accommodation with the nationalistic government. Also, in conformity with this investigation, it accepted the Comintern suggestion that it release Chiang Kai-shek, after he had been "kidnapped" in the famous Sian incident of December 1936. These moves are but two of many examples of the principle-oriented flexibility displayed by the Chinese Communists.

Today, the Chinese Communist party's "investigation" of the concrete state of affairs has produced the principle that the "main contradiction" is the conflict between American imperialism and the Chinese people.[73] This principle has defined two major neutral "zones" outside of China. In the first zone—Asia, Africa, and Central-South America—all the people, it says, are fighting American imperialism, while in the second zone—New Zealand, Canada, Japan, and Western Europe—many of the people are fighting American imperialism. In both zones, the Chinese Communists are prepared to encourage any and all anti-American sentiments and movements, whether or not they be directed or organized by local communist parties. In the case of Japan, for example, the party has enough flexibility to cultivate close contacts with those Japanese conservative groups that advocate anti-American policies. Indeed, in the logic of the Chinese Communists, any action that produces conflict with American imperialism must contribute to the ultimate resolution of the existing basic principle—the contradiction between American imperialism and the Chinese people. Therefore, within the confines of this principle, the Chinese government has unusual flexibility in the specific actions and programs it can pursue.

4. The fourth characteristic of Chinese thought has been Mao's four principles of guerrilla warfare. After the failure of the Autumn Harvest insurrection of 1927 in the four provinces of South China, Mao and his troops, exhausted by defeat and hunger, found their way to Chingkangshan. Here, as is well known, Mao and Chu Teh devised a strategy of guerrilla warfare based on their painful experiences. Mao summarized these tactics in four easily remembered principles: "Enemy advances, we retreat; enemy camps, we harass; enemy tires, we attack; enemy retreats, we pursue."[74] The first principle may be interpreted as a policy of prudence. Mao, for example, warned that the party should not fight when it does not have the ability to win. In striking contrast to militarist leaders in prewar Japan, the Chinese Communists have avoided great risks comparable to the attack on Pearl Harbor, and it is inconceivable that Communist

---

[73] *People's Daily*, January 21, 1964.

[74] "A Single Spark Can Start a Prairie Fire," in *Selected Works of Mao Tse-tung*, Vol. 1, p. 124.

China will resort to an aggressive policy that entails a strategic risk to the People's Republic.

The second principle, "enemy camps, we harass," is the strategy of pursuing disturbing activities. Thus, for example, as soon as General de Gaulle began to pursue policies that created friction in the NATO alliance, Communist China promptly approached France. De Gaulle responded by recognizing the Peking government, and the ensuing entente between Paris and Peking shocked the United States. Another application of this second maxim was Communist China's wholehearted support of Indonesia's withdrawal from the United Nations. Branding the existing United Nations as an organ manipulated by imperialist powers, Chou En-lai stated unhesitatingly that it would be a good idea to create a new United Nations, entirely different from the present organization. In fact, Communist China consciously promotes all efforts that disturb the present organization of the United Nations, which includes Nationalist China as one of the permanent members of the Security Council.

In the present context, the third principle, "enemy tires, we attack," can be taken to mean that the Chinese ultimately aspire to win an overwhelming victory over American imperialism. Still, Mao, in his essay "On Protracted War," advocated that a decisive attack should be made only when victory was absolutely certain.[75] In fact, Mao's strategy in the war against Japan was to concentrate at least three times the strength of his enemy at their weakest point. In the fall of 1937, for example, the powerful Japanese Fifth Division was marching through P'ing-hsing-kuan valley in Shansi province. The Chinese Eighth Route Army remained quietly in the hills and did not move until the major part of the Japanese division had passed through the valley. Then it ambushed the last part of the marching division, a transport corps, defeating it quite easily. Before it could be reinforced, the Chinese Communist army had quietly disappeared.

The fourth principle of guerrilla tactics, "enemy retreats, we pursue," suggests that Communist China will capitalize on any advantage in order to widen its sphere of influence. For example, wherever and whenever there emerges an independent country in the first neutral zone (which the Chinese Communists consider the major battlefield in the attempt to defeat American imperialism), the Chinese will continue to attempt to infiltrate this zone and promote anti-American movements.

5. These guerrilla-warfare maxims are part of a broader militaristic orientation that has characterized the Chinese Communist movement. As is well known, Mao attaches great importance to weapons and warfare. "Political power," he declared, "grows out of the barrel of a gun."[76] And, he added, "Yes, we are advocates of the omnipotence of revolutionary war.

[75] "On Protracted War," in *Selected Works of Mao Tse-tung*, Vol. 2, pp. 180–83.
[76] "Problems of War and Strategy," in *Selected Works of Mao Tse-tung*, Vol. 2, p. 224.

. . . We may say that only with guns can the whole world be transformed."[77] Since Mao and other leaders of his generation have survived continuous revolutionary wars, they know well the importance of weapons in the realization of political aims. This lesson has been applied in the Sino-Soviet dispute, in which the Chinese Communists repeatedly insist that peace will be obtained not by begging for it but by fighting for it. In brief, it is impossible to detect any pacifistic elements in the philosophy of the Chinese Communist party. Imperialism, Mao proclaimed, is a tiger. "Either kill the tiger or be eaten by him—one or the other."[78] In line with this attitude, Communist China has not hesitated to produce nuclear weapons, and it will continue in its efforts to catch up with American military power. Moreover, the Chinese Communists will be prepared to use these weapons whenever they may feel it necessary to do so. Moreover, although many Asian nations were surprised at the Chinese invasion of India, it was perfectly consistent with China's philosophy of relying on military power in order to achieve political purposes.

6. Notwithstanding the centrality of weapons and warfare in Communist thinking, the Chinese have also emphasized the spiritual elements in policies, politics, and war. "Whatever is done," Mao wrote, "has to be done by human beings; protracted war and final victory will not come about without human action."[79] Political mobilization, Mao insisted, "is crucial; it is indeed of primary importance, while our inferiority in weapons and other things is only secondary."[80] In fact, the Chinese Communist party appears to believe that victory in war depends less on the weapons used than on the human element involved. Given this orientation, it is unlikely that Chinese troops would be sent to any foreign country without local support. Rather, the Chinese Communists are more likely to lend "spiritual" support to any movement or insurrection against the United States in any foreign country, striving, of course, to develop and widen such efforts by this ideological technique.

Communist China: A Prognosis

In retrospect, this essay has examined the onset of the Great Cultural Revolution in the context of a moderate-radical pendulum movement that has been characteristic of Chinese history since 1949. It has also outlined six general traits that have distinguished the thought and behavior of the

[77] Ibid., p. 225.

[78] "On the People's Democratic Dictatorship," in Selected Works of Mao Tse-tung, Vol. 4, p. 416.

[79] "On Protracted War," in Selected Works of Mao Tse-tung, Vol. 2, p. 151.

[80] Ibid., p. 154.

Chinese Communist movement. The most hazardous task for a China specialist is to predict, on the basis of his understanding of Communist China, the future pattern of events and policies there. In this difficult assignment, six questions must be considered: (1) the question of political unity, (2) the role of Mao Tse-tung, (3) the dynamics of moderation and radicalism, (4) the importance of external pressure, especially by the United States, (5) China's relations with its neighbors, including the Soviet Union, and (6) the problem of demography and agricultural productivity.

Political unity was realized in 1949. This unity, however, rests on three pillars that have yet to demonstrate their long-term resiliency—namely, a particular form of nationalism, the personal prestige and authority of Chairman Mao, and the People's Liberation Army. Although nationalism in China may have reached the grassroots level, it remains a pubescent nationalism, similar in many respects to the nationalism of Meiji Japan. The centrality of the army and of Mao's role in China's political unity has been repeatedly conceded by the Communists themselves. On August 9, 1967, Lin Piao declared:

> It is thanks to two conditions that we are able to start the Great Proletarian Cultural Revolution. The first is nothing but the thought of Mao Tse-tung and Chairman Mao's supreme prestige. The second is the strength of the Liberation Army. Only these two conditions made it possible for us to venture to mobilize the masses as we thought proper. . . . At present both the Party and the Government are all paralyzed. On the surface this is disorder, but this disorder is absolutely necessary. But for disorder in a normal situation, it is impossible to expose the reactionary. It is because we had Chairman Mao's highest prestige and the strength of the Liberation Army that we could venture to do this.[81]

Since Chinese political unity is sustained by these elements, any prognosis of its future must be based on them. In my judgment, it is unlikely that the present system of Maoist absolutism will continue indefinitely. Sooner or later, China will shift to a style of political unity of the Soviet type or of the Latin American *junta* type. Or, if the Liberation Army were to fractionalize, one might see a militaristic decentralization of power, with each local ruler claiming to represent Marxist-Leninist orthodoxy— in effect, an up-to-date version of the warlord era. The first two possibilities, however, seem more viable. Which of these two forms ultimately prevails will depend, in large measure, on the foreign policy of the United States.

External pressure, as well as internal tension, has played a prominent role in strengthening Chinese nationalism. Indeed, it has been the prime

[81] *Kuangchou Feng-lai* (periodical issued by the Yenan Commune of the Kuangchou Huanan Technical School), September 22, 1967.

stimulant to Chinese political unity. It is reasonable, therefore, to assume that the Chinese communists will seek to foster among the people a sense of external crisis. In other words, they will continue to stress the dangers of American imperialism—which raises interesting (but, for the present, unanswerable) questions about the connections between the United States' bombing of North Vietnam and Chinese domestic policies, including the Great Cultural Revolution. For the moment, one may speculate that if the present American policy of containment were perfectly and powerfully implemented, the People's Republic of China would probably turn into a military state that would be ruled for a long time by a *junta* of the Latin American type. If, on the other hand, American external pressures were weakened, one could anticipate a shift to a Soviet-type government espousing the doctrine of peaceful coexistence.

The second question to consider is that of Mao's political leadership. Lin Piao has eulogized Mao's "supreme prestige" to the extent of claiming that China's political cohesion was sustained by Mao's personal leadership. If this is so, after Mao Tse-tung's death the loss of his charismatic personality must naturally produce major changes, one way or another, in China. Presently, it is impossible to ascertain with any accuracy the actual political role played by Mao, or even whether or not he is healthy. What is clear, however, is that Mao is deified in China as the omnipotent, flawless leader of the Chinese (and the world) Communist revolution. Still, the same was true in the past, and it did not prevent the Peking government from making major changes in policies. At the moment, the Cultural Revolution is apparently ending. Not only actions, but slogans as well, have recently changed. For instance, Mao Tse-tung's Twelve Article Directive of December 1967 was prudently followed throughout 1968, and this statement no longer advanced such slogans as "Rebellion is justified," or "Disorder is a good thing." Priority was given to the necessity of self-criticism and to a cautious handling of the problem of cadres and the reconstruction of party organizations. Along with this change, the party no longer advocated the fundamental goals of the Cultural Revolution—for example, the call for a remolding of the human soul. Instead, Mao Tse-tung's directive redefined the Cultural Revolution as a concrete political revolution that was connected with the class struggle and as a continuation of the long struggle against the Kuomintang reactionaries.[82] Moreover, specific action programs are becoming moderate at a faster tempo than are the slogans, as reflected, most recently, in the way the Chinese delegates negotiated the 1968 Sino-Japanese trade agreement. Whatever political role Mao may be playing, in my judgment Chinese policies are shifting toward moderation, albeit on a zigzag course. If the Cultural Revolution has not quite terminated, de-Maoization may never-

[82] *People's Daily*, April 10, 1968.

theless already have begun quietly. In addition, party organizations are being reconstructed, not by reinstituting the former organizations but by forming new groups under such names as the Revolutionary Committee and Congress of Active Members Studying the Thought of Mao Tse-tung. Along with the reconstruction of the party, the administrative system is also being quickly reconstructed, apparently in the search for a more simplified system that can be incorporated into party organizations.

In regard to the question of external pressure, especially American pressure, any softening in the attitude of the United States toward China should substantially increase the possibility of internal changes in China. Although one cannot be certain of the direction these changes would take, at least it is clear that if the United States' policy of containment remains fixed and continues to be carried out with the strength it has been since the Korean War, no major change in Chinese Communist diplomacy can be expected. Furthermore, the Taiwan issue remains a matter of crucial importance in American-Chinese relations. If both sides maintain their present attitudes concerning that issue, there could be only a very limited degree of softening in Sino-American relations.

Judging from the complicated developments in the Sino-Soviet dispute since 1961, it is also unlikely that China and the Soviet Union will again form a united front against American imperialism. More probably, they will keep struggling for the leadership of the world communist movement and continue to have minor confrontations along their borders. Concerning other countries on China's periphery, we have already pointed out that the Chinese Communists do not, in theory, believe that China can export revolution. From their viewpoint, the key issue is whether or not a revolutionary situation exists locally. Not even during the most radical period of the Cultural Revolution did the Peking government do anything except voice support for indigenous revolutionary movements. One may reasonably conclude that China will spur any insurrection in which an indigenous revolutionary force is strong and that it will strive to maintain friendly relations with any central government in which the revolutionary force is weak. In brief, the Chinese Communists will not resort to direct aggression, they will stabilize diplomatic relations with the countries on their borders, and they will champion ideologically all indigenous revolutionary movements in these countries.

The last issue to consider in any prognosis is the problem of agricultural productivity. According to the information available, the annual net increase in the Chinese population is around 2 percent. Demographers, on the basis of past experience, believe that a developing country whose population increases annually by 2 percent must raise its food production by 3 percent annually in order to satisfy the people's demand for a higher standard of living. This type of agricultural productivity seems a sheer impossibility for China, which has a population of between 750 and 780 million people. Japan, the most outstanding developing economy in Asia, was able to double its food production in the first forty years of the Meiji era mainly through technical innovation in agriculture. Nonetheless, the average rate of the annual increase in this period was actually no more than 1.79 percent. In light of this record, it is obvious how difficult it will be for China to achieve a 3 percent annual increase in food production. Still, China must accomplish this impossible task if it is to develop as a viable nation.

Considering the awesome economic and political problems confronting the Chinese Communists, the People's Republic of China will scarcely be able to engage in global politics. Red China is too weak militarily, industrially, and agriculturally to play the role of a world power. Unquestionably, China will utter bombastic rhetoric, especially in domestic propaganda, and will direct its ideology toward indigenous revolutionary movements in all foreign countries. Still, despite its stress on forming a united anti-American front, it is doubtful whether China could actually provide much material or technical assistance to such a movement. In short, one should never slight the realistic actions of the Chinese Communists. Since they came to power in 1949, despite violent slogans and radical revolutionary ideology, they have acted prudently, and this gap between rhetoric and behavior will doubtless continue to exist. Whatever the future holds, the observer of China will have to cope with the arduous assignment of measuring behavior against ideology in the quest to understand the subsequent history of Communist China and the Chinese revolution.

Selected Readings

Brzezinski, Zbigniew K. *The Soviet Bloc: Unity and Conflict*. Rev. ed. Cambridge, Mass.: Harvard University Press, 1967. A brilliant analysis of the tensions between ideology and national interest in the communist world, providing a valuable complement to John Gittings' later volume.

Eckstein, Alexander. *Communist China's Economic Growth and Foreign Trade: Implications for U.S. Policy*. New York: McGraw-Hill, 1966. Although the Chinese statistics are not always reliable or complete, this is a cogent assessment of trade and growth in Communist China, covering both past performance and future prospects.

Fairbank, John K. *China: The People's Middle Kingdom and the U.S.A.* Cambridge, Mass.: Harvard University Press, 1967. A collection of essays, many written from the viewpoint of the mid-1960's, by the most respected American scholar of Chinese history.

Gittings, John. *Survey of the Sino-Soviet Dispute: A Commentary and Extracts from the Recent Polemics, 1963–1967.* London: Oxford University Press, 1968. A thorough account that includes excellent essays on the historical contexts of the many issues involved in this dispute.

Halpern, Abraham M., ed. *Policies Toward China: Views from Six Continents.* New York: McGraw-Hill, 1965. A collection of informed essays that show the different ways in which authorities from various nations evaluated China before the Cultural Revolution assumed its more dramatic features.

Ho Ping-ti and Tsou, Tang, eds. *China in Crisis.* 2 vols. Chicago: University of Chicago Press, 1968. The most recent collection of authoritative essays and discussions on contemporary Chinese affairs, providing the best single introduction to responsible academic thinking on the issues and controversies surrounding the People's Republic of China.

Lifton, Robert Jay. *Revolutionary Immortality: Mao Tse-tung and the Chinese Cultural Revolution.* New York: Random House, 1968. A provocative interpretation by a professional psychiatrist who has closely studied the psychological and historical aspects of Communist China.

Mao Tse-tung. *The Political Thought of Mao Tse-tung.* Edited by Stuart R. Schram. New York: Praeger, 1963. By far the best analysis of this difficult and vital subject.

――――. *Selected Works of Mao Tse-tung.* Peking: Foreign Language Press, 1961–65. As the authoritative English translation of Mao's major essays, this is indispensable reading.

Mehnert, Klaus. *Peking and Moscow.* London: 1963. A shrewd and knowledgeable presentation, written from a German perspective.

Schurmann, Franz. *Ideology and Organization in Communist China.* 2nd ed. Berkeley, Calif.: University of California Press, 1968. Easily the most suggestive sociological analysis of the dynamics of ideology and organization in present-day China.

Steel, Archibald T. *The American People and China.* New York: McGraw-Hill, 1966. A thoughtful critique of American attitudes and assumptions about modern China.

Steel, Ronald. *Pax Americana.* New York: Viking Press, 1967. A pungent and sometimes abrasive challenge to the official rhetoric and the assumptions underlying a great deal of American policy in Asia and elsewhere.

Tsou, Tang. *America's Failure in China, 1941–50.* 2 vols. Chicago: University of Chicago Press, 1967. The most exhaustive and penetrating dissection of American policy in China during the decade in which the United States smashed Japan, only to witness the triumph of Mao's forces on the mainland.

Zagoria, Donald S. *The Sino-Soviet Conflict, 1956–1961.* Princeton, N.J.: Princeton University Press, 1962. The pioneering and still valuable study of this important subject.

Index

A 0
B 1
C 2
D 3
E 4
F 5
G 6
H 7
I 8
J 9